THE REMEMBRANCE OF DEATH AND THE AFTERLIFE

Kitāb dhikr al-mawt wa-mā baʿdahu

Book XL of
The Revival of the Religious Sciences
Iḥyāʾ ʿUlūm al-Dīn

Dear Paula,

May this book serve as a fitting reminder of the wonderful times you had at Vanguard!

All the best for the future!

Yours Ever,

Sabbir

x

OTHER TITLES IN THE ISLAMIC TEXTS SOCIETY
AL-GHAZĀLĪ SERIES

FROM THE *Iḥyāʾ ʿulūm al-dīn*

Al-Ghazālī on Invocations and Supplications

Al-Ghazālī on the Manners Relating to Eating

Al-Ghazālī on Disciplining the Soul & Breaking the Two Desires

Al-Ghazālī on Patience & Thankfulness (forthcoming)

OTHER WORKS

Al-Ghazālī on the Ninety-nine Beautiful Names of God

Al-Ghazālī Letter to a Disciple (*Ayyuhā 'l-walad*)

AL-GHAZĀLĪ

THE REMEMBRANCE OF DEATH AND THE AFTERLIFE · *Kitāb dhikr al-mawt wa-mā baʿdahu* · BOOK XL of THE REVIVAL OF THE RELIGIOUS SCIENCES *Iḥyāʾ ʿulūm al-dīn* · translated with an INTRODUCTION and NOTES by T.J. WINTER

THE ISLAMIC TEXTS SOCIETY
CAMBRIDGE 1989

First published in 1989 by
The Islamic Texts Society
Botanic House
100 Hills Road
Cambridge CB2 1JZ, UK

Reprinted 1995, 1999, 2004, 2006, 2009

British Library Cataloguing-in-Publication Data.
A catalogue record for this book is
Available from the British Library.

ISBN: 978 0946621 09 5 cloth
ISBN: 978 0946621 13 2 paper

Printed in Turkey by Mega Printing.

CONTENTS

THE REMEMBRANCE OF DEATH
AND THE AFTERLIFE '

Prologue

THE FIRST PART

ABBREVIATIONS

Ājurrī	al-Ājurrī, *K. al-Sharīʿa*
ʿAṭṭār	Arberry (tr.), *Muslim Saints and Mystics*
Azami	M.M. Azami, *Studies in Early Hadith Literature*
ʿĀriḍat al-aḥwadhī	Ibn al-ʿArabī, *ʿĀriḍat al-aḥwadhī* ...
Bayḍāwī	al-Bayḍāwī, *Anwār al-tanzīl* ...
Bidāya	Ibn Kathīr, *al-Bidāya wa'l-nihāya*
BSOAS	*Bulletin of the School of Oriental and African Studies*
De Anima	Ibn Sīnā, *De Anima*
Ḍuʿafā'	al-Nasā'ī, *K. al-Ḍuʿafā' wa'l-matrūkīn*
Durra	al-Ghazālī, *al-Durra* ..., ed. Gautier
EI	*Encyclopaedia of Islam* (First edition)
EI²	*Encyclopaedia of Islam* (Second edition)
Escatología	M. Asín Palacios, *La Escatología* ...
Fatḥ al-Bārī	Ibn Ḥajar, *Fatḥ al-Bārī* ...
Fihrist	Ibn al-Nadīm, *K. al-Fihrist*
Fiṣal	Ibn Ḥazm, *al-Fiṣal fī'l-milal* ...
GAL	Brockelmann, *Geschichte* ...
GALS	Brockelmann, *Geschichte* ... (*Supplement*)
GAS	Sezgin, *Geschichte* ...
Ghāya	Ibn al-Jazarī, *Ghāyat al-nihāya* ...
Ḥākim	al-Ḥākim al-Nīsābūrī, *al-Mustadrak* ...
Ḥalīmī	al-Ḥalīmī, *al-Minhāj fī Shuʿab al-īmān*
al-Ḥakīm al-Tirmidhī	al-Ḥakīm al-Tirmidhī, *Nawādir al-uṣūl* ...
al-Ḥāwī	al-Suyūṭī, *al-Ḥāwī li'l-fatāwī*
Hujwīrī	Nicholson (tr.) *Kashf al-maḥjūb*
Ibn Abī Shayba	Ibn Abī Shayba, *al-Muṣannaf*
Ibn Aʿtham	Ibn Aʿtham, *al-Futūḥ*
Ibn al-Daybaʿ	Ibn al-Daybaʿ, *Tamyīz al-ṭayyib* ...
Ibn Rajab	Ibn Rajab, *Ahwāl al-qubūr* ...
Ibn al-Mubārak	Ibn al-Mubārak, *al-Zuhd wa'l-raqā'iq*

Ibn Shaddād	:	Ibn Shaddād, *al-Aᶜlāq al-Khaṭīra ...*
Ibn al-Sunnī	:	Ibn al-Sunnī, *ᶜAmal al-yawm wa'l-layla*
Iljām	:	al-Ghazālī, *Iljām al-ᶜawāmm ...*
Inbāh	:	Ibn ᶜAbd al-Barr, *al-Inbāh ...*
Iqtiṣād	:	al-Ghazālī, *al-Iqtiṣād fi 'l-iᶜtiqād*
Iṣāba	:	Ibn Ḥajar, *al-Iṣāba fī tamyīz al-Ṣaḥāba*
Istīᶜāb	:	Ibn ᶜAbd al-Barr, *al-Istīᶜāb ...*
JAOS	:	*Journal of the American Oriental Society*
JRAS	:	*Journal of the Royal Asiatic Society*
Kāshif	:	al-Dhahabī, *al-Kāshif ...*
Khālid	:	Ḥasan Khālid, *al-Islām wa-ru'yatuhu ...*
Lane	:	Lane, *An Arabic-English Lexicon*
Mashāhīr	:	Ibn Ḥibbān, *Mashāhīr ᶜulamā' al-amṣār*
Ma'thūr	:	al-Daylamī, *al-Firdaws bi-ma'thūr ...*
Māturīdī	:	al-Māturīdī, *Kitāb al-Tawḥīd*
MIDEO	:	*Mélanges de l'Institut Dominicain d'Etudes Orientales*
MW	:	*The Muslim World*
Nawawī, *Sharḥ*	:	al-Nawawī, *al-Minhāj fī sharḥ ...*
Pensée	:	Gardet, *La Pensée Religieuse d'Avicenne*
Q.	:	*al-Qur'ān al-Karīm*
Quḍāᶜī	:	al-Quḍāᶜī, *Musnad al-Shihāb*
Qurṭubī	:	al-Qurṭubī, *al-Tadhkira ...*
Qushayrī	:	al-Qushayrī, *al-Risāla fī ᶜilm al-taṣawwuf*
Ṣafadī	:	al-Ṣafadī, *al-Wāfī bi'l-wafayāt*
Sakhāwī	:	al-Sakhāwī, *al-Maqāṣid al-Ḥasana ...*
Schimmel	:	Schimmel, *And Muhammad is His Messenger*
SEI	:	*Shorter Encyclopaedia of Islam*
Sharnūbī	:	al-Sharnūbī, *Taqrīb al-maᶜānī ...*
Shawkānī	:	al-Shawkānī, *al-Fawā'id al-majmūᶜa ...*
Smith and Haddad	:	Smith and Haddad, *The Islamic Understanding...*
Sulamī	:	al-Sulamī, *Ṭabaqāt al-Ṣūfiya*
Ṭabarānī, *Ṣaghīr*	:	al-Ṭabarānī, *al-Muᶜjam al-Ṣaghīr*
Tahdhīb al-Tahdhīb	:	Ibn Ḥajar, *Tahdhīb al-Tahdhīb*
Taᶜjīl	:	Ibn Ḥajar, *Taᶜjīl al-manfaᶜa ...*
Tārīkh Baghdād	:	al-Khaṭīb al-Baghdādī, *Tārīkh Baghdād*

Abbreviations

Ṭayālisī	:	al-Ṭayālisī, *al-Musnad*
ʿUqaylī	:	al-ʿUqaylī, *al-Ḍuʿafāʾ al-Kabīr*
Wakīʿ	:	Ibn al-Jarrāḥ, K. *al-Zuhd*
Zabīdī	:	al-Zabīdī, *Itḥāf al-sādat al-muttaqīn ...*

PREFACE

'DEATH and the sun are not to be looked at steadily.' The maxim of La Rochefoucauld centrally represents modern man's attitude to this alarming yet most fascinating of subjects. And indeed, to the reader whose roots lie in the soil of secular Europe the prospect of reading a text (and not an overly brief one at that) the declared object of which is to remind him just how quick and fragile his life must be, might seem unpromising, or even distasteful. One must not, however, lose sight of the fact that an interest in the Grand Leveller, far from reflecting bad taste or morbidity, has historically provided man with many of his finest literary and religious achievements. From the time of the *Egyptian Book of the Dead* more than two millennia before Christ, through the age of Dante to Donne and Milton, the steady contemplation of human mortality and the possibility of survival has bequeathed to us a recurrent literary theme, which, by shedding light on how earlier generations died provides us with profound insights into the way they chose to live.

The text here presented in translation lays a particular claim to our attention, for it is the principal work on the matter of death to have issued from the pen of the most celebrated theologian of Islam. The *Imām* al-Ghazālī designed it to be the final flourish to his forty-'book' *Revival of the Religious Sciences* (in Arabic, *Iḥyā' ʿulūm al-dīn*), his magisterial exposition of the Islamic faith which is generally acclaimed as the definitive *summa theologica* of Islam. In view of the wide circulation of the work, the *Remembrance of Death and the Afterlife* (*Kitāb Dhikr al-mawt wa-mā baʿdahu*) may well be considered the most influential treatment of orthodox Muslim belief in this signally important field. Further, while its academic interest is substantial, the appeal of al-Ghazālī's tract today extends far beyond the confines of University libraries, for the world which its author addressed, despite almost a thousand years of change and (as some would have it) corrosion, still lives, worships and dies. It is this abiding relevance of al-Ghazālī's message which I have endeavoured to bear in mind during the labour of translation, hoping that some glimmer of the literary quality of the original may shine through, and that perhaps, with the help of Providence, our author's text may still serve the purpose for which it was intended.

I would like to record my indebtedness to a number of scholars who have assisted me with this work. In particular, Dr. Ibrāhīm al-Baṭṭāwī of al-Azhar University and Shaikh Aḥmad Mashhūr al-Ḥaddād elucidated a number of difficult passages and helped me with the identification of certain of the sayings of the Prophet in which this text abounds. Professor Malcolm Lyons of Cambridge University and Seemi Ghazi kindly read the Introduction and parts of the translation, and made several useful suggestions. To these and a number of others I extend my thanks.

In the absence of a critical edition of the *Revival* I have made use of the following editions: (1) the Amīrīya edition of 1289 AH as reprinted at the margin of al-Murtaḍā al-Zabīdī's commentary *Itḥāf al-sādat al-muttaqīn bi-sharḥ asrār Iḥyā' ʿulūm al-dīn*, second edition (Cairo: al-Maymanīya, 1311 AH) (referred to as A); (2) the text reproduced in the *Itḥāf* itself, irregularities in which are sometimes pointed out by the commentator (Z); (3) the al-Maktaba al-Azharīya edition of 1317 AH (MA). Attention is drawn to significant discrepancies only; obvious typographic errors are omitted.

Square brackets have been employed for explanatory material added to the text, and also for the Arabic original of certain locutions for which no satisfactory equivalent exists in English. Qur'ānic material, for which I have drawn heavily on Pickthall's *Meaning of the Glorious Koran*, is in italics and numerated in accordance with the King Fu'ād Edition, while references to the *ḥadīth* literature follow the system used in Wensinck's *Concordance*, with the more recondite Traditions being identified according to the volume and page numbers of the printed editions of those works listed in the Bibliography. Where such material has not been identified in printed works the reader has been referred to the *takhrīj* of Zabīdī and the *zawā'id* literature. Roughly following the system of al-ʿIrāqī, all Traditions have been divided into three groups: those included by al-Bukhārī and

Muslim, for which no reference to other sources has been made, those covered by the other collections used by Wensinck, for which other sources are mentioned but rarely, and thirdly, the less important texts; this for the sake of economy. The pagination in references to the *Iḥyā'* is that of the Cairo edition of Muṣṭafā al-Ḥalabī (1347 AH) as being perhaps more widely available than the three texts listed above.

INTRODUCTION

FROM the first days of the Muslim experience the remembrance of death and the chastening facts of eschatology provided a characteristic underpinning to the devotional life. The earliest declarations of the Qur'ān, God's new revelation of His will, were charged with the most eloquent and urgent exhortations to erring man, warning him that before long the Last Trump would sound,[1] ushering in a Day of Judgement *which will turn children's hair to grey.*[2] On that day, *mankind shall issue forth in scattered groups to be shown their works.*[3] Man's actions shall be weighed in Scales[4] and a final consignment to Heaven or Hell shall be decreed,[5] *and they shall not be wronged in aught.*[6] The pleasures or chastisements which await them are depicted vividly: *For the Godfearing shall be a triumph – gardens and vineyards, maidens for companions, and a cup overflowing.*[7] But man is not to forget that *Hell lurks in ambush, a home for the profligate, where they shall abide for ages. Therein taste they neither coolness nor any drink, save only boiling water and a bitter cold: a proportioned reward.*[8]

This picture becomes further expanded when we turn to the Traditions (*aḥādīth*, sing. *ḥadīth*) of the Prophet. We are told that man undergoes a period of sepulchral life in the grave, which, as 'either a garden of Heaven or an abyss of Hell,'[9] prefigures his ultimate fate. To the landscape of the Day of Judgement we find added a 'Pool' (*ḥawḍ*), where the faith community assembles around Muḥammad,[10] and a 'Traverse' (*ṣirāṭ*), which is 'a bridge suspended over the gulf of Hell, sharper than a sword and finer than a hair',[11] which must be crossed as part of the material manifestation of the Judgement. The *ḥadīth* material also presents a concept of intercession (*shafāʿa*) exercised by the Prophets on behalf of their various communities.[12]

This fearsome picture of the eschaton profoundly informed the early believers' awareness of their central role in the created order. Certain figures among the Prophet's companions, such as Abū Bakr, Abū Dharr al-Ghifārī and Salmān al-Fārisī, responded with a deep asceticism, and their saintly and austere lives provided the inspiration for a vast corpus of hagiographic material, much of which found its place in folklore and, as we shall see, in later devotional literature. An attitude of indifference to the vanities of this world continued in the next generation, that of the 'Followers' (*tābiʿūn*) and that of their successors, and became epitomised in the personalities of al-Ḥasan al-Baṣrī (d.110AH/728AD), the Damascene Abū Sulaymān al-Dārānī (d. *c* 215/830) and other heroes of renunciation, styled *al-bakkā'ūn*, 'the weepers', by their contemporaries for their constant penitential recollection of death and the Judgement.

This attitude produced its own literature of asceticism (*zuhd*)[13] which assembled suitable anecdotes current in the *bakkā'ūn* milieu into book form. Among the best known of these writers whose works are still extant were ʿAbd Allāh ibn al-Mubārak[14] (d.181/797), Aḥmad ibn Ḥanbal[15] (d.241/855), and the prolific author of tracts Ibn Abi'l-Dunyā[16] (d.281/894). In the same period, the great *ḥadīth* compilers such as al-Bukhārī (d.256/870) and Muslim ibn al-Ḥajjāj (d.261/875) added chapters on *zuhd* and the related genre of *raqā'iq* to their own works.[17]

This literature contributed substantially to the evolution of the systematised Muslim esoterism known as *taṣawwuf*, or Sufism. A cursory glance at the works of the major early Sufis such as al-Muḥāsibī (d.243/857), al-Junayd (d.298/910) and Abū Ṭālib al-Makkī (d.386/996) reveals the importance of *zuhd* asceticism and the contemplation of death in the *via purgativa* such men expounded.[18]

During these same years, however, Islam found itself obliged to come to terms with the newly translated philosophy of the Greeks. A formal theology known as the *kalām*[19] came into being and, although put to work by a variety of sects,[20] was also used in defence of the crystallising *sunnī* orthodoxy against the more unassimilable conclusions of the Greeks, one of which was the Aristotelian denial of personal survival after death.[21] By Ghazālī's time, Sunnī thought had already investigated and ordered the eschatological content of the Qur'ān and the *ḥadīth* as part of magisterial expositions such as the *Discourses* of al-Ashʿarī[22] (d.324/935) and the *Preliminary* of al-Bāqillānī[23] (d.403/1013). Yet despite this growing intellectualisation of the life to come, the traditional idiom was never dominated by the *kalām*. By the beginning of the fifth Muslim century the two approaches, of the mind and of the heart, coexisted in uneasy harmony. The reconciliation of the two was part of the achievement of Abū Ḥāmid al-Ghazālī.

The Life of Ghazālī

(From the biographical dictionary of al-Ṣafadī [d.764/1363].)[24]

'Muḥammad ibn Muḥammad ibn Muḥammad ibn Aḥmad, the Proof of Islam, Ornament of the Faith, Abū Ḥāmid al-Ṭūsī (al-Ghazālī), the Shāfiʿite jurist, was in his later years without rival. At the outset of his career he studied under Aḥmad al-Rādakānī at Ṭūs,[25] and then proceeded to Nīsābūr[26] where he frequented the classes of the Imām al-Ḥaramayn.[27] He laboured most diligently, so that in a brief space of time he graduated (*takharraj*) and became a master, composing his own works in the lifetime of his preceptor, with whom he remained until the latter's demise.

'He then (478/1085–6) left for the Camp-Court and joined Niẓām al-Mulk,[28] who accorded him much honour and respect. With the vizier there was a group of men of virtue, who debated with him. He triumphed over them, and his name became celebrated and his fame spread.

> Because of him the lame walked briskly,
> And the songless through him burst into melody.

'The vizier conferred upon him the professorship of the Niẓāmīya[29] (484/1091–2), and there at Baghdad his followers grew in multitude until they outnumbered even the retinues of the emirs and magnates. The people of Iraq were greatly pleased with him.

'Then, in (the month of) Dhu'l-Qaʿda in the year 488 (1095) he gave up the entirety of his worldly estate and followed the way of renunciation and solitude. He made the Pilgrimage, and, upon his return, directed his steps towards Syria, where he abided awhile in the city of Damascus, giving instruction in the mosque retreat (*zāwiyat al-jāmiʿ*) which now bears his name in the Western quarter. He then voyaged to Jerusalem, exerting himself greatly in worship and in visiting the holy sites and places. Next he travelled to Egypt, remaining for a while at Alexandria. It is said that he there determined to set sail to join the emir Yūsuf ibn Tāshfīn, the ruler of Marrakesh, for he had heard of his love for scholars and that he bade them welcome.

'However, news reached him of the death of the aforementioned emir, and he returned to his native city of Ṭūs (shortly before 492/1099). Here he compiled a number of valuable books before returning to Nīsābūr, where he was obliged to give lessons at the Niẓāmīya[30] (499/1106). He subsequently (500/1107) forsook this and made his way back to his home city, where he assumed the directorship of a retreat (*khānqāh*) for the Sufis and of a neighbouring college for those occupied with learning. He divided his time among sundry good works such as reciting through the Qur'ān and holding lessons for the Sufis (*ahl al-qulūb*) ... He passed away on Monday, the fourteenth of Jumādā al-Ākhira in the year 505 (1111) at Ṭābarān[31] ... the citadel (*qaṣba*) of Ṭūs, where he was interred.'

The above account provides an accurate general summary of the Imām's career.[32] What Ṣafadī does not tell us, however, is the story of his troubled interior journey: his horror of the *odium theologicum* of the day,[33] and his climactic defence of orthodoxy[34] against the Arab philosophers[35] and the secret sect of the Bāṭinites,[36] which nevertheless failed to dislodge an underlying scepticism which was made only more intense by his spectacular success at Baghdad. It was during this time that, disillusioned, he began to think of renouncing his academic career. As he himself describes this time in his autobiography:[37]

> One day I would determine to leave Baghdad and these circumstances, and the next day change my mind ... The desires of this world pulled at me and entreated me to remain, while the voice of faith cried out 'Go! Go! Only a little of your life remains, yet before you there lies a lengthy voyage. All the knowledge and works that are yours today are but eyeservice and deceit. If you do not prepare now for the Afterlife then when shall you do so?'

It was the remembrance of death which finally triumphed. A ten-year period of wandering was given over to the Sufi path of self-purification and the quest for the direct knowledge of God.[38] The many works which he composed during and in the aftermath of this voyage bear witness to his sincerity and spiritual accomplishment, and none more so than the most celebrated among these, his *Revival of the Religious Sciences*, the crowning intellectual achievement of classical Islam, which, informed by his powerful conviction that the two were mutually indispensable to the balanced religious life, wedded inextricably the traditional exoteric sciences to Sufism. The scale of his accomplishment was summed up in a sentence which is quoted by almost all of the Imām's biographers: 'were all the books of Islam to be lost save the *Revival* alone, it would supply for them in full'.[39]

The *Revival of the Religious Sciences* and the *Remembrance of Death and the Afterlife*

As we have seen, Ghazālī's historic decision to devote his life to Sufism was occasioned largely by his awareness of the imminence of death and the Judgement, and it is not surprising that in the works ascribed to the latter part of his career he should have expressed a powerful and abiding concern with this theme.[40] Whereas in the *Just Mean in Belief*, composed before his period of wandering, the issues of eschatology are accorded the conventional treatment of the theologians as a category of saving beliefs, with no trace of hortatory appeal,[41] the *Revival* stands in full contrast, for the Afterlife finds mention on almost every page and forms the most characteristic leitmotif of the book.[42] It is Ghazālī's purpose, as he tells his readers at the very outset of the work, to treat the spiritual infirmity of his contemporaries with a reminder of the precariousness of their lives. In Book I, with a grand rhetoric that would not look out of place in the *Remembrance*, he cries out that 'the Afterlife approaches and this world passes by; the journey is long, but the provisions are scanty and the dangers great ...'[43] Because of the lamentable *ghafla*, or heedlessness, of the commonalty, and the pride and worldliness of the *ᶜulamā'*, the divines, who may no longer be relied upon to lead men to the 'way of the Afterlife', Ghazālī finds himself driven to create a work with no less dramatic a brief than the 'Revival of the Religious Sciences'.[44]

The *Revival*, then, is an attempt to universalise the central transformative experience of the author's career. It reflects his conviction that the conventional learning of the age, treating as it did only the more superficial aspects of man's condition, had failed to shake him from preoccupation with his sublunary concerns. The answer, as Ghazālī had discovered for himself, lay only in internalising the formalities of religion through 'tasting' (*dhawq*): personal religious experience. That such a knowledge is possible is the message reiterated by many of its forty 'books',[45] beginning with the *Book of Knowledge*, until a secure epistemology, the quest for which had so tormented the author at Baghdad, is laid down. Key terms such as *ᶜilm* (knowledge), *ḥikma* (wisdom), and *fiqh* (jurisprudence), are examined and defined, and *dhawq* put forward as the only way to certitude (*yaqīn*). It is fortified with this certitude that the range of traditional Islamic sciences is to be approached, and an exposition of these, beginning with the *kalām*, proceeds through the four 'quarters' of the book: on Worship, Usages, Mortal Vices and Saving Virtues, to an elegiac climax, where the voice of the Afterlife, which has run throughout the work as a *cantus firmus*, finally sounds alone.

In the main, the books of the *Revival* follow a set pattern, being ordered in Chapters (sing. *bāb*), which subdivide into smaller units characteristically named 'Expositions' (sing. *bayān*). It was

Ghazālī's intention that his work should be easily accessible,[46] and modern scholars commonly praise its 'clarity of style, the logical exactness of its divisions, and its mode of exposition'.[47] The *Remembrance*, perhaps partly due to its length (it is in fact the longest book in the *Revival*), itself divides into two 'halves' (sing. *shaṭr*), the first of which deals with the traditional questions of Muslim thanatology, while the second proceeds sequentially through the events which follow the Last Trump. In keeping with his accustomed method in the *Revival*, the author typically introduces each topic, and then cites in turn Qur'ānic verses, Prophetic traditions, and a range of *exempla* attributed to the early Muslims (the *salaf*, or 'predecessors'), and to Jesus and the Jewish patriarchs. These narratives, many of which are laconic and border on repetitiveness,[48] often redeem themselves by a terse and aphoristic quality which must necessarily suffer in translation. It should be borne in mind that the protagonists of these tales were in many cases the 'household names' of the day, and that this lore must have elicited an interest more lively than modern perusal might sometimes suggest.

All of this material, with certain variants, is to be found in earlier sources, many of which Ghazālī is known to have read. In particular, the works of Ibn Abi'l-Dunyā of Baghdad, the popular writer on *zuhd* subjects,[49] can be shown to include at least two-fifths of the stories Ghazālī tells, despite the fact that many of these works are no longer extant.[50] Abū Nuʿaym of Iṣfahān (d.430/1038),[51] together with al-Sulamī (d.465/1073),[52] al-Qushayrī (d.465/1072),[53] al-Muḥāsibī[54], and al-Ḥakīm al-Tirmidhī (d.285/898)[55] also include much of this material. Clearly, however, the presence of such stories in the *Remembrance* does not prove that its author had taken them directly from the earlier works in which they appear, for many of them must have been in very wide circulation in pietist circles. Although the influence of writers such as Abū Ṭālib al-Makkī on other tractates of the *Revival* may easily be demonstrated (whole passages of al-Makkī's *Qūt al-qulūb* are reproduced almost verbatim in some places),[56] the direct influence of Ghazālī's predecessors which may be proved conclusively is largely confined to Chapter Two ('On

Lengthy Hopes'), which reproduces much of the content of Ibn Abi'l-Dunyā's *Kitāb Qiṣar al-amal*,[57] and Chapter Three, which draws very heavily upon the chapter entitled 'On Preparation for Death' in al-Muḥāsibī's *Kitāb al-Riʿāya*, many lines of which are echoed or reproduced.[58] The account of the death of the Prophet bears some resemblance to the version given in the *Sīra* of Ibn Isḥāq.[59] In addition, the *Risāla* of al-Qushayrī contains most of the material in Chapter Six and of certain sections of Chapter Eight.[60] The second 'half' of the *Remembrance*, written in a rather more traditional idiom, is derived mostly from the *ḥadīth* collections and an eschatological treatise by al-Bayhaqī (d.458/1066),[61] and although it does reveal the sporadic influence of al-Muḥāsibī's eschatological excursion, the *Kitāb al-Tawahhum*, the charge of wholesale plagiarism brought by some is not borne out by a close comparison of the two texts.[62] The final chapter, which, with its soaring and joyful reminders of God's mercy, must rank among the finest examples of Arabic devotional writing, is wholly original.

The anecdotes relating to the Prophet himself, which are less numerous than those ascribed to the *salaf* and the Hebrew patriarchs,[63] are for the most part to be found in the major 'canonical' collections of *ḥadīth*. Although the remainder have all been traced to other collections by the commentator al-Murtaḍā al-Zabīdī (d.1205/1791)[64] they have regularly been criticised as 'weak' or even 'spurious' by certain of Ghazālī's biographers and opponents. In particular, writers such as Ibn al-Jawzī,[65] whom Ghazālī had, as it were, left behind in Baghdad, and who were concerned to question the concept of a religious knowledge based on *dhawq*, lent support to their polemic by accusing Ghazālī of incorporating large numbers of such *ḥadīth* into his *Revival*.[66] A majority of authorities, however, would seem to acquiesce in his use of such material, repeating in various ways that 'it cannot be criticised, since to use such Traditions is legitimate when inspiring hope or fear.'[67]

In another controversial field, that of the literal or symbolic interpretation of traditional teachings on the Afterlife, the Imām has but rarely been subjected to criticism. For Ghazālī's interweaving of the external sciences (*ᶜulūm al-muᶜāmala*) with those that treat of the spirit (*ᶜulūm al-mukās͟hafa*) is unceasingly conditioned by the belief that these two knowledges stand in a hierarchical relationship. The common people (*al-ᶜawāmm*) who live solely by the formalities of religion are inferior to the elect (*al-k͟hawāṣṣ*) who have united the two.[68] Quoting the Tradition 'Speak unto people in accordance with their understanding,' he states that the ordinary man may not be spoken to of certain metaphysical truths, which may only be attained through 'tasting', and where the significance of words is transformed. As he repeats, 'to divulge the secret of Lordship is unbelief'.[69]

The *Remembrance* is written on the level of understanding shared by the generality of mankind. Nowhere is there any trace of an esoteric symbolism. The punishment in the grave, the Scales, the Traverse, and all the features of the eschaton are literal fact by revelation. That G͟hazālī's belief in this was passionate is demonstrated in a theological polemic composed during the same period, in which he states unequivocally that 'the man who denies the existence of physical punishment in the Afterlife ... must be considered an unbeliever'.[70] But in the *Revival*'s *Book of Penitence* he states that the world of the Attributes (*ᶜālam al-malakūt*[71]) cannot be interpreted in the material world (*ᶜālam al-mulk*) without having resort to metaphor (*amt͟hāl*).[72] It is obvious to all, he remarks, that to interpret such statements as that of the Tradition: 'The believer's heart lies between two of the fingers of the All-merciful God'[73] as signifying that God might be possessed of actual fingers and a hand could only be the product of an ignorant mind. 'And in like fashion,' he continues,

> it may be that with matters concerning the Afterlife use is made of metaphors which the unbeliever (*mulḥid*) rejects due to the fixity of his gaze upon the metaphor's outer aspect and what seems to him to be its incoherence. For example, the Prophet, may God bless him and grant him peace, said, 'On the Day of Arising, death shall be brought in the form of a white ram, which is then slaughtered'.[74] The foolish unbeliever is angered, and rejects this, and infers from it that the Prophets lied, saying, 'Good God! Death is

> an accident (ᶜ*araḍ*) and the ram a body, and how could an accident become a body? Can this be other than impossible?' But God (Exalted is He!) has excluded these fools from the knowledge of His mysteries, saying, *And none shall comprehend them save those that know.*[75] The poor unfortunate is unaware that someone might well say, 'I saw in my dreams a white ram being brought,' to be told that 'It (represents) the plague which has descended upon the land'. 'And it was slaughtered' (he continued), to which the interpreter of dreams would say, 'You speak truly; the matter is as you beheld it. It signifies that the plague shall end, never to return, because when a thing is slaughtered it is at an end.' Here the interpreter is correct in believing him, while he himself is correct in what he sees . . . [76]

For Ghazālī there is no contradiction between such a symbolic interpretation and the strict literalness that he maintains elsewhere.[77] God has willed that men shall not comprehend Him equally. Although there can be only one factual description of what lies beyond death, that description will be variously interpreted, being bound by the limitations which inhere in human discourse.[78] Thus, the images of the Afterlife granted through the Prophets, while authentic, overlie and indicate a further dimension of truth.[79]

This insight is brought out most clearly in another passage of the *Revival*, where Ghazālī gives a division of mankind into four categories.[80] Firstly, there are the 'damned' (*al-hālikūn*), 'those wholly given over to the world, who have denied God and His Prophets,' and who shall remain eternally in hellfire. Secondly, there are the 'punished' (*al-mu*ᶜ*adhdhabūn*), 'who have the basis of faith but have failed to act in accordance therewith', and who shall abide in Hell until the Prophets sent to their respective communities intercede on their behalf. Then there is the category of the 'saved' (*al-nājūn*), made up of those with neither good nor evil works for which they might justly be called to account, 'such as madmen, the children of unbelievers, and those never reached by a prophetic summons,' who are to occupy a limbo known as *al-A*ᶜ*rāf*.[81] Finally, there are the 'victorious' (*al-fā'izūn*), who are the 'companions of the right hand' (*aṣḥāb al-yamīn*) praised in the Qur'ān,[82] and who 'have their abode in Heaven', and who include among their ranks a smaller elect, the 'ones brought nigh' (*al-muqarrabūn*), who are blessed with the beatific vision:[83]

> What these people shall encounter lies beyond the limits of language (*yujāwizu ḥadd al-bayān*). That which it is possible to say has already been said in the Qur'ān, for there is no discourse higher than that of God. And that which cannot be expressed in this world has been summed up in His statement (Great and Glorious is He!), 'I have prepared for My righteous bondsmen that which no eye has seen, no ear heard, and which has never occurred to mortal mind'.[84] This station constitutes the aspiration of the gnostics (*al-ʿārifūn*). The gnostic's aim is to attain to this station, which cannot be imagined by mortal mind in this world. As regards the houris and the palaces, the fruit and the milk and the honey, the wine, the jewellery and the bracelets: these people have no yearning for them, and would take no pleasure in them were they to be given them. They seek nothing save the delight of gazing into the noble Countenance of God (Exalted is He!), which is the utmost happiness, and the greatest of joys.[85]

Notes to Introduction

1 Q. XXXIX:68.

2 Q. LXXIII:17.

3 Q. XCIX:6.

4 Q. XXI:47. For these Scales, and some parallels in other religions, see M. Asín Palacios, *La Escatología Musulmana en la Divina Comedia*, 299–303. Although primarily concerned with the extensive debt of mediaeval Christian lore to Islamic eschatological beliefs, Asín Palacios's work remains the definitive study of Muslim 'leyendas de ultratumba' in its own right.

5 Q. LXXXII:13,14.

6 Q. XIX:60.

7 Q. LXXVIII:31–34.

8 Q. LXXVIII:21–26.

9 Tirmidhī, Qiyāma, 6. The other well-known Traditions on this subject are assembled in al-Bayhaqī, *Ithbāt ʿadhāb al-qabr* and Ibn Rajab, *Ahwāl al-qubūr wa-aḥwāl ahlihā ila'l-nushūr*. Ḥasan Khālid, the present Mufti of the Lebanon, provides a useful exposition of the subject in his *al-Islām wa-ru'yatuhu fīmā baʿd al-mawt* 103-163. For a detailed study of the doctrine of life in the grave from a Western perspective see R. Eklund, *Life Between Death and Resurrection According to Islam*; also Jane Smith and Yvonne Haddad, *The Islamic Understanding of Death and Resurrection*, 31–63.

10 The *ḥadīth* literature is unclear as to the stage of the Judgement at which the *ḥawḍ* will be encountered, but the verdict of later Ashʿarī thought, based on the same material, generally sets it after the *ṣirāṭ*; this is the view of Ghazālī in the *Iḥyā'* (I. 81–2), and also of e.g. al-Zabīdī (op. cit., X. 482), al-Suyūṭī, Ibn Ḥajar and the Qāḍī ʿIyāḍ (according to Khālid, 328) and the pillar of Azharite orthodoxy ʿAbd al-Salām al-Laqqānī (*Irshād al-murīd ilā maqām al-Tawḥīd*, 146). According to al-Qurṭubī, however, there are in fact two *ḥawḍs*, one before and one after the *ṣirāṭ* (*al-Tadhkira fī aḥwāl al-mawtā wa-umūr al-Ākhira*, 302); this opinion also gained fairly wide acceptance. Cf. A. Wensinck *The Muslim Creed*, 232. For the controversy see Khālid, loc. cit.

11 Muslim, Īmān, 306. For the *ṣirāṭ* see Asín Palacios, *Escatología*, 181–3.

12 For the *shafāʿa* see A. Wensinck, 'Shafāʿa', *SEI*, 511–512; Annemarie Schimmel, *And Muhammad is His Messenger*, 81–104. The best-known Traditions on the subject are given in the *Jamʿ al-fawā'id* of al-Rawdānī II. 475–8.

13 For which see F. Rosenthal, *"Sweeter than hope": Complaint and Hope in Medieval Islam*, passim.

14 ʿAbd Allāh ibn al-Mubārak, *K. al-Zuhd wa'l-raqā'iq*.

15 Aḥmad ibn Ḥanbal, *K. al-Zuhd*.

16 For Ibn Abi'l-Dunyā see below, note 49.

17 It may be that the independant *zuhd* genre developed out of such chapters as *ajzā'* works. With the exception of the *Muwaṭṭa'* of Mālik ibn Anas, all the canonical collections included in Wensinck's *Concordance* include separate sections devoted to the subject. To these should be added the important chapters found in the

Mustadrak of al-Ḥākim al-Nīsābūrī, IV. 306–332, and the *Muṣannaf* of Ibn Abī Shayba, XIV. 5–67.

18 It cannot be said that early Sufism itself affected the traditional picture of life after death, although authors such as al-Muḥāsibī did lay special emphasis on themes already present, such as the vision of the *lumen gloriae* in Paradise. (Cf. Q. LXXV:22–23; al-Muḥāsibī, *K. al-Tawahhum*, ed. A.J. Arberry, 56ff.)

19 Literally 'speech', 'discourse', but used technically to signify the 'scholastic' theology of Islam. See H.J. Wolfson, *The Philosophy of the Kalam*, 1–2.

20 For a good survey of the early history of the *kalām* see ibid., pp.3–43; also L. Gardet and M.-M. Anawati, *Introduction à la théologie musulmane*, 21–93.

21 One of the three points which induce Ghazālī to condemn the philosophers as unbelievers. (Cf. *al-Iqtiṣād fi'l-iʿtiqād*, 209; *Tahāfut al-falāsifa*, 344; Anawati, 'Introduction historique à une nouvelle traduction de la Métaphysique d'Avicenne', *MIDEO* 13 (1977), 200–7; also p.122n below.) The philosophers' relationship to traditional Islam has been studied by Gardet (*La Pensée Religieuse d'Avicenne*), who, however, is perhaps inclined to overestimate their Islamic loyalties.

22 *Maqālāt al-Islāmīyīn wa'khtilāf al-muṣallīn*.

23 *K. al-Tamhīd*.

24 *al-Wāfī bi'l-wafayāt*, 274–277. The classic account is that given by al-Subkī, *Ṭabaqāt al-Shāfiʿīya*, IV. 101–182, which may usefully be read in conjunction with F. Jabre, 'La biographie et l'oeuvre de Ghazālī réconsidérées à la lumière des Ṭabaqāt de Sobkī', *MIDEO* 1 (1954), 73–102. Also useful are M. Bouyges, *Essai de chronologie des oeuvres d'al-Ghazālī (Algazel)*; W. Montgomery Watt, *Muslim Intellectual*; D.B. Macdonald, 'The Life of al-Ghazzālī', *JAOS* 20 (1899), 70–133; ʿAbd al-Raḥmān Badawī, *Mu'allafāt al-Ghazālī*; Margaret Smith, *Al-Ghazālī the Mystic*.

25 A town of Khurāsān, the north-eastern region of Persia. (Cf. Yāqūt, *Muʿjam al-buldān*, III. 560; Le Strange, *Lands of the Eastern Caliphate* 388–391.)

26 City and, at the time, intellectual centre of Khurāsān. (Cf. Yāqūt, I. 630; III. 228–231; Le Strange, 382–388.)

27 Abu'l-Maʿālī al-Juwaynī, known as the Imām al-Ḥaramayn (419/1028–478/1085), the celebrated Ashʿarite theologian and Shāfiʿite jurist. Although their eschatological interest is slight (the relevant chapter being absent from extant manuscripts of *al-Shāmil*, his magnum opus; cf. M. Allard, *Le problème des attributs divins*, 380; Gardet and Anawati, 181–4), Juwaynī's influential tracts on *kalām* were the direct antecedents of Ghazālī's formal theological works.

28 The powerful Seljuq vizier (408/1018—485/1092). See H. Bower, art. 'Niẓām al-Mulk' in *EI*.

29 Niẓām al-Mulk's great college at Baghdad. See J. Pedersen and G. Makdisi, art. 'Madrasa', in *EI*², v. 1123–34, passim.

30 The college founded by Niẓām al-Mulk's son Fakhr al-Mulk.

31 According to al-Iṣṭakhrī, one of the four districts of Ṭūs. (*Masālik al-mamālik*, 257.)

32 The journey to Alexandria has been contested, although it is fairly consistently reported by the biographers, for example Subkī, op. cit., IV. 105; Ibn Khallikān (*Wafayāt*

al-aʿyān wa-anbā' abnā' al-zamān,) I. 587.

33 For which see e.g. his *Fayṣal al-tafriqa bayn al-Islām wa'l-zandaqa*, 202–205.

34 This word, although not entirely at home in an Islamic context, shall be used for the purposes of the present study to denote the *ahl al-sunna wa'l-jamāʿa.*

35 In his *Tahāfut al-falāsifa.*

36 *Faḍā'iḥ al-Bāṭinīya*, also known as *al-Mustaẓhirī*. Cf. Badawī, *Mu'allafāt*, 82–84.

37 *Al-Munqidh min al-ḍalāl*, Ar. pp. 36–37.

38 Curiously enough, al-Juwaynī had been through a crisis comparable to that of his great pupil: 'I had read fifty thousand books times fifty thousand, and then left behind all the people of Islam and their external sciences, sailing upon the boundless ocean, plunging into that which they had forbidden, all for the sake of the quest for truth. From an early age I had fled from imitation [*taqlīd*]; now I have renounced all that and returned to the word of truth: "follow the religion of old women".' (Subkī, III. 260). The last quotation is a popular *ḥadīth* (al-Suyūṭī, *al-Durar al-Muntathira fi'l-aḥādīth al-mushtahira* 136).

39 Ṣafadī, I. 275; Zabīdī, I. 27; Tāshköprüzāde, *Miftāḥ al-saʿāda wa miṣbāḥ al-siyāda*, II. 202.

40 Another work on eschatology is ascribed to this period of Ghazālī's life. The treatise known as *al-Durra al-Fākhira fī kashf ʿulūm al-Ākhira* (partially edited with partial French translation by L. Gautier, Leipzig, 1877, as *ad-Dourra al-Fākhira: La Perle Précieuse de Ghazali*; English translation by Jane Smith: *The Precious Pearl: A Translation from the Arabic*, Missoula, Montana, 1979) is thought by many European scholars to be spurious: for example M. Asín Palacios asserts that 'its authenticity is very doubtful; the editor (Gautier) bases it upon a single citation from the *Iḥyā'* on page 27, but al-Ghazālī does not mention it as his in any of his books, and the eschatological doctrine which it contains—a very poor résumé of the last tractate of the *Iḥyā'*—offers nothing to support the contention that this devout compendium is the work of al-Ghazālī himself.' (*La Espiritualidad de Algazel y su sentido Cristiano*, IV. 385.) However, to characterise the *Durra* as a résumé of the *Remembrance* would seem unwarrantable, for although a small number of the same *āthār* do appear, the former work is for the most part the author's own prose, and describes death and the Resurrection with only sporadic references to authorities. Almost half of the *Remembrance* is given over to a description of Heaven and Hell, which is nowhere attempted in the later work. The *Durra* makes regular use of the terms *mulk* and *malakūt* which figure hardly at all in the *Remembrance*, which largely confines itself to the *dunyā/ākhira* opposition. Asín Palacios supports his argument with the comment that the *Iḥyā'* is cited once only, but this carries no more weight, since, as Allard points out (in Bouyges, op. cit., 79—80) there are at least three other references to the *Iḥyā'* in the *Durra.*

W. Montgomery Watt ('The Authenticity of the Works Ascribed to Al-Ghazālī', *JRAS* 1952, 24—45) offers more substantial reasons to doubt the authenticity of the *Durra.* 'It is inconceivable', he says, '... that al-Ghazālī could express himself as the *Durra* does, since he so regularly preaches a *praeparatio mortis*' (p.32).

Yet, given the circumstances of Ghazālī's last years (during which the *Durra* was probably composed, according to Bouyges, p.79) it might not be unreasonable to suggest that Ghazālī intended this book, like the *Mishkāt al-anwār*, to be read primarily by his initiates, for whom the didactic approach of the *Iḥyā'* and other works intended mainly for popular consumption was inappropriate; this might also be supported by the presence of the key word *kashf* in the title. Montgomery Watt's further point that the 'ascension' story found in the *Durra* on pp. 11—15 'is in strong contradiction to the tradition of Muʿādh in the *Bidāya*' might also be explained in this way.

More confident still that the *Durra* is spurious is Hava Lazarus-Yafeh, who states that it is 'definitely not written by Al-Ghazzālī' (*Studies in Al-Ghazzālī*, 36), but without giving reasons, referring her readers instead (p.330) to the work of Bouyges, who, however, seems inclined to accept the work as authentic (Bouyges, loc. cit.).

To the arguments already adduced for the work's lack of authenticity might well be added the fact that the *Durra* puts the *ḥawḍ* sequentially before the *ṣirāṭ* (pp.83, 106), whereas the *Iḥyā'* (IV. 447–8; 452) envisages the opposite.

Perhaps the best answer to the controversy is that given long ago by al-Suyūṭī (in *al-Ḥāwī li'l-fatāwī*, I. 383) who, after pointing out that the *Durra* was accepted as authentic by such authorities as al-Qurṭubī (in his *Tadhkira*) and Ibn Ḥajar, suggests that although 'the *Durra* which is extant today contains poorly-worded phrases and faulty inflection, it would seem that this was the consequence of the very frequent use of the book by the common people, whereby the copyists added some parts and removed others, and corrupted and changed the text.'

41 *Iqtiṣād*, 180—189.

42 In the *Iḥyā'* (I. 14–15), Ghazālī classes the study of matters relating to the next life as *farḍ ʿayn*, a duty incumbent upon every Muslim.

43 *Iḥyā'*, I. 3.

44 ibid.

45 For the significance of the number 40 see Pouzet, *Une Herméneutique de la tradition islamique*, 42–52, who quotes (p.43) Massignon (*Essai sur les origines du lexique technique de la mystique musulmane*, 133) as telling us that it represents 'le nombre sémitique traditionnel pour désigner la pénitence et l'expiation'. According to Annemarie Schimmel (*And Muhammad is His Messenger*, 117), it is the number of 'patience, maturing, suffering, preparation. (Israel was forty years in the desert; Jesus spent forty days in the desert; Muhammad was forty when his calling came; the forty days of Lent; the forty days of complete retirement as practiced by the Sufis ...)'. Schimmel reminds us that 40 is also the numerical value of the letter *mīm*, and that the Sufis find endless scope for contemplation in the *ḥadīth qudsī* in which God says, *Anā Aḥmad bilā mīm*: 'I am Aḥmad (a name of the Prophet) without the "m" ': for when one removes this letter, only *Aḥad*, 'the One' remains. Speculation concerning this number flourished particularly at the hands of ʿAṭṭār and Ibn ʿArabī.

46 However, certain parts of the *Iḥyā'*, such as part II, book 4 (*al-Ḥalāl wa'l-ḥarām*) are technical and can only have been written for *ʿulamā'*. Other books, in particular II, 8 (*Ādāb al-samāʿ wa'l-wajd*), III, 10 (*Dhamm al-*

ghurūr), IV, 2 (*al-Ṣabr wa'l-shukr*), IV, 5 (*al-Tawḥīd wa'l-tawakkul*), and IV, 6 (*al-Maḥabba wa'l-shawq wa'l-uns wa'l-riḍā*) seem to have been written with fairly advanced practitioners of *taṣawwuf* in mind.

47 M. Asín Palacios, *Algazel, Dogmática, Moral y Ascética*, 156.

48 A criticism voiced by, e.g. Asín Palacios, *Algazel*, 175–176; A.J. Arberry, *Revelation and Reason in Islam*, 64.

49 For Ibn Abi'l-Dunyā see now Ella Appelrot-Almagor, ed. and introd., *The "K. Dhamm al-dunyā" by Ibn Abi'l-Dunyā*, 1–36; also the introduction provided to Ibn Abi'l-Dunyā's *K.al-Shukr*, 9–59. See also A. Wiener, 'Die Farağ ba'd aš-šidda Literatur', I/II, *Der Islam*, 4 (1913) pp.270–298, 387–420; A.J. Arberry, 'Ibn Abi'l-Dunyā on penitence', *JRAS* (1951) pp.48–63; J. A. Bellamy (ed. and introd.) *K. Makārim al-akhlāq* of Ibn Abi'l-Dunyā; Brockelmann, *GAL* I. 160, *GALS* I. 247–248.

50 Appelrot-Almagor includes in her list of Ibn Abi'l-Dunyā's books the following lost works, all mentioned by Zabīdī, *passim*, as sources for the *Remembrance*: *K. al-Baʿth wa'l-nushūr*; *K. Ṣifat al-Janna*; *K. Ṣifat al-Ṣirāṭ*; *K. Ṣifat al-Mīzān*; *K. Ṣifat al-Nār*; *K.* (or *Akhbār*) *al-Qubūr*; *K. al-Mawt* [said by al-Sawwās (introd. to *K. al-Shukr*, p.32n) to have been in seven parts; it was probably identical with a work called, perhaps significantly, the *K. Dhikr al-mawt* also listed by Appelrot-Almagor]. Appelrot-Almagor identifies (p.24) several points of correspondence between the *K. Dhamm al-dunyā* and the *Iḥyā'* (the opening section of the latter's own *K. Dhamm al-dunyā* [III, book 6] is derived almost exactly from the earlier work), but is surely on more hazardous ground when she says that 'one may perhaps venture to suggest that Al-Ghazālī may have deliberately introduced certain changes, so that his borrowings would not be too glaringly obvious.' Ibn Abi'l-Dunyā's *K. al-Ṣamt wa-ḥifẓ al-lisān* was also a source for the *Iḥyā'*; cf. ʿĀshūr's introduction, p.24.

51 In his *Ḥilyat al-awliyā' wa-ṭabaqāt al-aṣfiyā'*. According to Appelrot-Almagor (p.23), Abū Nuʿaym owed a considerable debt to Ibn Abi'l-Dunyā.

52 For instance, his *Jawāmiʿ ādāb al-Ṣūfiya* and his *ʿUyūb al-nafs wa-mudāwātuhā*).

53 His *al-Risāla fī ʿilm al-taṣawwuf* (*GAL* I. 432–433) seems to have provided a key precedent for the *Iḥyā'*'s fusion of the Law and Sufism, for example: 'Every Law unsupported by mystical truth is unacceptable; likewise every mystical truth unsupported by the Law' (I. 296).

54 See below, notes 58, 62. For Muḥāsibī's influence on Ghazālī see Margaret Smith, 'The Forerunner of al-Ghazālī', *JRAS* (Jan. 1936), pp.65–78.

55 For the influence of this figure on Ghazālī see M. al-Jayūshī, *al-Ḥakīm al-Tirmidhī. Dirāsa li-āthārihi wa-afkārihi*. Cf. also Lazarus-Yafeh, 268–277; for his influence on the *K. Dhikr al-mawt* see p.272.

56 Although it touches on the subject of the Afterlife when it deals with penitence and the distribution of ranks in Heaven and Hell (*Qūt*, I. 179–193), the issue of 'fear and hope' (I. 213–242) and the judgement of unbelievers (II. 157–158), the *Qūt al-qulūb fī muʿāmalat al-Maḥbūb* bears no apparent similarity to the *Remembrance*.

57 Cf. *GAL* I. 153.

58 *K. al-Riʿāya li-ḥuqūq Allāh*, pp.73—84.

59 *The Life of Muḥammad: A*

Translation of Ibn Isḥāq's Sīrat Rasūl Allāh. A. Guillaume, pp.678—682.

60 Particularly the *Risāla*'s chapter on the last moments of the Saints (II. 589–600) and the chapter on dream-visions (II. 714–30).

61 *K. al-Baʿth wa'l-nushūr*. Ed. and int. A. A. Ḥaydar. Beirut, 1406/1986. Ḥaydar states (int. pp. 5,6) that the manuscript upon which he bases his edition is probably incomplete.

62 *K. al-Tawahhum*, ed. and int. A.J. Arberry (Cairo, 1937), introduction, page D: 'Many phrases of the latter (i.e. the *Remembrance*) are either definitely borrowed from or modelled upon Muḥāsibī's book, while in scope and structure the whole section is profoundly indebted to it.' Even granting that Arberry is referring to *shaṭr* II, and although the tell-tale word *fatawahham* does appear three times, there would seem to be no more than a modest correspondence between the two works.

63 Twenty-eight percent of the word total compared to thirty-six percent. (Ghazālī's own prose accounts for less than thirty-five percent of the work.)

64 The remarkable erudition shown by Zabīdī in his *Itḥāf* owed much to the efforts of the earlier *takhrīj* work of Zayn al-Dīn al-ʿIrāqī (d.806/1404), the preceptor of Ibn Ḥajar and al-Subkī: his *al-Mughnī ʿan ḥaml al-asfār fi'l-asfār fī takhrīj mā fi'l-Iḥyā' min al-akhbār* has been printed as footnotes to several editions of the *Iḥyā'*, including that of Muṣṭafā al-Ḥalabī (Cairo, 1347 AH).

65 For these attacks see Margaret Smith, *Al-Ghazālī the Mystic*, 198.

66 E.g. Ibn al-Jawzī, *Talbīs Iblīs*, 177. Criticism was also offered by Ibn Kathīr, *al-Bidāya wa'l-nihāya*, XII. 174, who, although sympathetic to the *Iḥyā'*, states that it contains many 'strange' (*gharā'ib*) and 'disliked' (*munkarāt*) *ḥadīths*, and others which are apocryphal (*mawḍūʿ*); he cites the great *muḥaddith* Ibn al-Ṣalāḥ as being of the same opinion (Quoted in Badawī, 517). Al-Dhahabī, in his *Siyar aʿlām al-nubalā'* (quoted in Badawī, 539), takes a similar view: 'It contains a number of spurious *ḥadīth*' (*fīhi min al-aḥādīth al-bāṭila jumla*). Subkī, commenting that Ghazālī never excelled in this field ('*wa-lam yattafiq lahu al-riwāya*', *Ṭabaqāt*, IV. 109), provides a long list of weak *ḥadīth* found in the *Iḥyā'* (Subkī, IV. 145–182, of which pp.179–182 relate to the *Remembrance*).

67 '*li-jawāzihi fi'l-targhīb wa'l-tarhīb*': Tāshköprüzāde, loc. cit.; Ṣafadī, I. 276; cf. Ibn Kathīr, loc. cit. l.8. For this principle, well-known to the scholars of *uṣūl al-ḥadīth*, see also al-Nawawī, *Sharḥ matn al-Arbaʿīn al-Nawawīya*, in Pouzet, p.12 (Ar.) repeated in the same author's *al-Tibyān fī ʿulūm al-Qur'ān*, 17: 'The ulema are agreed on the legitimacy of using weak *ḥadīths* in the realm of virtuous works (*faḍā'il al-aʿmāl*)'.

68 *Iljām al-ʿawāmm ʿan ʿilm al-kalām*, 91.

69 *K. al-Imlā' fī ishkālāt al-Iḥyā'*, 54; *Iḥyā'*, III. 3.

70 *Fayṣal*, 191.

71 For which see below, p.150n.

72 *Iḥyā'*, IV. 20; German translation by Gramlich, p.63.

73 Muslim, Qadar, 17; *Iḥyā'*, IV. 21; Gramlich, 64 (with notes).

74 Bukhārī, Tafsīr Sūrat Maryam, 1; Muslim, Janna, 50. Cf. Suyūṭī, *al-Ḥāwī*, II. 95—96 (*K. Rafʿ al-ṣawt fī dhabḥ al-mawt*); Gramlich, 64n.

75 Q. XXIX:43. The full text runs: *And We coin these similitudes for mankind, and none shall comprehend them save those that know.*

76 *Iḥyā'*, loc. cit.

77 Mention should be made here of the *Mīzān al-ʿamal*, an ethical tract attributed to Ghazālī which presents an explicit denial of physical reward and punishment after death (pp.15–16). According to Montgomery Watt, however, 'the *Mīzān* is an unintelligent compilation from very varied sources' ('The Authenticity', p.39), and this verdict, although recently challenged by M. Sherif (in his *Ghazali's Theory of Virtue*, 170–6) may stand. Although it would appear that the work contains an admixture of genuine Ghazālīan material, the assertion referred to above is too remote from Ghazālī's usual position to be accepted as a reliable indicator of his views.

78 Chapter VII of the present work develops this theme by positing three 'degrees of belief', ranging from the literal to the partly allegorical: all of these 'lie within the realm of possibility', and are correct. However, the doctrine must be accepted by simple acceptance (*taqlīd*) of revealed authority, for those 'who know it by realisation (*taḥqīq*) are few'. (Infra, pp.139–140.)

79 This was not necessarily seen as being a later development. Cf. the saying attributed to Ibn ʿAbbās: 'In Paradise there exist none of the things of this world, save only their names' (Musaddad ibn Musarhad, *al-Musnad*, quoted in Ibn Ḥajar al-ʿAsqalānī, *al-Maṭālib al-ʿĀliya bi-zawā'id al-Masānīd al-Thamāniya*, IV. 404, no.4692.) (For more on this *athar* see Asín Palacios, *Escatología*, 213. For symbolic interpretations of eschatology see ibid., 212–7 and passim; L. Massignon, *La Passion d'al-Hallâj*, II. 682–698.

80 *Iḥyā'*, IV. 21–28; Gramlich, 67–80.

81 For which see Asín Palacios, *Escatología*, 129–133, 180; Smith and Haddad, 90–91; Khālid, 335–339; Bayhaqī, *Baʿth*, 104–109. According to one *ḥadīth* (in al-Ṭabarānī, *al-Muʿjam al-Awsaṭ*, cited in al-Haythamī, *Majmaʿ al-zawā'id wa-manbaʿ al-fawā'id*, X. 378) the people of *al-Aʿrāf* will ultimately enter Heaven through the intercession of the Blessed Prophet.

82 Q. LVI:8.

83 Some remarks on this doctrine of the Vision (*ru'ya*) will be found in notes on pp.250–252 of this book.

84 Bukhārī, Tawḥīd, 35; Muslim, Janna, 4. Cf. Q. XXXII:17: *Those who forsake their beds to cry unto their Lord in fear and hope, and spend of what We have bestowed upon them—no soul knoweth what is kept hidden for them of joy [qurrat aʿyun], as a reward for what they used to do.*

85 *Iḥyā'*, IV. 28; Gramlich, 79–80.

THE REMEMBRANCE OF DEATH AND THE AFTERLIFE

Being the Tenth Book of the Saving Virtues
and the Conclusion of the Book of
the Revival of the Religious Sciences[1]

In the Name of God, Most Compassionate and Merciful

PRAISED BE GOD, Who with death did break the necks of tyrants, shattering with it the backs of Persia's kings, cutting short the aspirations of the Caesars, whose hearts were long averse to recalling death, until the true promise came to them and cast them into the pit. From the loftiest of palaces into the deepest of graves[2] they passed, and from the light of the cradle into the sepulchre's gloom. From dallying with servant-girls and boys into sustaining insects and worms they passed, and from revelling in food and drink[3] into wallowing in the earth; from the friendliness of company into the forlornness of solitude, and from the soft couch into woeful perdition.

See if they had found any strength and protection[4] from death, or taken against it a barrier and refuge. See *if you can perceive a single man of them, or hear from them the slightest sound.*[5]

So all glory to Him Who is unique in power and authority, Who has taken to Himself all claim to permanence, abasing all forms of creation through the extinction which He has written for them, then appointing death as a redemption for the Godfearing and as the promise to them of a meeting. The tomb made He a prison for the damned, a cramped gaol for them until the Day of Decision and Judgement. For His is the power to bestow manifest blessings and to take vengeance through irresistible acts of requital. His is the thanksgiving in the heavens and the earth; His is the praise in the Former World and the Afterlife.

May many blessings and most abundant salutations be invoked upon Muḥammad of the clear miracles and the evident signs, and upon his Family and Companions.

Now, it behoves him for whom death is his destruction, the earth his bed, the worm his intimate, Munkar and Nakīr[A] his companions, the tomb his abode and the belly of the earth his resting-place, the Arising his tryst and Heaven or Hell his destiny, that he should harbour no thought or recollection but of death. No preparedness or plan should he have save for it, and his every expectation, concern, energy, waiting and anticipation should be for its sake alone. It is right that he should account himself among the dead and see himself as one of the people of the graves. For all that comes is certainly near; the distant is what never comes.

The Prophet (may God bless him and grant him peace) has said, 'The intelligent man is he who judges himself and acts for what follows death'.[6] Preparation for something can never be easy unless its memory is constantly renewed in the heart, and this can only be done through reminding oneself by paying attention to those things which cause it to be recalled and by looking to those matters which tell of it. Of the business of death, with its preludes and consequences, the conditions of the next world, the Resurrection, and Heaven and Hell, we shall mention that which the servant of God must repeatedly bring to mind and keep with him in his thinking and his meditation, so that this may act as an encouragement to preparedness. For the journey to what follows

[A] Munkar and Nakīr: the angels who question the newly dead. See Chapter VII below; also A. Wensinck, art. 'Munkar wa-Nakīr' in *SEI*, 411–2; Gardet, *Pensée*, 102n.

death is near at hand, and only a little of life remains; yet of this the people are inattentive. *Their reckoning draweth nigh for mankind, while they turn away in heedlessness.*[7]

We shall mention that which relates to death in two Parts.

THE FIRST PART

Concerning the preludes and consequences of death up to the Blast on the Trump

(Being composed of eight Chapters)

CHAPTER ONE: On the Merit which is in the Remembrance of Death, and an Encouragement to Remember it.

CHAPTER TWO: On Lengthy and Brief Hopes.

CHAPTER THREE: On the Agonies and Violence of Death, and the States Preferable upon its Advent.

CHAPTER FOUR: On the Death of the Emissary of God (may God bless him and grant him peace), and of the Rightly-guided Caliphs after him.

CHAPTER FIVE: On the Sayings of the Caliphs, Princes, and Righteous Men when Nearing Death.

CHAPTER SIX: On the Sayings of the Saints at Funerals and Cemeteries, and the Legal Verdict Concerning the Visitation of Graves.

CHAPTER SEVEN: On the True Nature of Death, and what the Dead Man Undergoes in the Grave prior to the Blast on the Trump.

CHAPTER EIGHT: On the States of the Dead which have been Known through Unveiling in Dreams.

CHAPTER ONE

On the Remembrance of Death, and an Encouragement to Remember it Abundantly

KNOW THAT the heart of the man who is engrossed in this world and is given over to its vanities and harbours love for its appetites must certainly be neglectful of the remembrance of death. Thus failing to recall it, when reminded of it he finds it odious and shies away. Such are the people of whom God has said: *Say: Lo! the death from which ye shrink will surely meet you, and afterward ye will be returned unto the Knower of the Invisible and the Visible, and He will tell you what ye used to do.*[8]

Now, men may be either engrossed [in the world], penitent beginners, or arrived gnostics. The man engrossed does not remember death, or, if he does, it is with regret for his world, and he busies himself with disparaging death. The remembrance of death increases such a one in nothing but distance from God.

The penitent man recalls death frequently, so that fear and apprehension might thereby proceed from his heart, making his repentance complete. It may be that he is in fear of death lest it carry him off before his repentance is complete and before his provisions for the journey are replenished; he is excusable in his aversion to death, and is not included in the saying of the Prophet (may God bless him and grant him peace): 'Whosoever would abhor meeting with God, God abhors meeting with him'.[9] Such a man does not abhor death and meeting God, but only fears the meeting with God passing him by as a result of his deficiency and remissness. He is like the man who is made late for a meeting with his beloved by busying himself with preparations for the encounter in a way that will find approval: he is not deemed to be reluctant about the meeting! The distinguishing mark of the penitent man is his constant preparation for this matter and his lack of any other concern. Were he to be otherwise he would associate with the man engrossed in the world.

As for the gnostic, he remembers death constantly, because for him it is the tryst with his Beloved, and a lover never forgets the appointed time for meeting the one he loves. Usually such a man considers death slow in coming and is happy upon its advent, that he might have done with the abode of sinners and be borne away into the presence of the Lord of the Worlds.[A] Such was the case with Ḥudhayfa, of whom it is related that when death came he said, 'A dear friend has come at a time of poverty. Whoever repents [at such a moment as this] shall not succeed. O Lord God! Should You know that poverty is dearer to me than wealth, and sickness more beloved to me than health, and death more dear to me than life, then make my death easy for me until I meet You.'

Thus it is that the penitent man may be excused the aversion he feels for death, while another is excusable in loving it and longing for it. And higher than either of them is the degree of he that has entrusted his affair to God (Exalted is He!) and no longer prefers death or life for himself, for the dearest of things to him is that which is more beloved in the sight of his Lord. By virtue of profound love and loyalty this man has arrived at the station of absolute surrender and contentment, which is the goal, and the utmost limit.

But whatever the situation may be, in the recollection of death there is reward and merit. For even the man engrossed in the world benefits from it by acquiring an aversion to this world, since it spoils his contentment and the fullness of his pleasure; and

[A] In the Islamic context the remembrance of death and the belief in the worthlessness of this world have traditionally been circumscribed by a prohibition on *tamannī al-mawt*, 'hoping for death'. Cf. the Prophet's statement as reported in the *ḥadīth*: 'let none of you hope for death' (Bukhārī, Marḍā, 19). Ghazālī writes elsewhere (*Iḥyā'*, IV. 270; tr. Gramlich, 669) that 'knowledge (*maʿrifa*) becomes more perfect if one's life is long, through constant meditation, combatting of the lower self and divesting oneself of worldly attachments . . . and all of this calls for time.'

everything which spoils for man his pleasures and his appetites is one of the means of deliverance.

An exposition of the excellence of the remembrance of death, however done

The Emissary of God (may God bless him and grant him peace) has said, 'Remember often the Ender of Pleasures,'[10] by which he meant, 'Make pleasures distasteful thereby until your inclination towards them is broken and you devote yourselves to God (Exalted is He!).' And he said also (may God bless him and grant him peace), 'Were the beasts of the field to know what the son of Adam knows of death you would not find a single plump one to eat.'[11]

Said ᶜĀ'isha (may God be pleased with her), 'O Emissary of God! Shall anyone be resurrected alongside the martyrs?' 'Yes,' he replied. 'He who recalls death twenty times in one day and night.'[12]

The entire reason for this merit is that the remembrance of death must needs result in an aversion to the abode of beguilement and demand that one make preparations for the Afterlife, while heedlessness of death summons one to indulgence in worldly desires.

The Prophet (may God bless him and grant him peace) has said, 'Death is a precious gift to the believer'.[13] This he said because 'the world is the believer's prison,'[14] in which he is incessantly in difficult circumstances due to suffering [the passions of] his soul, and because of the struggle with his desires and the repulse of his devil.[A] Death for him is a release from this torment, and for him this release is a 'precious gift'.

And the Prophet said (may God bless him and grant him peace), 'Death is an atonement for every Muslim'.[15] By this he

[A] Every man having been assigned an angel and a devil, respectively the instruments of his guidance and temptation (Muslim, Tawba, 62, 63).

was referring to the true Muslim and the sincere believer, from whose tongue and hand the Muslims are secure and in whom the qualities of the faithful are realised, who has not been polluted by any but the smallest and most trivial of sins. From these he is purified by death, which atones for him following his avoidance of the major sins and his performance of the obligatory works of religion.

ᶜAṭā' al-Khurāsānī once said: 'The Emissary of God (may God bless him and grant him peace) passed by a gathering from which laughter was ringing out. "Disturb your assembly by recalling the Spoiler of Pleasures," he said. "And what is the Spoiler of Pleasures?" they asked. "Death," he replied'.[16]

According to Anas (may God be pleased with him) the Emissary of God (may God bless him and grant him peace) said, 'Remember death abundantly, for to recall it wipes away sins and makes one abstemious in the world'.[17]

Also he said (may God bless him and grant him peace), 'Sufficient is death as a divider',[18] and also, 'Sufficient is death as a warner'.[19]

The Emissary of God (may God bless him and grant him peace) once went out to the mosque and noticed a group of people talking and laughing. 'Remember death!' he said. 'By Him in Whose hand lies my soul, if you knew what I know you would laugh little and weep much.'[20]

A man was once mentioned and highly praised in the presence of the Prophet (may God bless him and grant him peace). 'How is your companion's remembrance of death?' he asked. 'We have scarcely heard him mention it,' they replied. 'Then your companion', he said, 'is not as you suggest'.[21]

Said Ibn ᶜUmar (may God be pleased with him), 'I once came to the Prophet, may God bless him and grant him peace, in a group of ten people. A man from the Helpers [*al-Anṣār*] enquired, "Who is the most intelligent and generous of men, O Emissary of God?" And he replied, "The most diligent in recalling death, and the one who is best prepared for it. Such are the intelligent ones, who have gained the honour of this world and the dignity of the next".'[22]

Let us now turn to the Narratives.[A]

Al-Ḥasan, may God (Exalted is He!) have mercy upon him, said, 'Death has exposed the world's faults, and has left no joy to any thinking man'.

Said al-Rabīʿ ibn Khuthaym, 'There is nothing concealed for which the believer waits that is better than death'. He also used to say, 'Let no-one know of me, and throw me in to my Lord.'

A philosopher once wrote to one of his brethren as follows: 'O my brother! Beware of death in this abode before you travel to an abode in which you long for death but find it not.'

When death was mentioned in the presence of Ibn Sīrīn all his limbs would become lifeless.

ʿUmar ibn ʿAbd al-ʿAzīz used every night to gather together the doctors of the Law, and they would remind one another of death, the Arising and the Afterlife until they broke out in tears as though at a funeral.

Ibrāhīm al-Taymī said, 'Two things have severed me from the pleasures of this world: the remembrance of death, and calling to mind the standing before God (Great and Glorious is He!).'[B]

Said Kaʿb, 'The world's misfortunes and[23] cares become trivial for the man who is conscious of death.'

Said Muṭarrif, 'In a dream I once saw someone declaiming in the very centre of the mosque of Basra, "Remembering death the hearts of the Godfearing has broken. In nought save distraction, by God, is how you see them".'

Said Abū Ashʿath, 'We used to call on al-Ḥasan, and [his conversation] was of nothing but Hell, the Afterlife, and the remembrance of death.'

Ṣafīya (may God be pleased with her) told of an old woman who once complained to ʿĀ'isha (may God be pleased with her) of the hardness of her heart. 'Remember death frequently', she told her, 'and your heart will be softened'. This she did, and her heart was indeed made soft. She went to thank ʿĀ'isha (may God be pleased with her).

[A] *āthār*: traditions of the early Muslims, usually distinct in Ghazālī's writings from *akhbār*, traditions ascribed to the Prophet.

[B] i.e. on the Day of Judgement.

When David (upon whom be peace) remembered death and the Resurrection he would weep and his joints would become dislocated; when he remembered the [Divine] attribute of Mercy he would become himself again.

Said al-Ḥasan: 'Never have I seen an intelligent man without finding him to be wary of death and saddened by it.'

Said ᶜUmar ibn ᶜAbd al-ᶜAzīz to one of his divines, 'Admonish me.' 'You shall not be the first caliph to die,' he replied. 'Tell me more,' he asked. 'Of your ancestors from Adam,' he said, 'not one has not tasted death; now, your turn is come.' At this, ᶜUmar wept.

Al-Rabīᶜ ibn Khuthaym dug a grave in his house, and used each day to sleep therein so that by this expedient he might remember death unceasingly. 'Were the remembrance of death to leave my heart for a single hour', he was wont to say, 'it would become corrupted.'

Muṭarrif ibn ᶜAbd Allāh ibn al-Shikhkhīr said, 'This death has indeed spoilt the pleasure of those that seek pleasure, therefore seek out that pleasure in which there is no death.'

ᶜUmar ibn ᶜAbd al-ᶜAzīz once said to ᶜAnbasa, 'Remember death abundantly, for if your life is easy it will make it hard, while if your life is hard it will make it easy.'

Said Abū Sulaymān al-Dārānī, 'I once asked Umm Hārūn whether she loved death. "I do not," she replied. "Why not?" I enquired, and she said, "Were I to disobey a human being I would not wish to meet him. So how can I wish to meet Him when I have disobeyed Him?"'

An exposition of the way to bring about the recollection of death in the heart

Know that death is a terrible and most perilous thing. The heedlessness with which the people treat it is the consequence only of their insufficient meditation upon it and remembrance thereof. Even the man who does remember it does not do so with an unoccupied heart, but rather with one that is busy with the desires of this world, so that the remembrance of death does not have a salutary effect upon his heart. The way forward here is for the bondsman to void his heart of all things save the recollection of the demise which lies before him, in the way that the man who intends a dangerous voyage to a desert place or to set sail upon the ocean does not think of any other matter. When the remembrance of death touches his heart and comes to make some impression upon it his contentment and pleasure in the world will wane and his heart will break. The most productive method of bringing this about is for him to make frequent remembrance of those of his peers and associates who have passed away before him: he should contemplate their death and dissolution beneath the earth and recall how they appeared in their former positions and circumstances, and meditate upon the way in which the earth has now obliterated the beauty of their forms, and how their parts have been scattered in their tombs, and how they made widows of their wives and orphans of their children; how they lost their property, and how their mosques and gatherings have become voided of them, and of how their very traces have been wiped away. To the extent that a man recalls another, and pictures clearly in his mind his state and how he died, and imagines his form, and remembers his sprightliness and how he used to come and go, and the care which he devoted to living and to continuing, and his forgetfulness of death, and how he was deceived by the propitious means of his subsistence, and his trusting in his strength and his youth,[24] and his inclination to laughter and fun, and his heedlessness of the imminent death and the speedy destruction which lay before him; how he used to go hither and thither, and that now his feet and joints have rotted away, how he used to speak, while now the worm has devoured his tongue, how he used to laugh, while now the dust has consumed his teeth; how he used to arrange for himself that which he would not need for ten years at a time when there lay between him and death only a month, while he was in ignorance of what was planned for him, until death came at an hour he had not reckoned upon, and the Angel's form stood revealed before him, and the summons struck his ears—either to Heaven or to

Hell!—at that time he will see that he is like them, and that his heedlessness is as theirs, and that as theirs shall be his end.

Said Abu'l-Dardā' (may God be pleased with him), 'When you recall the departed count yourself as one of them.'

Said Ibn Masʿūd (may God be pleased with him) 'The happy man is he who draws an admonition from someone else.'

Said ʿUmar ibn ʿAbd al-ʿAzīz, 'Do you not see that each day, by morning and night, you prepare a traveller to God (Great and Glorious is He!), setting him in a crevice in the earth, who has taken the dust for his pillow, left his loved ones behind, and put himself apart from his means of subsistence?'

Holding fast to these and other similar ideas, and also entering graveyards and seeing ill people, is the way to refresh the remembrance of death in the heart until it takes possession of it and stands before one's eyes. At this point one will almost be ready for it, and will shun the world of vanity. Otherwise, a remembrance with the superficial aspect of the heart and a sweet tongue will be of little avail in warning and informing. However contented one's heart may be with some worldly thing, one should at once recall that it must needs be parted with.

One day, Ibn Muṭīʿ looked at his house, and was delighted by its beauty. He then broke out in tears, saying, 'By God, were it not for death I would rejoice in you, and but for the narrowness of the graves towards which we travel we would be entranced by this world.' Then he sobbed loudly and violently.

CHAPTER TWO

On Lengthy Hopes, and the Merit of Brief Hopes, together with the Reason for their Prolongation and How this may be Cured

The merit of brief hopes

GOD'S EMISSARY (may God bless him and grant him peace) once said to ʿAbd Allāh ibn ʿUmar, 'In the morning-time, do not speak to yourself of the evening, and in the evening-time do not speak to yourself of the morning. Take from your life something for your death, and from your health something for your infirmity, for in truth, O ʿAbd Allāh, you do not know what your name shall be tomorrow.'[A]

ʿAlī (may God ennoble his countenance) related that the Prophet (may God bless him and grant him peace) said, 'Two things fear I for you above all else: the pursuit of desire and lengthy hopes. For the pursuit of desire bars one from the Truth, while lengthy hopes are the very love of this world.' Then he said, 'Indeed, God (Exalted is He!) bestows the world upon the man He loves and the man He abhors; and when He loves His bondsman He gives him faith. Indeed, religion has its sons, as does the world; therefore be with the sons of religion, and be not with the sons of the world. Indeed, the world has moved by and passed on, while the Afterlife has moved close and drawn near. Indeed, you are in a day in which there is action without reckoning, but

[A] This is in fact Ibn ʿUmar's advice to Mujāhid usually appended to the well-known *ḥadīth* in which the Prophet says, 'Be in the world as though you were a stranger or a wayfarer'. (Bukhārī, Riqāq, 3.) According to Ibn Ḥajar the somewhat curious final phrase can mean either 'whether you will be called "sorrowful" or "blessed", or whether you will be alive or dead.' (*Fatḥ al-Bārī*, XI. 235.)

have well-nigh come to a day in which there shall be reckoning and no action.'[1]

Said Umm al-Mundhir, 'The Emissary of God (may God bless him and grant him peace) came out before the people one evening and said, "O people! Are you not ashamed before God?" "How should that be, O Emissary of God?" they asked, and he replied, "You gather in what you shall not eat, you hope for what you shall never accomplish, and build what you shall never inhabit".'[2]

Said Abū Saʿīd al-Khudrī, 'Usāma ibn Zayd once purchased a slave-girl from Zayd ibn Thābit for a hundred dinars, the payment of which was to be deferred for one month. The Emissary of God (may God bless him and grant him peace) came to hear of this and said, "Are you not amazed at Usāma, who pays a month after he buys? Truly, Usāma has lengthy hopes! By Him in Whose hand lies my soul, never have I closed my eyes without thinking that my eyelids would not close again before God took my spirit, neither have I opened them again in the belief that I would close them once more before passing away. Not once have I partaken of a morsel without thinking that I should not swallow it before death choked me on it." Then he said, "O children of Adam! If you have sense, then account yourselves among the dead. For by Him in Whose hand lies my soul, *that which is promised you shall come, and you shall not escape*".'[3]

It is related on the authority of Ibn ʿAbbās (may God be pleased with them both)[A] that God's Emissary (may God bless him and grant him peace) used to go out to pass water and would then perform the dust-ablution.[B] 'O Emissary of God,' I [Ibn ʿAbbās] would say to him. 'There is some water not far from you.' 'How may I know?' he replied. 'It may be that I shall not reach it.'[4]

It is related that he once picked up three twigs, setting one before him, another at its side, and the third at a distance. 'Do you know what this is?' he asked. 'God and His Emissary know best!'

[A] That is, with Ibn ʿAbbās and his father.

[B] *tayammum*, a wiping of the face and hands with clean dust which, in cases of illness or the absence of water, may be performed in place of the customary *wuḍū'* ablution required before most acts of worship. (*Iḥyā'*, I. 116, 121.)

we replied. 'This is man,' he said, 'and this is his lifespan, while that is hope, which the son of Adam pursues. His lifespan, however, shall overcome him before he can realise his hope.'[A][5]

And he said (may God bless him and grant him peace), 'It is as though the son of Adam were beset by ninety-nine deaths; if they fail to strike him down he falls into old age.'[6]

Said Ibn Masᶜūd [having sketched out a diagram in the dust], 'This is man, and these around him are ways by which death may come to him. Beyond them lies old age, and beyond that again lies his hope, which he cherishes while these deaths approach him. He will be seized by whichever of them is ordered to do so. Should they miss the mark, however, he will be slain by old age, while his hope remains.'[B]

And ᶜAbd Allāh [ibn Masᶜūd] said, 'The Emissary of God (may God bless him and grant him peace) once drew for us a square, setting a line down its centre and then drawing other lines by its side and another leading outside it. "Do you know what this is?" he asked, and we replied, "God and His Emissary know best!" He pointed to the line which lay at the centre, and said, "This is man, and this is his lifespan encircling him. These"—indicating the lines which lay round about it—"are chance happenings, which snap at him; when one misses him he is snapped at by another. And this"—indicating the line leading outside—"is his hope".'[7]

Said Anas, 'The Emissary of God (may God bless him and grant him peace) said, "The son of Adam may grow old, but two things remain with him: greed and hope".'[8] And in an alternative version: 'For him two things remain young: greed for wealth and greed for longevity.'[9]

And he said (may God bless him and grant him peace), 'The first people of this nation shall be saved by certainty and renunciation, while the latecomers shall be destroyed by greed and hope.'[10]

[A] The meaning of this Tradition is somewhat obscure. Perhaps the diagram was as follows, 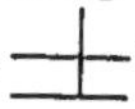 the vertical line representing man's hope, which is cut short by death.

[B] The diagram  is printed at the margin of Zabīdī's commentary, evidently as an elaboration of this account. It would also seem to illustrate the next Tradition. The meaning is reasonably clear; for a closer analysis, however, see Rosenthal, *Sweeter than hope*, 109.

It is said that Jesus (upon whom be peace) once sat down by an old man who was digging the earth with a spade. Said Jesus, 'O Lord God, take away his hope,' and the old man put down his spade and lay down. After an hour had passed, Jesus said, 'O Lord God, restore hope to him,' and he arose, and set about his task. And when Jesus asked him concerning what had transpired he said, 'While I was at work my soul said to me, "How much longer shall you labour, now that you are an old man?" so I cast aside my spade and lay down. Then it said to me, "By God, you must live out that which is left to you," so I arose, and took up my spade once more.'

Said al-Ḥasan, 'The Emissary of God (may God bless him and grant him peace) once asked, "Do all of you wish to enter into Heaven?" and they [his Companions] said, "Yes indeed, O Emissary of God!" And he said, "Then cut short your hopes, bring your deaths before your eyes, and be rightly ashamed before God".'[11]

In his prayers he used to say (may God bless him and grant him peace), 'O Lord God! I seek refuge in Thee from a worldly estate which precludes the good of the Afterlife. I seek refuge in Thee from a life which bars the good of death. And I seek refuge in Thee from hopes which make against good works.'[12]

From the Narratives

Said Muṭarrif ibn ᶜAbd Allāh, 'Were I to know the time of my demise I would fear for my reason. God has blessed His bondsmen by granting them heedlessness of death; were it not for this heedlessness they would take no pleasure in life, and no markets would be established among them.'

Said al-Ḥasan, 'Forgetfulness and hope are two mighty blessings upon the progeny of Adam; but for them the Muslims would not walk in the streets.'

Said al-Thawrī, 'I have heard it said that man is created foolish, and that were it otherwise life would hold no pleasure for him.'

Said Saᶜīd ibn ᶜAbd al-Raḥmān, 'The world is peopled only through the dimwittedness of its inhabitants.'

Said Salmān al-Fārisī, 'There are three things which have surprised me enough to make me laugh: a man who sets his hopes in the world while death is seeking him out, a heedless man who does not go unheeded, and a man who fills his mouth with laughter although he does not know whether the Lord of the Worlds is angry with him or satisfied. And three things have grieved me enough to make me weep: taking leave of the loved ones, Muḥammad and his people, the terror of the Resurrection, and the time when I shall stand before God not knowing whether I am to be consigned to Heaven or to Hell.'

A man once said, 'After Zurāra ibn Abī Awfā's death I beheld him in a dream. "Which actions proved to be of most value to you?" I asked, and he replied, "Reliance [*tawakkul*] upon God, and brief hopes".'

Said al-Thawrī, 'Renunciation of the world consists in the brevity of one's hopes, not in eating rough food or donning a mantle.'

Al-Mufaḍḍal ibn Faḍāla once asked his Lord to take away his hope, and he lost his appetite for food and drink; then he called on his Lord again, and He restored his hope to him, whereupon he returned to his food and his drink.

Al-Ḥasan once was asked, 'O Abū Saʿīd! Do you not wash your shirt?' and he replied, 'The matter is too hurried for that.'

Said al-Ḥasan, 'Death is bound to your forelocks, while the world folds away behind you.'

Someone said, 'I am as a man who stretches forth his neck while a sword is poised, waiting for the moment when his head will be severed.'

Said Dāūd al-Ṭāʾī, 'Were I to hope for one month of life I would consider that I had committed something dire. How might I hope for such a thing when I behold calamities descending upon mankind at every hour of the night and the day?'

It is told that Shaqīq al-Balkhī once repaired to a [spiritual] instructor [*ustādh*] of his named Abū Hāshim al-Rummānī, carrying something bound up in the side of his garment. 'What's that you've got with you?' his instructor demanded, and he replied, 'Some almonds given to me by one of my brethren; I would like you to break your fast with them.' 'O Shaqīq!' he said. 'Do you tell yourself that you shall live until nightfall? May I never again speak to you!' And Shaqīq said, 'And he went inside, and closed the door in my face.'

Said ʿUmar ibn ʿAbd al-ʿAzīz in one of his sermons, 'For every voyage there must be provisions; therefore adopt the fear of God as provisions for your voyage from this world into the Afterlife. Be as though you had seen the reward and chastisement which God has prepared: harbour longing and fear! Do not suffer your time to grow long for you lest your hearts become hard and you grow submissive before your enemy,[A] for, by God, the man who does not know whether he will awaken at the end of the night, or live through the morning to the evening, can have no high hopes, for it may be that between these times lie the hooks of fate. How many men have I seen, and have you seen withal, who were beguiled by this world; yet contentment is the lot only of he who is certain of deliverance from the chastisement of God (Exalted is He!). Only the man who is safe from the terrors of the Day of Arising can be content. As for the man who dresses his wound only to be afflicted by another coming from a different direction, how can he be of cheer? I ask God's protection from enjoining upon you something which I forbid myself, for then my transaction would be in loss, and my fault would stand revealed, and my indigence would be plain on that Day when wealth and poverty shall stand forth, and when the Scales are erected. You have been burdened with something which would cause the very stars to fall were they to be charged likewise, and the mountains to melt down and the earth to be riven asunder. Know you not that there exists no degree between Heaven and Hell, and that you are voyaging either to one or to the other?'

A man wrote the following to a brother of his: 'To proceed. Truly, this world is a dream, while the next is wakefulness. Between the twain lies the intermedium of death. Thus we are in jumbled dreams. Goodbye.'

Another man wrote to one of his brethren as follows: 'Sorrow in this world is long indeed, and death is ever near to man. Each

[A] i.e. the devil.

day brings its determined portion of decline as decay steals through his frame. Make haste, then, before you are summoned to depart. Goodbye.'

Said al-Ḥasan, 'Before Adam (upon whom be peace) committed his sin, his hope was behind his back and his fate before his eyes. But when he committed it he was transformed, so that he set his hope before his eyes and his fate behind his back.'[13]

Said ʿAbd Allāh ibn Sumayṭ, 'I once heard my father say, "O man, who is beguiled by abiding health! Have you ever beheld a man dead without cause? O man, who is beguiled by a lengthy respite! Have you ever beheld a man seized without forewarning? Truly, were you only to give some thought to the length of your life you would forget every pleasure which you have until now enjoyed. Is it by health that you are beguiled, or because of long haleness that you make merry? Are you secure from death, or hold you the Angel of Death in contempt? For that Angel, when he appears, will not be deflected from you by a king's fortune, nor by all the profusion of your retinue. Know you not that death is the hour of woe and sobbing, and lamentation over one's prodigality? At that time shall it be said, "May God have mercy upon that one of His bondsmen who acted for what follows death. May God have mercy upon His bondsman, who looked to himself before death befell him".'

Said Abū Zakarīyā al-Taymī, 'Once, when Sulaymān ibn ʿAbd al-Malik was in the Sacred Mosque,[A] an engraved stone was brought to him. He ordered that someone be found who could read it, and Wahb ibn Munabbih was brought. And there upon it was [this legend]: "O son of Adam! Could you only behold the brevity of your remaining span you would renounce your lengthy hopes and would long to increase in works,[B] and would cut short your ambitions and your stratagems. On the morrow, grief will be your lot only if your foothold has slipped and your family and retinue forsake you, if your father and relations

[A] *al-Masjid al-Ḥarām*: the mosque-sanctuary at Mecca where the Kaʿba stands.

[B] As in several of the stories in this section, use is made here of a play on words common in the ascetic milieu: *ajal* ('lifespan', or 'death'), *amal* ('hope') and *ʿamal* ('works').

abandon you, and your son and kinsman deny you. Neither shall you return to your worldly estate, nor shall you increase in good works. Therefore, work for the Day of Arising before you are overtaken by grief and contrition." At this, Sulaymān wept bitterly.'

Someone said, 'I once saw a letter from Muḥammad ibn Yūsuf to ᶜAbd al-Raḥmān ibn Yūsuf [which ran]: "Peace be upon you. I praise God unto you, even Him besides Whom there is no other deity. To proceed. I would caution you regarding your voyage from your place of respite to your lasting abode and the requital for your works, whereby you shall come to rest in the depths of the earth after abiding upon its superficies. At that time shall come unto you Munkar and Nakīr, who shall sit by you and reproach you. Should God be with you, then there shall be neither hurt, loneliness nor need, but should it be otherwise, then may God protect you and me from an evil doom and a straitened resting-place! Then the Shout of the Concourse shall overtake you, and the Blast upon the Trump, and the Almighty shall commence to pass judgement upon His creatures. The earth shall be voided of her people, and the heavens of their denizens, as all secrets stand revealed, and as the Fire is stoked up, the Scales erected, *and the Prophets and the Martyrs are brought,*[14] *and they are judged with verity, and it is said, Praised be God, the Lord of the Worlds!*[15] How great will be the number of men both shamed and screened; how many will be destroyed, and how many delivered; how many will be chastised and how many shown mercy! Would that I could know how my state and yours shall be on that Day! In this there is something to make away with pleasure and to distract one from one's desires, and to cut short one's hopes, to arouse the sleeping and to alert the heedless. May God assist us, and you also, in the face of this great peril, and set this world and the next in our hearts as they lie in the hearts of the Godfearing, for we are but His, and live by Him alone. Goodbye".'

ᶜUmar ibn ᶜAbd al-ᶜAzīz, delivering once a sermon, said, after having praised and magnified God: 'O people! You were not created in jest, neither shall you be abandoned to no purpose. For yours is a place of return, where God shall gather you together for decision and judgement between you. On the morrow a bondsman shall be defeated and dejected only if God should expel him from His mercy, which embraces all things, and from His Heaven, the compass of which is as the heavens and the earth. Tomorrow there shall be security only for the man that was in fear and trembling before God, who sold little for much, something which must needs perish for something which shall abide, and misery for beatitude. Perceive you not that you are among those that shall pass away, and that you shall be succeeded by others that remain behind? Perceive you not that every day, by morning and eve, you pay your last respects to a traveller to God (Great and Glorious is He!), who has run his course and whose hope is at an end? You lay him in the depths of a crevice in the earth with neither pillow nor preparation. He has cast off the instruments of subsistence, and departed from his loved ones, and now confronts the Reckoning. By God! I pronounce this statement of mine not knowing whether any one of you has more sins than I know I myself bear, but it is a just, Divine usage whereby I enjoin His obedience and discommend transgression against Him. I seek God's pardon.' Thereupon he covered his face with his sleeve and began to weep until his beard became soaked with his tears. And scarcely had he resumed his seat before he passed away.

Said al-Qaᶜqāᶜ ibn Ḥakīm, 'For thirty years have I been preparing myself for death; were it to come to me now there would be nothing I would wish to postpone.'

Said al-Thawrī, 'I once heard an old man in the mosque at Kūfa saying, "I have abided in this mosque for thirty years waiting for death to descend upon me. Were it to come now I would not require anything of it, nor forbid it anything. I am owed nothing by anyone; neither do I have anything which is the property of another".'

Said ᶜAbd Allāh ibn Thaᶜlaba, 'You laugh, but perhaps the fuller has already finished with your winding-sheets!'

Said Abū Muḥammad ibn ᶜAlī,[16] the ascetic, 'We once went forth to a funeral at Kūfa in the company of Dāūd al-Ṭā'ī. While the burial was taking place he withdrew and sat down to one side. I came and sat down near him, and he said, "Whoever fears the

Promise,[A] to him shall be brought near that which is remote. Whosoever extends his hopes, his actions shall be enfeebled. All that shall come is near. And know, O my brother, that everything which distracts you from your Lord is an evil omen for you. Know also that all the world's people are also the people of the graves, who lament for what they have left behind and rejoice at that which they have sent before them. But that for which the people of the graves lament is that over which the people of this world make argument and war, and concerning which they make their disputations before the judges".'

It is related that Maᶜrūf al-Karkhī (may God, Exalted is He! have mercy upon him) was once beginning the Prayer. Said Muḥammad ibn Abī Tawba, 'He told me to step forwards, and I said, "If I lead this Prayer for you I will never lead you in one again." And Maᶜrūf said, "And you tell yourself that you shall pray again! We seek refuge with God from lengthy hopes, for truly they make against good works!" '

In a sermon, ᶜUmar ibn ᶜAbd al-ᶜAzīz once said, 'This world is not the place of your final residence. It is an abode which God has decreed shall be extinguished, and from which He has ordained that its indwellers shall pass. How many confident men shall ere long rot away, and how many cheerful inhabitants shall soon pass on! Therefore (may God have mercy on you), make good your voyage with the aid of the best transports you have. *And make provision, for verily, the best provision is the fear of God.*[17] The world is nothing but a shadow which is shrinking and vanishing away. And while the son of Adam competes in the world in great happiness, God summons him through his fate, and impales him with the arrow of his demise, stripping him of his chattels and his worldly goods, so that other men come to possess what he has made and gained. In truth, the world does not delight as much as it causes harm; rather, it gives a little joy, and long melancholy.'

It is recorded of Abū Bakr al-Ṣiddīq (may God, Exalted is He! be pleased with him) that he was in the habit of saying in his sermons, 'Where are the men of fine, clear faces? Those who were delighted with their youth? Where are the kings that built the

[A] *al-waᶜīd*: 'promise' or 'threat'; in this case, of the Day of Judgement.

cities, and fortified them with walls? Where are they that used to receive victory on the fields of battle? Time has swept them away, and they have gone on to the shadows of the graves. So make haste! Make haste! And be saved! Be saved!'

An exposition of the cause of lengthy hopes, and how they may be cured

Know that lengthy hopes have two causes, the first of which is ignorance, and the second of which is love of the world.

As regards the latter, [the problem is that] when man comes to love the world, and its desires, pleasures and attachments, then taking leave of it weighs heavily upon his heart, which will thus avoid thinking of death, which is the instrument of this separation; for everyone who conceives a dislike for something will fend it off. Man is infatuated with vain hopes, and ever fills his soul with hoping for that which is conformable to his preferences; and the only thing which conforms to them is that he should remain in the world. Thus he never ceases to imagine this and count upon it within himself, along with the accessories of such permanence, including the wealth, family, accommodation, acquaintances, riding beasts and other means of life which he needs in the world. In this manner his heart becomes attached to this notion and cannot progress beyond it, being distracted thereby from the remembrance of death and not deeming it to be nigh.

When in certain circumstances the question of death and the need to prepare for it occur to him, he procrastinates, and makes promises to himself, saying, 'There are yet many days before you until you grow mature; then you can repent'. And when he grows to maturity he says, 'Not until you become an old man.' But when he becomes an old man he says, 'Not until you finish building this house,' or 'establishing this farm,' or 'return from this voyage,' or 'conclude the setting-up of this son, and provide for him and arrange a house for him,' or 'not until you have subdued this enemy who takes such pleasure in your misfortunes.'

Thus it is that he unceasingly procrastinates and delays, never plunging into one task without there being consequent upon its completion ten others, and in this gradual fashion procrastinates day after day, led by one task to another, or rather, to several others, until he is snatched away by his fate at some moment he never expected, at which his sorrows grow long and protracted.

The most frequent cry of the dwellers in the Inferno is 'shall'. 'O woe,' they cry, 'because of "shall!"' For the unfortunate procrastinator is unaware that what induces him to postpone something today will still be with him tomorrow, and that it will, with the passage of time, grow in strength and firmness. He thinks it conceivable that the man who plunges into the world and pays it heed might have time to spare. What folly! No-one has time to spare from it save he who has cast it aside.

No man has had his needs fulfilled therein;
one desire ends only in another.

The root of all these hopes is the love of the world, and finding comfort therein, neglecting the saying [of the Prophet] (may God bless him and grant him peace): 'Love whomso'er you will, for you shall surely leave him.'[18]

As for the matter of ignorance, this consists in a man's setting his confidence in his youth, and considering that death cannot be near while he remains young. This unfortunate wretch fails to consider that were the old men of his land to be tallied up they would amount to no more than a tenth of the men of the land. They are so few simply because death is more common in youth: for every old man that dies a thousand children and young men pass away. Alternatively, he may consider death to be unlikely by reason of his health, and discount the possibility of sudden death, being quite unaware that it is far from unlikely, or that, should it truly be unlikely, then sudden illness is not; and every illness makes its appearance suddenly, and when it has come death is no longer improbable.

If this heedless man would but think, and come to realise that death has no fixed time as to youth, middle age or decrepitude, and that it does not know winter from summer, autumn from spring, or day from night, his awareness would be greater and he would busy himself with preparing for it. But ignorance of these matters, combined with the love of this world, invites him to prolong his hopes and to neglect any consideration of the proximity of death. Always does he think that death is ahead of him, but does not reckon upon its befalling him and that before long he will tumble into it. Constantly does he imagine that he will be following funeral cortèges, and never imagines that his own cortège will some day be followed, because witnessing the demise of others is something which is often repeated and has become familiar. But as far as his own death is concerned, he has no experience of it, and cannot imagine that he will experience it, for it has never transpired; and when it does it will never do so again: it will be the first and the final time.

The way forwards for him is to compare himself with others, and to appreciate that his own funeral cortège must itself be followed, and that he himself must needs be interred in his grave, and that it may well be that the unfired brick with which his tomb will be covered has already been made, all unbeknown to him. Thus it is that his procrastination is sheer ignorance.

Upon thus having grasped that its cause is ignorance and the love of the world, one must cure oneself by destroying this cause. Ignorance is effaced by clear meditation with an aware heart, and through hearing eloquent wisdom issuing from hearts that are pure.

In the case of the love of the world, the cure by which it is driven from the heart is harsh, for this is a chronic illness the treatment of which sorely exercised the ancients and the moderns alike. Its treatment lies only in faith in the Last Day, and the great punishment and generous reward which shall then be assigned. In proportion to one's degree of certainty with regard thereto, the love of the world will leave one's heart, for it is only the love of something great that may erase from the heart the love of something paltry. When one perceives the meanness of this world and the great preciousness of the next, one will despise any inclination towards worldly things; and this would be so even if one were to be given authority over the earth from East to West.

How then could it be, when one has nothing of this world save a meagre, polluted and adulterated portion, that one might rejoice over it or feel its love take root in the heart, if faith in the Afterlife is present? We pray God (Exalted is He!) that He should make us behold this world as He has given His righteous bondsmen to behold it.

There exists no medicine which will induce one to contemplate death with one's heart comparable to that of looking to those of one's peers and companions who have passed away, and to the manner in which death came to them at a time they had never expected. At this time, the man who had made preparations *has triumphed mightily*,[19] but as for him who was beguiled by lengthy hopes, *he has failed most manifestly*.[20]

Let man in every hour look to his limbs and his extremities. Let his thoughts dwell upon how the worms must needs devour them, and upon the fashion in which his bones shall rot away. Let him wonder whether the worms are to begin with the pupil of his right eye or of his left; for there is no part of his body that shall not be food for the worm. He can do nothing for himself but to understand, and to act sincerely for the sake of God (Exalted is He!). And in like fashion, let him meditate upon that which we shall presently relate concerning the Punishment of the Grave, the Inquisition of Munkar and Nakīr, and the Congregation and Quickening, together with the terrors of the Resurrection, and the sounding of the Call on the Day of the Greatest Exposition. For it is thoughts such as these which prompt anew the remembrance of death in the heart, and summon one to make ready for it.

An exposition of people's diverse ranks in lengthy and brief hopes

Know that mankind is arrayed in different ranks in this regard. Among men there are some who hope for immortality, and long for it always. God (Exalted is He!) has said, *One of them would fain be given a thousand years of life*.[21] And of their number are others who hope to survive until old age, the greatest age witnessed and beheld. It is they who have conceived a violent love for the world. The Emissary of God (may God bless him and grant him peace) has said, 'The old man is like a youth in his worldliness, even should his collar bones have twisted from age, save those that are pious, *and they are few indeed.*'[22]

Others there are among them whose hopes extend for a year, and who do not occupy themselves with plans for what will transpire subsequently. Such a man does not reckon upon existing in the following year, although he makes preparations in the summer for the winter, and in the winter for the summer, occupying himself with worship when he has gathered enough for his year. And there are others who hope for the summer's or the winter's span, not setting aside in summer any garments for the winter, neither any summer garments during the wintertime.

Amongst them also are people whose hopes extend as far as a day and a night, so that they prepare for the day only and not for the morrow. Said Jesus (upon whom be peace), 'Pay no attention to your provisions for tomorrow, for if tomorrow is to be part of your lifetime then your provisions will come with it, whereas if it is not to be, then you should pay no attention to the lifetimes of others.'

There are other men amongst them whose hopes do not extend beyond an hour. As our Prophet said (may God bless him and grant him peace): 'O ᶜAbd Allāh![23] In the morning time do not speak to yourself of the evening, and in the evening do not speak to yourself of the morning.'[24] The Emissary of God (may God bless him and grant him peace) used to perform the dust-ablution even when able to obtain water a while later, saying, 'It may be that I shall not reach it.'[25]

Among them also are men for whom death stands before their very eyes, as though it had already befallen them, so that they live in [constant] expectation of it. These are the people who pray like men who are saying farewell.[A] Regarding them there is [the saying] related of Muᶜādh ibn Jabal (may God, Exalted is He!, be

[A] The Prophet is reported to have said, 'Pray like a man who is saying farewell.' (Ibn Māja, Zuhd, 15; Ibn Ḥanbal, *Musnad*, v. 412).

pleased with him), when he was asked by the Emissary of God (may God bless him and grant him peace) about the reality of his faith: 'Never have I taken a single step', he said, 'believing that I would follow it with another.' And it is told of al-Aswad, the Abyssinian, that when he prayed at night he used to turn to his left and his right, and that he said, when asked what he was doing, 'I am looking to see from which direction the Angel of Death shall come to me.'

Such, then, are the ranks of mankind. Each man occupies a certain degree before God: the man whose hopes are restricted to a month is not like the one whose hopes extend to a month and a day; between the two is a discrepancy in degree in God's sight. For truly, God does not work injustice, even so much as an atom's weight: *he who works an atom's weight of good shall see it.*[26] Then the effect of short hopes makes itself manifest in the celerity with which men act. Everyone claims that he has short hopes, yet he lies, for these can only reveal themselves in his actions. He may be concerning himself with things which he will not need for a year, and this indicates the length of his hopes. The sign of providential success is that death stands before a man's very eyes, and that he is not heedless of it for a single hour. Let him therefore make[27] his preparations for death, which shall come to him at its appointed time. Should he live to the evening he will render thanks to God (Exalted is He!) for having been granted obedience to Him, and will rejoice that he has not let his day go to waste, and that he has rather obtained his share thereof and laid up something for himself. Then he shall continue in the same wise until, in turn, the morning comes.

This is possible only for the man who has emptied his heart of the morrow and what might then transpire. When such a man dies, he receives felicity and bounty, and while he lives he contentedly makes good preparations, and enjoys the pleasure of hidden communion [with God]. For him, death is rapture, and life is gain.

Therefore, O unfortunate one, let death occupy your thoughts, for the voyage is urging you ever onward, while all the time you are in heedlessness of your own self. It may well be that you have drawn close to your resting-place and have covered the distance; and never should you be in such a position unless you have made haste to act, seizing an advantage from every breath for which you have been granted respite.

An exposition of making haste to works, and a warning about the unworthiness of delay

Know that whosoever has two absent brethren, and is anticipating the return of one of them the following day and of the other in a month's or a year's time, will not make preparations for the latter, but only for the one whose advent is expected on the morrow, for preparation is occasioned when something is expected soon. Thus the heart of the man who anticipates the arrival of death in a year's time will be concerned with this period and be oblivious of that which will come thereafter. But then each day will he awake and expect the year in its entirety, undiminished by the day which has just gone by. This will prevent him from making haste to works indefinitely, for he will invariably behold a generous span lying before him in that year, and postpone his [righteous] works, as [the Prophet] said (may God bless him and grant him peace): 'Not one of you may expect from this world aught but wealth which leads to excess, or poverty which leads to forgetfulness, or a destructive illness, or an enfeebling old age, or a speedy death, or the Antichrist (and the Antichrist is the worst of all absent things), or the Hour, *and the Hour is more wretched and bitter*.'[28]

Said Ibn ᶜAbbās, 'The Prophet (may God bless him and grant him peace) once said to a man he was admonishing: "Take advantage of five things before five others occur: your youth before your old age, your health before your sickness, your wealth before your poverty, your leisure before your work, and your life before your death".'[29]

And he [the Prophet] said (may God bless him and grant him peace), 'There are two blessings in which many people are cheated: health and leisure.'[30] In other words: they do not take advantage of them, and only know their value when they are gone.

And he said also (may God bless him and grant him peace), 'Whoever is afraid begins his journey in the early morning, and whoever does so reaches the halting-place. Truly, the merchandise of God is dear; truly, the merchandise of God is Heaven.'[31]

Said the Emissary of God (may God bless him and grant him peace), 'The First Blast [of the Trump] has come, followed by the Second, and death has come and all it entails.'[32]

The Emissary of God (may God bless him and grant him peace) used whenever he perceived any heedlessness in his Companions[33] to call out to them in a loud voice, saying, 'Your destiny has come to you, inevitable and inexorable, either with grief or with happiness.'[34]

Said Abū Hurayra, 'The Emissary of God (may God bless him and grant him peace) said, "I am the Warner, death is the Transformer, and the Hour is the tryst".'[35]

Said Ibn ᶜUmar, 'The Emissary of God (may God bless him and grant him peace) once went out while the sun was upon the tips of the palm branches,[A] and said, "Nothing remains of this world save a time proportionate to that which remains of this day".'[36]

And he said (may God bless him and grant him peace), 'The similitude of this world is that of a garment torn from end to end, but which remains attached by a thread at one extremity. That thread is almost broken.'[37]

Said Jābir, 'The Emissary of God (may God bless him and grant him peace) used, when delivering a sermon, to make mention of the Hour. His voice would be raised and his cheeks would show red as though he were warning them of the approach of an army. "Morning and evening I greet you," he

[A] i.e. at the very end of the day.

would say, " while my mission and the Hour are like so," and he would hold up two fingers held close together.'[A] [38]

Said Ibn Mas^cūd (may God be pleased with him), 'The Emissary of God (may God bless him and grant him peace) once recited *And whosoever God wills to guide, He opens his breast to Islam,*[39] and said, "When light enters into a heart it opens up." Upon being asked, "O Emissary of God! Is there a sign whereby this may be recognised?" he said, "Yes: turning aside from the abode of beguilement to the abode of eternity, and preparing for death before it comes".'[40]

Said al-Suddī [commenting on the verse] *He who did create life and death to try you: which of you is best in works?*,[41] 'This means: "Which of you recalls death most frequently, and treats it with the greatest fear and attention?" '

Said Ḥudhayfa, 'Not one morning or evening goes by without a herald crying out, "O people! Move on! Move on!" The proof of this is His word (Exalted is He!): *It is one of the Most Great. A warning to mankind, to whichever of you wills to go forward or to hold back*,[42] meaning, "in death".'

Said Suḥaym, the *mawlā*[B] of the clan of Tamīm, 'I once sat by ^cĀmir ibn ^cAbd Allāh while he was at prayer. He finished his prayer quickly, and then turned to me and said, "Set my mind at rest, what is your errand? For I am in a hurry." "Why so?" I enquired, and he replied, "Because of the Angel of Death, may God have mercy upon you." So I arose and left him, while he returned to his prayers.'

[A] Although the imminence of the Apocalypse is a recurrent theme in the Qur'ān (e.g. XVI: 77; LIV:1) and in the Islamic tradition in general, the Qur'ān states clearly that its time is known only to God (Q. VII: 187; XXXIII:63). Apparently drawing on Traditions related by al-Ḥakīm al-Tirmidhī, Ghazālī states in the present work that the total age of the world shall not exceed seven thousand years, which is a common view among the ^c*ulamā*'. An unusually specific and somewhat alarming *fatwā* is given by Suyūṭī, who states that the great events which will usher in the Day of Judgement must occur before the end of the fifteenth Islamic century (*al-Kashf* ^c*an mujāwazat hadhihi al-ummat al-alf* in *al-Ḥāwī*, II. 86).

[B] A *mawlā* was a person attached to an Arab tribe in a client relationship, or a freedman who enjoyed certain legal privileges.

Dāūd al-Ṭā'ī was once passing by when a man asked him a question about a Tradition. 'Let me be,' he said, 'for I am making haste before my soul departs.'

Said ʿUmar (may God be pleased with him), 'Leisureliness in all things is fine, save in the good works which are for the Afterlife.'

Said al-Mundhir, 'I once overheard Mālik ibn Dīnār say, "Woe betide you! Make haste before the Command overtakes you! Woe betide you! Make haste before the Command overtakes you! Woe betide you! Make haste before the Command overtakes you!" This he repeated sixty times, while I heard him, all unseen.'

Al-Ḥasan was in the habit of saying when he delivered an exhortation, 'Hurry! Hurry! If the breaths which you take were denied you they would signal the end of your works, through which you draw nearer to God (Great and Glorious is He!). May God's mercy be upon that man who looks to himself and sheds tears over the profusion of[43] his sins.' Then he recited the verse, *We do but number unto them a certain sum*,[44] and said, 'This refers to your breaths, the last of which shall be accompanied by the departure of your soul, the separation from your family, and your entry into the grave.'

Before he died, Abū Mūsā al-Ashʿarī was intensely occupied [with devotional practices]. Upon being asked why he did not forbear or have some pity on himself, he said, 'Horses which have been let loose give all they have when they draw near to their destination. That which is left of my lifespan is shorter even than that.' Thus he remained until he passed away. He took to saying to his wife, 'Make ready for hardship, for no passage exists through Hell.'

One of the Caliphs said from his pulpit: 'O bondsmen of God! Fear God as much as you are able. Be as a nation awakened by a great shout, which has come to understand that this world is no abode for it, and which therefore exchanges it for another. Make ready for death, for its shadow has already fallen over you; be off, for it pursues you assiduously. For truly, a span of time eroded by an instant and extinguished by an hour is of necessity fleeting, just as something which is at present absent will, since it is brought ever nearer by the days and the nights, return with celerity; and just as one who shall be granted either triumph or suffering should make the best of preparations. The man who is pious in his Lord's sight is he who counsels himself, offers his repentance, and overcomes his desires (for his lifespan is veiled from him); lest hope deceive him and he be entrusted to the care of Satan, who causes him to live only in hope of repentance so that he postpones it, and who makes iniquity fine in his sight, so that he commits it, until such time as his fate assails him at the moment when he least anticipates it. Between each one of you and Heaven or Hell there lies only the advent of death. Therefore, what sorrow shall be the lot of the man of heedlessness, that his life should be a warrant against him, and that his own days should cast him into misery! May God make you and I among those who are not made vainglorious by His blessings, or drawn from His obedience by some act of sin, and who are neither afflicted by any sorrow after their demise. Truly He is the Hearer of Prayer; in His hand is goodness always, Who acts as He will.'

A certain exegete gave the following commentary in connection with His word (Exalted is He!), *you tempted yourselves*: 'Through desires and pleasures,' *and you waited*, 'for repentance,' *and you felt doubts*, 'you were unsure,' *and vain hopes beguiled you*[45] *until there came the Command of God*, 'death,' *and you were beguiled by the deceiver*, 'by the devil.'[46]

Said al-Ḥasan, 'You must have perseverance and fortitude, for there are only a few days left, and you are no more than a troop of horsemen, one of whom is on the brink of being summoned, and who, responding, does not turn around. Thus pass on fortified with the best of that which is within your grasp.'

Said Ibn Masᶜūd, 'Each one of you when he awakens in the morning is a guest whose property is on loan; the guest must move on, while his property is to be returned.'

Said Abū ᶜUbayda al-Nājī,[47] 'We came in upon al-Ḥasan during the course of his final illness, and he said, "Welcome to you, and good cheer! May God greet you with peace, and cause you to dwell in the Abode Eternal! Should you have patience, truthfulness and piety, this matter augurs well indeed, so let not your share of this news (may God have mercy upon you) be that you listen to it with one ear and expel it from the other. For he that saw Muḥammad (may God bless him and grant him peace) saw him come and go without laying a single brick or piece of straw upon another; instead, a banner was raised up over him and he rolled up his sleeves for its sake. So make haste! Make haste! Be saved! Be saved! Why do you vacillate? By the Lord of the Kaᶜba, you and the Command[A] have well-nigh arrived as one. May God show His mercy to that bondsman who makes his life simple and eats crusts of bread, who wears patched rags and sits upon the floor, who exerts himself in worship, weeps over his transgressions, flees from God's chastisement and quests for His mercy, until, while he is in this condition, his appointed term comes to its close".'

Said ᶜĀṣim al-Aḥwal, 'I was once told by Fuḍayl al-Ruqāshī in answer to a question which I had put to him: "What! Do not let the people's multitude distract you from yourself, for the Command shall come to you despite them. Say not, 'Go hither, and thither,' for thereby your day would be consumed to no end. The affair is safeguarded for you; never will you see a finer purpose or a thing more rapidly realised than a new act of virtue for an old transgression".'

[A] i.e. the Day of Judgement.

CHAPTER THREE

On the Agonies and Violence of Death, and the States Preferable upon its Advent

KNOW THAT were there to lie before the hapless bondsman no terror, calamity or torment save that of the death agonies alone, these would suffice to render his life miserable and to cloud his happiness, and would banish his heedlessness and his distraction. It is right that his thoughts should dwell at length upon this matter, and that he should take the greatest care in preparing himself for it, not least because he is with every breath in its vicinity. As a philosopher once remarked, 'a calamity in another's hand cannot be foretold'. And Luqmān once told his son, 'O my son! Something whose advent you cannot foresee must be prepared for before it takes you unawares.'

It is a matter for some astonishment that a man, even if he should be indulging in the finest of diversions and the most delightful gatherings of play, will, if he is anticipating the entrance (for example) of a man-at-arms who is to strike him five blows with a wooden stick, find his pleasure spoilt and his life marred; yet with every breath that he draws the Angel of Death is liable to come in upon him with the agonies of death, but he pays no heed to this. There can be no reason for such a thing save ignorance and distraction.

Know, too, that the extreme pain of the death pangs is known in its fullness only to those who have tasted it. The man who has not done so may only come to know it through comparing it to the pains which he has actually experienced, or by inference from the violent states of other people during their death agonies, thereby drawing an analogy which bears witness to him. This is as follows.

No extremity from which the spirit is absent can feel pain. When, however, the spirit is present, then the faculty which perceives pain is the spirit: whenever the extremity suffers some injury or burn the effect makes its way to the spirit, which will feel pain in proportion to the amount which reaches it. The sensation disperses through the blood, the flesh and the remaining extremities, so that only a certain part of it reaches the spirit itself.[A]

However, should any pain travel directly to the spirit and not come into contact with anything else, then how terrible will that pain be, and how intense! For the pangs of death constitute nothing but a source of pain which invades the spirit itself and diffuses itself until the fractions of the spirit which are distributed throughout the body's depths have all been afflicted by it. If one is pricked by a thorn, then the pain which one feels runs only in that fraction of the spirit which is present in the place where the thorn prick occurred. The effect of a burn is more intense simply because the fractions of the fire spread out through the other parts of the body as well, so that no inner or outer part of the extremity remains unaffected by it, and the fractions of the spirit spread out through the other parts of the body come to feel it also. A wound only afflicts the place where the blade has touched, which is why its pain is inferior to that consequent upon a burn.

The pain felt during the throes of death, however, assails the spirit directly, and engulfs every one of its fractions. The dying man feels himself pulled and jerked from every artery, nerve, part and joint, from the root of every hair and the bottom layer of his skin from head to foot. So do not ask about the suffering and pain which he endures!

[A] According to the *Iḥyā'* (III.3), the seat of the spirit [*rūḥ*] is a cavity in the corporeal heart, with which it has a subtle relationship which may be understood by the saints but never disclosed. From there it spreads out [*yanshur*] along the arteries to the remainder of the body. Cf. McCarthy, *Freedom and Fulfillment*, 365–366; Nakamura, *Ghazālī on Prayer*, 8n.; Calverley, 'Doctrines of the Soul in Islam' *MW* 33, 254–264; Tritton, 'Man, *nafs*, *rūḥ*, *ʿaql*', *BSOAS* 34, 491–495 .

For this reason it has been said that 'death is crueller than the stroke of a sword, or being carved up with saws, or cut with scissors,' since to cut the body with a sword only produces pain though its association with the spirit, and how much worse must the pain be when it impinges directly upon the spirit itself! The man who has been stabbed cries out only because there is some remainder of strength in his heart and tongue; while the voice and screams of the dying man are cut off due to the severity of his pain, as his suffering bears down upon him and mounts up in the heart until it reaches[1] his every part, breaking his every strength and enfeebling all his limbs, leaving him with no strength left to cry for relief. It overwhelms his mind and deranges it, it strikes dumb his tongue, and it enfeebles his extremities. He longs to be able to seek relief in groaning, screaming and calling for aid, but he cannot. Should there remain in him any strength at all, a lowing and rattling sound is audible from his throat at the time when his spirit is pulled and dragged forth.

His colour changes also, to an ashen grey, until it is as though the dust which is the root of his nature has made itself manifest. Each vein is drawn out individually as the pain spreads through his surface and his innards, until his eyes roll up to the top of their sockets, and his lips are drawn back, and his tongue contracts to its root, and his testicles rise up, and his fingertips turn a greenish-black. So do not ask concerning a frame from which every artery is being pulled: were one of them alone to be pulled his agony would be intense, so how must it be when the percipient spirit itself is being pulled, and not just from one artery, but from them all?

Then, one by one, his extremities begin to die. First his feet grow cold, and then his shins and thighs, each limb suffering agony after agony, and misery after misery, until his spirit reaches his throat. At this point he gazes out for the last time at the world and its people, and the gate of repentance is closed, and he is overwhelmed by sorrow and contrition.

Said the Emissary of God (may God bless him and grant him peace), 'A man's repentance is accepted until he gives the death rattle'.[2]

Said Mujāhid [interpreting] His statement (Exalted is He!), *Repentance is not for those who work evil, and then, when death comes to one of them he says: Now I repent:*[3] 'When he sees the messengers'.[A]

At this juncture the face of the Angel of Death appears before him. Do not ask regarding the bitter taste of death, and its miseries as its agonies mount up! It was for this reason that the Emissary of God (may God bless him and grant him peace) used to say, 'O Lord God! Lessen for Muḥammad the agonies of death!'[4] People only ask for refuge therefrom and hold it in awe out of their ignorance of it, for things can only be known before their occurrence through the light of Prophethood and Sainthood. This is why the Prophets (upon them be peace) and the Saints were in such great fear of death, to the extent that Jesus (upon whom be peace) said, 'O company of disciples! Pray to God (Exalted is He!) that he may lessen these agonies for me,' (by which he meant the agonies of death) 'for I have feared death in a way which has brought me to its brink'.

It is related that a company of Israelites once passed by a graveyard, and that one of their number said to the others, 'What if you were to pray to God (Exalted is He!), that He should quicken before you a corpse from this graveyard so that you could put some questions to him?' So they prayed to God (Exalted is He!) and lo and behold! there before them was a man with the sign of prostration between his eyes, who had emerged from one of the tombs. 'O people!' he said. 'What would you have of me? Fifty years ago I tasted death, yet its bitterness is not yet stilled in my heart!'

Said ʿĀ'isha (may God be pleased with her), 'I feel no envy for anyone whose death is easy after having seen the rigour of the death of God's Emissary (may God bless him and grant him peace)'.

It is related that [the Prophet] used to say (may God bless him and grant him peace), 'O Lord God! Truly You draw out the spirit from the sinews, the nasal bone and the fingertips. O

[A] i.e. the angels.

Lord God! Grant me Your support in death, and render it easy for me to bear.'[5]

It is related on the authority of al-Ḥasan that the Emissary of God (may God bless him and grant him peace) once made mention of death, and its choking and its pain, and said, 'It is equal to three hundred blows with a sword'.[6]

He was once asked (may God bless him and grant him peace) about death and its severity, and replied, 'The easiest death resembles the branch of a thorn-tree caught in some wool. Shall the branch be extracted from the wool without some remaining with it?'[7]

Once he came in upon a sick man, and said, 'I know what he is experiencing. There is in him not a single artery that does not individually endure the pain of death.'[8]

ᶜAlī (may God ennoble his countenance) used to rouse the people to fight by saying, 'Should you not fight, then you shall die [a natural death]. By Him in Whose hand lies my soul, a thousand sword-strokes are easier to bear than death in one's bed'.

Said al-Awzāᶜī, 'We have heard it said that the dead man continues to feel the pain of death until he is resurrected from his grave.'

Said Shaddād ibn Aws, 'Death is the most fearsome terror that the believer will encounter in this world or in the next. It is worse than being carved up with saws, or being cut with scissors, or being boiled in cauldrons. If a dead man could be brought back to life to tell this world's people of death they would find no profit in life, and take no pleasure in sleeping.'

Zayd ibn Aslam related that his father once said, 'Whenever there remain for the believer certain degrees which he had not attained in the world through his works, death is made rigorous for him so that through its agonies and woe he might attain to his degree in Heaven. Whereas, should the unbeliever have to his account some act of kindness for which he has not been rewarded, then death is made easy for him to bear until his reward becomes complete and he takes his place in Hell.'

It is related of a certain man that he would question a large number of sick people about how they found [the advent of] death. And when he [in turn] was taken ill he was asked, 'And you, how do you find it?' 'It is as though the very heavens were being folded back against the earth,' he replied, 'and as though my soul were being drawn through the eye of a needle.'

And [the Prophet] said (may God bless him and grant him peace), 'Sudden death is relief for the believer, and grief for the profligate'.[9]

It is related on the authority of Makḥūl that the Prophet (may God bless him and grant him peace) said, 'Were a single hair from a dead man to be laid upon the dwellers of the heavens and the earth they would die, by the leave of God (Exalted is He!), because death lies in every hair, and it never falls upon anything without slaying it.'[10]

It has been related that 'were one drop of the pain of death to be distributed over all the mountains of the earth they would melt away'.

It is related that when Abraham (upon whom be peace) died, God, Exalted is He, asked him, 'How did you find death, O My Friend?' and he replied, 'Like a skewer pushed into damp wool and then tugged'. 'Yet We made it easy for you to bear,' He said.

It is related of Moses (upon whom be peace) that when his spirit passed away to God (Exalted is He!) his Lord asked him, 'O Moses! How did you find death?' 'I found myself', he said, 'to be like a sparrow being roasted alive, unable either to die and find rest, or to escape and fly away.' It is also related that he said, 'I found myself to be like a sheep being flayed alive at the hands of a butcher'.

It is related of the Prophet (may God bless him and grant him peace) that upon his death he had by him a vessel of water into which he took to dipping his hand in order to wipe his face, saying, 'O Lord God! Mitigate for me the agonies of death!'[11] At the same time, Fāṭima (may God be pleased with her) was saying, 'How great is my sorrow at your sorrow, father!' But he said, 'There shall be no more sorrow for your father after this day'.[12]

Said ʿUmar (may God be pleased with him) to Kaʿb al-Aḥbār, 'O Kaʿb! Speak to us of death!' 'Certainly, O Commander of the

Faithful,' he said. 'Death is as a thorny twig made to enter the stomach of a man, so that each thorn becomes attached to an artery. Then a powerful man pulls at it, and it takes what it takes, and leaves what it leaves.'

Said the Prophet (may God bless him and grant him peace), 'The bondsman shall surely undergo the misery and pangs of death, and his joints shall surely greet each other saying, "Peace be upon you; from each other we part now until the Day of Arising".'[13]

Such were the agonies of death as they were endured by God's Saints and dear ones. What, then, shall be our state, we who are engrossed in sins?

The agonies of death shall be followed in succession by its other calamities, of which there are three.

The first is the violence of the death throes, as we have already mentioned. The second consists in the vision of the Angel of Death, and the fear and terror which he inspires in the heart. For even if the strongest of men were to see him in the aspect he assumes when taking the spirit of a sinful bondsman he would not be able to bear the sight. It is related of Abraham, the Friend of God (upon whom be peace) that he once asked the Angel of Death, 'Are you able to show me the form you assume when taking the spirit of an evildoer?' 'You could not bear it,' he replied. 'But yes, I could,' he said. 'Then turn away from me,' he commanded, and he did so. Then Abraham turned round, and there before him stood a black man with hair erect, evil-smelling and garbed in black, from whose mouth and nostrils sparks and smoke were issuing forth. At this, Abraham fainted, and when he regained his wits the Angel had resumed his former guise. 'O Angel of Death!' he said. 'Were the evildoer to confront nothing but your visage after his death it would quite suffice him!'

And Abū Hurayra reported that the Prophet (may God bless him and grant him peace) said, 'David (upon whom be peace) was a solicitous[A] man, who would lock the doors whenever he left his house. One day, after he had locked them and gone out, his wife looked out and saw that there was a man in the house.

[A] In the sense of being concerned for his wife.

"Who admitted this man?" she demanded. "He will certainly have cause for dismay when David returns!" And when David came and saw him he asked, "Who are you?" "I", he replied, "am the one who fears no king, and who is not stopped by any chamberlain." "Then, by God, you are the Angel of Death," he said, upon which he died, there and then.'

It is related that Jesus (upon whom be peace) once passed by a skull. Striking it with his foot, he said, 'Speak, by God's leave!' And it said, 'O Spirit of God! I was the king in such-and-such a time. One day, when I was seated upon the royal couch in my dominion, wearing my crown and surrounded by my courtiers, the Angel of Death appeared before me, and my every limb became numb, and my soul went out [of my body] towards him. O would that those gatherings had never been! O would that that intimacy had rather been solitude!'

This is a calamity which afflicts sinners and from which the obedient are exempt. The Prophets only told of the convulsions of death, and not of the horror felt by those who behold the form of its Angel. Even if he were to be beheld during one's sleep at night the entire remainder of one's life would be marred; so how must it be to behold him [awake] when he has assumed such an aspect?

The obedient man, however, shall see him in the best and most beautiful of forms. ʿIkrima has related on the authority of Ibn ʿAbbās that 'Abraham (upon whom be peace) was a solicitous man. He had a house in which he would make his devotions and which he would lock upon leaving. One day when he repaired to this house he saw that there was a man within. "Who admitted you to my house?" he asked, and was told, "I was admitted to it by its Master". "But I am its master," said Abraham, but was told, "I was admitted to it by One Who has mastery over it more than you or I." "Then which of the Angels might you be?" he inquired. "I am the Angel of Death," came the reply. "Are you able to show me the form in which you take the soul of a believer?" "Yes," he replied. "Turn away from me." This he did, and when he turned round again, there before him stood a young man, handsome of face, perfumed, and finely-attired. "O Angel of Death!" he told him. "Were the believer to encounter only your form upon his death it would quite suffice him!"'

A further calamity consists in the vision of the two Recording Angels.[A] Said Wuhayb, 'We have heard it said that no man dies without being shown his works by the two Recording Angels. If he had been obedient, then they say, "May God reward you well! For you made us sit at many a gathering of truth, and caused us to be present at many a righteous act." But if he had been an evildoer they say to him, "May God not reward you well! For at many a gathering of iniquity did you make us sit, and you caused us to be present at many an act of unrighteousness, and obliged us to hear many a foul discourse. So may God not reward you well!" At this, the gaze of the dying man is fixed upon them, never to behold this world again.'

The third calamity is the witnessing by the sinful of their places in Hell, and the apprehension they feel even before this vision obtains. During their death agonies their strength grows increasingly feeble as their spirits yield to their departure from their physical frames. Their spirits, however, do not depart until they have heard the voice of the Angel of Death conveying one of the Two Tidings. Either this shall be: 'Rejoice, O enemy of God, at [the prospect of] Hell!' or: 'Rejoice, O friend of God, at [the prospect of] Heaven!' It is from this that the fear of people of understanding is ever inspired.

The Prophet (may God bless him and grant him peace) said, 'Not one of you shall leave this world before knowing his destination, and before beholding the place he is to occupy in Heaven or in Hell'.[14]

And he said (may God bless him and grant him peace), 'Whosoever would love meeting with God, God loves to meet him; but whosoever would abhor meeting with God, God abhors meeting with him.' 'Yet all of us are averse to death,' [his Companions] said. 'It is not the same,' he replied. 'For when the

[A] According to a Tradition ascribed to the Prophet, 'God has entrusted His bondsman to two angels, who record his works'. (Aḥmad ibn Manīʿ, *al-Musnad*, cited in Ibn Ḥajar, *Maṭālib*, III. 56.) For this doctrine see *Escatología*, 344–5; Khālid, 282.

sorrow to which the believer is travelling is banished, he takes delight in the meeting with God, and God takes delight in the meeting with him.'[15]

It is related that Ḥudhayfa ibn al-Yamān once said to Ibn Masʿūd early one morning, 'Arise, and see what hour it is'. Ibn Masʿūd did so, and when he returned said, 'The sky is red.' 'I seek refuge with You,' said Ḥudhayfa, 'from a morning voyage to Hell'.

Marwān once came in upon Abū Hurayra and said, 'O Lord God! Lighten his burden!' But Abū Hurayra said, 'O Lord God! Render it yet heavier!' Then he began to weep, saying, 'By God, I do not weep out of sorrow over losing this world, neither out of grief at being separated from you; rather I am awaiting one of the Two Tidings from my Lord: either to Heaven or to Hell!'

It is related in Tradition that the Prophet (may God bless him and grant him peace) said, 'When God (Great and Glorious is He!) is satisfied with His bondsman He says, "O Angel of Death! Make your way to So-and-so, and bring Me his spirit that I may grant him rest. His works I find sufficient: I tested him and found him to be as I desired." And so the Angel of Death descends in the company of five thousand angels all bearing rods of sweet basil and roots of the saffron plant, until each angel tells him different good tidings from his Lord. And then, holding their rods of basil, they form two ranks in preparation for the spirit's departure. When Satan beholds them he sets his hand upon his head and screams aloud. "What is the matter, O our lord?" his legions ask. "Do you not see the honour that has been accorded this bondsman?" he cries. "Where were you with respect to him?" And they reply, "We exerted our every effort with him, but he was invulnerable".'[16]

Said al-Ḥasan, 'There is no relief for the believer save in the encounter with God, and whosoever is given this, then for him the day of his death is a day of joy, rapture, security, glory and honour.'[17]

Jābir ibn Zayd was asked on his deathbed whether there was anything that he desired, and he replied, 'A glimpse of al-Ḥasan'. And he was told, when al-Ḥasan came in to see him, 'Here is al-

Ḥasan'. He raised his eyes to look at him and said, 'O my brother! In this hour, by God, shall I take my leave of you, either to Heaven or to Hell.'

Muḥammad ibn Wāsiᶜ said on his deathbed, 'O my brethren! Farewell! To Hell, or to the forgiveness of God!'

It was the wish of one man that he should remain forever in his death throes and never be raised to face reward or punishment.

In this wise, the fear of an evil end has torn apart the hearts of the gnostics, constituting as it does one of the terrible calamities which accompany death. We have already mentioned the significance of the 'evil end' [*sū' al-khātima*] and the intense fear which the gnostics harbour for it in the *Book of Fear and Hope*; it is relevant in this context, but we shall not commit prolixity by mentioning it again.[A]

An exposition of the states preferable in the dying man

Know that it is desirable for the dying man to have an aspect of peacefulness and tranquillity. He should be uttering the Two Testimonies[B] with his tongue, and should be maintaining in his heart a favourable opinion of God (Exalted is He!). For it is related that the Prophet (may God bless him and grant him peace) once said, 'Watch for three signs in the dying man. If his forehead sweats, his eyes shed tears and his lips become dry, then the mercy of God (Exalted is He!) has alighted upon him. But if he should choke like a man being strangled, and if his colour should turn to

[A] The *Iḥyā'*'s *Book of Fear and Hope* (IV, book 3) devotes a long section (pp.151–157) to the question of the *khātima*, the mental and spiritual condition prevailing at the moment of death. In particular, the author points out that even the righteous man is vulnerable to two types of 'evil end', the more dangerous one being that 'when undergoing the agonies and terrors of death his heart may be overwhelmed by either doubt or denial, so that the spirit comes to be taken away in this condition'; alternatively, 'at the moment of death, the love of some worldly thing or pleasure may prevail over it ... so that he turns his face in the direction of this world, and in proportion to one's inclination towards the world the veil [i.e. that which bars man from seeing the Kingdom], which induces the chastisement, will descend.' (IV. 151.)

[B] These being the formula 'I testify that there is no deity save God, and that Muḥammad is the Emissary of God'.

red, and if he should foam at the mouth, then this is from the chastisement of God which has befallen him.'[18]

It is a favourable sign that his tongue should be pronouncing the words of the Testimony. Said Abū Saᶜīd al-Khudrī, 'The Emissary of God (may God bless him and grant him peace) said, "Rehearse to your dying [the words] 'There is no deity save God'."' And in a version related by Ḥudhayfa [the Prophet continued as follows], 'For truly this effaces one's previous sins'.[19]

Said ᶜUthmān, 'The Emissary of God (may God bless him and grant him peace) said, "Whoever perishes knowing that there is no deity save God shall enter into Heaven".'[A] [20]

Said ᶜUbayd Allāh [in place of 'knowing that there is no deity save God']: 'While uttering the Testimony'.

Said ᶜUthmān, 'When the dying man nears death you should repeat "there is no deity save God" to him, for no bondsman shall end his life therewith without it becoming his travelling-provisions to Heaven.'

Said ᶜUmar (may God be pleased with him), 'Be present with your dying ones, and cause them to remember, for they see what you do not; and prompt them to say, "there is no deity save God".'

Said Abū Hurayra, 'I heard the Emissary of God (may God bless him and grant him peace) say, "The Angel of Death once came to a dying man. Having looked into his heart and found nothing therein, he parted his beard and found the tip of his tongue adhering to his palate as he said, 'There is no deity save God.' For this utterance of pure single-heartedness he was forgiven his sins".'[21]

It is best for the prompter to abstain from being insistent; he should rather use gentleness, for it may be that the sick man's tongue is unable to pronounce the formula and that the resultant distress leads to his finding the prompting burdensome and causes

[A] This Tradition is often cited in defence of the Ashᶜarite doctrine of justification by faith, and is typically accompanied by a word of qualification on the part of the theologians; for example al-Nawawī (quoting the Qāḍī ᶜIyāḍ's commentary on the *Ṣaḥīḥ* of Muslim): 'Even if such a man is not forgiven and is punished, he must ultimately be taken out of Hell and brought into Heaven'. (Nawawī, *Sharḥ*, I. 219.) See also the last chapter of the present work.

him to dislike the formula; it is to be feared that this might result in an evil end. The significance of [repeating] the formula lies only in ensuring that a man passes away without there being anything in his heart save God. For if he harbours no longing but for the Unique, the True, then his approach to his Beloved through death will be for him the ultimate felicity. But should his heart be infatuated with the world and incline towards it, and be in a state of lamentation over the loss of its delights, then even though the formula is present on his tongue his heart may utter nothing in confirmation. In such an instance the matter falls into the hazardous province of the divine will, for a mere wagging of the tongue is of little avail unless God (Exalted is He!) should through His grace grant it acceptance.

As regards having a favourable opinion [of God], this is recommended at this time, as we have already mentioned in the *Book of* [*Fear and*] *Hope*. A number of Traditions are forthcoming concerning the virtue of maintaining a favourable opinion.

Wāthila ibn al-Asqaᶜ once came in upon a sick man and asked him, 'Tell me, how is your opinion of God?' 'I am immersed in my sins,' said the man, 'and am on the very brink of destruction, but yet I hope for the mercy of my Lord'. At this, Wāthila cried out, 'God is Most Great!' and the people of the house did the same. 'God is Most Great!' he said. 'I once heard the Emissary of God (may God bless him and grant him peace) say, "God (Exalted is He!) says, 'I am as My bondsman thinks me to be; so let him think of Me what he will' ".'[22]

The Prophet (may God bless him and grant him peace) once came in upon a young man who was dying. 'How are you?' he asked, and he replied, 'I have set my hope in God, and fear my sins'. And he said (may God bless him and grant him peace), 'Never have these two things been united in the heart of a bondsman in circumstances such as these without God granting him that for which he hopes, and delivering him from what he fears'.[23]

Said Thābit al-Bunānī, 'There was once a youth much given to frivolity, whose mother would frequently reproach him, saying, "O my son! Your time will come, so remember it." And when that which God (Exalted is He!) had ordained befell him she leaned over him and said, "O my son! I warned you of this your fate, and told you that your time would come." "O mother," he said, "I have a Lord Who is greatly kind, and it is my hope that some part of His kindness might not pass me by on this day".' And Thābit said, 'So God had mercy upon him because of his good opinion of his Lord'.

Said Jābir ibn Wadāʿa, 'There was once a young man who was disposed towards foolishness. When he drew near death his mother said to him, "O my son! Do you have any last wishes?" "Yes," he said. "Do not take my ring from me, for upon it God (Exalted is He!) is mentioned; perhaps He will have mercy upon me." After he had been buried he was seen in a dream, saying, "Tell my mother that that utterance benefited me, and that God has granted me His forgiveness".'

A nomad once fell ill, and upon being told that he was dying, asked, 'Where shall I be taken?' 'To God,' they replied. 'I cannot dislike being taken,' he said, 'to One from Whom all that is good proceeds'.

Said al-Muʿtamir ibn Sulaymān, 'When he drew near to death, my father said, "O Muʿtamir! Speak to me of the concessions [*rukhaṣ*] [in the Law], that I may meet God (Great and Glorious is He!) thinking well of Him".'

They[A] preferred that the bondsman's good works be mentioned to him on his deathbed so that he would think well of his Lord.

An exposition of the sorrow felt upon meeting the Angel of Death, through accounts uttered on the tongue of the Spiritual State[B]

Said Ashʿath ibn Aslam, 'Abraham (upon whom be peace) once put certain questions to the Angel of Death (whose name is

[A] The early Muslims

[B] Ar. *lisān al-ḥāl*: an utterance made during the '*ḥāl*', a brief state given the mystic by God, usually with emotional symptoms. (Cf. e.g. Qushayrī, *Risāla*, I. 236.)

ᶜAzrāʾīl, and who has two eyes: one in his face and the other at the back of his head). "O Angel of Death!" he said. "What do you do if there is one soul [dying] in the east and another in the west, or when the land is stricken by a plague, or when two armies clash?" "I summon the spirits," he said, "by God's leave, until they lie between these two fingers of mine". [And Abraham said,] "Then the earth is flattened out and left like a dish before him, from which he partakes as he wishes".' Ashᶜath said, 'It was then that He gave him the good tidings that he was the Friend [*khalīl*][A] of God (Great and Glorious is He!)'.

Said Solomon the son of David, to the Angel of Death (upon them be peace), 'Why do I not see you dealing justly with mankind? For you seize one man, while you leave another alone.' 'I know no more of that than you,' he replied. 'I am merely given scrolls and books containing names'.

Said Wahb ibn Munabbih, 'A certain king once conceived a wish to ride to a province. He called for a garment to wear, but it was not pleasing to him, so he demanded another until after several tries he donned one that was agreeable to him. In the same fashion he ordered a mount to be brought, but found it not to his liking when it came, so others were brought to him until he mounted the finest one amongst them. Then the devil came to him and blew into his nostril, and he puffed himself up with pride. Then he set out on his journey, never looking at anyone because of his haughtiness. But then he was approached by a man of threadbare appearance, who came up to him and greeted him. When the king failed to reply he took hold of the bridle of his horse. "Release my bridle!" cried the king, "for you have committed something most heinous!" "I have a request to make of you," he said. "Have patience", the king said, "until I dismount." "No," he replied. "At this instant!" and he pulled at the reins of his horse. "Then say what it is," said the king. "It is a secret," he replied. So he leaned his head down to him, and [the stranger] confided his secret to him, saying, "I am the Angel of Death!" At this, the king's complexion changed colour, and his tongue stammered, and he said, "Leave me, so that I may return

[A] Cf. Q. IV:125: *And God did take Abraham to be His Friend.*

to my family to bid them farewell, and wind up my affairs." "No, by God," he told him. "Never will you see your family and wealth again!" Thereupon he took away his spirit, and the king fell dead, as though he were a wooden log.

'Then the Angel continued on his way. Presently, he came across a believer, whom he greeted and who greeted him in return. "I have a request which I would mention in your ear," he said. "Let me hear it," said the man. And he confided in him his secret, saying, "I am the Angel of Death." "Welcome!" he said. "Welcome to the one who has long been absent from me. By God, there is no-one on earth whom I have wanted to meet more than you!" At this, the Angel of Death said to him, "Conclude the business for which you had set out." But he replied, "I have no business which is more important and beloved to me than meeting God (Exalted is He!)." And the Angel said, "Then choose the state in which you would prefer me to take your spirit." "Are you able to do that?" he asked. "Yes," he replied, "and thus have I been instructed." "Leave me awhile, so that I may perform the ablutions and pray, and then take my spirit while I am prostrating." And this he did.'

Said Bakr ibn ᶜAbd Allāh al-Mazanī, 'A man from the tribe of Israel once amassed a large fortune. When he drew near death he gave instructions to his sons, saying, "Show me the varieties of my wealth!" And he was brought a huge quantity of horses, camels, slaves and other things. When he looked at them he began to weep out of sorrow at their loss. The Angel of Death, seeing him in this state, asked him, "What has made you weep? Truly, by Him Who blessed you with these things I shall not leave your house before cleaving your spirit from your body." "Give me some respite," he pleaded with him, "that I may distribute my wealth." "What folly!" said he. "Your period of respite has come to an end; it would have been better had you acted before you had run your course." And saying this, he took his spirit.'

It is told that a certain man once accumulated great wealth, until there remained not a single kind of property in which he had not invested. He raised up a palace to which he set two powerful gates, and gathered around his person a guard of young men. Then he called together his family and regaled them with food, and sat back on his couch with one leg over the other, while they set to eating. And when they had finished he said to himself: 'Revel for years, for I have accumulated all that you need!' But hardly had he finished uttering these words when the Angel of Death came by in the guise of a man dressed shabbily like a pauper. He struck the gates a tremendous blow, terrifying the rich man upon his couch. The young men leaped up and said, 'What is your business here?' 'Call your master for me,' he said. 'And should our master come out', they asked, 'for the likes of you?' 'Yes indeed,' he said. And when they told their master of what had transpired he said, 'You have done well'. But then the door was knocked even more violently than before, and when the guards leaped up to speak to him [the stranger] said, 'Tell him that I am the Angel of Death'. When they heard this they were aghast, and their lord was covered in ignominy and humility. 'Speak to him politely,' he instructed them, 'and ask him whether he is to take anyone from this house'. But [the Angel] came in, and said, 'Do with your wealth as you please, for I shall not leave this place before I draw forth your spirit'. So he called for his wealth, and said, when it was laid out before his eyes, 'May God curse you! For you distracted me from the worship of my Lord, and diverted me from devoting myself to Him'. And God caused his wealth to speak, and it said, 'Why do you insult me, when it was through me that you entered into the presence of the sultan, while the Godfearing were turned away from his door? It was through me that you married women of pleasure, sat in the company of kings, and spent me in the way of evil. Yet never did I withhold myself from you. And had you spent me in the way of righteousness I would have brought you profit. You and all the sons of Adam were created from dust, then some set out with charity, and others with iniquity.' Then the Angel of Death took away his spirit, and he fell to the ground.

Said Wahb ibn Munabbih, 'The Angel of Death once took away the spirit of a great tyrant, the likes of whom had never been seen on the face of the earth before. When [the Angel] had ascended up to heaven again, the other angels asked him, "Of all those whose spirits you have taken, to whom did you show the most mercy?" "I once was commanded", he replied, "to take the soul of a woman in a desert place. When I came to her she had just given birth to a son, and I dealt with her mercifully on account of her remoteness from her homeland, and with her son because of his young age and his presence in the desert where there was no-one who might care for him." And the angels said, "The tyrant whose soul you just took away was that very same child to whom you showed mercy." And the Angel of Death declared, "Glory be to Him Who shows kindness as He will!"'

Said ᶜAṭā' ibn Yasār, 'On the middle night of Shaᶜbān[A] the Angel of Death receives a scroll and is told, "This year you are to take the people whose names are recorded on this scroll." A man may sow crops, marry women and raise up buildings, while his name is upon that scroll and he knows it not.'

Said al-Ḥasan, 'With every passing day the Angel of Death inspects every house three times, and takes away the spirits of those whose provision has been exhausted and whose lifetimes have drawn to a close. When he has done so the inhabitants of that house take to lamentation and weeping, and the Angel of Death, holding onto the doorjambs, says, "By God, I did not eat of his provision, nor did I consume any part of his life, nor yet did I shorten his allotted span. I shall return amongst you again and again until I have left not one of you remaining!"' And al-Ḥasan said, 'By God, if they could only see him standing there and hear his words they would forget the dead man and weep for their own sakes instead!'

Said Yazīd al-Ruqāshī, 'Once, when a tyrant of the Israelites was sitting in his residence alone with one of his wives, a man entered through the door of his house. The tyrant flew into a rage, and went up to him, saying, "Who are you? Who admitted you to my house?" "As for the one who admitted me to this house," the man answered, "it was its Lord. And as for myself, I am the one who is barred by no chamberlain, who does not ask for permission even of kings when he would enter, who fears not

[A] Shaᶜbān: the eighth month of the Muslim year.

the force of imperious monarchs, and who is never refused by any stubborn tyrant or rebellious devil." At this, the tyrant buried his head in his hands and began to tremble, and then fell down, hiding his face. Then he raised his head towards him imploringly and in great humility. "Then you are the Angel of Death," he said. "I am he," he replied. "Will you grant me respite so that I may mend my ways?" "What folly!" he told him. "You have run your course; your every breath is expended, and your hours are all consumed; there is no way by which you may be granted respite." "Where will you take me?" he asked. "To the works which you sent before you," he replied, "and to the house which you have prepared." "How shall it be, then," he asked, "as I have neither sent before me any righteous works nor prepared a goodly house?" And he replied, "Then to *hellfire, which snatches at the edges of men's bones*."[24] Then he took away his spirit, and he fell down dead in the midst of his family, who set to wailing and to screaming.' Remarked Yazīd al-Ruqāshī, 'If they had only known the balefulness of their own destination they would have wept more bitterly still.'

Al-Aᶜmash has related on the authority of Khaythama that the Angel of Death once came in upon Solomon, the son of David (upon both of whom be peace) and took to scrutinising one of his companions at some length. When he had left again the man asked, 'Who was that?' and was told that it was the Angel of Death. And he said, 'I saw him looking at me as though he wanted me.' 'So what do you want?' asked Solomon. 'I want you to deliver me from him by ordering the wind to carry me off to the farthest part of India.'[A] And this the wind did. Then, when the Angel of Death came again, Solomon said to him, 'I saw you looking closely at one of my companions'. 'Yes indeed,' he replied. 'I was surprised to see him, because I had been instructed to take his spirit in the farthest part of India shortly afterwards; yet there he was with you, and I was astonished at this.'

[A] According to Muslim belief, Solomon had the ability to direct the winds (Q. XXI:81).

CHAPTER FOUR

On the death of the Emissary of God (may God bless him and grant him peace), and of the Rightly-guided Caliphs after him

The death of the Emissary of God (may God bless him and grant him peace)[1]

KNOW THAT in the Emissary of God (may God bless him and grant him peace) there is a goodly example in life and in death, in word and in deed. His every circumstance is a lesson to the beholders and an illumination to those who seek understanding. For never was any man more honourable in the sight of God than he, who was the friend [*khalīl*][A] of God, His well-beloved and His intimate, His Chosen One, Emissary and Prophet. Yet see if He granted him one hour's respite when his time came to an end. Did He prolong his life by one instant when it had run its course? Nay, rather He despatched to him the noble Angels, those entrusted with taking the spirits of men, who took hold of his pure and noble spirit to bear it away. They tended to it so as to carry it from his immaculate body into mercy and good-pleasure, and the *fine and beautiful*[B],[2] even to a *Seat of Truth*[3] in the presence

[A] *Khalīl Allāh* is customarily an epithet of Abraham; Muḥammad is rather *Ḥabīb Allāh*: God's Beloved. Ghazālī's use of the former title here (assuming the text is stable) is apparently an archaism (Cf. Schimmel, 57, and pp.213–216 below).
[B] A reference to the houris of Paradise.

of the All-Compassionate. But despite this, his affliction was great when the agony of death came, and his groaning plain. His disquiet became compounded, and his voice was raised in moaning. His colour changed, sweat appeared on his brow, and as he breathed in and out his left and right sides shook until those present at his demise wept at it and until those who witnessed his appearance sobbed at the extremity of his condition.

Did you think that the office of Prophethood would ward off from him that which was destined? Did the Angel respect family and relations for his sake ? Did he comply with his wishes because he had aided the Truth, and had been to mankind[4] a *bringer of good news and a warning*?[5] Absurd! Rather he followed that which he had been commanded to perform, and that which he found inscribed upon the Tablet. Such was his state, although he was of a Praiseworthy Station[A] with God, and possessed of the Frequented Pool[B], the first around whom the earth shall split asunder, the exerciser of the Intercession on the Day of Exposition. Astonishing it is that we draw no lesson from him, despite our uncertainty regarding what we shall encounter.[6] Instead, we are the prisoners-of-war of our desires, the boon-companions of evil deeds and iniquities. What ails us that we draw no admonition from the demise of Muḥammad, Master of the Messengers, Leader of the Godfearing and the beloved of the Lord of the Worlds? Perhaps we think ourselves immortal, or imagine that despite the evil of our works that we are ennobled in God's sight? Absurd! Absurd! Instead we must be confident that we shall all come to Hell, and that none shall then escape therefrom save the Godfearing. Thus we are certain of coming to it, but only conjecture when we think of thence emerging. Nay, if such is our state then we have done an injustice to our own selves by thinking wishfully. By

[A] *al-Maqām al-Maḥmūd* (Q. XVII:79): generally understood to refer to the Prophet's intercession in the Afterlife (cf. Bayḍāwī, 382; Bayhaqī, *Baʿth*, 327; Baghdādī, *Uṣūl*, 244). It is sometimes more specifically described as a hill on the plain of resurrection, upon which the Prophet, dressed in a green robe, shall stand, surrounded by the community of believers (Cf. Khālid, 188, 460–1, where four possible meanings of the phrase are examined).

[B] *al-Ḥawḍ al-Mawrūd*: see below pp.217–219.

God! We fear not Him! For God, the Lord of the Worlds, has said, *There is not one of you but shall come to it. This is a fixed ordinance of thy Lord. Then shall We deliver those that were Godfearing, and leave the wrongdoers therein crouching*[A].

Let each bondsman look to himself, and to whether he is closer to the wrongdoers or to the Godfearing. And look to yourself after having seen the conduct of the righteous Predecessors. For despite the success they were granted they were among the fearful. Then look to the Master of the Messengers: he was of a certainty regarding his case, for he was indeed Master of the Messengers and Leader of the Godfearing. Draw a lesson from how his affliction was upon parting from this world, and from how fierce was the matter of his wayfaring to the *Garden of the Refuge*.[7]

Said Ibn Masᶜūd (may God be pleased with him), 'We went in to visit the Emissary of God (may God bless him and grant him peace) in the house of our mother ᶜĀ'isha[B] when the parting drew near. He looked at us (may God bless him and grant him peace) and tears welled up in his eyes. Then he said, "Welcome to you! May God preserve you! May God give you refuge! May God support you! I commend to you the fear of God, and I commend you to Him. *I am a clear warner unto you*,[8] that you should not exalt yourselves before Him in His land and among His bondsmen. The appointed time has drawn near, and the return is to God and to *the Lote Tree of the Boundary*,[C] [9] the *Garden of the*

[A] Q. XIX: 71,72. Whether *wurūd* in this context means *dukhūl*, actual entry into the infernal fires, is a question that has never been resolved. Six traditional interpretations are given by Ḥasan Khālid (321–4). Perhaps the most common view (cf. al-Ḥakīm al-Tirmidhī in his *Nawādir*, 25) is that all shall enter Hell, but that the righteous shall not be harmed by it, and shall be delivered from it immediately; this as a means of making their delight in Heaven complete.

[B] The Prophet's wives being 'mothers of the believers' (Q. XXXIII:6).

[C] This tree is said to be the closest point to the Divine Presence which man can hope to attain. Depicted with myriad details in the *ḥadīth* and in Sufi literature, it is said that it is a symbol of faith and virtue, and that its fruit represents the experience of the mystic. From its foot four rivers, the Pentateuch, the Psalms, the Gospel and the Qur'ān pour forth; beyond it lie the sphere of the fixed stars and, finally, the *lumen gloriae*. (Palacios, *Escatología*, 20–1, 39, 78, 83—largely from Ibn al-ᶜArabī.)

Refuge[10] and the Most-fulfilling Chalice. So give to yourselves and to those who enter your religion after me the salutation of peace and the mercy of God".'[11]

And it is related that the Prophet (may God bless him and grant him peace) said to Gabriel (upon whom be peace) at his demise, 'Who will support my nation after me?' and God (Exalted is He!) inspired in Gabriel: 'Give My beloved the good tidings that I shall not disappoint him regarding his nation. And give him the good tidings that he shall be the swiftest of mankind in coming forth from the earth when they are resurrected, and shall be their master when together they are congregated, and that Heaven shall be forbidden to all the nations until his nation has gone in.' And he said, 'Now am I content'.[12]

Said ᶜĀ'isha (may God be pleased with her), 'The Emissary of God (may God bless him and grant him peace) instructed us to wash him from seven vessels from seven wells. This we did, and he found some relief, going outside and leading the people in prayer. He asked for forgiveness for the people of Uḥud[A] and prayed for them. He advised us to treat the Helpers well, saying, "To proceed, O company of Emigrants! Truly you are rising to a position of ascendancy, while the Helpers will rise no higher than the circumstances in which they are today. The Helpers are my intimates to whom I had resort, so honour whomsoever amongst them is honourable"—meaning: those among them who act righteously—"and pardon their wrongdoers." Then he said, "A bondsman has been given the choice between this world and what is with God. He has chosen the latter."

'At this, Abū Bakr wept (may God be pleased with him) thinking that he meant himself. And the Prophet said (may God bless him and grant him peace), "Be in less haste, Abū Bakr! Close up these street doors of the Mosque, except the door of

[A] A mountain near Medina where in the year 3 AH the second great battle between the Muslims and the idolators of Mecca took place, to the temporary advantage of the latter.

Abū Bakr, for truly, I know of no man who has been more worthy of companionship than he".'[A] [13]

Said ᶜĀ'isha (may God be pleased with her), 'He passed away (may God bless him and grant him peace) in my house, on my day,[B] between my chest and throat. And at death God joined my saliva to his. For when my brother ᶜAbd al-Raḥmān entered carrying a tooth-stick in his hand, he [the Prophet] began to look at it, and I knew that it pleased him, so I said, "Shall I bring it to you?" Yes, he nodded, so I handed it to him. He put it into his mouth, but it was too hard for him. "Shall I soften it for you?" I asked. Yes, he nodded, so I made it soft. And by him there lay a leather vessel containing water into which he started dipping his hand, saying, "No deity is there save God! Truly death has agonies!" Then he lifted up his hand and said, "The Highest Companion! The Highest Companion!" and I said, "So, by God, he will not prefer us".'[14]

Saᶜīd ibn ᶜAbd Allāh related the following from his father: 'When the Helpers saw that the Emissary of God (may God bless him and grant him peace) was increasingly burdened they encircled the Mosque. Al-ᶜAbbās (may God be pleased with him) went inside to the Prophet (may God bless him and grant him peace) and told him of of their position and their sympathy. Then al-Faḍl entered, and appraised him likewise, and ᶜAlī (may God be pleased with him), who did the same. He stretched out his hand and said, "Here," so they grasped it. "What say you?" he asked, and they replied, "We fear that you shall die."[15] And their women wailed at their menfolk's gathering around the Prophet (may God bless him and grant him peace).

'Then the Emissary of God (may God bless him and grant him peace) arose, and went outside leaning upon ᶜAlī and al-Faḍl, with al-ᶜAbbās in front. His head was bandaged and his feet

[A] This symbolic gesture of closing the mosque doors, mentioned elsewhere in the Traditions (Bukhārī, Manāqib al-Anṣār, 45; Muslim, Faḍā'il al-Saḥāba, 2; etc.) is discussed by Suyūṭī (*K. Shadd al-athwāb fī sadd al-abwāb*, in *al-Ḥāwī*, II. 12–31), who quotes (p.16) Ibn Ḥajar's opinion to the effect that by making this gesture the Prophet was designating Abū Bakr as the first successor to his temporal authority.

[B] It having been the Prophet's custom to divide his time among his wives on a principle of daily rotation.

dragged along the ground, but he gained the pulpit and sat down upon its lowest step. The people collected around him.

'He praised and glorified God, and then said, "O people! I have heard that you fear I shall die, as though you considered death to be something odious. What is it that you resent in the death of your Prophet? Has not my death-notice already been given you; have not you yourselves already been given your death-notices? Was any Prophet of those that were sent before me rendered immortal that I might also be granted eternal life? Nay, I shall go to join my Lord, as shall you all. I advise you to act kindly towards the First Emigrants, and to them I counsel mutual favour, for truly God (Great and Glorious is He!) has said, *By the Afternoon! Truly man is in loss. Save they that have faith . . .*"[16] He recited [the chapter] to its end,[A] and then continued, "Affairs run by the leave of God. Never permit the [inherent] slowness of something to induce you to try hastening it, for truly, God (Exalted is He!) hastens not by reason of the haste of anyone. Whoever seeks to overthrow God, God shall overthrow him, and whoever seeks to deceive Him will be deceived by Him. If you turn away, will you work corruption in the earth and sever your family ties? I counsel you to honour the Helpers, for they it was *who made ready the land and the faith before you came.*[B] [17] Be good to them, for did they not share with you half their crops and make room for you in their houses? Did they not prefer you over themselves, although theirs was the greater need? Thus whoever is given authority to judge between two men, let him accept from the virtuous amongst their number and deal indulgently with their wrongdoers. Do not prefer anyone over them.

' "I am preceding you, but you shall join me. Our tryst is at the Pool, my Pool whose breadth exceeds the distance which is between Bostra of Syria and Ṣanʿā' of the Yemen. Into it from the spout of al-Kawthar[C] pours a water which is whiter than milk,

[A] The chapter continues: *and perform deeds of righteousness, and exhort one another to truth and to endurance.*

[B] The Helpers [*Anṣār*] had prepared the ground for Islam in Medina before the Prophet's arrival.

[C] al-Kawthar: the name of a river in Heaven. See below pp.217–218.

softer than foam and sweeter than honey; whosoever drinks of it shall never thirst again. Pearls are its pebbles; musk is its bed. Whosoever is deprived of it tomorrow at the Standing Place[A] is deprived of all good. Therefore, let him who is desirous of meeting me there tomorrow restrain his tongue and hand from all save what is meet."

'Al-ᶜAbbās said, "O Prophet of God, advise us concerning Quraysh!"

"I only commend," he said, "this affair[B] to Quraysh, to whom the people are followers: their righteous men [shall rule] the righteous, and their evildoers [shall rule] their evildoers. O tribe of Quraysh! Deal with the people in a goodly fashion! And O people! Blessings and gifts are transformed by sin. Thus it is that whenever the people are good that their rulers are good towards them; and that whenever they are iniquitous that they are harsh to them. God (Exalted is He!) has said, *Thus do We give some of the wrongdoers authority over others because of what they had been earning*".'[18]

Ibn Masᶜūd (may God be pleased with him) related that the Prophet (may God bless him and grant him peace) said to Abū Bakr (may God be pleased with him), 'Ask me your question, O Abu Bakr!' 'O Emissary of God!' he replied. 'The time has drawn near!' 'The time has drawn near', he said, 'and is almost come.' 'What is with God shall surely gladden you, O Prophet of God,' he said. 'But would that I could know the place of our return!' And he told him, 'To God, and to the *Lote Tree of the Boundary*, then the *Garden of the Refuge*, the Highest Paradise, the Most-fulfilling Chalice, the Highest Companion, good fortune and the life made pleasant.' 'O Prophet of God!' he said. 'Who shall take charge of washing you?' 'Men from the closest of the people of my Household,' he replied. 'In what shall we shroud you?' he asked. 'In these clothes of mine, and a Yemenite cloak, and bound white cloth.' he replied. 'How are we to pray over you?' he asked. And we wept, and he wept with us, and then said, 'Gently now! May God forgive you, and reward you on behalf of your

[A] i.e. at the Judgement.

[B] i.e. leadership of the Muslim state.

Prophet well. When you wash and shroud me, set me on my bed in my house here at the side of my grave, then depart from me for an hour, for the first to pray for me will be God (Great and Glorious is He!): *He it is who blesses you, and His angels.*[19]

'Then He will give the angels leave to pray for me. The first of God's creatures to enter and pray for me shall be Gabriel, then Michael, Seraphiel, and the Angel of Death, together with a great host; then the angels in their entirety, may God bless them all.[20] Then you: enter in groups and pray for me in groups, one group at a time, and offer your salutations. Injure me not with excessive praise, or shouting or moaning. Let the prayer-leader [*imām*] commence, then the people of my Household, the nearest first, and then the companies of women and children.'

'Who shall set you in your grave?' he asked, and he replied, 'Groups of the people of my Household, first the closest, with many angels, whom you cannot see but who see you. Arise, and act on my behalf towards those who shall come after me'.[21]

Said ᶜAbd Allāh ibn Zamᶜa, 'Bilāl came at the beginning of Rabīᶜ al-Awwal[A] and delivered the Call to Prayer. The Emissary of God (may God bless him and grant him peace) said, "Instruct Abū Bakr to lead the people in prayer". So I went out, but could see no-one in the vicinity of the door save ᶜUmar, who was with a group of people which did not include Abū Bakr. "Arise, ᶜUmar!" I said, "and lead the people in prayer." So ᶜUmar got up, but when he declared, "God is Most Great,"[B] being a man of stentorian voice, he was heard by the Emissary of God (may God bless him and grant him peace) who said three times, "Where is Abū Bakr? God and the Muslims refuse this! Command Abū Bakr to lead the prayer!"

'And ᶜĀ'isha said (may God be pleased with her), "O Emissary of God! Abū Bakr is a man whose heart is delicate; whenever he stands in for you he is overcome with tears." But he said, "You are indeed the female companions of Joseph! Enjoin Abū Bakr to lead the prayer!" '[22]

[A] The third month of the Muslim year.

[B] This formula, the *takbīr*, is the first element in the Muslim prayer (*Iḥyā'*, I. 137).

And so it was that Abū Bakr led a prayer after the one which ᶜUmar had already said. And ᶜUmar used to say to ᶜAbd Allāh ibn Zamᶜa ever afterwards, 'Confound you! What was it that you did to me? By God, had I not thought that the Emissary of God (may God bless him and grant him peace) had given you instructions I would not have done what I did.' And ᶜAbd Allāh would reply, 'I saw no-one more worthy of it than you'.

And ᶜĀ'isha said (may God be pleased with her), 'I only spoke thus and turned him from Abū Bakr because I wanted to spare him this world and the peril and destruction which lie in leadership for all save those for whom God grants deliverance. I was also afraid that, unless God willed otherwise, the people might not have affection for a man who had prayed in the Prophet's stead (may God bless him and grant him peace) while he still lived, for they might then be envious of him, and feel hostile towards him and draw an ill omen from his act. But the matter rests with God; His is the decree, and He safeguarded him from all I had feared in the affairs of this world and of religion.'

And ᶜĀ'isha said (may God be pleased with her), 'When the day of the Emissary of God's death came (may God bless him and grant him peace), the people saw an improvement in him at the day's beginning, and the men went apart from him to their homes and tasks rejoicing, leaving him with the women. While we were there we were in a state of hope and joyfulness the likes of which we had never known. And then the Prophet of God said, "Go out, away from me; this Angel seeks leave to enter". At this, everyone but myself left the house. His head had been in my lap, but now he sat up and I retired to one side of the room. He communed with the Angel at length, and then summoned me and returned his head to my lap, bidding the women enter. "I did not sense that that was Gabriel, upon him be peace," I said. "Indeed, ᶜĀ'isha," he replied. "That was the Angel of Death, who came to me and said, 'I am sent by God (Great and Glorious is He!), Who has commanded me not to enter your house without your consent. So if you should withhold it from me I shall go back, but should you give it me, then shall I enter. And He has enjoined me not to take your spirit until you so instruct me; what, then, might your instructions be?' 'Hold back from me', I said, 'until Gabriel has come to me, for this is his hour'." '

And ʿĀ'isha [continued, and] said, (may God be pleased with her), 'So we came into the presence of a matter for which we had neither answer nor opinion. We were downcast; it was as if we had been struck by a calamity about which we could do nothing. Not one of the people of the Household spoke because of their awe in the face of this affair and because of a fear which filled our depths. At his hour, Gabriel came (I felt his presence) and gave his greeting. The people of the Household left, and he entered, saying, "God (Great and Glorious is He!) gives you His greetings, and asks how you are, although He knows better than you your condition; yet He desires to increase you in dignity and honour, and to render your dignity and honour greater than that of all creatures, that this may be a precedent [*sunna*] for your nation."[A] "I am in pain," he said. And the Angel replied, "Be glad, for God (Exalted is He!) has willed to bring you to that which He has made ready for you." "O Gabriel," he said. "The Angel of Death asked for permission to enter!" and he told him of what had transpired. And Gabriel said, "O Muḥammad! Your Lord longs for you! Has He not given you to know His purpose for you? Nay, by God, never has the Angel of Death sought permission of anyone, no more than is his permission to be sought at any time. It is only that your Lord is making perfect your honour while He longs for you." "Then do not leave until he comes," he said.

'Then he allowed the women to enter, and said, "Fāṭima, draw near." She leaned over him and he whispered in her ear. When she raised her head again she was weeping, and could not bear to speak. Then he said again, "Bring your head close," and she leaned over him while he whispered something to her. Then she raised her head, and was smiling, unable to speak. What we saw in her was something most astonishing. Afterwards we questioned her about what had happened, and she said, "He told me, 'Today I shall die,' so I wept; then he said, 'I have prayed to God to let you be the first of my family to join me, and to set you with me,' so I smiled."[23]

[A] i.e. that all should greet the sick in the same fashion.

'Then she brought her two sons[24] close by him. He drew in their fragrance.[25] Then the Angel of Death came, greeted him, and asked leave to enter. He granted it him, and the Angel said, "What are your instructions, O Muḥammad?" "Take me now to my Lord," he said. "Yes indeed," he responded, "on this day of yours. Truly your Lord longs for you. He has not paused over any man as He has paused over you, nor has He ever forbidden me to enter without permission upon anyone else. But now, your hour is come." And he went out. Then came Gabriel, who said, "Peace be upon you, O Emissary of God! This is the final time I shall ever descend to the earth. Revelation is folded up, the world is folded up, and I had on the earth no business save with you. Upon it now I have no purpose save being present with you, after which I shall remain in my place. No! By He Who sent Muḥammad with the Truth, there is no-one in the house able to change one word of what I have said. He will never be sent again despite the greatness of the discourse concerning him which shall be heard, and despite our affection and sympathy."'

'I got up and went to the Prophet (may God bless him and grant him peace) to put his head between my breasts, and clutched onto his chest. He began to swoon until he was overcome. His forehead was pouring forth sweat in a way that I have never seen from any man; I took to wiping away this sweat, and never had I found the scent of anything to be sweeter than it. I would say to him when he came round, "May my father and mother be your ransom, and myself and all my family! How your forehead perspires!" And he said, "O ʿĀ'isha, the soul of the believer departs with his sweat, while that of the unbeliever departs through his jaws like that of the donkey." At this, we were afraid, and sent for our families.

'The first man to come not having seen him was my brother,[A] whom my father had sent. But the Emissary of God (may God bless him and grant him peace) died before the arrival of anyone. For God held them back from him, as He had now set him in the charge of Gabriel and Michael. And when the swooning came he took to saying, "Rather, the Highest Companion!" as though the

[A] ʿAbd al-Raḥmān ibn Abī Bakr.

choice had been restored to him. And he would say whenever he was able to speak, "The Prayer! The Prayer! You shall always hold together as long as you pray together. The Prayer! The Prayer!" He commended it until he passed away, saying, "The Prayer! The Prayer!" '[26]

And ʿĀ'isha said (may God be pleased with her), 'The Emissary of God (may God bless him and grant him peace) died between the forenoon and midday, on a Monday.'

Said Fāṭima (may God be pleased with her), 'What is it that afflicts me on Mondays? By God, always is the [Muslim] nation afflicted by some great calamity on that day!'

Likewise, Umm Kulthūm (may God be pleased with her) said on the day that ʿAlī (may God ennoble his face) was struck down at Kūfa, 'What is it that afflicts me on Mondays? On that day the Emissary of God (may God bless him and grant him peace) passed away, and on it my husband ʿUmar was killed,[27] and on it my father was killed also. So what is it that afflicts me on Mondays?'

Said ʿĀ'isha (may God be pleased with her), 'When the Emissary of God (may God bless him and grant him peace) died, the people were thunderstruck, and a great wailing rose up, as the angels covered him with a garment of mine. The people differed amongst themselves: some denied his death, others were struck dumb and did not speak for a long while, whereas others became delirious and babbled without meaning. Others retained their reason, but there were still others who were unable even to walk. ʿUmar ibn al-Khaṭṭāb was among those who denied his death; ʿAlī was one of those unable to walk, while ʿUthmān was of those who had been struck dumb.

'Then ʿUmar went out to the people and declared, "The Emissary of God (may God bless him and grant him peace) has not died! God (Great and Glorious is He!) shall most certainly bring him back. May the hands and feet be struck from those hypocrites who desire the Emissary of God's death (may God bless him and grant him peace). For God (Great and Glorious is He!) has only taken him for a meeting, as He did for Moses, and he shall yet come to you." And according to another account he said, "O People! Restrain your tongues from speaking [thus] of the Emissary of God (may God bless him and grant him peace), for truly he has not passed away. By God, I shall attack with this sword of mine anyone who says that the Emissary of God (may God bless him and grant him peace) has died!"

'As for ᶜAlī, he was unable to walk, and remained in the house. And as for ᶜUthmān, he spoke to no-one, and would be taken by the hand and led here and there. There was no-one among the Muslims in a state comparable to that of Abū Bakr and al-ᶜAbbās, for God (Great and Glorious is He!) had succoured them both with guidance and good sense. The people paid attention to the speech of Abū Bakr alone until al-ᶜAbbās came and said, "By God, besides Whom is no other deity! The Emissary of God (may God bless him and grant him peace) has tasted death. While still among you he had declared, '*You will die, and they will die. Then, on the Day of Arising before your Lord you will dispute*'."[28]

'The news came to Abū Bakr while he was in the quarter of Banu'l-Ḥārith ibn al-Khazraj[A]. He came, and entered into the presence of the Emissary of God (may God bless him and grant him peace). He looked at him, then leaned over him and kissed him. Then he said, "May my father and mother be your ransom, O Emissary of God! Never was it God's will to make you taste death twice. Indeed, by God, the Emissary of God (may God bless him and grant him peace) has passed away." Then he went out to the people and said, "O people! Whoever has worshipped Muḥammad [let him know that] Muḥammad has died. But whoever has worshipped the Lord of Muḥammad [then let him know that] He is Alive, and does not die. For God (Exalted is He!) has said, *Muḥammad is but an emissary; emissaries have passed away before him. Will it be that when he dies or is slain, you will turn back on your heels?*"[29] And it was as though the people had never heard this verse before that day'.

In another account, when the news reached Abū Bakr he went into the house of the Emissary of God (may God bless him and grant him peace) and invoked blessings upon him, weeping abundantly and choking loudly like the camel on its cud, although his movements and his speech were firm. He leaned

[A] A tribe of Medina (*Inbāh*, 105).

over him and uncovered his face, and kissed his brow and cheeks, and wiped down his face. Weeping,[30] he said, 'May my father and mother be your ransom, and myself and all my family! How fine you are in life and in death! At your decease something was cut off which was never cut off at the death of any Prophet [before you]: Prophecy itself. Too great are you for description, too exalted even for the shedding of tears. You were unique so that you became a source of joy, and were universal so that through you we became equals. Were it not that your death had been of your own choosing we would perish also for grief over your loss, and had you not forbidden weeping[A] we would exhaust on your account our eyes' every tear. But what we cannot banish from us is an abiding sorrow and grief which shall never pass away. O Lord God! Convey this to him from us! O Muḥammad, may God grant you His blessings, recall us in the presence of your Lord! Let us be on your mind. Were it not for the serenity you have left behind no-one could withstand the loneliness which you have bequeathed to us. O Lord God! Convey this to Your Prophet, and supply his place amongst us.'[31]

It is related on the authority of Ibn ᶜUmar that when Abū Bakr entered the house and praised and magnified God, the people of the Household raised their voices in a clamour which was audible to the people in the Mosque; and each time he made mention of something they would clamour still more loudly. Their din did not subside until a salutation came from a sturdy and stentorian-voiced man at the gate. 'Peace be upon you, O people of the Household!' he said, [and then recited] *Every soul shall taste of death*[32] until he had reached the end [of the verse]. 'Truly in God there is a successor to every man, and an attainment for every desire, and a deliverance from every fear. Thus set your hopes in God, and trust in Him.' Although they did not recognise him, they hearkened to his words and ceased to weep. And when the weeping stopped his voice vanished; someone looked about, but could see no-one. Then they fell to weeping once again. But another caller whose voice they did not recognise cried out and said, 'O people of the Household! Remember God, and praise

[A] i.e. over his death.

Him in every circumstance, that you might be granted single-heartedness. Truly, in God there lies a consolation for every misfortune and a compensation for everything loved. Thus obey God. Work by His ordinance.' 'That', said Abū Bakr, 'was al-Khiḍr and Elias [al-Yasaᶜ] (upon them be peace), who have attended the Prophet (may God bless him and grant him peace).'[A]

The entire text of Abū Bakr's sermon has been given by al-Qaᶜqāᶜ ibn ᶜAmr, who said, 'When the people had finished weeping, Abū Bakr stood up before them to preach a sermon, the greater part of which was an invocation of blessings upon the Prophet (may God bless him and grant him peace). He praised and glorified God for every state [which He may bring about], and then said:

' "I bear witness that there is no deity save God, Alone, Who brought about His promise, gave victory to His bondsman, and overcame the Factions[B] Alone. To Him alone is the praise. And I bear witness that Muḥammad is His bondsman and Emissary, and the seal of His Prophets. And I bear witness that the Book is now as it was when revealed, and that the Faith is now as it was when laid down, and that the Tradition now is just as it transpired, and that the discourse is just as he uttered it, and that God is the Manifest Truth. O Lord God! Bless Muḥammad, Your bondsman and Emissary, Your Prophet, Your beloved one, trusted one, preferred and chosen one, with the most excellent blessings ever granted by You to any one of Your creatures. O Lord God! Bestow Your blessings and protection from ill, and Your mercy and Your grace upon the Master of the Messengers, the Seal of the Prophets, the Leader of the Godfearing, Muḥammad, the Commander and Leader of Good, the Emissary of Mercy. O

[A] For other versions of the tradition of the appearance of al-Khiḍr/al-Khaḍir, the mysterious wandering immortal (for whom see A. Wensinck, art. 'al-Khaḍir' in *SEI*, 232–5) at the Prophet's death see Ibn Kathīr, *Bidāya*, I. 332; V. 277. Ibn Kathīr is sceptical that such an event took place, and does not mention any tradition that might suggest that al-Yasaᶜ was also present. However, al-Khiḍr and al-Yasaᶜ are often portrayed as carrying out their tasks together. According to Ghazālī (*Iḥyā'*, I. 285) they meet together every year during the Pilgrimage.

[B] A reference to the tribe of Quraysh and their confederates, who had unsuccessfully besieged Medina in the year 5/627.

Lord God! Bring close to You his degree, make mighty his proof, ennoble his rank, and raise him up to a Praiseworthy Station which shall be the envy of the first and the last [of mankind]. Grant us the benefit of his Praiseworthy Station on the Day of Arising and supply his place for us in this world and in the next, and lead him to the Rank and the Means[A] in Heaven. O Lord God! Bless Muḥammad and the family of Muḥammad, and grant grace to Muḥammad and to the family of Muḥammad, as You did grant blessings and grace to Abraham; truly You are Praiseworthy and Majestic.

'"O people! Whosoever used to worship Muḥammad, [let him know that] Muḥammad has died. But whosoever has worshipped God, God lives and has not died. God revealed His will to you through him, so do not pray to Him in anguish, for God (Great and Glorious is He!) has preferred for His Prophet (may God bless him and grant him peace) that which is in His presence to that which is in yours, and has taken him to his reward. He has left with you His Book, and the Precedent of His Prophet (may God bless him and grant him peace). Whosoever holds to them both has acted in accordance with good custom, and whosoever separates them has trespassed against it. *O you that believe! Be staunch in justice.*[33] Do not allow the devil to preoccupy you with the decease of your Prophet, or to tempt you away from your religion. Make haste to good works, and you shall disable him. Give him no respite lest he catch up with you and work with you his sedition".'

Said Ibn ʿAbbās, 'When Abū Bakr (may God be pleased with him) had finished his sermon he said, "O ʿUmar! I hear that you say that the Prophet of God (may God bless him and grant him peace) has not died. Do you not see that the Prophet of God (may God bless him and grant him peace) used to say that such-and-such a thing would transpire on such-and-such a day, and that such-and-such a thing would transpire on such-and-such a day, and that God (Exalted is He!) has said in His Book, *You will die, and they will die*?"[34]

[A] *al-daraja wa'l-wasīla*: According to a *ḥadīth* (Muslim, Ṣalāt, 13), an exalted position in Heaven which may be occupied by one man only. Cf. also Khālid, 380–1.

'And ᶜUmar said, "By God, it is as if I had never heard this in the Book of God before this moment, due to what has befallen us. I bear witness that the Book is now as it was when revealed, and that the Tradition is now as it transpired, and that God is Alive and dies not. *Truly we are God's, and truly unto Him is our return.*[35] God's blessings be upon His Emissary. We hold that he has gone to God to receive his reward." Then he sat down with Abū Bakr.'

Said ᶜĀ'isha (may God be pleased with her), 'When the men gathered to wash him they said, "By God, we do not know how to wash the Emissary of God (may God bless him and grant him peace)! Are we to remove his garments as we do with our dead, or should we wash him in them?" And God sent down sleep upon them, until each one of them was resting his beard on his chest in slumber. Then someone—we knew not whom—spoke, and said, "Wash the Emissary of God (may God bless him and grant him peace) in his garments." Then they regained their senses and did so. Thus the Emissary of God (may God bless him and grant him peace) was washed in his long shirt [*qamīṣ*], until, when they had finished washing him they set him in his shrouds.'

And ᶜAlī said (may God ennoble his face), 'We had wanted to take off his shirt, but were called and told, "Do not remove the garments of the Emissary of God (may God bless him and grant him peace)," so we abided by this and washed him dressed in his shirt and laid out on his back, just as we wash our dead. And every time we wanted a limb which the water had not reached turned over it was turned over for us until we had finished. There was a rustling sound like a soft breeze with us in the house, which said, "Be gentle with the Emissary of God (may God bless him and grant him peace), for you shall indeed be rewarded".'

Thus, then, was the demise of the Emissary of God (may God bless him and grant him peace). He did not leave anything save that which was buried with him. Abū Jaᶜfar said, 'His grave was floored with a mat, and then with the garments he used to wear when awake, and then he was set upon them in his shrouds.' He left after his death no property, and never in his life had he laid one brick or piece of straw upon another. In his death there lies a most perfect lesson, and in him the Muslims have an excellent example.

The death of Abū Bakr al-Ṣiddīq (may God be pleased with him)

When Abū Bakr (may God be pleased with him) drew near to death, ᶜĀ'isha came (may God be pleased with her) and recited the following verse:

By your life! no use to a man is wealth
When he has the death rattle, and when his chest is tightened.

He uncovered his face, and said, 'Do not speak thus. Say instead, "*And the agony of death has come in truth. This is what you used to shun!*"[36] Mark my two garments here. Wash them and enshroud me in them, for the living are in more need of new things than the dead.'

And ᶜA'isha said (may God be pleased with her) shortly before his death,

Many a man so white that the doves took him for a cloud,
Is the orphan's springtime, a protection for the widows.

But Abū Bakr said, 'Thus was the Emissary of God (may God bless him and grant him peace)'.

They came in and said, 'Shall we not call a physician to look at you?' and he said, 'My Physician has looked at me, and has said, "I am the One Who acts as He will".'[37]

Salmān al-Fārisī (may God be pleased with him) came in to visit him in his illness. 'O Abū Bakr!' he said. 'Give us your last advice!' And he said, 'God is opening up the world for you in conquests. But do not ever take from it more than that which suffices you. Know that whoever says the Morning Prayer is under God's protection. Do not challenge God's protection, lest He cast you down in Hell upon your face.'

And when his affliction weighed heavily upon him the people asked him to appoint a successor. But when he appointed ᶜUmar (may God be pleased with him) they said to him, 'You have chosen as your successor a man harsh and stern! What shall you say to your Lord?' 'I shall say,' he replied, 'that I have chosen as my successor over Your creatures the finest of them all.'

Then he sent for ʿUmar (may God be pleased with him) and when he arrived, told him, 'I am going to give you a final injunction. Know that God has rights over you in the daytime the discharge of which He will not accept at night, and that He has rights over you at night which He will not accept to be discharged by day. He does not accept the supererogatory act of worship until that which is mandatory has been performed. The only man whose balance is heavy is he for whom it weighs down on the Day of Arising by virtue of his following the Truth in this world although it was a heavy burden upon him, for it is the nature of a balance in which only Truth is placed to be weighed down. And the only man whose balance is light is he for whom it is light on the Day of Arising because of his pursuing vanity and its easiness to bear for him; and lightness is the nature of a balance in which nought is placed save vanity.

'Know that God has described the people of Heaven according to their best works, choosing to overlook their sins, so that a man might say, "I am beneath these people and shall not attain their rank." And that He has described the people of Hell according to their most evil acts, rejecting the good which they had worked, so that a man might say, "I am superior to these people". Know that He has given you verses of mercy and verses of torment, so that the believer may both desire and fear,[38] and not be cast by his own hands into ruin,[39] or wish for anything from God save the Truth. If you should respect this injunction of mine, then no absent thing will be more beloved to you than death, which you cannot escape; should you cause it to be lost, however, then nothing which is absent will be more hateful to you than death, which you can neither escape nor hinder.'

Saʿīd ibn al-Musayyib said, 'When Abū Bakr (may God be pleased with him) drew near to death, a group of the Companions came and said, "O Successor to the Emissary of God (may God bless him and grant him peace), give us some provisions for the journey, for your condition is very evident to us!" And Abū Bakr said, "Whomsoever says certain words before dying, God shall set his spirit on the Clear Horizon." "What is the Clear Horizon?" they asked, and he replied, "A vale which lies before the Throne. In it lie the Gardens of God,[40] and rivers and trees. A hundred mercies cover it each day. God shall set in this place the spirit of whomsoever says these words: "O Lord God! Truly You did create mankind, although You had no need for them. Then You did render them two parties: a party for bliss, and a party for the Blaze. Make me, therefore, of the former party. O Lord God! Truly You did create[41] humanity in groups, and divided them before their creation. From them did You appoint the damned and the saved, the strayer and the rightly-guided. Do not damn me through acts of disobedience to You! O Lord God! Truly You knew what every soul would acquire before creating it; no escape has it from that which You have known. Render me, therefore, amongst those You make to act in obedience to You. O Lord God! No-one may wish for anything until You have willed it to transpire. So make it Your will that You decree that which brings me closer to You. O Lord God! You have determined the movements of Your bondsmen; nothing moves save by Your leave. Make, then, my movements to be in piety to You. O Lord God! Truly You have created good and evil, and appointed men who act by each. Make me, therefore, of the better party. O Lord God! Truly You did create Heaven and Hell,[A] and appoint people for each of them. Make me, then, of the dwellers in Your Heaven. O Lord God! Truly You did will misguidance for some people, constricting with it their breasts. Open, then, my breast to faith, and adorn with it my heart. O Lord God! Truly You have disposed all things, making their final destiny unto Yourself. Raise me up, then, after my death into a goodly life, and grant me great nearness to You. O Lord God! Despite he whose hope and trust, morning and night, is not in You, still You are my hope and trust. No power is there, and no strength, save in God".

[A] The orthodox doctrine being that Heaven and Hell are both created, but eternal (Ashʿarī, *Maqālāt*, 474; Rāzī, *Maʿālim*, 127–9).

'And Abū Bakr said, "All of this is in the Book of God (Great and Glorious is He!)".'

The Death of ᶜUmar ibn al-Khaṭṭāb (may God be pleased with him)

ᶜAmr ibn Maymūn said, 'On the day that ᶜUmar was struck down I was standing [in prayer] behind him, there being only ᶜAbd Allāh ibn ᶜAbbās between us. He walked between the rows, and, whenever he saw any irregularity, said, "Straighten out!" until at last he saw no further unevenness and went out in front,[A] saying "God is Most Great!" It was his custom to recite the chapter of Joseph, or The Bees,[B] or some such text in the first *rakᶜa*[C] so that the people had time to gather.

'No sooner had he begun the prayer when I heard him say, "He has slain me!" or "The dog has bitten me!" when Abū Lu'lu'a stabbed him. The foreigner ran amok with a two-pointed dagger, stabbing all he passed on his left and his right until he had stabbed thirteen men, of whom nine died (seven, according to another account). Upon seeing this, one of the Muslims threw a cloak over him, and the foreigner, seeing that he was captured, took his own life.

"ᶜUmar took hold of ᶜAbd al-Raḥmān ibn ᶜAwf and put him in front. Those who were behind ᶜUmar saw what I saw, but those who were at the back of the Mosque did not know what was the matter, only that they had lost ᶜUmar's voice. "Glory be to God!"[D] they said, "Glory be to God!" ᶜAbd al-Raḥmān led them in a brief prayer, and when they had left ᶜUmar said, "O Ibn ᶜAbbās! See who it is that has slain me." He disappeared for a while, and then came back and announced, "The servant-boy of

[A] One of the Imām's duties is to ensure that the rows of worshippers are straight before the prayer is begun (*Iḥyā'* I. 157).

[B] Both of these chapters of the Qur'ān (*sūras* XII and XVI) being reasonably long.

[C] *rakᶜa*: the basic unit of the regular Muslim prayer.

[D] *subḥān Allāh*: a common formula traditionally used to express surprise. In particular, uttered by any member of the congregation to inform the prayer-leader that he has made an error in the liturgy.

al-Mughīra ibn Shuʿba." "May God slay him!" said ʿUmar. "I had ordered that he be treated well." Then he said, "God be praised for not making my death be at the hands of a Muslim.[A] It was you and your father who wanted there to be many foreigners at Medina. Al-ʿAbbās was the one who had the most of them, as slaves." "If you wish, I will act," said Ibn ʿAbbās, meaning, "If you wish, I will put them to death." "After they have spoken your language, prayed in the direction you pray, and followed the rites of pilgrimage that you follow?" he asked.

'He was then carried to his house, and we set off with him. It was as though the people had never been afflicted by any disaster before that day. One man said, "I am afraid for him," while another said, "There is no danger." Some grape juice[B] was brought from which ʿUmar drank, but it came out from his belly; then they brought some milk, but when he drank this it too came out from his belly, and they knew that he would die.

'We went in to visit him with the people, who lavished praises on him. A young man came forward and said, "Rejoice, O Commander of the Faithful, at good news from God (Great and Glorious is He!). Yours was companionship with the Emissary of God (may God bless him and grant him peace) and such precedence in Islam as you have known. Then you were given to rule, and ruled with justice, until martyrdom came to you." "I only hope that that will balance out," he said, "and count neither for nor against me". And when the speaker had turned to leave, his waist-wrapper [*izār*] was to be seen trailing along the ground. ʿUmar asked that he be brought back, and then said to him, "O my nephew! Raise up your garment somewhat, for that will make it last longer and shows more piety to your Lord."[C] Then

[A] Abū Lu'lu'a was probably a Christian. His assassination of the Caliph is said to have been out of resentment at high taxes.

[B] *Nabīdh*: a beverage commonly made from grapes, and fermented, although not always (as presumably it was not in this case) to the extent of making it intoxicating. Cf. Lane, 2757.

[C] It being a recommended practice not to allow one's garment to extend lower than the ankles. The purpose of the story is of course to show that the Caliph, although *in extremis*, was undiminished in his zeal for the reform and improvement of his subjects.

he said, "O ᶜAbd Allāh! Look to my outstanding debts." They calculated them, and found that they amounted to eighty-six thousand [dirhams], or thereabouts. "If the wealth of the family of ᶜUmar will cover them," he said, "then pay them from my wealth. If not, then ask the tribe of ᶜAdī ibn Kaᶜb.[A] Should their wealth be insufficient, then ask among Quraysh. Do not go beyond them to anyone else, but pay back this money for me.

' "Go to ᶜĀ'isha, the Mother of the Believers, and say to her that ᶜUmar sends her his salutations. Do not say, 'Commander of the Faithful,' for today I am no longer their commander. Say, "ᶜUmar ibn al-Khaṭṭāb seeks leave to be buried beside his two companions'."

'And so ᶜAbd Allāh went, and gave his greetings, and asked leave to enter. When he entered he found her sitting down and weeping. "ᶜUmar ibn al-Khaṭṭāb sends his greetings to you", he said, "and seeks leave to be buried with his two companions". "I had wanted to have that place for myself," she said, "but today I will certainly put him first."

'When he returned, someone said, "Here is ᶜAbd Allāh ibn ᶜUmar, who has returned." "Lift me up," ᶜUmar said, and a man supported his weight. "What news do you bring?" "That which you have longed for, O Commander of the Faithful! She has given her consent." "God be praised!" he said. "Nothing was more important to me than that. Now when I have passed away, carry me thence, greet her, and say, "ᶜUmar seeks your leave to enter.' If she grants it me, then take me in; and should she send me back, then take me on to the cemetery of the Muslims."

'At this, Ḥafṣa, Mother of the Believers came, with the women veiling her. When we saw her we rose to our feet. She made her way over to ᶜUmar's house, where she wept awhile. Then she asked the men to let her enter, and she went inside, where we heard her weeping.

' "Give us your final injunction, O Commander of the Faithful," they said, "and appoint your successor!" "I see none with more right to this affair", he said, "than those people with whom the Emissary of God (may God bless him and grant him peace)

[A] His own clan of ᶜAdī ibn Kaᶜb ibn Lu'ayy (cf. *Inbāh*, 48).

was satisfied when he passed away." And he named ʿAlī, ʿUthmān, al-Zubayr, Ṭalḥa, Saʿd [ibn Abī Waqqāṣ] and ʿAbd al-Raḥmān [ibn ʿAwf]. "Let ʿAbd Allāh ibn ʿUmar be a witness to this, although he shall have no share in rulership; it shall be a consolation for him.[A] Should the government pass into the hands of Saʿd, then so be it; if not then let whomsoever is assigned it seek his aid, for I did not dismiss him on grounds of inadequacy or treachery.[B] I enjoin the man who shall succeed me as Caliph to deal kindly with the First Emigrants, and to recognise their merit and to respect their inviolability. I enjoin him to deal kindly with the Helpers, *who made ready the land and the faith before they came,*[42] that the deeds of their good men should be accepted and their wrongdoers forgiven. And I enjoin him to deal kindly with the people of the garrison towns [*al-amṣār*], for they are the buttress of Islam, the tax-gatherers, and the rage of the enemy; and that only what they hold in surfeit should be taken, and that with their consent. I enjoin him also to deal kindly with the nomads, for they are the root of the Arabs and the very stuff of Islam. Their surplus wealth should be taken from them and redistributed among their paupers. And I enjoin him, by the covenant of God (Great and Glorious is He!) and that of His Emissary (may God bless him and grant him peace), to respect their compact, to fight wars on their behalf, and to burden them only with that which they can sustain."

'When he passed away, we went out along with him and set off walking. ʿAbd Allāh ibn ʿUmar gave the greeting, and said, "ʿUmar ibn al-Khaṭṭāb asks leave to enter." "Bring him in," she said. And they brought him in, and laid him in a place there beside his two companions.'

It is reported that the Prophet (may God bless him and grant him peace) said, 'Gabriel (upon whom be peace) has told me that upon the death of ʿUmar all Islam shall weep'.[43]

[A] Ibn ʿUmar was appointed an advisor to the council which chose the new Caliph in the year 23/644. He himself was not eligible for the post.

[B] Saʿd ibn Abī Waqqāṣ had been appointed governor of Kūfa in the year 17 of the Hegira, and was subsequently discharged (Cf. *SEI*, art. 'Saʿd', 482 [K.V. Zettersté-en]).

According to Ibn ʿAbbās, "ʿUmar was set down on his bed, and the people crowded around him making supplications and prayers before he was lifted up. I myself was among them. No-one disturbed me until a man placed his hand on my shoulder. I turned, and there was ʿAlī ibn Abī Ṭālib (may God be pleased with him) who asked God to show mercy to ʿUmar, and said [to him] "There is not a single man with whose works I should prefer to meet God than with yours. By God, I had already believed that God would set you with your two companions, for how often did I hear the Prophet (may God bless him and grant him peace) say, 'I went with Abū Bakr and ʿUmar,' 'I entered with Abū Bakr and ʿUmar,' and 'I went out with Abū Bakr and ʿUmar,' so that I hoped, or suspected, that God would set you with them".'

The Death of ʿUthmān (may God be pleased with him)

The Tradition concerning his slaying is well-known.[A] ʿAbd Allāh ibn Salām said, 'At the time of the siege of my brother ʿUthmān I went in to visit him. "Welcome, my brother!" he said. "This same night, in this alcove here (meaning an alcove in the house [where he slept]), I saw the Emissary of God (may God bless him and grant him peace). He said to me, 'O ʿUthmān! They have laid siege to you!' and I said, 'Yes.' 'They have made you thirsty,' he said. 'Yes,' said I. And he drew me a pail of water, and I drank until my thirst was quenched, and I could feel its coolness between my breast and shoulders. 'Should you so wish', he said, 'you will be given victory over them; or, if you prefer, you may break your fast with me.' And I decided to break my fast with him."

'On that day he was killed, may God be pleased with him.'

ʿAbd Allāh ibn Salām once asked those who had been present at the death agonies suffered by ʿUthmān after he had been

[A] Towards the end of his reign he was widely accused of nepotism. This, combined with his policy of permitting only one authorised version of the Qur'ān, aroused enough enmity to bring about his assassination in the year 35/656.

wounded, 'What did ʿUthman say while he was in his death throes?' 'Three times we heard him say,' they replied, ' "O Lord God! Unify the nation of Muḥammad (may God bless him and grant him peace)!" ' And he said, 'By Him in Whose hand lies my soul, had he prayed God never to allow them to unify, never would they do so again until the Day of Arising.'

Said Thumāma ibn Ḥazn al-Qushayrī: 'I was watching the house from which ʿUthmān was looking out over them when he said, "Bring to me your two companions who called you out against me!" And they were brought as though they were a pair of camels or donkeys. ʿUthmān leaned out and said, "I adjure you both by God and Islam! Did you know that when the Emissary of God (may God bless him and grant him peace) came to Medina there was no sweet water there save the well of Rūma.[A] 'Who will buy Rūma,' he asked, 'setting his own bucket along with those of the Muslims in exchange for something better than it in Heaven?' And I purchased it with my own wealth. Are you going to bar me from drinking from it today, or even from any other well?" And they said, "Yes, by God!" "I adjure you by God and Islam!" he said [again]. "Did you know that I equipped the Army of Difficulty[B] from my own wealth?" "Yes, by God," they replied. "By God and Islam I adjure you!" he said. "Did you know that at one time the Mosque became too small for those who frequented it, and that God's Emissary (may God bless him and grant him peace) said, 'Who will buy the land of So-and-so's family and add it to the Mosque in exchange for something better than it in Heaven?' upon which I purchased it from my own wealth. Shall you today bar me from praying two *rakʿas* therein?" "Yes, by God!" they said. "By God and Islam I adjure you! Did you know that the Emissary of God (may God bless him and grant him peace) was once on [Mount] Thabīr at Mecca in the company of Abū Bakr, ʿUmar and myself, when the mountain moved so that stones rolled down to the valley floor?

[A] This well, now known as Bi'r ʿUthmān, is still pointed out in Medina in the vicinity of al-ʿAqīq.

[B] The force sent to Tabūk in the ninth year of the Hegira, so called because it set out at the time of the date harvest in Medina.

He scuffed it with his foot, and said 'Be still, Thabīr, for there is no-one upon you save a Prophet, a Truthful One, and two martyrs'!" "Yes, by God!" they replied. "God is Most Great!" he exclaimed. "They have testified to me, by the Lord of the Kaᶜba, that I am to be a martyr!" '

It is related on the authority of a shaykh of Ḍabba[A] that when ᶜUthmān was struck down, and when the blood was flowing out onto his beard, he took to saying, '*No deity is there but Thee! Glory be to Thee! Assuredly I have been among the wrongdoers.*[44] O Lord God! I implore Thy protection against them, and ask for Thy support in all my affairs, and I ask Thee to grant me steadfastness in that with which Thou hast tried me.'

The death of ᶜAlī (may God ennoble his face)

Said al-Aṣbagh al-Ḥanẓalī: 'At daybreak, shortly before the time when ᶜAlī (may God ennoble his face) was struck down, Ibn al-Tayyāḥ[45] came to him to call him to the Prayer. He was reclining and sleepy, and remained so when he returned to him. But when he came for the third time ᶜAlī arose and walked, saying:

Gird up your loins for death.
    Death shall surely meet you.
Do not be angry at death
    When it comes to your valley.

'When he reached the small door Ibn Muljam bore down upon him and dealt him a blow.'[B]

Umm Kulthūm, the daughter of ᶜAlī (may God be pleased with him) came out and cried repeatedly, 'What is it that afflicts me at the Morning Prayer? My husband the Commander of the

[A] The tribe of Ḍabba ibn Udd (*Inbāh*, 60).

[B] Ibn Muljam belonged to the Khārijite rebels, whom ᶜAlī had defeated in battle at Nahrawān.

Faithful,[A] and my father were both slain at the Morning Prayer!'

It is told on the authority of a shaykh of Quraysh that ʿAlī (may God ennoble his face) said, when Ibn Muljam stabbed him, 'I have triumphed, by the Lord of the Kaʿba!'[B]

According to Muḥammad ibn ʿAlī, after he was stabbed he counselled his sons, and then said nothing but 'There is no deity but God' until he died.

When al-Ḥasan ibn ʿAlī (may God be pleased with them both) became increasingly ill, al-Ḥusayn (may God be pleased with him) entered and said, 'O my brother, why do you sorrow? You are going on to join God's Emissary (may God bless him and grant him peace) and ʿAlī ibn Abī Ṭālib, who are your fathers; and Khadīja bint Khuwaylid and Fāṭima bint Muḥammad, who are your mothers; and Ḥamza and Jaʿfar, who are your paternal uncles.' And he replied, 'O my brother! I am going to something the likes of which I have never been to before.'

Said Muḥammad ibn al-Ḥusayn,[46] 'When the people bore down upon al-Ḥusayn (may God be pleased with him), and he became certain that they would kill him,[C] he stood up in the midst of his followers and delivered a sermon. He praised and lauded God, and then said, "The matter is as you have seen. The world has changed and been befouled, its good customs passing away; and it has shrivelled up so that all that remains of it is as a drop in the bottom of a vessel. Enough of a life like bad pasturage! Do you not see that the Truth is not acted by, and that falsehood is not denounced? Let the believer aspire to the meeting with God (Exalted is He!). Truly, I see death as nothing but happiness, and life in the company of the wrongdoers as nothing save transgression".'

[A] Umm Kulthūm had been married to the Caliph ʿUmar.

[B] By winning the martyr's crown.

[C] For the death of al-Ḥusayn see his notice in the Appendix.

CHAPTER FIVE

On the Sayings of the Caliphs, Princes, and Righteous Men when Nearing Death

WHEN DEATH came to Muʿāwiya ibn Abī Sufyān he said, 'Help me to sit down,' and they did so. He then began glorifying God (Exalted is He!) and making remembrance of Him, until he wept and said, 'You have remembered your Lord, O Muʿāwiya, after the onset of decrepitude and decline. Would that you had done so while the bough of youth was fresh and verdant!' He wept more loudly still, and then said, 'O Lord! Have mercy on the sinful old man with the hard heart! O Lord God! Overlook my stumblings, and forgive my lapses, and by Your clemency relent towards him who has set his hopes in none save You, and has trusted in You alone.'

And an elder of Quraysh relates that a group of people came in to visit him in his sickness, and beheld his dire condition. He [Muʿāwiya] praised and lauded God, and said, 'To proceed. Is the world in its entirety anything more than that which we have experienced and seen? In truth, by God, we turned to face its attractions with our strivings and our revelling in our lives, yet not long was it before the world began to diminish us, condition after condition, and attachment after attachment, until it defrauded and exhausted us. So how unworthy an abode is the world! How unworthy an abode is the world!'

It is related that in the last sermon Muʿāwiya preached he declared, 'O people! I am of a crop that was sown and then reaped. I have been set in authority, and none shall rule you after me save that he be worse than myself, even as those who preceded me were my betters. O Yazīd! When my destined course is done, entrust the washing [of my body] to a man of intelligence, for truly, the intelligent man has a certain status in the sight of God. Let him carry out the washing gently and declare "God is Most Great" in a loud voice. Then go to find a certain cloth in the treasury, where there lies one of the garments of the Emissary of God (may God bless him and grant him peace), and some of his hair and his nail parings, which you should set in my nose, mouth, ears and eyes. Put the garment upon my body directly underneath my shrouds. And O Yazīd! Respect God's injunction with regard to parents! Then, when you have lowered me into the earth and set me in my crevice, leave Muᶜāwiya alone with the Most Merciful of all that show mercy.'

Said Muḥammad ibn ᶜUqba,[1] 'When death descended upon Muᶜāwiya he said, "Would that I were a man of Quraysh at Dhū Ṭuwā,[A] and had never assumed any of this authority!" '

When death came near to ᶜAbd al-Malik ibn Marwān he looked at a washerman in a district of Damascus who was folding a garment and beating it against a washing vessel. 'If only I were a washerman', he said, 'who eats from what his own hands earn each day, and that I had never assumed any authority over this world.' This came to the ears of Abū Ḥāzim, who said, 'Praised be God, Who has made them, when they draw near to death, long for what we already have, while when we approach death we do not long for what they have.'

During the course of his mortal illness, ᶜAbd al-Malik ibn Marwān was asked, 'How are you, O Commander of the Faithful?' and he replied, 'I am as God (Exalted is He!) has said: *You come unto Us singly as We did create you aforetime, having forsaken that which We conferred upon you behind your backs.*'[2] [He continued] to the end of the verse,[B] whereupon he passed away.[3]

[A] A place close to Mecca.

[B] The remainder of the verse runs: *We do not behold with you your intercessors of whom you claimed that they possessed a share in you. Now is the bond between you severed, and that which you presumed has failed you.*

Said Fāṭima bint ᶜAbd al-Malik ibn Marwān, the wife of ᶜUmar ibn ᶜAbd al-ᶜAzīz: 'During the course of the sickness from which he died, I would hear ᶜUmar saying, "O God! Conceal my death from them, if only for one hour of the day."[A] And when the day in which his soul was taken came, I left his presence and sat in another chamber which was separated from him by a door. I could hear him in a domed chamber of his saying, "*That Abode of the Afterlife: We have appointed it for those who wish for no grandeur upon the earth, neither any corruption. And the outcome is for the Godfearing.*"[4] Then he fell silent, and I could hear neither movement nor utterance from him, so I said to one of his pages, "Look and see if he is asleep." But when he entered the chamber he shrieked, and I jumped up; and lo and behold! he had passed away.'

When he had drawn near to death he was asked, 'O Commander of the Faithful! Give us your final injunction!' 'I warn you of a death such as mine,' he replied, 'for you shall not escape it.'

It is related that when ᶜUmar ibn ᶜAbd al-ᶜAzīz grew increasingly weighed down [by his illness] a physician was summoned for him. When he looked at him he said, 'I believe that the man has been poisoned, and I cannot protect him from death.' ᶜUmar looked up and said, 'Neither can you protect from it the man who has not been poisoned.' 'Did you feel it, O Commander of the Faithful?' the physician asked, and he replied, 'Yes, I knew it as soon as it entered my belly.' 'Accept treatment, O Commander of the Faithful', he said, 'for I fear that your spirit will pass away!' 'My Lord is the best destination,' he replied. 'By God, if I knew that my cure lay at my earlobe I would not raise my hand to take it. O Lord God! Allow ᶜUmar to choose to meet You!' And no more than a few days later he died.

It is said that he wept upon the advent of death and was asked, 'What has made you weep, O Commander of the Faithful? Rejoice, for through you God has revived [Prophetic] precedents [*sunan*], and made justice to prevail!' But he wept anew, and asked, 'Am I not to be stood up and questioned about my authority over His creation? By God, even had I been just to

[A] A civil conflict being expected to erupt upon his death.

mankind I would still fear that my spirit might not stand firm with its plea before God, unless taught its plea by Him. So how shall it be when I have done so much?' His eyes brimmed with tears, and only a short while later he died.

It is related of Hārūn al-Rashīd that he chose his shrouds with his own hands shortly before he died, and gazed at them, saying, '*My wealth has not availed me. My dominion has passed away*.'[5]

Al-Ma'mūn sprinkled ashes on the ground and lay down upon them, saying, 'O Thou Whose reign is never-ending, have mercy upon him whose reign has ended!'

Al-Muᶜtaṣim said on his deathbed, 'Had I only known that my life would be so short I would not have acted as I did.'

Al-Muntaṣir grew restless as he approached death, and, when he was told, 'There is no danger, O Commander of the Faithful!' replied, 'It is simply this: the world has receded and the Afterlife has drawn near.'

When near to his death, ᶜAmr ibn al-ᶜĀṣ looked at some chests, and said to his sons, 'Who will take them and what they contain? Would that they were no more than dung!'

Al-Ḥajjāj said on his deathbed, 'O Lord God! Grant me Your forgiveness, for the people say that You will not forgive me.' ᶜUmar ibn ᶜAbd al-ᶜAzīz was pleased by this utterance of his and envied him for it. But when it was related to al-Ḥasan he asked, 'Did he truly say this?' 'Yes,' he was told. 'Perhaps,' he remarked.

An exposition of the sayings of a number of the most righteous men among the Companions, the Followers, and the Sufis who came after them

When death came to Muᶜādh (may God be pleased with him) he said, 'O Lord God! I used to fear You, but today in You have I set my hopes. O Lord God! Truly You know that never have I harboured love for this world or for a long sojourn therein; neither for the flowing[6] of streams or the planting of trees; rather have I loved thirsting in the midday heat, enduring the hours, and joining the crowds around the Divines on my knees in the circles of remembrance.'[A] And when the pangs of death mounted up as they had mounted up for no other man, he would open his eyes whenever he awoke from his mortal agonies and say, 'O my Lord! Choke me as You will, for by Your glory, You know that my heart loves You.'

When Salmān drew near to his death he wept. 'What has made you weep?' he was asked, and he replied, 'I do not weep out of regret for losing this world, for the Emissary of God (may God bless him and grant him peace) instructed us that our share of it should be as the travelling-provisions of a rider.' And when he had passed away, all that he had left behind was inspected, and its value amounted to little more than ten dirhams.[7]

When death came to Bilāl his wife cried, 'O sorrow!' But he said, 'Rather say, "O rapture!" For tomorrow we shall meet those we love, Muḥammad and his company.'

It is said that at the moment of death ᶜAbd Allāh ibn al-Mubārak opened his eyes and laughed, saying, '*For the likes of this, then, let those who would work, work*!'[8]

When death came to Ibrāhīm al-Nakhaᶜī he wept. 'What has made you weep?' he was asked, and he replied, 'I am awaiting a messenger from God who will give me the tidings either of Heaven or of Hell'.

When death came to Ibn al-Munkadir he wept. Upon being asked why, he said, 'By God, I am not weeping over a sin which I know I have committed; rather I fear that I might have done something which I considered *trivial but which in God's sight is grave*'.[9]

When death came to ᶜĀmir ibn ᶜAbd al-Qays he wept. 'What has caused you to weep?' he was asked, and he replied, 'I do not weep from fear of death, nor out of greed for this world; rather I weep for the thirsting daytimes and the night vigils in winter which have passed me by'.

When death came to Fuḍayl he swooned. Then he opened his eyes and said, 'O! How long is the voyage! And O! How scant the provisions!'

[A] i.e. classes on religion.

And when death came to Ibn al-Mubārak he said to his *mawlā* Naṣr, 'Lay my head upon the dust.' Naṣr wept, and when asked why, said, 'I recalled the felicity which once was yours, and now [see] you dying impoverished and estranged'. 'Hush,' he said. 'I once prayed God (Exalted is He!) to make me live the life of the wealthy and die the death of the poor.' Then he said, 'Rehearse [the Confession of Faith] to me, and do not repeat it unless I speak again.'

Said ᶜAṭā' ibn Yasār, 'The devil once appeared before a man on his deathbed and told him that he was saved. However, he retorted, "I am not safe from you yet!" '

A man who was weeping on his deathbed was asked why he wept. 'Because of a verse in the Book of God (Exalted is He!),' he replied, 'in which He says (Great and Glorious is He!): *God only accepts [good works] from the pious*'.[10]

Al-Ḥasan once came in upon a man who was giving up the ghost, and said, 'To be sure, any matter with a prelude such as this must have an ending to be feared, and any matter with such an end as this must have a prelude to be lived in austerity.'

Said al-Jurayrī, 'I was in the presence of al-Junayd at the time of his death agonies. It was a Friday, and the day of Nayrūz.[A] He was reciting the Qur'ān, and when he finished I said to him, "O Abu'l-Qāsim! Shall it be in this state?" And he said, "And who deserves it more than myself, as my scroll has now been folded up?" '

Said Ruwaym, 'I was present at the demise of Abū Saᶜīd al-Kharrāz. He was saying:

> The yearning of the hearts of the gnostics is for Remembrance, and their remembrance of the Secret is at the time of their intimate communion.
> Cups of fate were passed among them,
> thus they turned from the world as the drunkard turns.
> Their yearnings circulate in an encampment
> wherein are the folk of God's love like shining stars.
> Their bodies lie dead on the earth from His love,

[A] The Persian New Year; cf. Ahsan, 286–90.

and their spirits pass by night through the veils towards the sublime.
Never do they halt save in the vicinity of their Beloved;
nor are they deflected by touch of misery or harm.'

It was said to al-Junayd that Abū Saʿīd al-Kharrāz had been in a state of overpowering divine love[A] as he approached death. 'It would not have been a wonder,' he remarked, 'had his spirit flown away from passion [*ishtiyāq*]!'

It was said to Dhu'l-Nūn upon his death: 'What do you desire?' And he replied, 'To know Him before my death by one instant.'

It was said to one of them[B] while he was undergoing the pangs of death: 'Say: "God"!' 'How much longer will you say this to me,' he replied, 'when I am burning up in God?'

One of them said: 'I was in the company of Mumshād al-Dīnawarī when a dervish came up and said, "Peace be upon you! Is there a clean place here where a man might die?" They pointed out a place to him, and the dervish renewed his ablutions in a spring of water, and then prayed for as long as God willed. Then he went over to that place, stretched out his legs, and died.'

Abu'l-ʿAbbās al-Dīnawarī was once speaking in his assembly when a woman screamed from Divine love [*tawājud*]. 'Die!' he said to her, and she rose to her feet. When she reached the door of the building she turned to him and said, 'I have died!' and she fell down, having died indeed.[C]

It is told that Fāṭima, the sister of Abū ʿAlī al-Rūdhbārī, said, 'When the time drew near for the death of Abū ʿAlī al-Rūdhbārī[11] his head was in my lap. He opened his eyes and said,

[A] Ar. *tawājud*: 'a thrill of emotion in contemplation of God' (Hujwīrī, tr. Nicholson), a prelude to the higher 'station' of *wajd*, in which the mystic is rapt from himself in contemplation of his Beloved.

[B] The Sufis.

[C] This rather enigmatic anecdote was probably meant in its original context (Qushayrī, *Risāla*, II. 562) as an illustration of the danger of excessive emotionality which usually accompanies *tawājud*, which is a problem of the beginner on the spiritual path. Qushayrī tells us elsewhere (I. 246–7) that the Baghdad Sufi al-Jurayrī once stood in ecstasy during a mystical session and asked al-Junayd, 'Master, are you gaining nothing from this?' But he only replied with the Qur'ānic verse, *The mountains which you think to be firm pass away as do the clouds.*

"Behold the gates of Heaven which have been opened! Behold the gardens which have been decked out! Behold a speaker who says, 'O Abū ʿAlī! We have brought you to the furthest degree, although you sought it not.' " Then he recited:

By Your Truth, never may I look at what is not You
with the eye of love until I see You.
I see You as my Tormentor, who made my glance feeble,
and made my cheek rosy from shyness of You.

It was said to al-Junayd, 'Say: "There is no deity but God"!' and he replied, 'I have not forgotten it that I might thus recall it.'

Jaʿfar ibn Nuṣayr asked Bakrān al-Dīnawarī, the servant of al-Shiblī, 'What did you see him do [in his last hours]?' And he replied, 'He said, "I was once in unjust possession of one dirham, and although I [later] bestowed thousands upon its owner in charity there is no greater worry in my heart than this." Then he asked me to wash him in preparation for prayer, and I did so. But I had forgotten to pass my hand through his beard, and he, being unable to speak, grasped my hand and set it in his beard, upon which he passed away.' At this Jaʿfar wept, and said, 'What can one say regarding a man who at the last extremity of his life did not leave undone a single propriety of the Law?'

When Bishr ibn al-Ḥārith drew near to death in great suffering, he was told, 'It seems that you love life'. And he replied, 'The approach to God is severe'.

It was said to Ṣāliḥ ibn Mismār, 'Shall you not entrust your son and family to anyone?' and he replied, 'I am ashamed to entrust them to anyone save God'.

When Abū Sulaymān al-Dārānī approached death his companions came to him and said, 'Be glad, for you are passing on to a Lord Who is Forgiving and Merciful'. And he said, 'Should you not rather say, "Beware, for truly you are passing on to a Lord Who shall call you to account for your small sins and punish you for the major ones"?'

When death came to al-Wāsiṭī he was asked to give his companions a final injunction. 'Acquiesce in what the Truth has willed for you,' he said.

The wife of one of the Sufis wept when he approached death. 'What has made you weep?' he asked, and she said, 'I am weeping on your account.' 'If you must weep', he said, 'then weep for yourself, for I have wept over this day for forty years'.

Said al-Junayd, 'I came in upon al-Sarī al-Saqaṭī when he was in his mortal illness. "How are you?" I enquired, and he recited:

How may I complain to my physician of what ails me,
when what ails me from my Physician comes?

I picked up a fan in order to fan him, but he said, "How may the one whose innards are aflame find any relief in being fanned?" Then he recited:

The heart is aflame and the teardrops race;
adversity gathers and endurance departs.
Wherefore constancy for he that has none,
who is wronged by passion, love and disquiet?
O Lord, should there be in [life] anything of joy to me
then bestow it upon me as long as I draw breath!'

It is related that a group of al-Shiblī's companions came in to visit him when he was on the point of death. 'Say: "There is no deity but God"!' they told him. And he recited:

A house in which you dwell
is in no need of lanterns.
Your hoped-for face will be our justification
on the day when mankind shall come with justifications.
May God not grant me any relief
on the day when I implore for relief from you.[A]

It is told that Abu'l-ᶜAbbās ibn ᶜAṭā' came in upon al-Junayd during his death pangs. He greeted him, but al-Junayd did not respond until some time later, when he said, 'Forgive me; I was

[A] According to Annemarie Schimmel (pp. 126–7), these lines, which are still sung in mystical gatherings on the Subcontinent, are generally understood to be a eulogy for the Blessed Prophet. The final verse is problematic, and is not to be found in the original (*Risāla*, II. 560).

busy with my litany [*wird*].' Then he turned his face towards Mecca, declared 'God is Most Great!' and died.

Al-Kattānī was asked as he drew near to death: 'What were your works?' And he replied, 'Were it not for the imminence of my demise I would not tell you. I stood at the door to my heart for forty years, and whenever that which is not God [*ghayr Allāh*] passed by it I denied it entry.'

It is related of al-Muᶜtamir that he once said, 'I was among those who were in the presence of al-Ḥakam ibn al-Muṭṭalib at the hour of his death. "O Lord God!" I said, "Mitigate the agonies of death for him, for that which is past is past." And I made mention of his good qualities until he awoke and said, "Who is it that speaks?" "It is I," I replied. "Truly the Angel of Death," said he, "upon him be peace, says to me, 'I am tender to all who have been generous'." Thereupon he passed away.'

When death came to Yūsuf ibn Asbāṭ, Ḥudhayfa was watching him. Seeing him to be in a state of agitation he said, 'O Abū Muḥammad [ibn Asbāṭ]! Now is the time of distress and sorrow!' And he replied, 'O Abū ᶜAbd Allāh! How should I not be distressed and sorrowful when I do not know whether I have truly obeyed God in any of my works?' 'How wonderful is this Godfearing[12] man', said Ḥudhayfa, 'who swears upon his death that he does not know whether he has obeyed God in any of his works!'

Said al-Maghāzilī, 'I once came in upon a shaykh of mine while he was unwell and in this plight. "You are able to do with me as You will," he was saying, "so deal with me with gentleness".'

One of the Shaykhs came in upon Mumshād al-Dīnawarī at the hour of his demise and said to him, by way of a prayer, 'God (Exalted is He!) has acted and done'. He laughed and said, 'For thirty years Heaven was offered to me with all it contains, yet I did not so much as glance at it.'[A]

Ruwaym was told at his death to say 'There is no deity save God,' but he replied, 'I cannot say anything else correctly'.

[A] 'A reference to the station of absorption in God [*maqām al-istighrāq bi'llāh*] whereat one perceives no felicity save that which is in Him.' (Zabīdī, x. 344).

When al-Nūrī approached death he was told to say 'There is no deity save God,' and he replied, 'Is there no command?'[A]

Abū Yaḥyā al-Māzinī came in upon al-Shāfiʿī (may God have mercy upon them both) in his final sickness, and asked him, 'How are you faring this morning?' 'This morning I am travelling from this world', he said, 'and departing from my brethren, and going to meet my evil works, quaffing the cup of death, and coming unto God (Exalted is He!) Yet I do not know whether my spirit is travelling to Heaven, that I might congratulate it, or to Hell, that I might console it.' Then he recited:

> When my heart was hardened and my courses
>   constrained,
> I made my hopes a stairway to Your
>   forgiveness.
> My sin burdened me heavily, but when I measured it
>   by Your forgiveness, Lord, Your forgiveness
>   was the greater.
> Always are You forgiving of sin, and always
>   do You show generosity and forgiveness out of
>   munificence and bounty.
> Still, were it not for You no worshipper would be
>   tempted by the devil;
> How could that be, when he led astray Your
>   chosen one, Adam?

When Aḥmad ibn Khiḍrawayhi approached death a question was put to him. His eyes brimmed with tears, and he said, 'O my son! A door upon which I have been knocking for ninety-five years is now opening, yet I do not know whether it shall open into happiness or suffering. So how may I have time now to furnish you with an answer?'

Thus, then, were their sayings. They differed only in accordance with the discrepancy between the states of those that

[A] That is, 'Is there no command to that effect already?' The *Risāla* (II. 595) has *alaysa ilayhi aʿūd* for *alaysa thamma amr*.

pronounced them. For some men are dominated by fear, others by hope and still others by love and yearning; each man speaks in accordance with his state, and all of them, within the context of their states, are correct.

CHAPTER SIX

On the Sayings of the Gnostics at Funerals and Cemeteries, and the Legal Verdict concerning the Visitation of Graves

KNOW THAT funerals are a lesson to the man possessed of insight, and a reminder and a counsel to all save the people of heedlessness. For these latter are increased only in hardness of heart by witnessing them, as they imagine that for all time they will be watching the funerals of others, and never reckon that they themselves must needs be carried in a funeral cortège. Even if they do so reckon, they do not deem this to be something near at hand. They do not consider that those who are carried now in funeral processions thought likewise. Vain, then, are their imaginings, and soon their allotted lifespans will be done.

Therefore let no bondsman watch a funeral without considering that he himself is the one being borne aloft, for so he will be before long:[1] on the morrow, or on the day that follows: it is as if the event had already occurred.

It is related of Abū Hurayra that whenever he saw a funeral procession he would say, 'Continue, for we are following you.'

Whenever Makḥūl al-Dimashqī saw a funeral procession he would say, 'Continue, for we are leaving [also]. An eloquent exhortation soon followed by heedlessness, as the first goes by and the last remains without thinking!'

Said Usayd ibn Ḥuḍayr, 'Never have I witnessed the funeral of a man without telling myself what will be done with him and to what he is going'.

When the brother of Mālik ibn Dīnār died, Mālik followed his cortège, saying, 'By God, I shall never be content until I know to what you have departed, but never shall I know for as long as I live'.

Said al-Aᶜmash, 'We used to attend funerals, and did not know who to console because of the sorrow of everyone present'.

Said Thābit al-Bunānī, 'We used to attend funerals, and would see no-one who was not covering his face and weeping'.

Such, then, was their fear of death. But nowadays never do you see a group of people attending a funeral without the majority of them laughing and enjoying themselves, speaking of nothing but the inheritance and of what [the deceased] has bequeathed to his heirs; the sole thought in the minds of his friends and relatives being of the devices by which they might obtain some share in his legacy. Not a single one of them (save those whom God wills) meditates upon his own funeral and upon how he shall be when he himself is carried in a funeral cortège. The sole reason for this is the hardness which has afflicted people's hearts through their many acts of disobedience and sin, whereby we have come to forget God (Exalted is He!) and the Last Day, and the terrors which lie before us. We have taken to playfulness and neglect, and to busying ourselves with that which is of no concern to us. We pray God (Exalted is He!) to rouse us from this heedlessness! For truly, the best of states in those who attend funerals is that they should weep for the deceased; moreover, if they had any understanding they would weep for themselves rather than for him.

Ibrāhīm al-Zayyāt once watched a group of people who were praying for God's mercy upon a dead man, and said, 'It would be better for you if you were to pray for mercy for yourselves. For he has now been delivered from three terrors: the face of the Angel of Death, which he has now seen, the bitterness of death, which he now has tasted, and the fear of death, from which he has now obtained security.'

Said Abū ᶜAmr ibn al-ᶜAlā', 'I was once sitting in the company of Jarīr while he was dictating some poetry to a scribe. A funeral procession came past, and he stopped short, and said, "These funerals have turned my hair grey, by God!" Then he recited:

> Funerals alarm us when they approach,
> and we enjoy ourselves when they go away.
> Like a flock of sheep, which panics when the wolf descends,
> and pastures once again when it is gone.'

The proprieties of attending funerals include meditation, heedfulness, preparedness, and walking before the pall in humility, as we have already described in connection with its proprieties and Precedents when dealing with the science of Jurisprudence.[A] One of these proprieties is to have a good opinion of the deceased even if he had been corrupt, and to have a poor opinion of oneself even if one may outwardly be pious. This is because the last moment is a perilous thing the true nature of which is unknown.

It is told of ʿUmar ibn Dharr that one of his neighbours once died. He had been extravagant with himself, and for this reason many people refused to attend his funeral. However, Ibn Dharr attended it and took part in the prayers. When he [the neighbour] had been lowered into the grave he [Ibn Dharr] stood beside it and said, 'May God show you mercy, O father of So-and-so! For throughout your life you kept with you the testimony to Divine Unity, and begrimed your face through prostration. Although they have called you a sinner and a transgressor, which one of us is not a sinner and has no transgressions to his account?'

It is related that a certain man deeply sunk in depravity once passed away in a district of Basra. His wife was unable to find anyone to help her carry him, since not one of her neighbours paid him any heed on account of his great wickedness. So she hired some carriers, who bore him out to the prayer-place, where there was no-one to pray for him. Then she carried him out into the desert to bury him. Now, on a mountain close by there was one of the great ascetics, whom they descried in the aspect of a man waiting for a funeral. [Sure enough,] he came and prayed for

[A] Cf. *Iḥyā'*, I. 183-184.

him. The news that the ascetic had done this spread throughout the city, and the people were greatly astounded that he should thus have prayed for him, but he told them, 'I was instructed in a dream to descend to such-and-such a place, where I would see a man's funeral attended only by a woman, and there to offer prayers for him, for he had been forgiven his sins'. The people's astonishment increased at this, until the ascetic summoned the woman and questioned her about the circumstances and behaviour of the dead man. 'As people know,' she said, 'his entire day was spent in the tavern where he occupied himself with drinking wine.' 'See now,' he said, 'do you know of any good deeds which were to his credit?' 'Yes,' she replied, 'three things. Every day at dawn he used to awaken from his drunkenness, change his clothes, perform the ablution, and offer the Dawn Prayer with the congregation. Then he would return to the tavern and occupy himself with vice. The second thing is that his house was never devoid of one or two orphans, to whom he showed even more kindness than he did to his own children, and for whom he was greatly solicitous. The third thing is that in the darkness of the night and in the very midst of his drunkenness he would awake, and weep, and say, "O Lord![2] Which corner of Hell do you wish to fill with this foul man?"—by which he meant himself.'

And so the ascetic went his way, the obscurity surrounding the affair having been cleared.

It is told of Ṣila ibn Ashyam that when a brother of his died he said at his graveside:

> If you are saved, then you are saved from something
> most momentous;
> If not, then truly I cannot see you saved.

An exposition of the condition of the grave and of their sayings at the graveside

Said al-Ḍaḥḥāk, 'A man once said, "O Emissary of God! Who is the most ascetic of men?" And he replied, "He who does not forget the grave and decay, and abandons the surfeit of this world's bedizenment; he who prefers what abides to that which must pass away; he who does not reckon that tomorrow will be among his days, and who accounts himself among the people of the graves".'[3]

ʿAlī (may God ennoble his face) was asked why it was that he lived near to the cemetery. 'I find [its inmates] to be the best of neighbours,' he replied. 'I find them to be neighbours of truthfulness, who hold their tongues and remind one of the Afterlife.'

Said the Emissary of God (may God bless him and grant him peace), 'Never have I seen a spectacle more fearsome than the grave'.[4]

Said ʿUmar ibn al-Khaṭṭāb (may God be pleased with him), 'We once went out to the cemetery with the Emissary of God (may God bless him and grant him peace). While I was the nearest of the people to him, he sat down by a grave and wept. I wept at this, and so did the other people. "What has made you weep?" he asked, and we replied, "We weep because you are weeping." And he said, "This is the grave of my mother, Āmina bint Wahb. I asked permission of my Lord to visit her, and was granted it. Then I asked His permission to pray that she should be forgiven, but this was denied me, and I was afflicted with the sensibility which is the lot of sons".'[A] [5]

Whenever he stopped by a grave, ʿUthmān ibn ʿAffān (may God be pleased with him) used to weep until his beard became soaked. 'How is it', he was asked, 'that you make mention of Heaven and Hell and do not weep, yet weep when you stop by a grave?' And he replied, 'I once heard the Emissary of God (may

[A] Orthodox opinion has generally held that the Prophet's parents gained salvation, having died before his mission commenced and thereby joining the ranks of all whose lives were lived out in a *fatra*, an age following the decay of one prophetic dispensation and before the advent of the next, and who therefore had no opportunity to submit themselves to the authority of revelation. See Suyūṭī's summary of the issue (*Masālik al-ḥunafā' fī wāliday al-Muṣṭafā*, in *al-Ḥāwī*, II. 202–233). Suyūṭī suggests that the reason which prevented the Prophet from asking for pardon for his mother might have been that she had been in debt, and that 'in the early days of Islam it was prohibited to offer prayers for the soul of a debtor'. (Ibid, II. 227.)

God bless him and grant him peace) say, 'The grave is the first stage of the Afterlife. Should the one who occupies it be delivered therefrom then what follows will be easier than it, but if he is not delivered therefrom then what follows is to be more severe".'[6]

It is said that ᶜAmr ibn al-ᶜĀṣ once saw a graveyard, dismounted, and prayed two *rakᶜas*. 'This is not something you used to do,' he was told, and he replied, 'I remembered the people of the graves, and what has come between them and such acts, and wished to draw closer to God by praying thus'.

Said Mujāhid, 'The first to address the son of Adam [after his death] is his grave, which says, "I am the house of worms! I am the house of loneliness and solitude and darkness! This is what I have prepared for you, so what, then, have you prepared for me?"'

Said Abū Dharr, 'Shall I not tell you of the day of my poverty? It is the day when I shall be set in my grave.'[A]

Abu'l-Dardā' was in the habit of sitting at gravesides. When this was remarked upon, he said, 'I sit with a people who remind me of my fate, and who, when I rise to depart, do not then slander me'.

It was the custom of Jaᶜfar ibn Muḥammad to visit the cemetery by night and to say, 'O people of the graves! What ails me, that when I call you you make no response?' Then he would say, 'They have been barred from replying to me, by God! And now, it is as though I were one of them.' Then he would pray until the dawn broke.

Said ᶜUmar ibn ᶜAbd al-ᶜAzīz to a man with whom he was sitting, 'O So-and-so! Tonight I have not slept because of thinking about the grave and its occupant. Truly, if you were to behold a dead man after three days in his grave you would be repelled by his presence even had you been familiar with him for a long while. You would see a house with a changed smell in which vermin move about, and where pus flows, where worms penetrate, and where the shrouds have decayed, where once there was a sweet odour, pure garments and an excellent appearance.' Then he moaned, and fell down in a swoon.

[A] This despite his celebrated poverty and asceticism.

Yazīd al-Ruqāshī used to say, 'O you who are buried in your pit, all by yourself in the grave, who find solace in the belly of the earth only in your works. Would that I could know at which of your actions and companions you have rejoiced!' Then he would weep until he made his turban-cloth damp, and say, 'By God! He rejoices at his righteous works, and at those of his companions who assisted one another to obey God (Exalted is He!).' And whenever he looked at a grave he would low like a bull.

Said Ḥātim al-Aṣamm, 'Whosoever passes by a graveyard and neither thinks about himself nor prays for its occupants has betrayed them, and himself also.'

Bakr al-ᶜĀbid used to say, 'O my mother! Would that you had been barren and never begotten me! For before your son there lies a lengthy sojourn in the grave, and after that, the journey onwards.'

Said Yaḥyā ibn Muᶜādh, 'O son of Adam! Your Lord has summoned you to the Abode of Peace, so look, then, to the place from which you have responded. You shall enter [that abode] if you have responded from your stay in this present world and have busied yourself with the voyage, but should you respond from your grave you shall be barred therefrom.'

Whenever al-Ḥasan ibn Ṣāliḥ looked out over a cemetery he would say, 'How excellent is your external prospect; the terrors lie only in your interior!'

When nightfall came, ᶜAṭā' al-Salīmī would go out to the cemetery and say, 'O people of the graves! You have died, and O! what a death! And you have seen your works, and O! what works!' Then he would say, 'Tomorrow ᶜAṭā' will be in the graveyard! Tomorrow ᶜAṭā' will be in the graveyard!'[7] This would be his practice the whole night long.

Said Sufyān, 'He who remembers the grave frequently shall find it to be one of the gardens of Heaven, while he who is in heedlessness of it shall find it to be one of the chasms of Hell.'[A]

Al-Rabīᶜ ibn Khuthaym dug a grave in his house, and whenever he felt some hardness in his heart would enter it and lie

[A] An echo of the *ḥadīth*, 'The grave is either one of the chasms of Hell or one of the gardens of Heaven'. (Tirmidhī, Qiyāma, 26.)

prone. After waiting for as long as God willed, he would say, '*O Lord! Send me back, that I may work righteousness in that which I have left*',[8] and then say to himself, 'O Rabīʿ! I have returned you, so act!'

Said Aḥmad ibn Ḥarb, 'The very earth is amazed at the man who lays out his bed and prepares to sleep. "O son of Adam!" it says. "Why do you not remember your long decay at that time when there shall be nothing between us?" '

Said Maymūn ibn Mihrān, 'I once went out to the cemetery with ʿUmar ibn ʿAbd al-ʿAzīz. When he looked at the graves he wept, and came over to me, saying, "O Maymūn! These are the tombs of my forefathers, the house of Umayya. It is as though they had never taken part in the life and delights enjoyed by the people of this world. See you not that they were felled to the ground, *afflicted by exemplary punishments*?[9] Corruption has taken hold of them, and vermin have found an abode in their bodies." Then he wept, and said, "By God! I do not know of a happier man than he who has entered these graves safe from the chastisement of God!" '

Said Thābit al-Bunānī, 'I once entered a cemetery, and when I made to leave heard a voice addressing me. "O Thābit!" it said. "Be not deceived by the silence of its people, for how many an unhappy soul is lying within!" '

It is related that Fāṭima bint al-Ḥasan, while watching the funeral of her husband al-Ḥasan ibn al-Ḥusayn,[10] covered her face and declaimed:

> They were a hope, and then turned to losses;
> Severe and mighty indeed were those losses.

It is said that she then pitched a tent over the grave and went into a retreat there for a whole year. When the year had passed they struck the tent and she returned to Medina. Then they heard a voice rising from one side of al-Baqīʿ,[A] saying, 'Did they find what had gone astray?' and another voice from the other side, saying, 'No, they despaired and went away'.

[A] The cemetery of Medina.

Said Abū Mūsā al-Tamīmī, 'When the wife of al-Farazdaq died, her funeral was attended by the great men of Basra. Among them was al-Ḥasan, who asked, "O Abū Firās![A] What have you set aside for this day?" "Sixty years of the testimony that there is no deity save God," he replied. Then, when she had been interred, he stood by her grave and said:

I fear beyond the grave, should You not pardon me,
something tighter than the grave, and more fiercely burning.
When on the Day of Arising a stern captain comes,
and a marshal who drives al-Farazdaq onwards.
Defeated is that son of Adam who does walk
to the Inferno, blue, and necklaced with chains.'[11]

People have declaimed on the subject of the graves' inhabitants:

Pause by the graves and say to their expanses:
'Which of you is buried in their shadows?
Which of you is honoured in their depths,
and has tasted the coolness of safety from their terrors?'
As for their tranquillity, to the onlookers it is one,
the discrepancy between their degrees cannot be seen.
If they replied to you they would inform you with tongues
which describe their realities through a number of their conditions.
As for the obedient one, in a garden shall he dwell,
led where he will among its tall trees.
The rebellious sinner turns round and about in it,
in a pit, taking refuge with its serpents.
Scorpions scuttle to him, and his spirit
is in dire torment from their stings.

[A] i.e. al-Farazdaq.

Dāūd al-Ṭā'ī once passed by a woman who was weeping by a grave and saying:

> You lost your life, and gained it not
> when they buried you in your grave.
> How, then, may I taste the savour of sleep,
> when on your right side they have laid you?

Then she said, 'O father![12] Would that I knew with which of your cheeks the worms began!' At this, Dāūd was thunderstruck, and fell down in a swoon.[A]

Said Mālik ibn Dīnār, 'I once passed by the cemetery and declared:

> I came to the graves and called out to them:
> "Where is the mighty and where the despised?
> Where is he who was pleased with his power?
> Where the self-righteous man who did brag?"

Then he said, 'I was called from the graves, and, although I saw no-one, I heard a voice that said:

> They are all extinguished, and no one can tell of them.
> They died all together, and all news as well.
> The daughters of the earth may come and may go,
> but it will erase the charms of their forms.
> O you who ask me of people departed,
> is there no lesson for you in those that you see?

'I returned in tears,' he said.

[A] According to al-Qushayrī (*Risāla*, I. 93), it was this incident which occasioned al-Ṭā'ī's repentance and conversion to Sufism.

Chapter Six

Some verses found inscribed upon graves

The following was found inscribed upon a grave:

Tombs hold discourse with you, and yet are silent
  while their indwellers lie quietly under the dust.
O you gatherer of the world who will never gather it,
  for whom do you gather the world when you must die?

Upon another grave was found inscribed:

Abū Ghānim! Spacious is your shelter,
  and well-laid are the walls of your tomb.
Yet the one interred is not helped by the construction of
  his grave
  when his frame inside it is falling into ruin.

Said Ibn al-Sammāk, 'I once passed by the cemetery, and there beheld the following inscription upon a grave:

My relations pass by my graveside;
  it is as though they never knew me.
My heirs divide my wealth,
  caring not that they have repudiated my debts.
They have taken their shares and lived on.
  By God! How fast have they forgotten me!'

And upon a further grave was found inscribed:

One is taken from one's loved ones by embezzlement;
  death is not stopped by a doorman and guards.
So how can you delight in this world and its pleasures,
  you, whose words and breaths have been tallied up?
O heedless one! You are immersed in loss,
  while all your life you were immersed in pleasure.
Death shows no mercy to an ignorant man because of his
  fair complexion;
  nor yet to the man from whom knowledge was sought.

How often death has struck dumb, at some grave where I halt,
  a tongue never dumb before, lest it make reply!
Well built was your palace, and honourable indeed,
  yet today your tomb lies obliterated among the graves.

Upon another grave was found the following:

I stood among my loved ones, when their graves
  were ranked in line like racehorses.
When I wept, and as my tears poured forth,
  my eyes beheld my own place amongst them.

Upon the grave of a physician was found:

I said, when someone declared,
  'Luqmān has gone to his grave.
So where is the medicine he prescribed;
  where his bitter solutions and his feeling of
  temperatures?'
'What folly! He that cannot protect himself,
  can hardly ward off any harm from another.'

And upon another grave was found inscribed:

O people! I once had hopes,
  but my course was too short for me to realise them.
So let him fear God, his Lord, that man
  who was able to act in his lifetime.
Not alone am I in being taken to this place that you see;
  all shall be taken to its like.

These verses were inscribed on graves because of the failure of their inmates sufficiently to be admonished before they died. The man of insight looks to the graves of others and sees his own place amongst them, and then readies himself to join them, knowing that they will not move from their places before he comes among them. He should be fully aware that if but one wasted day of his life were to be offered them it would be more precious to them than the whole world. For they have known the value of their lifetimes,[13] and have had the true nature of things revealed to them. Their yearning for one day of life is so that the man with failings might make up for his shortcomings and thereby rescue himself from punishment, and so that the one who has already been granted providential success might seek to raise his degree so that his reward becomes multiplied.

They only become aware of the value of their lifetimes after they have departed them: thus their sorrow and yearning for one more hour of life. You are capable of living that hour, and perhaps more, yet you spend it to no profit. Prepare yourself, therefore, to lament over having thus wasted it when the decision is no longer in your hands, and when you have failed to grasp your share of your allotted time by way of forestallment.

One of the righteous once said, 'In a dream I once saw one of my brethren in God. "O So-and-so!" I said to him. "You are alive, *praised be God, the Lord of the Worlds*!"[14] And he said, "That I were only able to utter it" (meaning "*praised be God, the Lord of the Worlds*") "would be dearer to me than the world and all it contains". Then he said, "Did you not see where they buried me? So-and-so stood in that place and prayed two *rakᶜas*. That I were able to pray them would be dearer to me than the world and all it contains." '

An exposition of their sayings upon the death of a child

It behoves the man whose child or kinsman has passed away that he should treat his antecedence in death as though it were a journey in which his child has preceded him to a country which is his dwelling-place and homeland. His grief will not then overwhelm him, as he knows that soon he is to catch up with him, and that there lies between them nothing save an early and a later departure. Thus is death: its meaning is to precede another to the homeland until such time as the one who has tarried catches up. When one comes to believe this one's sorrow and anguish[15] will be lessened, most particularly because such news of reward has come to us as may console every person thus afflicted.

The Emissary of God (may God bless him and grant him peace) has said, 'That I should send before me one miscarried foetus is more beloved to me than leaving a hundred cavalry all fighting in the way of God.'[16] He mentioned the miscarried foetus only to suggest that the death of older children would bring a yet greater reward; otherwise, the reward is in proportion to the position occupied by the child in one's heart.

Said Zayd ibn Aslam, 'David (upon whom be peace) once lost a son, and fell into a state of intense grief. When asked what the child had been worth to him, he replied, "The whole earth filled with gold." "In the Afterlife," he was told, "yours will be a recompense like unto that".'

Said the Emissary of God (may God bless him and grant him peace), 'Never does a Muslim lose three children and suffer from their loss without their becoming a protection for him against Hell'. A woman who was in the presence of the Emissary of God (may God bless him and grant him peace) spoke up, and asked, 'Or two?' and he replied, 'Or two'.[17]

The parent should pray earnestly for a child which has perished, for such a prayer is the most likely to gain response. Muḥammad ibn Sulaymān once stood by the grave of his son, and said, 'O Lord God! This morning I hope for Your grace upon him, and fear Your chastisement of him; thus realise my hopes and grant him security from what I fear'.

Abū Sinān stood by the grave of his son, and said, 'O Lord God! I have forgiven him that which he owed to me, so forgive him that which he owed to You, for truly You are more Generous and Excellent!'

A nomad once stood by the grave of his son and said, 'O Lord God! I have overlooked his shortcomings in filial piety, so overlook his shortcomings in piety to You.'

When D͟harr ibn ʿUmar ibn D͟harr died, and after he had been laid in his tomb, his father ʿUmar ibn D͟harr stood up and said, 'O D͟harr! Sorrow on your behalf has distracted us from sorrowing for you. Would that I could know what you have said, and what was said to you!' Then he said, 'O Lord God! This is D͟harr. You gave me pleasure from him for as long as You willed, then, without wronging him, brought his course and sustenance to an end. O Lord God! You commanded him to obey You and myself. O Lord God! That recompense which You have promised me in my misfortune I make over to him. Give me his chastisement, and punish him not.' Having made those who were present cry, he made to leave, and then said, 'After you, O Dharr, we will have no poverty, and, God being with us, will neither have any need from any man. We pass on and leave you behind; were we to remain with you we would bring you no benefit.'

A man once looked at a woman at Basra and said, 'Never have I seen such cheerfulness! Such a thing can only be the result of a lack of grief'. 'Bondsman of God!' she said. 'I am in a state of misery shared by no-one else'. 'How is that?' he asked, and she replied, 'My husband slaughtered a sheep on the Feast of Sacrifices.[A] I had two beautiful sons who were playing at the time. One of them said to the other, "Do you want me to show you how father slaughtered the sheep?" "Yes," said the other. And he took hold of him and slaughtered him. We knew nothing of this until we found him writhing in his blood. And when the hue and cry started the boy fled and hid in the mountains, where he was caught and devoured by a wolf. Then his father went out to search for him, but died of thirst because of the great heat. Thus has fate left me in solitude, as you see.'

Such misfortunes as these should be brought to mind when children die so that in the midst of much grief some consolation may be had. For no misfortune is there without one greater being imaginable, for in every circumstance God prevents that which is more baneful.

An exposition of the visitation of graves, the offering of supplications for the deceased, and related matters

In general, the visitation of graves is a desirable thing, for it instils the remembrance of death and acts as an admonition. To

[A] *ʿīd al-aḍḥā*: the festival which closes the pilgrimage season.

visit the tombs of the righteous in order to obtain blessings and a lesson is desirable likewise. The Emissary of God (may God bless him and grant him peace) used to forbid the visitation of graves, but later allowed it: it has been related on the authority of ᶜAlī (may God be pleased with him) that the Emissary of God (may God bless him and grant him peace) said, 'I once forbade you to visit graves, but you should now visit them, for they remind you of the Afterlife. But do not utter defamations.'[18]

The Emissary of God (may God bless him and grant him peace) once paid a visit to the grave of his mother when he was riding with a thousand cavalry, and wept more profusely than he had ever been seen to do before. 'I am granted leave to pay a visit', he said, 'but not to ask for pardon'.[19]

Said Ibn Abī Mulayka, "ᶜĀ'isha (may God be pleased with her) repaired one day to the cemetery. "O Mother of the Believers!" I asked her. "Where have you been?" And she replied that she had been at the grave of her brother ᶜAbd al-Raḥmān. "But was that not forbidden by the Emissary of God (may God bless him and grant him peace)?" I asked. "Yes," she said, "but then he enjoined it".'[20]

However, this should not be adhered to in such a way as to suffer women to go out to the cemeteries. For they frequently utter defamations at the graveside, so that the advantage of their visit does not outweigh the harm it causes. Neither do they shrink from displaying themselves and playing up their charms in the street, and these are serious matters, whereas the visitation of graves is a Precedent [*sunna*].[A] How can such things be tolerated for the sake thereof? Certainly, there is no harm in a woman going out in chaste garments such as will ward off from her the eyes of men, but on condition that she restrict herself to praying, and avoid any discoursing by the grave.

Said Abū Dharr, 'The Emissary of God (may God bless him and grant him peace) said, "Visit graves, and you will be reminded of the Afterlife; wash your dead, for truly in the touching of an empty body there is an eloquent lesson; and offer

[A] The *sunnas* being of a supererogatory nature, and therefore less important than the maintenance of standards of decency and modesty.

prayers at funerals, that perhaps you may grieve, for truly, the grief-stricken are in the very shadow of God".'[21]

Said Ibn Abī Mulayka, 'The Emissary of God (may God bless him and grant him peace) said, "Pay visits to your dead, and give them your salutations, for in them there lies a lesson for you".'[22]

It is related on the authority of Nāfiᶜ that Ibn ᶜUmar would never pass by a grave without halting and giving a greeting.

Jaᶜfar ibn Muḥammad related from his father that Fāṭima, the daughter of God's Emissary (may God bless him and grant him peace) used to visit the grave of her [great-] uncle Ḥamza during the daytime, where she would pray and weep.

He said (may God bless him and grant him peace), 'Whosoever visits the grave of one or both of his parents every Friday shall be forgiven his sins, and shall be inscribed as having been faithful to them.'[23]

According to Ibn Sīrīn, the Emissary of God (may God bless him and grant him peace) said, 'A man's parents may die after he has severed his ties with them, but should he render prayers to God on their behalf after their decease God shall record him among those who showed filial piety.'[24]

Said the Prophet (may God bless him and grant him peace), 'My Intercession becomes mandatory for all who visit my grave.'[25]

And he said (may God bless him and grant him peace), 'Whosoever visits me at Medina, seeking thereby a reward from God, for him shall I intercede and bear witness on the Day of Arising.'[26]

Said Kaᶜb al-Aḥbār, 'Never does dawn break without there descending seventy thousand angels, who circle the [Prophet's] tomb, beating their wings and invoking blessings upon the Prophet (may God bless him and grant him peace), until, when the evening comes, they return aloft to be succeeded by a similar [host] which disposes itself likewise, until that time comes when the earth shall be split asunder, and he shall emerge at the head of seventy thousand angels paying homage to him.'

It is the preferred practice when visiting a grave to stand with one's back to the Direction of Prayer [*qibla*] and to orient oneself towards the countenance of the deceased before greeting him. The tomb should not be rubbed, touched or kissed, for such are the practices of the Christians.

Nāfiᶜ related that on a hundred occasions or more he saw Ibn ᶜUmar approach the [Prophet's] tomb and say, 'Peace be upon the Prophet. Peace be upon Abū Bakr. Peace be upon my father'. After this he would depart.

Said Abū Umāma, 'I once saw Anas ibn Mālik approach the tomb of the Prophet (may God bless him and grant him peace), halt, and lift up his hands so that I thought that he had begun the Prayer. Then he greeted the Prophet (may God bless him and grant him peace) and went his way.'

Said ᶜĀ'isha (may God be pleased with her), 'The Emissary of God (may God bless him and grant him peace) said, "No man who visits his brother's grave and sits with him shall not have him enjoy his company and return his greetings until he stands up".'[27]

Said Sulaymān ibn Suḥaym, 'I once saw God's Emissary (may God bless him and grant him peace) in a dream, and said to him, "O Emissary of God! Those people who come to you and greet you, do you hear their greetings?" "Yes," he said, "and I return them".'

Said Abū Hurayra, 'Whenever a man passes by the grave of a man he used to know and greets him, he is recognised and his greeting is returned. And when he passes by the grave of one unknown to him and gives a greeting, his greeting is returned also.'

A man from the family of ᶜĀṣim al-Jaḥdarī once said, 'I saw ᶜĀṣim in a dream two years after he had died. "Have you not died?" I asked him, and he said, "Of course." "Where are you?" I enquired. "I am, by God", he replied, "in one of the gardens of Heaven with a group of my friends. Each Thursday night, and on the following morning, we gather around Abū Bakr ibn ᶜAbd Allāh al-Mazanī and receive your news." "In your bodies?" I asked, "or as spirits?" "What folly!" said he, "the bodies have perished, and only as spirits is it that we congregate." And I enquired, "Know you aught of the visits we pay you?" and he replied, "Yes, we are aware of them on Thursday night, on

Friday in its entirety, and on Saturday until the rising of the sun." "How should that be," I asked, "to the exclusion of all other days?" And he replied, "By reason of the greatness of Friday, and its excellence".'[A]

Muḥammad ibn Wāsiᶜ was in the habit of visiting [graves] on Fridays. When asked why he did not postpone his visits until Monday he replied, 'I have heard that the dead are aware of those that visit them on Friday, and on the preceding and succeeding days also'.

Said al-Ḍaḥḥāk, 'The dead man knows of the visit of he who attends his grave before sunrise on Saturday.' Upon being asked why this should be so he replied, 'Because of the status of Friday.'

Said Bishr ibn Manṣūr, 'In the days of the plague there was a man who used to frequent the graveyard to attend the funerals there. In the evening he would stand at the gate of the graveyard and say, "May God send you comfort in your solitude! May He show you mercy in your loneliness! May He overlook your sins! May your good works be acceptable to Him!" He would say no more than these words. And the same man said, "One evening I returned to my family without repairing to the cemetery as had been my custom. When I fell asleep there appeared before me a great throng which had come to me. "Who are you?" I asked, "and what would you have of me?" "We are the people of the graveyard," they replied. "And what brings you here?" I enquired. And they said, "You have put us in the habit of receiving a gift from you each time you return to your family." "And what might that be?" I asked. "The prayers you used to say for us," they replied. "I shall resume them," said I, and never did I omit them thenceforth".'

[A] In an analysis of the relative suitability of times for religious practices (*Iḥyā'*, I. 274), Ghazālī explains that 'Friday is a time of united zeal and the gathering of hearts in the soliciting of God's grace, which is one reason for the nobility of certain times; there are others which man can never know'. Asín Palacios (*Escatología*, 338), who refers to this passage of the *Remembrance*, tells us that it is a 'universal Muslim doctrine' that the torment of sinners abates on Fridays, when wandering souls return to their graves; hence the recommendation to visit cemeteries on that day (a custom, incidentally, which is still widely observed).

Said Bashshār ibn Ghālib al-Najrānī, 'I once saw Rābiʿa al-ʿAdawīya, the worshipper [*al-ʿābida*] in my sleep, it having been my custom to pray for her abundantly. "O Bashshār ibn Ghālib," she told me. "Your gifts come to me covered with silken cloths upon salvers of light." "How should that be?" I asked, and she replied, "Thus are the prayers of the living believers: when they offer a prayer for the deceased and are granted a response, that prayer is set upon salvers of light and covered with silken cloths, after which it is brought to the one who has died with the words, 'This is So-and-so's gift to you' ".'

The Emissary of God (may God bless him and grant him peace) said, 'The dead man in his grave is like a drowning man shouting for help, as he waits for a prayer to come to him from his father, his brother or his friend. When it comes it is more beloved to him than the world and all it contains. Indeed, the gifts of the living to the dead are prayer and the petitioning of God for His forgiveness.'[28]

It was said by a certain man, 'A brother of mine once passed away. I saw him in my sleep, and asked, "In what state were you upon being lowered into the grave?" And he replied, "I was approached by someone bearing a brand of fire, and had someone not prayed for me I saw that he would have beaten me with it".'

Hence it is desirable to rehearse [the Confession of Faith] to the deceased after he has been interred, and to pray for him.

Said Saʿīd ibn ʿAbd Allāh al-Awdī,[29] 'I saw Abū Umāma when he was in the agonies of death. "O Saʿīd!" he said. "When I die, do with me that which was decreed by the Emissary of God (may God bless him and grant him peace): 'When one of you dies and you have levelled the soil above him, let one of you stand at the head of his grave and say, "O So-and-so!, the son of such-and-such a woman!" for truly he hears, unresponding. Then let him say, "O So-and-so, the son of such-and-such a woman!" when he will sit upright. Then let him say, "O So-and-so, the son of such-and-such a woman!" a third time, when he will say (although you cannot hear him), "May God have mercy upon you; we are guided aright." Then let him say, "Remember that with which you departed this world: the testimony that there is no deity save

God and that Muḥammad is the Emissary of God, and that you have been well-pleased with God as your Lord, with Islam as your religion, and with Muḥammad (may God bless him and grant him peace) as your Prophet, and with the Qur'ān as your guide [*imām*]." For verily both Munkar and Nakīr shall retreat at this, saying, "Let us be gone from here! What should induce us to sit with this man when his plea has been rehearsed for him?" And God (Great and Glorious is He!) shall be his advocate against the twain.' A man asked, 'O Emissary of God! What if his mother's name be not known?' And he replied, 'Let him ascribe him to Eve.' "[30]

There is no harm in reciting the Qur'ān over graves. It is told that ᶜAlī ibn Mūsā al-Ḥaddād said, 'I was once with Aḥmad ibn Ḥanbal at a funeral in the company of Muḥammad ibn Qudāma al-Jawharī. When the dead man had been interred a blind man came up and recited [the Qur'ān] beside the grave. "What is this?" Aḥmad said to him. "Recitation at the graveside is an innovation [*bidᶜa*]!" But when we had left the cemetery Muḥammad ibn Qudāma asked Aḥmad, "O Abū ᶜAbd Allāh, what is your opinion of Mubashshir ibn Ismāᶜīl al-Ḥalabī?" "A sound authority," he said. "Have you written anything down from him?" he enquired. "Yes," he replied. "Mubashshir ibn Ismāᶜīl related to me on the authority of his father, on the authority of ᶜAbd al-Raḥmān ibn al-ᶜAlā' ibn al-Lajlāj, on the authority of his father, that he had requested that upon his death the opening and closing verses of the Chapter of the Cow[A] should be recited over his grave, saying, 'I heard Ibn ᶜUmar requesting that this be done'." Thereupon, Aḥmad said to him, "Return to the man, and bid him recite".'

Said Muḥammad ibn Aḥmad[31] al-Marwazī, 'I once heard Aḥmad ibn Ḥanbal say, "Whenever you enter a cemetery recite the Opening Chapter of the Book, the Two Refuge-taking Chapters,[32] and [the chapter which begins] *Say: He is God, the One.*[33] Make the reward of all this over to the people of the cemetery, for it will reach them".'

[A] The second Chapter of the Qur'ān.

Said Abū Qilāba, 'Voyaging once from Syria to Basra, I came to al-Khandaq, where I made my ablutions and prayed two *rakʿas* of prayer, it being night. Then I laid my head upon a grave and fell asleep. All of a sudden I awoke, and there before me was the grave's occupant complaining to me. "All night long you have injured me," he said. "You act, and know not, whereas we know, and cannot act. The two *rakʿas* you have just prayed are better than the world and all it contains." And then he said, "May God richly reward the world's dwellers on our behalf. I send them my salutations, for with their prayers there can come into our midst a light as great as the mountains".'

The purpose of the visitation of graves is that the visitor should be admonished, and that the one visited should receive benefit from his prayers. The visitor should not neglect to pray for himself and for the one deceased, or to derive a lesson. This latter may only come about through picturing the deceased in one's heart, and the way in which his members have been scattered abroad, and how he shall be raised up from his grave, and that one shall be joining him before long.

In this connection it is told that Muṭarrif ibn Abī Bakr al-Hudhalī said, 'There once was an old woman of ʿAbd al-Qays,[A] who was much given to worship. Whenever night fell she would tighten her belt and stand up in her prayer-niche to pray,[34] then, when daybreak came she would go out to the graves, where the greater part of her day would be spent.[35] I was told that she was reproached for visiting graveyards so frequently, and that she replied, "The hard heart which has become rough is softened only by the tokens of decay. When I make my way to the graves it is as though their inmates have emerged from beneath their surfaces and I am gazing at those putrefied faces, those altered bodies, and those bloated shrouds. What a gaze that is! Were people to drink deeply of it into their hearts how great a bitterness would it engender in their souls, and how cruelly would it emaciate their bodies!" '

Indeed, an image of the deceased must be brought to mind, similar to that which ʿUmar ibn ʿAbd al-ʿAzīz, may God (Exalted

[A] An Arab tribe (*Inbāh*, 88–90).

is He) have mercy upon him, mentioned when a certain jurist came in to visit him and was taken aback by his changed aspect, the consequence of much strain and worship. 'O So-and-so!' [the Caliph] said, 'Could you but see me three days after having been set in my grave, when the pupils of my eyes have come forth and flowed across my cheeks, when my lips have shrivelled back over my teeth, when my mouth has opened and the pus run out, when my belly is inflated and rises above my chest, when my spine protrudes from my rear, and when the worms and the pus have emerged from my nostrils; then you would behold something far more remarkable than that which you see now.'

It is commendable to praise the deceased, and to make mention of him only in terms that are excellent and beautiful. ʿĀ'isha (may God be pleased with her) once said, 'The Emissary of God (may God bless him and grant him peace) has said, "When your companion dies, let him be, and do not be harsh with him".'[36] And he said (may God bless him and grant him peace), 'Insult not the dead, for they have gone to that which they sent before them'.[37] And he said (may God bless him and grant him peace), 'Do not mention your dead save to advantage. For otherwise, if they should be of the people of Heaven you would be sinning, while should they be of the people of Hell then their present predicament is quite sufficient for them.'[38]

Said Anas ibn Mālik, 'A funeral cortège once passed by God's Messenger (may God bless him and grant him peace), and those present condemned [the deceased] strongly. And [the Prophet] said, "It is mandatory". Then another passed, and they heaped praises upon [the deceased]. "It is mandatory," the Prophet said again. ʿUmar questioned him about this, and he said, "The latter you praised, and Heaven is mandatory for him, while the former you censured, and for him Hell is mandatory. You are God's witnesses upon the earth".'[A] [39]

[A] According to al-Nawawī (*Sharḥ*, VII. 19–20) this Tradition may be interpreted in two ways. Firstly, the meaning may be that the Companions were already aware of the dead man's standing in both cases, and that their comments merely confirmed

Said Abū Hurayra, 'The Emissary of God (may God bless him and grant him peace) said, "A bondsman may die, and the people may praise him abundantly, while God knows him to be otherwise. Then He says (Exalted is He!) to His Angels, "I bring you to witness that I have accepted the testimony of My bondsmen regarding My bondsman, and have disregarded My knowledge of him".'[40]

what had already been decreed. The second explanation, which Nawawī tells us is the sounder of the two, is that even should a dead man's actions not be sufficient to help him on his way to Heaven, God may still decide to forgive him, and will cause the righteous to praise him as a token of this. Commenting on the apparent contradiction between the general prohibition on speaking ill of the dead and the Companions' condemnation of the dead man in this *ḥadīth*, he states that the prohibition does not extend to hypocrites, unbelievers and heretics, and that the deceased man in question was in fact known to fall into one of these categories.

CHAPTER SEVEN

On the True Nature of Death, and what the Dead Man Undergoes in the Grave prior to the Blast on the Trump

An exposition of the true nature of death[1]

KNOW THAT men entertain many false and mistaken notions regarding the true nature of death. Some have imagined that death is extinction, and that there is to be neither Resurrection nor Concourse, nor any consequence to good or evil, and that man's death is as the drying up of plants and the death of animals. This is the opinion of the Atheists [*al-mulḥidūn*] and of all those who have no faith in God and the Last Day.[A]

Another group has it that man becomes nothingness with death, and that for the duration of his sojourn in the grave he neither suffers chastisement nor feels the delight of any reward until he is restored together at the time of the Concourse.[B] And

[A] Probably Ghazālī has in mind the Dahrīya atheists (*Iqtiṣād*, 209; Māturīdī, 141–5), together with such minor sects as the Manṣūrīya, the Muᶜammarīya and the Khaṭṭābīya, all of which denied the Resurrection (Baghdādī, *Firaq*, 245–47; Ashᶜarī, *Maqālāt*, 9–13). Zabīdī adds the pre-Islamic Arabs to this list. To deny the Afterlife is, of course, to set oneself outside the fold of Islam (*Iqtiṣād*, loc. cit.).

[B] This major heresy was a doctrine of the Khārijite sect (Ashᶜarī, *Maqālāt*, 127, 430), and the Jahmīya (Gardet and Anawati, 140), and was also professed by some of the Muᶜtazilites, and, perhaps, the Murji'ite thinker Bishr al-Marīsī (Ashᶜarī, *Maqālāt*, 430; al-Ījī, *Mawāqif*, 269–270).

still others hold that the spirit remains and is not extinguished by death, but that it is the spirits which experience reward or punishment rather than the bodies, which are not restored or resurrected at all.[A]

These beliefs are all unsound and far removed from the truth. For intellection, together with the pronouncements of the [Qur'ān's] verses and of many Traditions, testifies that death signals a simple alteration of state, and that after leaving the body the spirit survives to feel either torment or bliss. The significance of its separation from the body is that it acts no longer within it, since the body is no more subject to its dictates. Now, the members [of the body] are the tools of the spirit, which, when put to use, enable it to strike with the hand, to listen with the ear, to see with the eye, and to know the true nature of things with the heart. The 'heart' here is merely another expression for the

[A] The doctrine of certain Muʿtazilites (Ibn Ḥazm, *Fiṣal*, IV. 199). It was also held that most Christians denied the bodily resurrection (Baghdādī, *Uṣūl*, 235).

It is more probable, however, that our author has in mind the teachings of al-Fārābī and Ibn Sīnā, whom he anathematises elsewhere on these (and other) grounds (*Tahāfut*, 334; *Iqtiṣād*, 209). The position of the Arab philosophers is a necessary corollary of their theory of the rational soul, which alone constitutes the human creature (cf. *De Anima*, 234). The soul, being a simple and incorruptible substance, receives its individuation from the body (ibid., 227), and must therefore lose its individual nature, to a greater (al-Fārābī) or lesser (Ibn Sīnā) extent when the body perishes and the soul returns to the Active Intellect (Rahman, *Prophecy*, 25). According to Louis Gardet (*Pensée*, 94n), Ghazālī's major quarry of Avicennian pneumatology and eschatology seems to have been the esoteric *al-Risāla al-Aḍḥawīya fī (amr) al-maʿād*, the position of which is certainly irreconcilable with orthodoxy. Elsewhere, however, Ibn Sīnā (e.g. in the *Najāt*) asserts that 'The revealed Law affirms, and reason does not deny, that the body also shall enjoy felicity' (apud *Pensée*, 95), perhaps merely as an attempt to deflect charges of heresy. Regarding the 'lesser judgement' and the punishments of the grave, Ibn Sīnā again maintains a form of 'double truth': in the *Risāla* he presents these doctrines as symbols, which serve to assist the simple masses, while in the *Najāt*, and in his commentary on the (Neoplatonic) *Theology of Aristotle*, he attempts to reconcile his belief in a temporary 'purgatory' in a celestial or astral body (a Neoplatonic conception) with the Islamic doctrine of the sepulchral life (*Pensée*, 101–4; cf. *Prophecy*, 81, Plotinus, IV. 3.24 and IV. 4.5); the endeavour, while patently sincere, must be regarded as unconvincing. For a penetrating discussion of the issue see Anawati, *Etudes*, 263–289.

'spirit', which is able to learn things without the medium of any tool, which is why it may independently feel pain in the form of sadness, misery or sorrow, and pleasure in the form of various kinds of happiness and contentment; none of these things having any link with the members.

Thus, all that is purely an attribute of the spirit abides with it after it has been cleft from the body, while that which is associated with it through the medium of the members is extinguished with the body's death until the spirit is restored thereto. It is not an irrational belief that the spirit should be returned to it actually in the grave, nor yet that it should be withheld until the Day of Resurrection. (God is best appraised of what He has decreed for each one of His bondsmen.) The falling into disuse of the body through death resembles the incapacitation of certain limbs during one's life upon the affliction of an unsound humour, or a tension in the arteries which prevents the spirit from penetrating therein, so that the knowing, thinking, percipient spirit remains, making use of some of the members but being barred from the use of others.

Death signifies the incapacitation of the members in their entirety, all of which are the tools of the spirit. By the 'spirit' I mean that abstraction through which man apprehends the sciences, and the pains of sorrow as well as the pleasures of happiness. Now, however completely its authority over the members may be annulled, these sciences and perceptions continue on, as do joys and miseries, and as does its vulnerability to pain and pleasure. For man is in reality that abstraction which apprehends the sciences and feels pain and pleasure, and which may not die (or, in other words, be extinguished), for death means no more than the end of its control over the body and the end of the body's status as its tool. Just as the onset of an incapacitating disease may mean that the hand is no longer a tool of which use is made, so death is an incapacitating disease spread throughout all the members.

It is man's soul and spirit that constitute his real nature, which is immortal. [Upon death] his state changes in two ways. Firstly, he is now deprived of his eyes, ears and tongue, his hand, his feet and all his parts, just as he is deprived of his family, children, relatives, and all the people he used to know, and of his horses and other riding-beasts, his servant-boys, his houses and property, and all that he used to own. There is no distinction to be drawn between his being taken from these things and these things being taken from him, for it is the separation itself which causes pain. At times, separation may take place through the plundering of a man's wealth, and at others when a man is seized and led away from his power and[2] wealth: in both cases the pain is identical. The meaning of death is quite simply the deprivation of a man's property consequent upon his being pitched into another world which does not correspond to this. If there was anything in the world the presence of which had become familiar to him and in which he had found consolation and peace, then he will greatly lament for it after he dies, and feel the greatest sorrow over losing it. His heart will turn to thoughts of everything he owned: of his power and estates, even to a shirt which he used to wear, for instance, and in which he took pleasure.

However, had he taken pleasure only in the remembrance of God, and consoled himself with Him alone, then his will be great bliss and perfect happiness. For the barriers which lay between him and his Beloved will now be removed, and he will be free of the obstacles and cares of the world, all of which had distracted him from the remembrance of God. This is one of the aspects of the difference between the states of life and death.

The second lies in the fact that upon death there stand revealed before him certain things which were never disclosed to him in life, in the way that things may be revealed to a man who is awake which were concealed from him during his slumber, for 'people are asleep, and when they die they awake'.[A] The first thing to be revealed to him is his good and evil works, such as will benefit or harm him, and which have been inscribed in a book folded away in his innermost heart from the perusal of which he was distracted by his worldly concerns. When these concerns are cut away his actions all stand revealed before him, so

[A] Attributed to the caliph ʿAlī (Shawkānī, 256; Suyūṭī, *Durar*, 179).

that he is dismayed by every sin which he beholds; so much so that he would fain plunge into the depths of Hell in order to escape from this misery. It is at this time that he shall be told, *Sufficient for you today is your own soul as a reckoner!*[3]

All of this is revealed when his breathing ceases and before his interment. Kindled within him are the flames of separation, by which I mean separation from all the things in which he had felt confident in this transient world, rather than that which he did with the intention of laying up provisions and support, for whoever searches for provisions to bring him to his destination will surely be delighted at being separated from the remainder of them when he attains his goal, for he never sought the provisions for their own sake. This is the circumstance of the man who has taken from this world only what he needs, and who has longed for an end to these needs that he might dispense with [this quest for provisions]. Now that what he longed for has come about he no longer stands in need of them.

These varieties of punishment and torment are at their most vehement when they assail him before his burial. Then, when he has been interred, his spirit may be restored to him to face another species of chastisement (unless he is to be spared this). The state of the man who luxuriates in the world and sets his confidence therein is comparable to that of a man who, in the absence of a king, enjoys himself in his palace, kingdom and harem, trusting that the king will deal leniently with him or that he is unaware of the ugly deeds he is committing, until such time as the king suddenly seizes him and shows him a copy-book in which all his foulnesses and misdeeds have been recorded in full detail. The king, who is mighty and powerful, is greatly concerned for the welfare of his preserve and exacts retribution from all who would encroach on his authority, paying no heed to those that would intercede on behalf of any that have rebelled against him. Contemplate the plight in which such a man would be upon being caught, and the fear, shame, disgrace, sorrow and contrition which would be his lot before the king's chastisement descended upon him. Thus is the state of the dead evildoer who had been dazzled by this world and set his trust therein following his death and before the punishment of the grave has descended upon him. We seek refuge in God from such a thing! For truly, humiliation, disgrace and exposure are more dreadful than any torment which might afflict the flesh, whether through blows, cutting wounds, or anything else.

The foregoing constitutes an indication of man's state at the time of death. It has been witnessed by people of insight by virtue of an inner vision stronger even than the vision of the eye. Similarly, it is attested to by the authority of the Book and the Precedent of the Prophet. But to draw the veil from the true nature of death is impossible, since death cannot be understood by those that do not understand life, and life may only be understood through knowing the true nature of the spirit itself and by coming to understand the nature of its essence. The Emissary of God (may God bless him and grant him peace) was not given leave to speak of this more than by saying '*the spirit is by the command of my Lord*'.[4] Hence it is not given to any of the divines to reveal the secret of the spirit, even if one were to uncover it. It is permitted only to mention the state of the spirit after death.

That death does not constitute the extinction of the spirit and its consciousness is proved by a number of Verses and Traditions. Among the former is [the text] which treats of the Martyrs, wherein God (Exalted is He!) says, *And consider not those that were slain in the way of God to be dead. Rather they are alive, nourished in the presence of their Lord, all rejoicing.*[5] And when the heroes of Quraysh were slain on the day of Badr,[A] the Emissary of God (may God bless him and grant him peace) called out to them and said, 'O So-and-so! O So-and-so! O So-and-so! I have found what my Lord promised me to be true, so have you found what He promised you to be true also?' He was asked, 'O Emissary of God! Are you calling out to them when they are dead?' and he replied (may God bless him and grant him peace), 'By Him in Whose hand lies my soul, they hear my words more clearly than

[A] The first great battle between the Muslims and the idolaters of Mecca, which took place in the year 2 AH, and which resulted in the decisive defeat of the Meccan tribe of Quraysh and the death of many of its leaders.

you, it is only that they are unable to make reply'.[6] This constitutes a text which establishes the survival of the spirits of the damned, and of their intelligence and knowledge, just as the verse does for the spirits of the Martyrs.

The dead man must needs be either happy or woeful. The Prophet (may God bless him and grant him peace) once said, 'The grave is either one of the chasms of Hell or one of the gardens of Heaven'.[7] This text states unambiguously that death signifies no more than a change of state, and that the future sorrow or happiness of the dead man manifests itself immediately upon death without any delay whatsoever (although certain secondary varieties of punishment and reward will be deferred).

Anas relates that the Prophet (may God bless him and grant him peace) said, 'Death is the Resurrection; whoever dies, his resurrection has come'.[8] And he said also (may God bless him and grant him peace), 'When one of you dies his [future] seat is displayed before him morning and evening: should he be of the people of Heaven, then it is situated among them, while should he be of the people of Hell, then it is situated among them. And he will be told, "This is your seat until you are resurrected to meet Him on the Day of Arising".'[9] It is not difficult to see what states of torment and bliss would arise merely from seeing one's seat.

Said Abū Qays, 'We were once in the company of ʿAlqama during a funeral, when he said, "As far as he is concerned, his resurrection has come".'

Said ʿAlī (may God ennoble his face), 'It is not lawful for any soul to leave this world until it knows whether it is to be of the dwellers of Heaven or of Hell'.

Said Abū Hurayra, 'The Emissary of God (may God bless him and grant him peace) said, "Whosoever dies of a sickness dies a martyr, and receives a protection from the tormentors of the grave, and sustenance is brought to him from Heaven morning and evening".'[10]

Said Masrūq, 'There is no-one I envy more than a believer in his tomb, for he has found rest from the exertions of the world and safety from the chastisement of God.'

Said Yaʿlā ibn al-Walīd, 'I was walking one day with Abu'l-Dardā', and asked him, "What do you like to happen to those you like?" "Death," he replied. "But if one has not died yet?" I asked, and he answered, "That his progeny and wealth should be scanty. I feel a liking for death because it is liked only by the believer, whom it releases from his imprisonment. And I like one's progeny and wealth to be scanty because these things are a trial, and can occasion familiarity with this world, and familiarity with that which must one day be left behind is the very extremity of sorrow. All that is other than God, His remembrance, and familiarity with Him must needs be abandoned upon one's death".'

For this reason ʿAbd Allāh ibn ʿAmr said, 'When his soul, or spirit, emerges, the believer is as a man who was in a prison, from which he was released and travelled about and took pleasure in the world.'

This [Narrative just] mentioned refers to the state of the man who withdrew from the world, being wearied of it and finding no pleasure in it save that which is in the remembrance of God (Exalted is He!), and who was kept by the distractions of the world from his Beloved, and who was hurt by the vicissitudes of his desires. In death he found a release from every harmful thing, and won unrestricted solitude with his Beloved, who was ever his source of consolation. How right it is that this should be the pinnacle of bliss and beatitude!

The most perfect of delights is that which is the lot of the Martyrs who are slain in the way of God. For when they advance into battle they cut themselves off from any concern with the attachments of the world in their yearning to meet God, happy to be killed for the sake of obtaining His pleasure. Should such a man think upon the world he would know that he has sold it willingly for the Afterlife, and the seller's heart never inclines to that which has been sold. And when he thinks upon the Afterlife, he knows that he had longed for it, and has now purchased it. How great, then, is his rejoicing at that which he has bought when he comes to behold it, and how paltry his interest in what he has sold when from it he takes his leave!

Full absorption of the heart in the love of God may well take place in certain circumstances, but death may not overtake one in such a state before one changes again. Combat is one of the causes of death, and is also a means of coming to death in this state. For this reason one's bliss is intense, since the meaning of bliss is the attainment of desire. God (Exalted is He!) has said, *Theirs is whatsoever they desire*;[11] and this is the most comprehensive description of the delights to be enjoyed by the people of Heaven. Similarly, the greatest torment occurs when a man is denied what he desires, just as God (Exalted is He!) has declared, *And they were barred from what they had desired*:[12] in turn, the most comprehensive expression of the punishments endured by the people of Hell.

This delight is attained by the martyr as soon as his breath is cut short. This is a matter which has been disclosed to the Sufis [*arbāb al-qulūb*] by virtue of the light of certainty. But should you wish for proof from the realm of textual authority, then [know that] it is attested to by all the Traditions of the Martyrs; each Tradition, in different words, includes an intimation of their extreme bliss.

Thus it is related of ᶜĀ'isha (may God be pleased with her) that she said, 'The Emissary of God (may God bless him and grant him peace) once said to Jābir, "Shall I not give you good news, O Jābir?" (his father having been martyred on the day of Uḥud). "Yes indeed", he replied, "may God give you good news also!" And he said, "God (Great and Glorious is He!) has given your father life once more, and has seated him in His presence, saying to him, 'O my bondsman, ask of Me whatsoever you will, for I shall grant it you.' 'O my Lord!' he said, 'I did not worship You as was meet, so I implore You to send me back to the world that I might fight alongside Your Prophet and be killed again for Your sake.' But He said to him, 'I have already told you that you shall never return to the world'."'[13]

Said Kaᶜb, 'In Heaven there is a weeping man who, when asked, "Why do you weep, although you are in Heaven?" replies, "I weep because I was slain for God's sake no more than once; I yearn to go back that I might be slain many times".'

Know that after the believer dies there is revealed to him of the mightiness and[14] great majesty of God something in comparison to which this world is no more than a narrow gaol. He is like a prisoner in a gloomy chamber from which a door has been opened onto a spacious garden stretching as far as his eyes can see, containing diverse trees, flowers, birds and fruit, and cannot therefore wish to return to the gloomy gaol. The Emissary of God (may God bless him and grant him peace) provided such a simile when he said, regarding a man who had died, 'He has now voyaged from this world and left it to its inhabitants. If he is of the blessed then he will no more wish to return to it than would any one of you wish to return to his mother's belly.'[15] Thus he informs us that the relation between the expanse of the next world and that of this is as the difference between the breadth of this world and the darkness of the womb.

And he said (may God bless him and grant him peace), 'The believer in this world can be likened to a foetus in its mother's belly, which cries when it emerges, but when it sees the light and begins to suckle no longer wishes to return to its former abode. So it is with the believer, who suffers at death, but who, when brought to his Lord, no more desires to return to the world than a baby wishes to return to its mother's belly.'[16]

The Emissary of God (may God bless him and grant him peace) was once told that a certain man had died. 'He has either found rest', he said, 'or others are finding rest because of his absence'.[17] By the one who has 'found rest' he was referring to the believer, while by the other he referred to the evildoer, since the inhabitants of the world find rest when he is gone.

Said Abū ᶜUmar Ṣāḥib al-Suqyā, 'When we were children, Ibn ᶜUmar once passed by us. He glanced at a grave where there lay a rotten skull, and instructed someone to bury it, which was done. Then he said, "These bodies are not in the least harmed by the soil, rather it is the spirits which are to be punished and rewarded on the Day of Arising".'

Said ᶜAmr ibn Dīnār, 'No man dies without being aware of the condition of his family after his death. They wash and shroud him while he watches them'.

Said Mālik ibn Anas, 'I have heard it said that the spirits of the believers are let loose to go where they please'.[A]

Said al-Nuʿmān ibn Bashīr, 'I heard the Emissary of God (may God bless him and grant him peace) say from the pulpit, "Nothing of this world remains save that which is like the flies which fly about in the air.[B] So, by God I adjure you regarding your brethren in the graves, for your works are shown to them".'[18]

Said Abū Hurayra, 'The Emissary of God (may God bless him and grant him peace) said, "Do not shame your dead with your evil works, for they are shown to your companions in the graves".'[19]

It was for this reason that Abu'l-Dardā' said, 'O Lord God! Truly I seek refuge with You from committing some act of which I might be ashamed before ʿAbd Allāh ibn Rawāḥa', (the latter, who was his maternal uncle, having just died).

ʿAbd Allāh ibn ʿAmr ibn al-ʿĀṣ was once asked where the spirits of the believers reside after death. 'They are in the form of white birds in the shade of the Throne,' he replied. 'And the spirits of the unbelievers are in the seventh earth.'[C]

[A] According to the *Durra*, ascribed by some to Ghazālī, although the souls of some of the dead remain in their graves until the Judgement, others leave their tombs after their bodies have turned to dust, and either roam the earth or wait at the place where the Last Trump is to be sounded (*Durra*, 35, 37–38). (For more on this doctrine, which is supported by a number of Traditions, see Smith and Haddad, 50–56; al-Ḥakīm al-Tirmidhī, 213; Qurṭubī, 57–61; also Ḥasan Khālid [133, 153–5], who quotes at some length from the present chapter to establish this point.) A number of early sayings suggest that the spirits of dead unbelievers congregate in a well known as 'Barhūt' or 'Tarhūt', in the Ḥaḍramawt (cf. Bayhaqī, *Baʿth*, 266), while those of the faithful are in the well of Zamzam at Mecca (cf. Smith and Haddad, 58) or at al-Jābiya in Syria (cf. Ibn Rajab, 117-9); this is probably the memory of some pre-Islamic belief.

[B] i.e. very little.

[C] According to the Qur'ān (LXV:12) there are seven 'earths' just as there are seven heavens (Cf. also Ibn Ḥazm, *Fiṣal*, II. 109–110; Asín Palacios, *Escatología*, 73–89).

Said Abū Saᶜīd al-Khudrī, 'I once heard the Emissary of God (may God bless him and grant him peace) say, "The dead man recognises his washer and those that carry him and lower him into his grave".'[20]

Said Ṣāliḥ al-Murrī, 'I have heard that the spirits meet together at death, and say to the one that is newly come among them, "How was your abode, and in what variety of body were you ensconced, in one fair or foul?" '

Said ᶜUbayd ibn ᶜUmayr, 'The dwellers in the graves wait for any news. When a dead man joins them they ask, "What has So-and-so done?" And he replies, "Has he not already come amongst you, or did he not precede you here?" "*Truly we are God's, and truly unto Him is our return,*"[21] they say. "He was led along a different path from ours".'[A]

Said Jaᶜfar ibn Saᶜīd, 'When a man dies he is met by his son just as a man is met after a long absence'.

Said Mujāhid, 'The [dead] man is given to know of his son's circumstances in the grave'.

Abū Ayyūb al-Anṣārī relates that the Prophet (may God bless him and grant him peace) said, 'When the believer dies his soul is received by the people of mercy from God's presence, just as the bringer of good tidings is received in the world. "Grant your brother some respite," they say, "that he may rest, for he was formerly in great distress." Then they ask him what such-and-such a man had done, and how such-and-such a woman had occupied herself, and whether such-and-such a woman had married, until, when they ask him about a man who had passed away before him, to be told, "He died before me," they say, "*Truly we are God's, and truly unto Him is our return.* Then he has been taken to his mother, the Abyss!" '[22]

[A] i.e., that leading to Hell.

Chapter Seven

An exposition of the grave's discourse to the dead, and of their utterances, either on the tongue of common speech, or that of the Spiritual State[A]

Now, the tongue of the Spiritual State is even more eloquent in communicating with the dead than is that of speech when communicating with the living. The Emissary of God (may God bless him and grant him peace) said, 'When the dead man is laid in his grave it speaks to him, saying, "Woe betide you, O son of Adam! What distracted you from contemplating me? Did you not know that I am the house of trial, the house of darkness, the house of solitude and the house of worms? What distracted you from me? You used to pass me by, strutting on!" Now if he had worked well, then someone will reply to the grave on his behalf, saying, "Do you not see that it was his practice to enjoin good and forbid evil?" And the grave replies, "Then for him shall I turn to verdure, and his body shall become radiance, and his spirit shall soar up to God (Exalted is He!)".' (According to the narrator, 'strutting' [*faddād*] is to take large strides.)[23]

Said ᶜUbayd ibn ᶜUmayr al-Lay<u>th</u>ī,[24] 'Not a single man dies without being called by the pit in which he is buried, which declares, "I am the house of gloom, and of loneliness and solitude! If you were obedient to God during your lifetime then today I shall be a source of mercy for you, but if you were rebellious then I am an act of vengeance against you. The obedient who enter me shall come forth joyful, while the rebellious who enter me shall emerge in ruin".'

Said Muḥammad ibn Ṣabīḥ, 'I have heard that if a man is laid in his tomb to be tormented or afflicted by something which is odious to him, his dead neighbours call out to him, saying, "O you who leave your brethren and neighbours behind you in the world! Was there never any lesson for you in us? Was there no clue for you in our preceding you? Did you not see how our actions were severed from us while you still had some respite?

[A] *lisān al-ḥāl*: cf. p.50n above.

Why did you not achieve that which passed your brethren by?" Then the regions of the earth call out to him, saying, "O you who were beguiled by the outer aspect of the world! Did you not take heed from your relatives who had vanished into the earth's interior? Those who were beguiled by the world before you and then met their fate, and entered into their graves? You watched them being borne aloft,[A] availed in nothing by those they loved, and taken to the abode which they could not escape." '

Said Yazīd al-Ruqāshī, 'I have heard it said that when the deceased is set in his tomb his works amass around him and are given to speak by God, so that they say, "O bondsman, alone in his pit! Your family and friends are now separated from you, so that today we are your sole companions".'[25]

Said Kaᶜb [al-Aḥbār], 'When the righteous bondsman is laid in his tomb he is surrounded by his righteous acts, such as his prayer, his fasting, his pilgrimage, his engagement in the Holy War, and the charity he used to distribute. Then the Angels of Chastisement approach him from the direction of his feet, but are told by Prayer, "Get back from him, you have no authority over him, for upon those [feet] he stood in me at length for the sake of God". Then they approach him from the direction of his head, but Fasting says, "You have no authority over him, for in the world's abode he thirsted at length for the sake of God". Next they draw near to him from the direction of his trunk, but Pilgrimage and Holy War say, "Get back from him, for he exhausted himself and wearied his body when he accomplished the Pilgrimage and the Holy War for the sake of God; no authority do you have over him". Then they approach him from the direction of his hands, but Charity says, "Back! Retreat from my master, for how many an act of charity issued from those two hands to fall into the hand of God (Exalted is He!), while he acted only for His sake; no authority, therefore, do you have over him". Then he shall be told, "Rejoice! Good you have been in life and in death!" Next, the Angels of Mercy come, and spread a heavenly cloth and resting-place out for him, and his grave is widened around him for as far as his eye can see. A candle is

[A] To the cemetery.

brought from Heaven, and from it he has light until God resurrects him from his grave.'

Said ᶜAbd Allāh ibn ᶜUbayd ibn ᶜUmayr at a funeral, 'I have heard it said that the Emissary of God (may God bless him and grant him peace) once declared, "The dead man sits up and hears the footsteps of those that are present at his funeral, but none addresses him save his tomb, which says, 'Woe betide you, O son of Adam! Did you not fear me and my narrowness, and my corruption, terrors and worms? What have you prepared for me?' " '[26]

An exposition of the Punishment of the Grave, and the questioning of Munkar and Nakīr

Said al-Barā' ibn ᶜĀzib, 'I once went forth with the Emissary of God (may God bless him and grant him peace) to attend the funeral of one of the Helpers. The Emissary of God (may God bless him and grant him peace) sat down by the grave and bowed his head, saying three times, "O Lord God! I seek refuge with Thee from the punishment of the grave." Then he said, "When the believer travels into the Afterlife, God dispatches unto him angels whose faces are like the sun, who bear his shrouds and his perfume[A] with them. Then they sit down around him for as far as his eye can see, so that when his spirit issues forth every angel which is between heaven and earth, and every angel which dwells in heaven, prays for him. Then the gates of heaven are opened before him, not one of which would not have his soul enter through it. When his spirit has ascended it is said, 'O Lord! Your servant So-and-so!' But He says, 'Return him, and reveal to him the honour which I have made ready for him, for thus did I promise him: *From it did We create you; to it shall We return you* . . .'[27] And he hears the footfall of their sandals as they turn and depart.

[A] *ḥanūṭ*: a scent especially mixed for the perfuming of shrouds and the bodies of the dead, commonly including musk, sandalwood, ambergris and camphor (Cf. Lane, 657).

'"Then it is said, 'O man! Who is your Lord? What is your religion? Who is your prophet?' and he shall answer accordingly: 'My Lord is God, my religion is Islam, and my prophet is Muḥammad, may God bless him and grant him peace.' Then the two [Angels] chide him vigorously in the last trial to which the dead man is submitted, but when he has uttered these words a voice calls out, saying, 'You have answered correctly!' And this is the meaning of His word, *God stays those who believe with the word of steadfastness . . .* [28] At this, there approaches one who is beautiful of countenance, sweet-smelling and decked in finery, who declares, 'Rejoice at the mercy which is come to you from your Lord, and at gardens *in which there is bliss everlasting*'.[29] 'May God give you good tidings!' he replies. 'Who are you?' 'I am your righteous deeds,' he says. 'By God, I have known that you were quick to obey God and slow to disobey Him; therefore may God reward you well.' Then a voice calls out for furnishings from Heaven to be set out for him and for one of its gates to be opened before him. And when this is done, he cries, 'O Lord God! Hurry on the Hour, that I may return to my kinsmen and to my property!'"

'And [the Prophet continued, and] said, "As for the unbeliever, when he travels into the Afterlife and is severed from this world, there descend to him *Angels strong and severe*[30] bearing *garments of fire*[31] and *mail-coats of tar*,[32] who beset him on every side until, when his soul emerges, he is cursed by every angel between heaven and earth, and every angel that dwells in heaven. The gates of heaven are locked shut, for there is not a single one of them that would not loathe his entry by it. And when his spirit ascends it is cast back, as it is declared, 'O Lord! Your bondsman So-and-so, whom neither heaven nor earth will accept!' And He says, 'Return him, and show him the horror I have prepared for him, even as I promised: *From it did We create you; to it shall We return you . . .*' And he hears the footfall of their sandals as they turn and depart.

'"Then it is said, 'O man! Who is your Lord? What is your religion? And who is your prophet?' but he says, 'I know not.' 'You know not!' it is said, and he is approached by one of vile countenance, corrupt-smelling and meanly attired, who says, 'Receive the tidings of God's wrath, and of a painful and abiding torment!' 'God give you evil tidings!' he says, 'Who are you?' 'I am your foul deeds,' he makes reply. 'By God, you were hasty to disobey Him and tardy in giving Him your obedience; therefore may God reward you with ill.' 'And you,' he replies, 'may God reward you with ill also!' Then he is seized by one who is deaf, dumb and blind,[33] who bears a rod of iron which, were men and jinn all to combine to carry it they could not, and which would smite into dust any mountain struck with it. With it he strikes him a blow which turns him to dust, after which his spirit is restored, and he strikes him another blow between the eyes which is heard by every dweller upon the earth, saving only men and jinn. Then a voice calls for two slabs from Hell to be set down for him by way of furnishing, and for one of the gates of Hell to be opened before him, and this is done".'[34]

Said Muḥammad ibn ᶜAlī, 'Before every man that dies appear his good and his evil works. He fixes his gaze upon the former and averts it from the latter'.

Said Abū Hurayra, 'The Emissary of God (may God bless him and grant him peace) has said, "When the believer draws near to death he is approached by angels bearing bunches of sweet basil and a silken cloth perfumed with musk. They draw out his spirit as a hair is drawn from dough, and he is told, '*O soul at rest*![35] Come forth *satisfied, well-satisfying*[36] to the grace and generosity of God!' And when his spirit is drawn forth it is set among that musk and that sweet basil, and the silken cloth is folded over it, and it is sent to ᶜIllīyīn.[A]

'"When the unbeliever draws near death, however, the angels come to him with a piece of black cloth in which there lies a glowing coal, and pull his spirit forth violently. 'O vile soul!' he is told. 'Hating and hated, emerge to God's wrath and His chastisement!' When his spirit is taken forth it is laid upon that hissing

[A] Q. LXXXIII: 20 describes ᶜIllīyīn as a book in which the deeds of the righteous are recorded. The word is also used to denote the highest reaches of Paradise (Cf. Qurṭubī, 462, 464; al-Ḥakīm al-Tirmidhī, 273).

coal, and the black cloth is folded over it, and it is taken away to Sijjīn".'[A]

It is related of Muḥammad ibn Kaᶜb al-Quraẓī that he used to recite His statement (Exalted is He!): *until, when death comes, he says, O Lord! Send me back, that I might work righteousness in that which I have left.*[37] Then he would say, 'What is it that you want? What do you desire to have? Do you wish to return in order to gather wealth and plant crops, to erect buildings and to dig canals? Nay,[38] may I *work righteousness in that which I have left*! For the Almighty would [otherwise] say, *It is no more than a word which he utters,*[39] that is, "he will certainly say this at death!" '

Said Abū Hurayra, 'The Prophet (may God bless him and grant him peace) has said, "The believer in his grave is in a verdant garden. For his sake his tomb is widened by seventy cubits, and he shines with light until he becomes as the full moon. Know you in what regard [the text] *His shall be a miserable life*[40] was revealed?" And [his Companions] said, "God and His Emissary know best." "The unbeliever's punishment in his grave," he said. "Ninety-nine dragons [*tinnīn*] are let loose against him. Do you know what a dragon is? It is formed of ninety-nine serpents each of which has seven heads, which maul and savage him, and blow into his body until the Day of Resurrection." '[41]

One should not be astonished at such specific numbers, for these serpents and scorpions correspond in number to one's vices, such as pride, dissimulation, envy, malice, hatred, and all the other [blameworthy] attributes. For vice has a certain number of roots, and from these a certain quantity of branches divide out, which in turn ramify into a variety of categories. These very attributes, which are the mortal sins, then turn into scorpions and snakes: the stronger sting like dragons while the more feeble have a sting like that of a scorpion, while the vices which are intermediate [between these two] hurt like a snake-bite. Now,

[A] Sijjīn, although described in the Qur'ān (LXXXIII:7,8) as a book where man's evil deeds are recorded, is also held to refer to 'a rock beneath the seventh earth, under which the book of the unbeliever is placed.' (Attributed to Mujāhid in Ibn al-Mubārak, 434.) The *Durra* (p.18) describes Sijjīn as a rock in Hell to which the spirits of the wicked are brought (cf. also *Escatología*, 139). The *ḥadīth* is recorded by Nasā'ī (Janā'iz, 9).

the people of [illuminated] hearts and insight [*arbāb al-qulūb wa'l-baṣā'ir*] behold these mortal sins and their manifold ramifications through the light of spiritual insight [*nūr al-baṣīra*], although their exact number may be known only through the light of Prophethood.

Such tales as the above are possessed of external aspects (which are genuine) and also of hidden secrets which are clear only to people of spiritual insight: whoever has not been shown their true nature should not deny their outward aspect, for to believe and to accept are the very lowest of the degrees of faith. Should you say, 'We observe the unbeliever in his grave and watch him for some time, yet we behold none of these things; how, therefore, are we to believe in a matter which contradicts what we see?'[A] then you should know that there are three degrees[42] of belief in matters such as these.

The first, which is the most evident, and also the truest and the soundest, is to believe that these [creatures] exist, and that the stinging to which the dead man is subject is a fact, but that you are unable to perceive it. For our eyes are unequipped to behold the things of the Kingdom,[B] whereof are all affairs which concern the Afterlife. Do you not perceive how the Companions (may God be pleased with them) believed that Gabriel truly descended, even though they never beheld him, and that they believed that he was visible to the Prophet (may God bless him and grant him peace)? If you cannot believe in this then it is more important that you rectify the basis of your faith in the angels and in Revelation. However, if you do believe in it, and accept that the Prophet could see that which his nation could not, then how can you not accept that [what we have described] could befall a dead man? For just as an angel does not resemble a man or a beast, the snakes and the scorpions which sting in the grave are not of the same order of the snakes of our world; rather, they constitute a

[A] This was the customary argument of the Muʿtazilites, the majority of whom denied the punishment of the grave (Cf. *Iqtiṣād*, 182ff.; Ījī, *Mawāqif*, 270; Ashʿarī, *Maqālāt*, 430).

[B] The Kingdom: a tentative translation of *malakūt*, the highest of the three planes of existence found in Ghazālī's cosmology. See p.149ff. below.

different order, and are to be perceived with a quite separate faculty.

The second degree is attained by calling to mind the circumstances of the man asleep. For while he slumbers he may see a snake biting him and feel pain as a result, so that you behold him perspiring and screaming in his sleep, and perhaps shaking from his place. Yet he is truly seeing these things, deriving them from his own soul, and may suffer just as much as a man awake. You might also see him to be superficially tranquil, and behold no snake near by him, even though for him the snake is truly present and the pain is real, merely being imperceptible to you. Inasmuch as the torment lies in in the bite's pain, no difference exists between a snake imagined and one truly beheld.

The third degree consists in the knowledge that it is not the snake itself that produces pain, but rather that which afflicts one from it, namely, the venom. Furthermore, the venom is not the pain itself; rather one's suffering results from its effect upon one: were the same effect to obtain without the presence of any venom the pain would still be there. Yet this variety of suffering can only be defined by ascribing it to its usual cause. For example, were the pleasure of sexual union to be created in a man without any relation to its outward form it would be impossible to describe it without ascribing it thereto, so that the ascription to the cause becomes its definition. The cause's effect would have obtained even though the outward form of the cause had not; and the cause is not desired for itself, but only for its effect.

Mortal vices are transformed into sources of pain and torment in the soul after it has died, in such a way as to resemble snakebites, even though no snakes are present. The transformation of an attribute into a source of pain corresponds to the transformation of love into a source of misery upon the death of one's beloved: for it had been delightful, but this same delight turned, under new circumstances, into a source of pain, until the heart was assailed by so many varieties of suffering that one might well have wished that one had never enjoyed the pleasure of love and union. In fact, this is itself one of the varieties of punishment which the dead man undergoes, for in the world his soul had been susceptible to love: he had loved his wealth, his land, his power, his children, relatives and acquaintances, and if while he still lived all this had been taken from him by someone from whom he could never hope for its recovery, then how do you suppose his pain would have been? Would not his misery and his suffering have been intense, and would he not have declared in hindsight, 'Would that I had never possessed any wealth or power, that I would not suffer thus upon losing it!'?

Death signifies the loss of one's worldly loves altogether, and all at once. [As the poet said:]

What shall be the state of he that had just one,
when that one has vanished from him?

What, then, shall be the lot of he who rejoiced in the world and nothing else when it comes to be taken from him and is delivered up to his enemies? And when to this torment is added his lamentation over the bliss of the Afterlife which has passed him by, and over the barrier which has come between him and God (Great and Glorious is He!)? For in truth, the love of anything other than God shall bar one from the meeting with Him and the joy which therein consists. [Such a man] is overwhelmed by the pain of losing all that he loved, and by his grief over the bliss of the Afterlife which has forever and eternally passed him by, as well as by the disgrace of rejection and of being veiled from God (Exalted is He!). It is this which constitutes the torment with which he is punished, for the fire of separation can only be followed by the fire of the Inferno, as God (Exalted is He!) has said, *Nay, they are that day veiled from their Lord; then shall they be cast into the Blaze.*[43]

But as for the man who did not find his consolation in this world, and who loved none save God, and yearned for the meeting with Him: he has escaped from the prison of this world and the vicissitudes of the desires which lie therein. He has come to his Beloved, as all barriers and distractions are cut away; bliss is his abundantly, never to pass away in all eternity. *For the likes of this, then, let those who would work, work!*[44]

Our purpose is that a man may love a horse of his so dearly that were he to be offered the choice between losing it and being stung by a scorpion he would prefer to endure the latter, because the pain of losing the horse would be, for him, more dire than a scorpion sting. The very love of the horse would sting him were it to be taken away. He should, therefore, ready himself to be stung, for death shall take his horse from him, together with its saddle, his house, his land, his family, his loved ones and his friends, and shall confiscate his power and his influence; indeed, it shall deprive him even of his hearing, sight and limbs, so that he shall despair of their ever returning to him. Now if he had loved nothing more than these things, then when they are taken from him he shall suffer a torment greater than that inflicted by scorpions and snakes. Just as his suffering would be grievous if they were to be confiscated from him while he lived, so shall it be upon his demise.

We have already made it clear that the essence which perceives pain and pleasure is immortal, and that the suffering it endures may be greater after the advent of death, for although in life one may amuse oneself with[45] things which busy the senses, such as sitting with other people and making conversation, together with the anticipation of returning to such things or their like, there is no amusement after death; for every means by which one might find it stands blocked, and despair prevails. If a man had loved his every shirt and garment so that he would have found their confiscation hard to bear, then he shall remain in lamentation for them and be tormented by them. If, however, he had taken only a little of the world, he shall be saved; this is what is meant by the saying, 'Those who take little, make away'.[A] But if he had loaded himself heavily with it then his chastisement shall be severe, just as the condition of the man who is robbed of one dinar is less burdensome than that of he who is robbed of ten; likewise the state of he who has one dirham with respect to he who has two. This is the purport of [the Prophet's] statement (may God bless him and grant him peace): 'The man with one dirham shall be

[A] *najā al-mukhiffūn*. For this proverb in its more usual form *fāz al-mukhiffūn*, see Sakhāwī, *Maqāṣid*, 478–479; Ibn al-Daybaʿ, 109.

judged more lightly than the man who has two'.[46] Indeed, none of the worldly goods which you are to leave behind at death shall be anything but a source of woe for you in the Afterlife: thus take many of them if you will, or few. And should you take many, then you are acquiring many sources of woe, while if you take but few, then you are lightening only [the burden which is upon] your own back. The scorpions and snakes abound only in the graves of the rich, *who did prefer the life of the world to the Afterlife, and rejoiced therein, and were content with it.*[47]

Such, then, are the degrees of faith concerning the matter of the grave's snakes and scorpions, and of every other variety of its punishment.

Abū Saʿīd al-Kharrāz[48] (may God have mercy upon him) once beheld in a dream a child of his who had died. 'O my son,' he said, 'Admonish me!' And he replied, 'Do not differ with God in what He has willed'. 'Tell me more, my son!' he said. 'O father,' he replied. 'You could not bear it.' 'Tell me!' he said, and he replied, 'Do not set between yourself and God so much as a shirt'. And so it was that he would not wear a shirt for thirty years thereafter.

Now, should you ask which of these three degrees constitutes the truth, you should know that there are some people who affirm only the first and reject the remainder, while there are others who deny the first and affirm the second, while still others affirm the third alone. The truth, which becomes manifest to us through spiritual insight, is that all of these three degrees lie within the realm of possibility, and that a man who denies any one of them has shown a narrowness of understanding and an ignorance of the vast compass of God's power (Exalted is He!) and of the marvels of His purpose: such a person will deny such of God's acts as he has no familiarity and acquaintance with, and this is ignorance and a shortcoming. For these three means of punishment are all possible, and it is mandatory to believe in them. Some bondsmen are punished through one of them, while they act in concert in the case of others. We seek God's protection from this punishment, whether [in our case] it be slight or severe! This matter is true, and you must have faith in it by example [*taqlīd*], for the people of this world that know it by realisation [*taḥqīq*] are few. The counsel which I give you is that you should not look too intently into the details of this matter or busy yourself with trying to understand it. Occupy yourself instead with warding this chastisement off by whatever means, for if you were to neglect your works and worship and busy yourself with this matter instead you would resemble a man arrested and incarcerated by a sultan with a view to cutting off his hand or his nose, but who spent all night wondering whether he would be cut with a knife, a sword, or a razor, and neglected to devise a plan which might ward off the punishment itself, something which is the very height of folly.

It is known for certain that after his death the bondsman must meet either with dire punishment or with everlasting bliss. It is this that one should prepare for; to study the minutiae of chastisement and reward is superfluous and a waste of time.

An exposition of the questioning of Munkar and Nakīr, their aspect, and the straitening of the grave, and the remainder of what needs to be said regarding the Punishment of the Grave

Said Abū Hurayra, 'The Prophet (may God bless him and grant him peace) said, "When a bondsman dies he is visited by two blue-black Angels, one of whom is named Munkar and the other Nakīr. 'What say you of the Prophet?' they demand of him. Now if he is a believer he will reply, 'He is God's bondsman and Emissary.' 'We had known that you would speak thus,' they say, and his grave is widened for him by seventy cubits by seventy, and he is given light therein, and is told to sleep. 'But let me return,' he says, 'to my kinsfolk, that I might inform them!' But he is told to sleep, and he sleeps like a bridegroom, who is awakened only by the most beloved of his family, until he is raised up from his bed.

' "And if he is a hypocrite he will say, 'I know not; I used to hear the people saying something, so I said it also.' And [the

Angels] say to him, 'We had known that you would speak thus!' Then the earth is commanded to draw tightly around him, and it is so until his very ribs protrude. In torment he thus remains until God resurrects him from his bed." '[49]

Said ʿAṭāʾ ibn Yasār, 'The Emissary of God (may God bless him and grant him peace) once said to ʿUmar ibn al-Khaṭṭāb (may God be pleased with him), "O ʿUmar! How shall you fare when you are dead, and when your family go to measure out [shroud-cloth] three cubits by one and a span,[50] then return to you and wash you, then shroud and perfume you, and then carry you and set you in [your grave], then pour the earth over you and bury you? For when your family have departed, the two tormentors of the grave, Munkar and Nakīr, shall come, whose voices are as rolling thunder and whose eyes are like dazzling lightning, who trail their hair and scrutinise the grave with their fangs [apparent], terrifying and frightening you? How shall you fare, O ʿUmar?" And ʿUmar asked, "Will I have a mind like that which I have now?" and he said, "Yes." "Then," he said, "I shall be a match for them!" '[51]

This constitutes a clear statement that the mind does not change at death, but that only the body and limbs change. Thus, the dead man has intelligence and is able to perceive and know the varieties of pain and pleasure, nothing in his mind having been transformed. For the percipient mind does not consist of these members of ours; rather it is a thing concealed, without length or breadth. The faculty which perceives things consists of every part of one which does not rot away; and were a man's every limb to be scattered abroad leaving nothing but the percipient part, which can neither be dissolved or divided, then that man would be whole and would still exist and continue. So it is after death: for this part is not invaded by death and cannot be liable to extinction.

Said Muḥammad ibn al-Munkadir, 'I have heard it said that there shall be let loose against the unbeliever in his grave a deaf and blind beast, in the claw of which is an iron goad with something like a camel's foretooth at one end, with which he beats him until the Day of Arising. It cannot see him, that it might deliver him, neither can it hear his voice, that it might have mercy upon him.'

Said Abū Hurayra, 'When the deceased is set in his grave he is approached and surrounded by his righteous works. When they draw near him from the direction of his head his recitation of the Qur'ān comes forward, and when they approach him from the direction of his feet there comes his standing [in night prayers]. And when they approach him from the direction of his hands these speak out, saying, "By God! It was his custom to stretch us forth in charity and supplication; no authority do you have over him."[52] When they come to him from the direction of his mouth, his commemoration [of God] and his fasting appear. Likewise, Prayer and Fortitude stand at one side, and each declares, "As for me, if I behold any shortcoming I will stand by him".'

Said Sufyān [al-Thawrī], 'His righteous works will defend him as a man might defend his own brother, family and children. At this time he shall be told, "May God bless you in your resting-place; how fine are your friends, and how goodly your companions!" '

Said Ḥudhayfa, 'We were once at a funeral with God's Emissary (may God bless him and grant him peace). He sat down beside the grave and looked at it several times; then he said, "In here the believer shall be so straitened that his ribs will protrude as a consequence".'[53]

Said ᶜĀ'isha (may God be pleased with her), 'The Emissary of God (may God bless him and grant him peace) said, "The grave straitens, and if anyone has been delivered from its straitening it is Saᶜd ibn Muᶜādh".'[54]

Said Anas, 'When Zaynab, the daughter of the Emissary of God (may God bless him and grant him peace), passed away, having been a woman often afflicted with illness, [her funeral] was attended by God's Emissary (may God bless him and grant him peace), and we were much distressed at his condition. When we arrived at the grave he went inside it, and his face became pallid, but when he emerged once more his face was shining. "O Emissary of God!" we said. "We have seen something happening to you; what was it?" And he said, "I recalled the straitening to which my daughter will be subjected, and the intensity of the grave's punishment, but then I was approached to be told that God had relieved her of her punishment. She had been straitened in a way that was audible from East to West." '[55]

CHAPTER EIGHT

On the States of the Dead which have been known through Unveiling [*mukāshafa*] in Dreams

KNOW THAT the illuminative insights which may be derived from the Book of God (Exalted is He!) and from the Precedent of His Emissary (may God bless him and grant him peace) and from other means by which insight may be derived, all inform us of the dead's general circumstances, and of how they stand divided into people of joyfulness and of woe. However, the specific state of [say] Zayd or ᶜAmr is never disclosed in this fashion. For even if we had arrived at some conclusion regarding the faith of Zayd or ᶜAmr, we would yet remain in ignorance of his condition at the moment of death, and of how he was given to live his final moments. We might have judged him to be outwardly righteous, yet piety reposes obscurely in the heart, and if it may be concealed from the pious man himself then wherefore may others [know of it]?

Hence there can be no judgement of outward righteousness which does not take into account the piety which lies within. Since God (Exalted is He!) has said that *God only accepts [good works] from the pious,*[1] it is not possible to pass judgement on Zayd or ᶜAmr without watching him and scrutinising his conduct.

Upon his death, a man passes from the Terrestrial and Visible Realm [*ᶜālam al-mulk wa'l-shahāda*] to the Realm of the Unseen and the Kingdom [*ᶜālam al-ghayb wa'l-malakūt*], and is no longer to be beheld with the physical eye, but rather with an eye which is apart.[A] [2] This eye has been created within the heart of everyone. Man, however, draws over it a thick covering composed of his desires and his worldly activities, so that he becomes unable to perceive with it anything of the Kingdom. Indeed, for as long as this covering remains unremoved from the heart's eye it is quite unimaginable that one might see anything of it. The Prophets (upon whom be peace) had these blinds removed, and of necessity beheld the Kingdom and its marvels. The dead, who dwell in that Kingdom, were descried by them, and described.

It was in this wise that the Emissary of God (may God bless him and grant him peace) witnessed the contraction of the grave around Saᶜd ibn Muᶜādh and his daughter Zaynab, and beheld the condition of Abū Jābir following his martyrdom, when he told him that God had given him to sit before Him without any intervening veil. Such visions as these may be aspired to only by the Prophets and those Saints who approach them in degree; all that is possible for the likes of us is another, more feeble species of unveiling, but one which is, nevertheless, Prophetic in nature.

By this I refer to visions received in one's sleep, which are of the lights of Prophecy. God's Emissary (may God bless him and grant him peace) has said that 'The righteous dream is one forty-sixth part of Prophecy'.[3] For it resembles it, in that it too constitutes an unveiling which occurs only through the drawing back of the covering which lies over one's heart. Hence one is only to set confidence in the vision of the man who is righteous and truthful: that of a habitual liar should not be credited. For the man of much corruption and many acts of disobedience has brought darkness into his heart, and sees nothing more than

[A] In Ghazālī's psychology, the heart has two doors, one opening onto the *malakūt*, which is the realm of the *lawḥ* (the 'Tablet'—for which see below) and the Angels, and the other onto the *mulk wa'l-shahāda*, the domain of the five senses. The opening of the first door is termed *kashf*, or *mukāshafa*: 'unveiling'. When, as is the case with most men, the second door only is open, it is still possible to know of God, but only in the manner of a man who observes the sun's reflection in a pool of water (cf. Plato's Cave): a disturbed and refracted image, and one open to misinterpretation. (Cf. *Iḥyā'*, III. 18; also Wensinck, 'On the Relation between Ghazālī's Cosmology and his Mysticism'.)

jumbled dreams.[A] It was for this reason that God's Emissary (may God bless him and grant him peace) ordained ritual purity before going to sleep so that one might sleep in a condition of pureness.[B] [4] This constitutes a reference to inward purity also, which is the root with respect to which external purity is the fulfilment and perfection. In proportion to this inner purity there will stand disclosed before the pupil of the heart's eye that which shall come to pass in the future. Thus was the disclosure of the Entry into Mecca to the Emissary of God (may God bless him and grant him peace) while he slept, so that the [subsequent] revelation of God's Word (Exalted is He!) was *God has fulfilled the vision of His Emissary in truth.*[C] [5]

Indeed, it is quite uncommon for a man not to be given dreams which intimate certain things which he later finds to be true. Dreams, and the knowledge of the Unseen through sleep, are among the marvels of God's works (Exalted is He!) and the wonders of the primordial disposition [*fiṭra*] of man. They constitute one of the clearest indications of the Kingdom, yet of this mankind is heedless, just as it is heedless of the other marvels of the heart and of the world [*ᶜālam*].

Discourse concerning the true nature of dream-visions is one of the subtle sciences of unveiling, and cannot be mentioned within the context of the science of conduct [*ᶜilm al-muᶜāmala*]. That amount which it is possible to mention here [can be expressed] in a metaphor which will give you to understand what is intended. You should know that the metaphor of the heart is that of a mirror in which images and realities are reflected. Everything which has been decreed by God (Exalted is He!) from the beginning of the world's creation until its close has been written and maintained in something He created, which He at times calls the *Tablet*,[6] and at others the *Clear Book*[7] or the *Clear Example*[8], as has been mentioned in the Qur'ān. All that has passed in the

[A] In the story of Joseph in the Qur'ān, Pharaoh's counsellors dismiss his famous vision as *jumbled dreams* (Q. XII.44).

[B] For this practice see *Iḥyā'*, I. 121.

[C] The Prophet received this vision in the year 6 AH; the conquest of Mecca took place two years later.

world, together with all that is to come, is inscribed therein as an inscription invisible to our eyes. Never imagine that the Tablet is of wood or iron or bone, nor yet that the Book is of paper or parchment; rather you should understand absolutely that God's Tablet bears no resemblance to the tablets of men, and that His Book is in no wise similar to their books, any more than His Essence and Attributes resemble the essence and attributes of mankind. Instead, should you truly seek for a metaphor which might bring this matter closer to your understanding, then know that the maintenance of destinies on the Tablet is analogous to the maintenance of the words and letters of the Qur'ān in the mind and heart of a man that has committed it to memory. Therein it so lies recorded that when he recites it it is as though he were looking at it; yet if you were to search through his brain piece by piece you would not see a single letter of script.

It is in this fashion, whereby there is no script, and not even a letter to be seen,[9] that you should understand the Tablet's being inscribed with all that God (Exalted is He!) has destined and decreed. The Tablet's metaphor is indeed that of a mirror in which images appear. Should another mirror be positioned before it the images in the first mirror will be reflected therein, provided that there is no intervening obstruction. Now, the heart is a mirror which accepts the essences of knowledge, whereas the Tablet is the mirror in which the essences of all knowledges repose. The engagement of the heart with one's desires and with the demands of the senses constitutes a veil drawn between it and any apprehension of the Tablet, which is a thing of the Kingdom. If a wind should blow then this veil will move and lift, causing there to shine in the heart's mirror something of the Kingdom, like a sudden flash of lightning, which may or may not endure, the latter being the more common.

For as long as one is awake one is occupied by the senses' reports about the Terrestrial and Visible Realm, and this composes a veil between one and the Kingdom. Sleep, which signifies the quieting of the senses so that they convey nothing to the heart, and whereby it is rendered secure from them and from the imagination, allows the veil which lies between it and the Well-guarded Tablet to be raised (given that the heart is in essence pure), so that some part of what the Tablet contains alights upon the heart, just as an image may pass from one mirror to another when an obstructing veil is removed.

However, sleep, while preventing the operation of the other senses, does not suppress the operations and movements of the imaginative faculty. Everything which alights upon the heart is pre-empted by this faculty, which accommodates itself thereto by creating an image which approximates to it. Now, things imagined establish themselves more firmly in the memory than others, and, since the thing imagined is what remains in the memory it is all that stays remembered upon awakening. Thus it is that the interpreter of dreams needs to investigate the thing imagined as an 'imitation' [*ḥikāya*], that is, an abstraction, looking into its symbols according to the correspondence which exists between the dream and the abstraction. There are many clear examples of this for those who would look into the science of dream-interpreting, but just one will be sufficient for you. A man once said to Ibn Sīrīn, 'I saw in a dream that in my hand I held a seal with which I could seal the mouths of men and the pudenda of women'. And he said, 'Why then, you are a muezzin, who delivers the Call to Prayer before daybreak during Ramaḍān,' and he replied, 'It is as you say'.[A]

You will perceive that the essence [*rūḥ*] of sealing is 'prevention', and that it is this that 'sealing' here signifies. A man's circumstances in the Well-guarded Tablet are only disclosed to the heart as they are, [in this case] as his acting to prevent people from eating and drinking. The imaginative faculty, however, mixes 'prevention' with 'sealing', producing the image of a 'seal', which embodies the essence of the concept, after which nothing remains lodged in the memory save the image.

The above constitutes a brief dip into the ocean of the science of dream-interpreting, the marvels of which are unending; indeed, how should they end when sleep 'is the brother of death?'[10] Death is a wondrous thing because it bears a faint

[A] Eating, drinking and sexual relations being of course forbidden during the daylight hours of the fasting month.

similarity to it, in that sleep raises the cover from the unseen world so that the sleeper comes to know what will happen in the future. What, then, must be the situation in the case of death, do you surmise, which rends the veil apart and removes the cover completely, so that after having breathed his last a man forthwith beholds himself either set around with torments, degradations and humiliations (from which we seek refuge in God!) or alternatively, sheltered in everlasting bliss and great authority which shall never come to an end?

At this, it shall be said to the damned after the veil has been removed, '*You were in heedlessness of this, but today have We lifted your veil so that this day your vision is sharp*'.[11] And they shall be told likewise, '*Is this magic, or do you not perceive? Fall back therein! Persevere, or persevere not; it is the same for you; you are only requited for what you used to do*'.[12] And they are referred to [again] in His statement (Exalted is He!): *And from God there appeared before them that wherewith they had never reckoned.*[13] In this way, even the most learned and wise of men shall find disclosed to him after his death wonders and portents which had occurred not once to his intellect, nor ever impinged upon his mind. Surely, were the intelligent man to harbour no worry or concern save for the perilousness of this state, and for that which shall stand revealed upon the lifting of the veil, and the abiding woe or perpetual felicity which shall be disclosed before him once the covering is removed, these things would suffice to occupy his thoughts for his entire lifetime.

How astonishing is our heedlessness in the face of these weighty affairs; and how much more astonishing still is the pleasure which we take in our wealth, family, chattels and offspring, and in our limbs, our hearing and our sight, despite our certain knowledge that we shall come to leave all of these things. But where is the man into whose fear-stricken breast the Holy Spirit[A] shall cast his breath, and utter that which he declared to the Master of the Prophets: 'Love whomsoever you will, for you shall surely leave him; live howsoever you will, for you shall

[A] The 'Holy Spirit' (*al-Rūḥ al-Qudus*: Q. II:253; XVI:102 etc.) in Islam usually signifies the Archangel Gabriel.

surely die; and act as you will, for you shall surely be requited'?[14] Of a surety, whoever has this disclosed to him through the eye of certainty [ʿ*ayn al-yaqīn*] shall be 'like a wayfarer in the world',[A] and not set one brick upon another, nor one piece of straw upon the next,[B] neither will he bequeath a single dinar or dirham, or [even] take a friend or a companion.

Yes indeed, for [the Prophet himself] said, 'Were I to take any intimate [*khalīl*], I would take Abū Bakr as an intimate, but instead your companion is the intimate of the All-Merciful'.[15] By this he was explaining that intimacy [*khulla*] with the All-Merciful had pervaded [*takhallalat*] the interior of his heart, and that love for Him had become established in his innermost heart, leaving no place therein for any intimate or loved one.

God (Exalted is He!) said to his nation, *If you love God, then follow me; God shall love you.*[C16] For his nation is made up of those who follow him, and they alone are his followers who turn away from this world in favour of the next, for his summons was exclusively to God and the Last Day; just as he only turned men away from this world and its fleeting fortunes. Thus it is in proportion to your turning aside from this world in favour of the next that you walk his road, and in proportion to your walking his road that you follow him, and in proportion to your following him that you become one of his nation. Likewise, in proportion to your turning to this world you turn away from his road and from following him, and join those regarding whom God (Exalted is He!) has said, *As for the profligate, who has preferred the life of the world; for him hellfire is his place of resort.*[17]

O man! (who is every one of us.) Were you only to come forth from the hiding-place of your beguilement to deal justly with yourself, you would come to realise that from morning to night your every endeavour is wholly for the sake of fleeting fortunes, and that you move about and labour solely for the transient businesses of this world; yet still you hope that on the morrow you are to be among his nation and followers! How misguided

[A] Cf. Bukhārī, Riqāq, 3: 'Be in the world as though a stranger or a wayfarer'.

[B] Cf. above, p.73.

[C] The Prophet is being instructed to say this.

are your imaginings, and how simpleminded your hopes! *Shall We treat the Muslims like the workers of unrighteousness? What ails you? How do you judge?*[18]

But let us now return to our subject, for the course of our disquisition has strayed from our purpose. Let us now make mention of such dream-visions revelatory of the states of the dead as may provide some benefit: Prophecy is past, but the portents [*mubashshirāt*] remain,[A] and these are none other than the Visionary Dreams [*manāmāt*].

An exposition of visionary dreams which reveal the states of the dead and the works which have brought advantage in the Afterlife

One aspect of this is the vision which may be had of the Emissary of God (may God bless him and grant him peace), for he said, 'Whosoever sees me in his sleep[19] has seen me truly, for the devil does not assume my form'.[20]

Said ᶜUmar ibn al-Khaṭṭāb (may God be pleased with him), 'I once beheld the Emissary of God (may God bless him and grant him peace) in my sleep, and saw that he was not looking at me. "What have I done, O Emissary of God?" I asked, and he turned to me and enquired, "Do you not kiss while fasting?" And I said, "By Him in Whose hand lies my soul, never again shall I kiss a woman while fasting".'

Said Ibn ᶜAbbās (may God be pleased with him), 'I had been a close friend to ᶜUmar, and [after his death] longed to see him in my sleep. However, it was only at the year's ending that I saw him. He was wiping sweat from his brow and saying, "This is my time for rest, and my shade[B] would have collapsed had I not found Him to be All-Lenient, All-Merciful." '

[A] As related in a *ḥadīth* (Bukhārī, Taᶜbīr, 5): 'After I am gone, all that shall remain of Prophecy will be the *mubashshirāt*: the dream-visions of the believer'.

[B] *ᶜarsh*: perhaps here in its ancient signification of 'a booth or shed, or thing constructed for shade, mostly made of canes, or reeds'. (Lane, 2000.)

Said al-Ḥasan ibn ᶜAlī, "ᶜAlī (may God be pleased with him) once said to me, "God's Emissary (may God bless him and grant him peace) appeared to me tonight in a dream. 'O Emissary of God!' I said. 'How do you find your nation to be?' 'Call down curses upon it!' he said. 'O Lord God,' I said, 'replace them with others who are better for me than them, and replace me with someone who is worse for them than myself!'" Then he went out, and was stabbed by Ibn Muljam.'[A]

One of the Shaykhs said, 'I once beheld God's Emissary (may God bless him and grant him peace) [in a dream]. "O Emissary of God!" I said. "Ask forgiveness for me!" but he turned away. Then I said, "O Emissary of God! Sufyān ibn ᶜUyayna has related to me on the authority of Muḥammad ibn al-Munkadir on the authority of Jābir ibn ᶜAbd Allāh that you never refused any request." And he drew near to me and said, "May God grant you His forgiveness".'

It is related that al-ᶜAbbās ibn ᶜAbd al-Muṭṭalib once said, 'I had been as a brother to Abū Lahab, and used to keep his company. When he died, and God spoke of him as He did,[B] I felt grieved for him, and worried greatly over his condition. For a year I asked God (Exalted is He!) to grant me a vision of him in my sleep, and [in due course] I beheld him burning in flames. When I asked him of his condition he said, "I have been consigned to Hell, the torment of which is lessened and abated only on Sunday night out of all the days and nights of the week." "Why should that be?" I asked, and he replied, "On Sunday night Muḥammad was born, (may God bless him and grant him peace) and I was visited by a little slave-girl who gave me the good news that Āmina had been delivered of him. I was overjoyed at this, and gave one of my bondsmaids her freedom out of happiness. For this, God rewarded me by lessening my punishment every Sunday night."'

Said ᶜAbd al-Wāḥid ibn Zayd, 'I once set out on the Pilgrimage in the company of a man who would not stand, sit,

[A] The caliph is here expressing his disgust at the dissensions which ultimately brought about his murder.

[B] Cf. Q. CXI:1-5.

move or be still without invoking blessings upon the Prophet (may God bless him and grant him peace). When I questioned him about this he said, "I shall tell you about this matter. When I set out for Mecca for the first time in the company of my father, I went to sleep at a way-station. While I was asleep someone came to me and said, 'Arise, for God has caused your father to die and has blackened his face.'[A] Terrified, I arose, and removed the garment from his face, and behold, he was indeed dead, and his face had turned black. While I was in this state I was overcome by drowsiness and fell asleep. And behold! At my father's head there stood four negroes bearing poles of iron. Then there stepped forwards a man of handsome appearance dressed in two garments of green. 'Stand aside!' he commanded them, and he touched [my father's] face with his hand. Then he approached me and said, 'Arise, for God has whitened your father's face.' 'Who are you, may my father and mother be your ransom?' I asked. 'I am Muḥammad,' he replied. And I arose, and lifted the clothes from my father's face, and behold! it now was white. From that time on I have never ceased to invoke blessings upon God's Emissary, may God bless him and grant him peace." '

It is related that ᶜUmar ibn ᶜAbd al-ᶜAzīz once said, '[In a dream] I beheld God's Emissary (may God bless him and grant him peace) sitting in the company of Abū Bakr and ᶜUmar (may God be pleased with them). I greeted them, and then sat down. While I was seated, ᶜAlī and Muᶜāwiya were brought, led into a room, and the door was closed on them while I watched. At once, ᶜAlī, (may God be pleased with him) emerged, declaring, "By the Lord of the Kaᶜba, judgement is passed in my favour." Then Muᶜāwiya came out immediately behind him and said, "By the Lord of the Kaᶜba, I am forgiven!" '[B]

Ibn ᶜAbbās (may God be pleased with them both)[C] once awoke and said, '*Truly we are God's, and truly unto Him is our return!*[21] Al-

[A] This being a sign of damnation (cf. Q. III:106).

[B] The struggle between ᶜAlī and Muᶜāwiya for the Caliphate caused some discomfort for later orthodoxy, which came to favour ᶜAlī, while rejecting any criticism of his rival, who had also been a Companion of the Prophet (cf. e.g. Ashᶜarī, *Maqālāt*, 456–7).

[C] i.e. with both Ibn ᶜAbbās and his father.

Ḥusayn has been slain, by God!' (this being before his murder). His companions took exception to this, but he declared, 'I have [just] seen God's Emissary (may God bless him and grant him peace) holding a vial of blood. "Know you what my nation has done after me?" he asked. "It has slain my [grand-]son al-Ḥusayn! This is his blood, and that of his companions, which I hold aloft before God!" ' Then, twenty-four days on, the news came of his murder, which had taken place on the day that he had seen him.

Al-Ṣiddīq [Abū Bakr] (may God be pleased with him) was once seen [in a dream] and was asked, 'You used constantly to say of your tongue, "May this bring me to the sources [*al-mawārid*]!" How, then, did God deal with you?' And he said, 'With it I said, "There is no deity save God," and He brought me to Heaven'.

An exposition of the visionary dreams of the Shaykhs, may God be pleased with them all

One of the Shaykhs said, 'I once beheld Mutammim al-Dawraqī in a dream, and said, "O my master! How did God deal with you?" And he replied, "I was led around the gardens of Heaven and asked, 'O Mutammim! Is there anything here that you find pleasing?' 'No, my Lord,' I replied. 'Had you found anything pleasing herein,' He said, 'I would have turned you over to it, and not brought you to Me'." '

Yūsuf ibn al-Ḥusayn was once seen in a dream. 'How did God deal with you?' he was asked. 'He granted me His forgiveness,' he replied. 'For what reason?' he was asked, and he replied, 'Because I never mingled seriousness with jest'.

Said Manṣūr ibn Ismāʿīl, 'I once beheld ʿAbd Allāh al-Zarrād[22] in a dream, and asked him, "How did God deal with you?" And he replied, "He made me stand before Him, whereupon He forgave me every sin to which I confessed, there remaining only one sin which I was ashamed to acknowledge. Then He made me stand in my sweat until the very flesh on my face dropped away." "And what was that sin?" I enquired. "I had once looked at a handsome boy," he said, "and found him attractive, and was ashamed to mention this before God." '

Said Abū Jaᶜfar al-Ṣaydalānī, 'I once beheld the Emissary of God (may God bless him and grant him peace) in my sleep. He was surrounded by a group of dervishes [*fuqarā'*]. While we were thus disposed, the heavens split open and there descended two angels, one of whom bore a bowl and the other a ewer. The bowl was laid before God's Emissary (may God bless him and grant him peace) and he washed his hands. Then he instructed [the angels] to circulate [with the bowl and the ewer] until all had washed, upon which they set the bowl before me. One of them said, "Do not pour for him, for he is not one of them!" but I said, "O Emissary of God! Is it not related of you that you said, 'A man is of those he loves'?"[23] "Yes indeed," he said. "O Emissary of God!" I said. "I love you, and I love these dervishes." And he said (may God bless him and grant him peace), "Pour for him, for he is one of them".'

Said al-Junayd, 'In a dream I once saw myself addressing a group of people. An angel came before me and asked, "What is the finest thing by which those who are close to God have drawn near to Him?" "A hidden action in a fair balance," I said. The angel turned away, and said, "By God, a statement rightly-guided".'

Mujammiᶜ was once seen in a dream. 'How do you see matters?' he was asked, and he replied, 'I see that those who renounce the world are given the best of the world and of the Afterlife'.

A Syrian once said to al-ᶜAlā' ibn Ziyād, 'I saw you in a dream, and you were in Heaven!' He descended from the place where he had been sitting and approached him, saying, 'Perhaps the devil wished [to tempt] me somewhat, but I was protected, so he sent a man to slay me'.[A]

Said Muḥammad ibn Wāsiᶜ, 'The visionary dream gladdens the believer, but does not make him proud'.

Said Ṣāliḥ ibn Bashīr,[24] 'I once saw ᶜAṭā' al-Salīmī in a dream, and said to him, "May God have mercy upon you. Truly, you

[A] Complacency being a form of spiritual death.

were often saddened in the world." "Indeed, by God," he said. "And that sadness bequeathed to me long relief and unending bliss." "At which degree are you?" I enquired, and he recited, "With *those whom God has blessed, the Prophets and the Saints*",[25] to the end of the verse.'

Zurāra ibn Abī Awfā was asked in a dream [after his death], 'Which action proved the best for you?' And he replied, 'Satisfaction,[A] and brief hopes'.

Said Yazīd ibn Madhʿūr, 'In a dream I once beheld al-Awzāʿī. "O Abū ʿAmr!" I said. "Tell me of a deed whereby I may draw nearer to God (Exalted is He!)." And he replied, "I have not seen any degree here more exalted than that of the Divines, which is followed by that of the grief-sticken." ' At this, Yazīd, who was an old man, wept unremittingly until his eyes clouded over.

Said Ibn ʿUyayna, 'In a dream I once beheld one of my brethren. "O my brother!" I said to him. "How did God deal with you?" And he replied, "He forgave me every sin for which I had implored His forgiveness, but did not forgive me those for which I had not asked it".'

Said ʿAlī al-Ṭalḥī, 'In my sleep I once saw a woman who bore no resemblance to the women of this world. "Who are you?" I enquired, and she said, "An houri." "Marry me!" I said, but she answered, "Ask my Lord for my hand, and provide me with my bride-price." "And what might that be?" I asked. "That you keep your soul from its weaknesses," she said.'

Said Ibrāhīm ibn Isḥāq al-Ḥarbī, 'I once beheld Zubayda in my sleep, and asked her how God had dealt with her. "He granted me His forgiveness," she replied. "For the money you spent on the Mecca Road?"[B] I asked, but she replied, "The reward for the money I spent was returned to the money's owners; I was forgiven only on account of my intention".'[C]

[A] *al-riḍā*: i.e. with one's lot and mortal destiny.

[B] The princess had expended vast sums on the improvement of the pilgrim road from Iraq to Mecca and Medina, constructing water cisterns, fortresses to reduce the depradations of the nomads, and waymarks. A not inconsiderable number of these works are still visible today.

[C] In other words, the money she had spent had been unjustly acquired by the state by means of extortion and by taxes not sanctioned by Divine Law.

After Sufyān al-Thawrī died he was seen in a dream, and asked, 'How did God deal with you?' 'I set one foot on the Traverse', he said, 'and the next was in Heaven'.

Said Aḥmad ibn Abi'l-Ḥawārī, 'In a dream I once beheld the most beautiful girl I have ever seen. Her face was fairly shining with light. "Whence comes the light of your face?" I asked her, and she replied, "Recall you that night in which you wept?" "Yes," I said. "Your tears were caught," she said, "and my face was anointed with them, and from them proceeds the light of my countenance that you now behold".'

Said al-Kattānī, 'I once saw al-Junayd in a dream, and asked him, "How did God deal with you?" "Those allusions [*ishārāt*][A] have perished," he replied, "and those expressions have passed away; I had obtained nothing but two *rakᶜas* which it had been my custom to pray at night".'[B]

Zubayda was seen in a dream, and was asked how God had dealt with her. 'He forgave me', she replied, 'because of [my uttering] these four phrases: "With 'no deity save God' do I live out my life, with 'no deity save God' shall I enter my grave, with 'no deity save God' shall I be all alone, and with 'no deity save God' shall I meet my Lord ." '

Bishr al-Ḥāfī was once seen in a dream, and was asked, 'How did God deal with you?' He replied, 'My Lord (Great and Glorious is He!) showed me His mercy, saying, "O Bishr! Are you not ashamed before Me, seeing that you used to fear Me with such intensity?" '

Abū Sulaymān was seen in a dream and was asked, 'How did God deal with you?' 'He forgave me,' he answered, 'and nothing proved more harmful to me than the way the people used to point at me'.[26]

Said Abū Bakr al-Kattānī, 'In a dream I once beheld the most beautiful young man I have ever seen. "Who are you?" I

[A] Variously defined, the *ishārāt* are usually understood to be verbal or non-verbal pointers which allude to and may communicate a spiritual state. See P. Nwyia, art. 'Ishāra', in *EI²*, IV. 113–4.

[B] In other words, the symptoms of mystical grace do not in themselves bring a reward. The *Risāla* (II. 722) has *tasbīḥāt* for *rakᶜatayn*.

enquired, and he replied, "I am Piety." "And where do you dwell?" I asked, and he replied, "In every grief-stricken heart". Then I turned away, and behold! there before me stood a black woman. "Who are you?" I asked. "Sickness," she replied. "And where do you dwell?" I asked. "In every cheerful, exuberant heart," said she. At this I awoke, and vowed that I would never laugh again unless obliged to'.

Said Abū Saʿīd al-Kharrāz, 'In my sleep I once beheld the devil leaping at me. I brought forth a stick in order to strike him, but he showed no fear. Then a voice [*hātif*] called out to me, saying, "He will not fear that; he fears only the light which dwells in the heart".'

Said al-Masūḥī, 'I once saw the devil in a dream. He was walking naked, and I said, "Are you not ashamed to be naked in front of the people?" But he said, "By God, are these people? Were they really so I would not be able to play with them all day long as children do with a ball. Nay, 'people' are a different race, who have caused my body to sicken." And with his hand he pointed to our companions, the Sufis.'

Said Abū Saʿīd al-Kharrāz, 'When I was in Damascus I received a dream in which I saw the Prophet (may God bless him and grant him peace) approaching me, leaning for support on Abū Bakr and ʿUmar (may God be pleased with them). He stopped in front of me while I was uttering certain phrases and beating my chest. "The evil which is in this thing," he said, "outweighs its good".'[A]

Said Ibn ʿUyayna, 'In my sleep I once beheld Sufyān al-Thawrī in Heaven. He was flying from tree to tree, saying, "*For the likes of this, then, let those who would work, work!*"[27] "Counsel me!" I asked him, and he said, "Reduce the number of your dealings with people".'[B]

[A] A call to sobriety in mysticism.

[B] The arguments for and against *ʿuzla*, withdrawal from the world for devotional purposes, form the greater part of an entire 'book' of the *Iḥyā'* (II. 197–217: *K. Ādāb al-ʿuzla*), where Ghazālī concludes that it is recommended only under certain circumstances, and is certainly not for novices on the spiritual path.

Abū Ḥātim al-Rāzī related that Qabīṣa ibn ᶜUqba once said, '[In a dream] I once saw Sufyān al-Thawrī. "How did God deal with you?" I asked, and he replied:

I looked directly at my Lord, and He did say,
"Be joyful, Abū Saᶜīd,[A] for I am content with you.
For your custom it was to stand when the twilight drew on,
With the tear of a lover and a sturdy heart.
Before you now, choose which palace you desire,
And visit Me, for I am not far from you".'

Al-Shiblī was seen three days after his death, and was asked, 'How did God deal with you?' 'He disputed with me until I despaired,' he said, 'but when He saw my despair He encompassed me in His mercy.'

Majnūn of Banū ᶜĀmir[B] was seen after his death in a dream. When asked how God had dealt with him he replied, 'He forgave me, and made me a proof against all lovers'.

Al-Thawrī was once seen in a dream, and was asked how God had dealt with him. 'He showed me His mercy,' he replied. Then he was asked, 'What is the condition of ᶜAbd Allāh ibn al-Mubārak?' and he replied 'He is one of those that come before their Lord twice in every day'.

Someone was asked [in a dream] how he was faring, and said, 'They[C] called us to account and scrutinised us, then they were generous and let us go'.

Mālik ibn Anas was seen [in a dream] and was asked, 'How did God deal with you?' 'He forgave me', he replied, 'by virtue of a phrase which ᶜUthmān ibn ᶜAffān (may God be pleased with him) used to repeat whenever he saw a funeral: "Glory be to the Alive, Who perishes not!"'

On the night that he died, al-Ḥasan al-Baṣrī was seen in a dream. The gates of heaven had been opened, and a voice was

[A] Al-Thawrī's name was in fact Ibn Saᶜīd; his *kunya* was Abū ᶜAbd Allāh. (Cf. *Mashāhīr*, 169.)

[B] The Arabian tribe of Banū ᶜĀmir ibn Ṣaᶜṣaᶜa. (*Inbāh*, 71.)

[C] The Angels, presumably.

calling out, 'Al-Ḥasan al-Baṣrī has come to God, and He is well-pleased with him!'

When al-Jāḥiẓ was seen in a dream being asked, 'How did God deal with you?' he replied as follows:

> "Never write any words with your hand
> which you might not be happy to see on the Day of Arising."

Al-Junayd once saw the devil in his sleep. Since the devil was naked, he asked him, 'Are you not ashamed before the people?' 'These are not people,' he replied. 'Those in the mosque of al-Shūnīzīya[A] are people, those who have emaciated my body and burned up my liver.' And al-Junayd said, 'Upon awakening I made my way to that mosque, and there beheld a group of people who had set their heads upon their knees in contemplation. When they saw me they said, "Be not beguiled by the discourse of the vile".'

Al-Naṣrābādhī was seen in Mecca in a dream after he had died. 'How did God deal with you?' he was asked, and he replied, 'I was reproached most nobly, and then was called, "O Abu'l-Qāsim! Shall there be separation after union?" "No, O Lord of Majesty!" I replied. And no sooner had I been laid out in my tomb than I joined my Lord.'

In a dream, ʿUtba al-Ghulām beheld a beautiful houri. 'O ʿUtba!' she said. 'I long for you! See therefore, that you do not do anything that might cause us to be parted.' And ʿUtba declared, 'I have thrice-divorced this world, and shall never call it back before I come to you.'[B]

It is said that Ayyūb al-Sakhtiyānī once saw the funeral of a sinner, and turned into the entrance-passage of a house in order to avoid praying at it. [In time,] the dead man was seen by someone in a dream, and was asked, 'How did God deal with you?' 'He

[A] A celebrated mosque of Baghdad where al-Junayd used to teach. It stood beside a cemetery of the same name, in which were buried such luminaries as Ibn Abi'l-Dunyā, al-Sarī al-Saqaṭī, and, in due course, al-Junayd himself.

[B] The threefold divorce barring a man from remarrying the same woman until she has married another and been divorced again. (Cf. *Iḥyā'*, II. 51.)

forgave me,' he said. 'And tell Ayyūb to repeat, "*Were you to own the very treasure-houses of my Lord's mercy you would assuredly hold back from fear of expense*".'[28]

Someone once said, 'On the night that Dāūd al-Ṭā'ī passed away I beheld a radiance, and saw angels descending and ascending. "What night is this?" I asked, and they told me, "The night in which Dāūd al-Ṭā'ī has passed away, for all Heaven has been decked out for the advent of his spirit".'

Said Abū Saᶜīd al-Shaḥḥām,[29] 'In a dream I once beheld Sahl al-Ṣuᶜlūkī. "O shaykh!" I said. "Forbear from using that title," he said. "But what of those states which I witnessed?" I asked. "They proved of no benefit to me," he replied. And I asked, "How did God deal with you?" "He forgave me," he said, "on account of [my answering] certain questions put to me by the commonalty".'

Said Abū Bakr al-Rashīdī, 'I once saw Muḥammad al-Ṭūsī, the teacher, in my sleep. He spoke to me, and said, "Say to Abū Saᶜīd al-Ṣaffār al-Mu'addib:

It was our custom never to turn from love.
By the heart's life, you have turned away, but not we."

'Upon awakening I duly mentioned this to him, and he informed me, "I used to visit his grave every Friday, but this week failed to do so".'

Said Ibn Rāshid, 'After he had died I beheld Ibn al-Mubārak in a dream. "Have you not died?" I asked him. "Yes," he replied, and I said, "How, then, did God deal with you?" And he answered, "He granted me such forgiveness as encompasses every sin." "And what of Sufyān al-Thawrī?" I enquired, and he replied, "O rapture! He is of *those whom God has blessed, the Prophets and the Saints*,"[30] [and continued to the end of] the verse.'[A]

Said al-Rabīᶜ ibn Sulaymān, 'After his death I beheld al-Shāfiᶜī, may God have mercy upon him, in a dream. "O Abū ᶜAbd

[A] The remainder of the verse runs: *and the Martyrs and the Righteous. The best of company are they!*

Allāh!" I said. "How did God deal with you?" And he replied, "He seated me upon a throne of gold and cast glittering pearls over me".'

Al-Ḥasan al-Baṣrī was seen by one of his companions on the night that he died. A herald was crying out that '*God did prefer Adam and Noah, and the progeny of Abraham and the progeny of ᶜImrān*[A] *over all creatures,*[31] and He preferred al-Ḥasan al-Baṣrī over all the people of his age'.

Said Abū Yaᶜqūb al-Qāri' al-Daqīqī, 'In my sleep I saw a tall, brown-skinned man followed by a group of people. "Who is this?" I enquired, and they replied, "Uways al-Qaranī." So I approached him and said, "Counsel me, may God show you mercy!" He frowned into my face, but I said, "I am a seeker of guidance, so grant it me, may God grant it you also.", At this, he came up to me and said, "Pursue the grace of your Lord when you have loved Him; beware of His vengeance when you have disobeyed Him; and in all of this, never lose the hope you have set in Him." Then he turned and departed from me.'

Said Abū Bakr ibn Abī Maryam, '[In a dream] I once saw Waraqā' ibn Bishr al-Ḥaḍramī, and asked him, "How did you fare, O Waraqā'?" "I was saved, after every travail," he replied. "Which action did you find to be most valuable?" I enquired, and he told me, "Weeping from the fear of God".'

Said Yazīd ibn Naᶜāma, 'A girl once died in the great plague,[B] and was seen by her father in a dream. "O my daughter," he said. "Tell me of the Afterlife!" And she said, "O father, we are now in a fearsome condition: we know and do not act, while you act, and do not know. By God, uttering 'Glory to God' once or twice, or praying one or two *rakᶜas* in an opportunity for action would be more beloved to me than the world and all that it contains".'

Said one of the companions of ᶜUtba al-Ghulām, 'In a dream I once beheld ᶜUtba, and asked him how God had dealt with him. And he replied, "I entered Heaven by virtue of that prayer which

[A] According to the Muslim historians and exegetes ᶜImrān was the father of the Virgin Mary, and also of Elisabeth, the mother of John the Baptist.

[B] *al-ṭāᶜūn al-jārif*: a plague which afflicted Basra in the year 65 AH.

is written in your house." When I awoke I duly betook myself to my house, and there on the wall before me was written in the hand of ᶜUtba al-Ghulām: "O Guide of those that go astray! O Merciful towards those that sin! O Forgiver of those that stumble! Have mercy upon Thy bondsman, who is in great peril, and upon the Muslims in their entirety. Render us among the living and sustained, even those whom Thou hast blessed, *the Prophets and the Saints, the Martyrs and the Righteous.*[32] Amen, O Lord of the Worlds!"'

Said Mūsā ibn Ḥammād, '[In a dream] I once beheld Sufyān al-Thawrī in Heaven winging his way from one palm-tree to the next. "O Abū ᶜAbd Allāh!" I said. "How did you attain to this?" "Through scrupulousness [*waraᶜ*][A]," he replied. "What, then, of ᶜAlī ibn ᶜĀṣim?" I asked, and he said, "He can scarcely be descried, save in the way one might descry a travelling star".'

One of the Followers once beheld the Prophet (may God bless him and grant him peace) in a dream, and said, 'O Emissary of God! Give me an exhortation!' And he replied, 'Whosoever does not seek out loss,[B] he is himself the loser; and whosoever is in loss, for him death is the better circumstance.'

Said al-Shāfiᶜī (may God have mercy upon him), 'For several days latterly I was afflicted with a matter which alarmed and saddened me grievously. Only God (Great and Glorious is He!) was aware of my plight. But yesterday in a dream someone came to me and said, "O Muḥammad ibn Idrīs! Say: '*O Lord God! I possess not for my own soul any benefit, harm, death, life or resurrection.*[33] Only that which Thou hast bestowed upon me may I take, and only that from which Thou hast granted me safekeeping may I ward off. O Lord God! Therefore grant me guidance towards that which is beloved and pleasing in Thy sight, in word, in deed, and in my times of health.'" In the morning I duly repeated this. Later on that morning God (Great

[A] The precise observance of the Law, and more particularly the avoidance of matters which might be prohibited or discommended. A traditional virtue which goes hand in hand with *zuhd*. The best-known treatment of the subject is probably Ibn Ḥanbal's *K. al-Waraᶜ*. In the *Iḥyā'* (I. 17) four degrees of it are identified; for these see Morelon, pp. XI–XIV.

[B] i.e. the renunciation of worldly things.

and Glorious is He!) answered my prayer, and made easy for me an escape from my plight. Thus you must make use of these prayers, and never neglect them.'

The above constitutes an anthology of unveilings which have intimated the circumstances of the dead and the works which may bring one into the propinquity of God. Let us next make mention of those things which shall pass before the dead man from the commencement of the Trumpet-Blast until his final abiding in Heaven or in Hell.

And praised be God, with the praise of those that give thanks!

THE SECOND PART

OF THE BOOK OF THE REMEMBRANCE OF DEATH

Concerning the Circumstances of the Man Deceased from the time when the Trump is Blown to his Final Residence in Heaven or in Hell, together with a Detailed Account of the Perils and Terrors which shall Confront him.

(Containing an exposition of the following:)

The Trumpet-Blast.

The Land and People of the Concourse.

The Perspiration of the People of the Concourse.

The Length of the Day of Arising.

The Day of Arising, and its Calamities and Names.

The Inquisition of Sins.

The Scales.

The Adversaries, and the Restoration of Wrongs.

The Traverse.

The Intercession.

The Pool.

The Inferno, its Terrors, Torments, Snakes and Scorpions.

Heaven, and the Varieties of its Bliss.

The Number of Heavens, and their Gates, Chambers, Walls, Rivers and Trees.

The Raiment of Heaven's People, their Furnishings and Divans.

Their Food.

The Large-eyed Houris and the Pages.

The Vision of God's Countenance (Exalted is He!).

A Chapter on the Wide Compass of God's Mercy (Exalted is He!).

And thus shall be concluded the Book, if God (Exalted is He!) so wills.

The Trumpet-Blast

IN WHAT preceded you came to know how violent are a man's states during the agonies of death and how perilous is his condition as he fearfully awaits his fate, as he endures the grave's darkness and worms, and suffers the Questioning of Munkar and Nakīr, to be followed, should he have incurred God's wrath, by the perils of the Punishment of the Grave.

More fearsome than all of this, however, are the perils which shall confront him subsequently: the Trumpet-Blast, the Resurrection on the Day of Arising, the Presentation before the Almighty, the Inquisition regarding matters both important and minor, the Erection of the Scales in order that men's destinies might be known, and then the passage over the Traverse despite the fineness and sharpness of its edge. These things shall be followed by the awaiting of the Summons to final judgement, and either bliss or misery.

You are obliged to know of these circumstances and these terrible events, and to believe in them with a firm and convinced faith; you must ponder them at length so that there might issue from your heart a motivation to make ready for them. For faith in the Last Day has not entered or become firmly established in the hearts of the greater part of mankind, as is demonstrated by the great preparations they make for the summer's heat and the cold of winter, and their making light of the heat of the Inferno and its bitter cold, and the woes and terrors which it contains. Of course, if they are questioned regarding the Last Day their tongues wag in affirmation; however their hearts remain quite heedless of it. Any man who is told that the food set before him is poisoned, and admits this to be true to the friend who informed him of this, but who then stretches out his hand to partake of it has believed him with his tongue but has belied him with his deeds. Indeed, to deny something with an action is more eloquent by far than to deny it with the tongue: the Prophet (may God bless him and grant him peace) once said, 'God (Exalted is He!) has declared, "The son of Adam insults Me, although it is not right that he should do so. He cries lies to Me, although it is not right that he should do so. His insult is to say that I have a son, while he calls Me a liar by saying, 'He shall not restore me as He began me'." '[1]

The sole cause of the mind's insufficiently strong certainty and faith in the resurrection and quickening of mankind lies in the inadequacy of its understanding during its worldly[2] sojourn of such matters as these. If a man had never witnessed the reproduction of animals, and was told that man was moulded from a dirty drop of fluid by a Creator, and given intelligence, speech and movement, his mind would most energetically shrink from believing this. Thus God (Exalted is He!) has said, *Has man not seen that We created him from a drop of liquid, and behold! he is a manifest opponent?*[3] and also, *Does man reckon that he will be left to no purpose? Was he not a drop of seed poured forth, then a clot, while He created and gave proportion, making therefrom the two partners, the male and the female?*[4] In the diverse wonders of a man's creation, therefore, with the great variety of elements which comprise his parts, are marvels even more numerous than those which would consist in his resurrection and restoration. How can one who has seen that such a thing lies within the bounds of His creative ability and power deny that [resurrection] is within His capacity and wisdom also? If there is any weakness in your faith, then fortify it by contemplating the first growth [of man], for the second resembles it, and indeed is simpler than it. If, however, your faith in this matter is strong, then alert your heart to these terrors and perils, and ponder them at length, drawing a lesson from them so that all rest and repose might vanish from your heart and you make ready for the presentation before the Almighty.

You should think first of the force with which the Trumpet-Blast shall assail the ears of the people of the graves. It comprises *one shout,*[5] wherewith the graves open up over the heads of the deceased, who pour forth in a single rush. Picture how you shall be when you have leaped forth with your face disfigured and your body covered from head to toe with the soil of your grave, as you reel from the violence of the Blast, eyes turned upwards in the direction from which the Summons came. Mankind will have poured out as one man from their graves, in which they had suffered long, greatly agitated by terrors and horrors which increased their woe and trepidation, and by the harshness of their wait for the final outcome. As God (Exalted is He!) has said, *The Trump is blown, and all that are in the heavens and the earth fall down in a swoon, save those whom God wills; then shall it be blown again, and lo! they stand, beholding.*[6] And He has said (Exalted is He!), *When the Horn is blown; that day is hard, not easy for the unbelievers,*[7] and also, *And they say, When shall this promise come to pass, if you are truthful? They wait only for a single Shout which takes them while they are disputing. Then they cannot make bequests, neither shall they return unto their families. The Trump is blown, and behold! from their graves they hasten unto their Lord. They say, 'Woe betide us! Who resurrected us from our sleeping-place? This is what the All-Merciful promised, and the Messengers spoke the truth!'*[8]

Were there therefore to be no terror facing the dead save that of this Blast, it would still be right to fear it. For it comprises a Blast and a Shout at which all who are in the heavens and the earth shall swoon, that is, shall die, excepting only those whom God spares, who are a number of the angels. It was thus that God's Emissary, (may God bless him and grant him peace) said, 'How can I be happy, when the Angel of the Trump has taken up the Horn and moved his head towards it, and pricked up his ears, waiting to hear the command to blow?'[9]

Said Muqātil, 'The Trump [*al-ṣūr*] is [none other than] the Horn [*al-qarn*]. Seraphiel[A] (upon whom be peace) shall put his lips to it as though it were a trumpet [*būq*]. The mouth of the Horn is as the breadth of the heavens and the earth. He is looking upwards underneath the Throne, waiting for the time when he

[A] The angel responsible for this duty, which, it is said, will be carried out at the Rock of Jerusalem. Cf. A.J. Wensinck, art. 'Isrāfīl' in *SEI*, 184.

will be instructed to deliver the First Blast. When this is sounded, *all that are in the heavens and the earth shall fall down in a swoon,*[10] that is, every living thing shall die because of the greatness of this terror, *saving those whom God wills,*[11] who are Gabriel, Michael, Seraphiel and the Angel of Death. Then He shall order the latter to take away the spirit of Gabriel, then that of Michael and then Seraphiel; then shall He issue His command to the Angel of Death, who in his turn perishes.

'After the First Blast, all created beings shall abide for forty years in the Intermediate Realm [*barzakh*][A]. Then shall God quicken Seraphiel, and command him to deliver the Second Blast, as He has said (Exalted is He!): *Then shall it be blown again, and lo! they stand, beholding:*[12] they shall be on their feet, watching the Resurrection.'

Said the Prophet (may God bless him and grant him peace): 'When I received my mission the Herald of the Trump was sent for, and he raised the Horn to his lips, setting one foot before the other and waiting for the time when he would be commanded to blow. Beware, therefore, of the Blast!'[13]

Imagine, therefore, all the beings of creation, and the humility and lowliness which will be theirs at the Resurrection because of their fear of this swooning, and by reason of their anticipation of the joy or misery which shall be decreed for them.

And you are to be among them, bewildered just as much as they; had you been among the rich, the pampered and luxurious in this world, then [know] that it is the kings of this world that shall be on that day the most base, lowly and insignificant of the world's inhabitants, trampled underfoot like ants.

At this, the wild animals shall approach from the desert places and the mountains, lowering their heads and mingling with men despite their former wildness, so humbled are they by the Day of Arising. Although they have no sins to pollute them, they are gathered together by the violence of the Swooning and the

[A] Forty years is the period most commonly given (cf. Khālid, 173–4), a time which is descibed by a rich variety of Traditions (cf. Qurṭubī, 171–3). The use of the term *barzakh* in this context is unusual; although not employed regularly by Ghazālī it is the common term for the period of life in the grave (cf. Qurṭubī, 177).

dreadfulness of the Blast, which distract them from any flight from mankind or from feeling any fear of them. Thus is His saying (Exalted is He!): *And when the wild beasts are gathered together.*[14] Then the rebellious demons, despite their erstwhile rebelliousness and obstinacy, come forward in submission and humility, awed by the presentation before God (Exalted is He!), as He has said: *By thy Lord, We shall surely gather them and the demons; then We shall surely bring them to their knees around the Inferno.*[15]

Think, therefore, how your state, and the state of your heart, shall be at that moment.

The Land and People of the Concourse

THEN SEE how, after the Resurrection and Arising, they shall be driven barefoot, naked and uncircumcised to the Land of the Concourse, which is white and perfectly smooth, and *upon which is to be seen neither unevenness nor any protrusion.*[1] You will be unable to behold upon it any prominence behind which a man might hide, nor any hollow in which he might sink out of the sight of men; instead it is a single, uninterrupted plain devoid of any irregularity, to which they are driven in groups.

All glory, therefore, to Him Who shall unite from the provinces of the earth all creatures irrespective of their diverse natures, driving them on with the *Initial Blast, which shall be followed by the Succeeding Blast.*[2] The Initial Blast [*al-Rājifa*] is the First Blast [*al-nafkha al-ūlā*], while the Succeeding Blast [*al-Rādifa*] is the Second [*al-nafkha al-thāniya*]. It is right that men's hearts should be *trembling that Day*,[3] and that their eyes should be humble.[4] The Emissary of God (may God bless him and grant him peace) has said, 'On the Day of Arising, mankind shall be gathered upon an off-white land like pure flour, on which no sign has been left by anyone'.[5]

The narrator [of this Tradition] remarked that 'off-white' [ᶜ*ufra*] is 'an impure white,'[A] while 'pure' [*naqī*] is 'that which is free of husks and chaff'; and 'no sign' means that 'there is to be no building there to provide a place of concealment, neither any irregularity which might impede the vision.'

Do not imagine that that land will resemble the land of this world, for it corresponds thereto only in name. God (Exalted is He!) has said: *On that Day, when the earth shall be changed to other than the earth, and the heavens,*[6] and Ibn ᶜAbbās said [commenting on this text], 'It will be raised up and lowered; its trees, mountains, valleys and all else that it contains shall disappear, as it is stretched out like the leather of ᶜUkāẓ to form a land as white as silver, upon which no blood shall have been shed nor any sin committed. And in the heavens, the sun, moon and stars shall have vanished away.'

Therefore, O unfortunate one, contemplate the awesomeness and might of that Day. All created beings shall gather together on this plain, as the stars of heaven scatter above them, the sun and moon are extinguished, and the very earth is plunged into darkness because her lantern has been put out. While they[7] are in this state the sky turns over above their heads, and, despite all its strength and firmness, bursts asunder for five hundred years, while the Angels stand at its corners and its peripheries. O, the terror of the sound of its sundering in your ears! O, the majesty of a Day in which the very heavens are rent in spite of their strength and power, to collapse and flow like molten silver mixed with yellow, so that they become *rosy like red hide!*[8] The *heavens become as molten copper,*[9] *and the mountains as carded wool,*[10] and people mingle together *like thickly-scattered moths,*[11] barefoot and naked, none mounted.

Said the Emissary of God (may God bless him and grant him peace), 'All mankind shall be resurrected barefoot, naked and uncircumcised, engulfed by their sweat, which reaches to their very nostrils'. Said Sawda, the wife of God's Emissary (may God bless him and grant him peace), the narrator of this Tradition,

[A] So in Lane, s.v.. According to the Qāḍī ᶜIyāḍ, it is a white inclining to red, suggesting that it has been heated by the sun (Nawawī, *Sharḥ*, XVII. 134).

'How shameful! Are we to look at each other?' But he said, 'People will be too distracted for that. *Each man shall that Day have concern enough to make him heedless.*'[12]

Therefore, hold in awe a Day in which one's private parts will be revealed, but when no harm can be done by looking and beholding. How could it be otherwise, when some people will be crawling on their bellies and faces, and thus prevented from so much as glancing at others? Said Abū Hurayra (may God be pleased with him), 'The Emissary of God (may God bless him and grant him peace) said, "On the Day of Arising, mankind shall be resurrected in three groups: those who ride, those who walk, and those who walk on their faces." A man asked, "O Emissary of God! How could they walk on their faces?" and he answered, "The One Who made them walk on their feet is well able to make them walk upon their faces".'[13]

It is part of human nature to deny all that with which one is unfamiliar. If a man had never beheld a snake walking upon its belly like a flash of lightning he would deny the possibility of anything walking without a foot. Walking on feet would also be deemed impossible by a man who had never beheld it. So beware of denying any of the wonders of the Day of Arising because of their failure to accord with the measure of mundane things. Had you never seen the wonders of this present world, and they were intimated to you before you witnessed them you would deny them most vehemently.

Bring to mind, then, an image of yourself, as you stand naked, uncovered, outcast and ashamed, bewildered and dazed, awaiting the Judgement which will decide your rapture or misery. Make much of this state, for it shall be momentous.

The Perspiration

NEXT contemplate the crowding and congregation of all created beings, whereby the dwellers of the seven heavens and the seven earths, including the angels, jinn, men, demons, beasts, carnivores and birds shall come crowding together at the Standing-place. The sun will shine down upon them with redoubled heat, transformed from her former mildness, and shall be brought down *two bows' length*[A] [1] above the heads of the nations. No shade shall there be upon the earth save that cast by the Throne of the Lord of the Worlds, which only those who have been brought nigh unto Him may enjoy. Thus shall they either take shade under the Throne, or be exposed to the sun's blazing heat, and their sorrow and misery shall grow with its rays.

Then they press one against the other, forced by the intense crowding and the entanglement of their feet, to which is added their great shame and fear of being disgraced and humiliated at the time when they shall be presented before the Almighty of Heaven. The sun's burning and the heat of their breath conjoin with the conflagration produced in their hearts by the flames of shame and fear, and perspiration pours forth from the root of every hair until it flows upon the plain of the Arising and rises over their bodies in proportion to their favour with God. It reaches to the knees of some, to the loins of others, and to the nostrils of others still, while some well-nigh vanish into it.

Said Ibn ʿUmar, 'The Emissary of God (may God bless him and grant him peace) said [explaining the text], *On the Day when mankind shall rise to the Lord of the Worlds:*[2] "When one of them shall vanish into his own sweat up to the middle of his ears".'[3]

Said Abū Hurayra, 'The Emissary of God (may God bless him and grant him peace) said, "On the Day of Arising people shall

[A] A classical figure denoting a short distance or close proximity.

sweat until their perspiration reaches seventy spans deep upon the earth and engulfs them so that it reaches to their ears." ' Thus has it been related by al-Bukhārī and Muslim in their *Ṣaḥīḥs*.[4]

In another Tradition [we read], 'They shall stand raising up their eyes to heaven for forty years, as the perspiration engendered by their violent suffering engulfs them'.[5]

Said ʿUqba ibn ʿĀmir, 'The Emissary of God (may God bless him and grant him peace) said, "On the Day of Arising the sun shall draw nigh to the earth so that mankind shall perspire. For some the perspiration will reach to the ankles, for others to the middle of the shins, for others to the knees or to the thighs, the waist[6] or, for some, the mouth,"—and he raised his hand and set it in his mouth—"and there will be others quite submerged in it,"—and he put his hand upon his head—"like this".'[7]

Ponder then, O unfortunate one, the perspiration of the Concourse's people and the intensity of their suffering. For there will be some among them who shall cry out, saying, 'O my Lord! Grant me release from this suffering and this anticipation, even should it be to Hell!'[8] All this shall take place even though they have as yet received neither judgement nor chastisement. And you are to be one of them, and cannot tell how high the perspiration shall reach in your case. You should know that all the sweat which you did not shed through some effort in God's way, such as the Pilgrimage, the Holy War, the Fast, standing [in night prayer], regularly fulfilling the needs of a Muslim, and sustaining hardships in enjoining what is good and forbidding the wrong, will be driven forth by shame and fear on the plain of the Arising, thereby prolonging your suffering. Were the son of Adam only to be secure from ignorance and beguilement he would realise that to perspire through undertaking difficult works of obedience is easier to bear and less enduring than to perspire at the Arising in distress and misgiving. For truly, the Resurrection is awesome in might,[9] long in duration.

The Length of the Day of Arising

ON that Day all created beings shall stand heartbroken, their eyes raised aloft. They shall not speak, and no attention shall be paid to their circumstances for three hundred years, during which time they shall eat not a morsel and drink not a drop, and fail to find therein any cool breeze.

Said Kaᶜb and Qatāda [interpreting the text], *On the Day when mankind shall rise to the Lord of the Worlds:*[1] 'They shall stand for a period of three hundred years'.

Said ᶜAbd Allāh ibn ᶜUmar, 'The Emissary of God (may God bless him and grant him peace) recited this [same] verse, then asked, "How shall you fare, when God has gathered you together as arrows are gathered in a quiver for fifty thousand years and does not look at you?"'[2]

Said al-Ḥasan, 'What think you of a Day in which men shall stand on their feet for a period of fifty thousand years, eating not a morsel and drinking not a drop, until, when their throats are lacerated by thirst and their bellies burned up with hunger, they are taken away to Hell and given to drink from *a boiling spring,*[3] whose heat had already been prepared, and the scorching of which had grown intense? When they are at the end of their strength, and their endurance is exhausted, they ask around of one another, trying to find a man who is honourable in the sight of his Lord, that he might intercede on their behalf. But no sooner do they congregate around a Prophet then he sends them away, saying, "Leave me! Myself! Myself! My plight has made me heedless of the plight of others!" And each one asks to be excused [the duty of Intercession] because of the great wrath of God (Exalted is He!), saying, "Today our Lord is angered as He has never been before, and as He shall never be again". Then our Prophet (may God bless him and grant him peace) intercedes on behalf of those for whom this is permitted; none possesses the right of Intercession save *he who is permitted this by the All-Merciful and whose speech is pleasing to Him.*'[4]

Ponder, then, the length of that Day and the intensity of the anticipation which must then be endured, that perhaps endurance in the face of sin in your fleeting life in this world may grow easier for you. Know also that when one's waiting for death in this world becomes lengthy as a result of one's great acts of fortitude in the face of one's desires, then one's waiting upon that Day will be of especially brief duration.

The Emissary of God (may God bless him and grant him peace) said, upon being questioned about the length of that Day, 'By Him in Whose hand lies my soul, it shall be shortened for the believer until it becomes briefer for him than the prescribed prayer which he used to perform in the world.'[5]

Strive, therefore, to be among those believers. As long as a single breath of your lifetime remains this affair and the preparations for it lie in your hands. So labour during days that are short for others which shall be lengthy, and you shall reap a gain of unceasing joy. Consider your lifespan to be short, and that of the world itself (which is seven thousand years), for were you to remain steadfast for seven thousand years in order to escape from a Day the length of which is fifty thousand, your gain would be immense, and your effort paltry indeed.

The Day of Arising, and its Calamities and Names

PREPARE yourself, O unfortunate one, for that Day of great import and duration, which is irresistible in might and of near provenance. It is upon that Day that you shall see the heavens cleft asunder[1] and the travelling stars scattered about by reason of its dread authority.[2] The shining stars shall have tumbled down,[3] as the sun's radiance is overthrown[4] and the mountains are moved away.[5] The she-camel ten-months pregnant shall be ignored[6] and the wild beasts gathered together.[7] Poured forth shall be the oceans[8] as souls and bodies are paired once more;[9] the infernal fires shall be stoked and flamed,[10] Heaven shall be brought nigh,[11] and the mountains blown away,[12] and stretched out shall be the earth.[13] On that Day shall you behold the earth convulsed with her earthquake, and *bringing forth her burdens;*[14] *on that Day shall mankind come forth in scattered groups to be shown their works.*[15] *On that Day, when the earth and the mountains are laden and spread out as one plain; on that Day the Event shall have come to pass. The very heavens shall be rent, for on that Day they will be frail, as the Angels stand at the peripheries thereof, and as eight bear above them the Throne of your Lord. On that Day shall you be shown to your Lord,*[16] *and not one of you shall be hidden.*[17] *On that Day shall the mountains be moved away, and you shall behold the earth protruding.*[18] On that Day the earth shall be violently shaken, and the mountains ground to powder *so that they become scattered dust.*[19] *On that Day mankind shall be as thickly-scattered moths, and the mountains as carded wool.*[20] *On that Day shall each nursing mother be oblivious to her suckling, and every woman great with child deliver, and you shall see mankind as drunken; yet they are not drunken, but the chastisement of God is severe.*[21] *On that Day shall the earth be changed for other than the earth, and the heavens, and they shall appear before God, the One, the Almighty.*[22] On that Day the mountains shall be shaken to dust *and left as a level plain upon which is to be seen neither unevenness nor any protrusion.*[23] On that Day *you shall see the mountains which you think to be firm passing away as do the clouds.*[24] On that Day the heavens shall be split apart, and become *rosy like red hide.*[25] *On that Day neither man nor jinn shall be asked regarding his sins.*[26] On that Day the sinner shall be deprived of speech and shall not be questioned about his evildoing, rather *shall he be seized by the forelocks and the feet.*[27] *On that Day every soul shall find in attendance all that it had wrought of good and ill, and shall yearn that there be between it and its works a great gulf.*[28] On that Day each soul shall know *what it has brought*[29] and shall witness *what it sent before it and what it left behind.*[30] On that Day tongues shall be struck dumb, and limbs shall speak out loud.

It was that Day the very mention of which turned grey the hair of the Master of the Messengers, when al-Ṣiddīq[A] (may God be pleased with him) said to him, 'I see that your hair has turned grey, O Emissary of God!' and he replied, 'It has been turned grey by [the Qur'ānic chapter of] Hūd, and its sisters, which are[31] the Event, the Winds Sent Forth, What Do They Ask Concerning, and When the Sun is Dimmed.'[32]

O hapless reader! Mumbling[33] the Qur'ān and wagging your tongue with it is the sum total of your recitation! If you but pondered what you read your heart would be broken by that which greyed the hair of the Master of the Messengers; but should you remain content with tongue-wagging then the fruit of the Qur'ān will be denied you. Resurrection is the most terrible thing which it describes: God has portrayed certain of its calamities and has given it an abundance of names so that through the multiplicity of its titles you might come to understand the great diversity of the things it signifies. Now the reason for such a plethora of names does not lie in the merit of a mere repetition of names and appellations, but rather in the awakening of people who understand. For within each name of the Day of Arising there lies a secret, and there is a significance to every attribute described. Strive, therefore, to know these things.

[A] al-Ṣiddīq: Abū Bakr, the first Caliph.

We shall now assemble for you its names.[A]

It is the Day of Arising, the Day of Lament, the Day of Sorrow, the Day of Reckoning, the Day of Inquisition, the Day of Racing, the Day of Dispute, the Day of Competing, the Day of the Earthquake, the Day of Overwhelming, the Day of Swooning, the Day of the Event, the Day of the Rattler, the Day of the Initial Blast, the Day of the Succeeding Blast, the Day of the Coverer, the Day of the Befaller, the Day of the Imminent Event, the Day of the True Event, the Day of the Calamity, the Day of the Shouter, the Day of Uniting, the Day of Separation, the Day of Driving, the Day of Retaliation, the Day of Mutual Cries, the Day of Reckoning, the Day of Return, the Day of the Torment, the Day of Flight, the Day of the Settling, the Day of Encounter, the Day of Abiding, the Day of Decision, the Day of Requital, the Day of Tribulation, the Day of Weeping, the Day of the Concourse, the Day of the Warning, the Day of Exposition, the Day of the Balance, the Day of the Truth, the Day of Judgement, the Day of Separation, the Day of Gathering, the Day of Resurrection, the Day of Opening, the Day of Humiliation, the Mighty Day, the Barren Day,[34] the Difficult Day, the Day of Recompense, the Day of Certitude, the Day of Rising, the Day of Destiny, the Day of the Trumpet-Blast, the Day of the Shout, the Day of the Convulsion, the Day of Shaking, the Day of Reproach, the Day of Drunkenness, the Day of Terror, the Day of Anguish, the Day of Conclusion, the Day of Refuge, the Day of Time, the Day of the Appointed Hour, the Day of Ambush, the Day of Alarm,[35] the Day of Perspiration, the Day of Poverty, the Day of Changing Hues, the Day of Spreading Stars, the Day of the Sundered Heavens, the Day of Standing, the Day of Departure, the Day of Eternity, the Day of Mutual Deceit, the Day of Scowling, the Day which is Known, the Day which is Promised, the Day which is Witnessed, the *Day in which there is no doubt*,[36] the *Day on which the secret things are rendered public*,[37] the *Day on which no soul shall aid another*,[38] the *Day on which the eyes are raised aloft*,[39] the *Day on which no master shall relieve another*,[40] the *Day on which no soul may aid another*,[41] the *Day on which they are*

[A] These names seem to be almost entirely drawn from the Qur'ān.

summoned towards the infernal fire,[42] the *Day on which they are cast on their faces into Hell,*[43] the *Day on which their faces shall be turned over in Hell,*[44] the *Day on which no father may assist his son,*[45] the *Day on which a man shall flee from his brother, his mother and his father,*[46] the *Day on which they shall not speak, when they are given no leave to make apology,*[47] the *Day on which one shall have no refuge from God,*[48] the *Day on which they shall stand forth,*[49] the *Day on which they are tried by Hell,*[50] the *Day on which neither wealth nor sons avail one,*[51] the *Day on which the evildoers' excuses succour them not: theirs is the curse and theirs the evil abode,*[52] the Day on which apologies are rejected, when the secret things are revealed and what was hidden is made plain, and when the veils are lifted; the Day on which eyes are made humble and when voices fall silent, when turning is rare, when the concealed things come forth and the transgressions appear, the Day when the bondsmen are driven with their witnesses, when the little child's hair turns grey, and the adult falls down in drunkenness.

On that Day are the Scales set up and the Scrolls undone. Hellfire is brought near and its simmering water brought to a boil; the Inferno moans, the unbelievers despair, the fires are stoked up, the colours alter, the tongue falls dumb and men's[53] extremities speak out.

So, *O man! What beguiled you from your Generous Lord,*[54] when the doors were locked and the screens raised and you committed acts of vileness while you were hidden from mankind? What shall you do now that your own limbs have borne witness against you? Woe, woe to us all, the company of neglect; God (Exalted is He!) did send to us the Master of the Messengers, vouchsafing to him the Clear Book, appraising us of these, the attributes of the Day of Requital, then causing us to know of our heedlessness, saying, *The people's reckoning draws nigh for mankind, while they turn away in heedlessness. Never comes there to them anew a reminder from their Lord but that they listen to it and play, with hearts distracted.*[55] Then He tells us of the imminence of the Day of Arising, saying, *The hour drew nigh and the moon was rent in twain,*[56] and *Truly they behold it afar off, while We behold it nigh,*[57] and *how should you know, perhaps the Hour is nigh.*[58]

The most excellent circumstance for us, then, is to adopt the practice of Qur'ānic study. For we have failed to ponder the meaning of the Book or to look into the copiousness of the descriptions and names of the Day; we do not prepare ourselves to be redeemed from its terrors. Therefore do we seek refuge in God from this heedlessness, and pray that He should encompass us in His abundant mercy.

The Inquisition

AFTER these circumstances, O unfortunate one, you should next meditate upon the questioning' which shall face you orally and without any intermediary. You are to be asked regarding the great and the small, even every jot and tittle. For as you linger in the torment of the Arising with its perspiration and the violence of its great events, there shall descend from the provinces of heaven powerful and harsh Angels, who are mighty and vast in form. They have been ordered to seize the forelocks of the workers of unrighteousness, and to bear them to their place of presentation before the Almighty.

Said the Emissary of God (may God bless him and grant him peace), 'God (Great and Glorious is He!) has an angel between the edges of whose eyes lies a distance of one hundred years' journeying'.[1]

How, then, do you picture yourself at the time when you behold the likes of these angels, who have been sent to take you to the place of presentation, and who, in spite of the magnificence of their frames, are abject before the severity of the Day, having perceived the wrath of the Almighty made manifest towards His bondsmen? Upon their descent, every Prophet, Saint and righteous man shall fall down upon his knees fearing that perhaps it is he that shall be taken. And if such is to be the condition of the devout, how shall be the state of the rebellious and the sinful?

At this moment companies of men hasten forth, urged on by the intensity of their fear, and ask of the Angels, 'Is our Lord among you?' for they are deceived by the splendour of their procession and their fearful appearance. But the Angels are dismayed by their question, knowing their Creator to be exalted far above being present amongst them, and they cry out that their King is far beyond that which terrestrial mankind can imagine. 'Glory be to our Lord!' they say. 'He is not among us, but after us shall He come.'

Now the Angels stand in one array, gazing intently at mankind from every side. On the countenance of each one of them is the sign of humiliation and ignominy, and the aspect of fear and awe before the harshness of the Day. At this point, God (Exalted is He!) brings to pass His word, *And We shall surely question those to whom the Messages were sent, and We shall surely question the Messengers. With knowledge shall We speak to them, and never were We absent,*[2] and also, *And, by your Lord, We shall surely question them all together about that which they used to do.*[3]

He shall commence, glory be to Him, with the Angels,[4] and then the Prophets, *on the Day that God gathers together the Emissaries, saying: What response did you receive? And they say: No knowledge have we; truly You, only You, are the All-Knower of the Unseen.*[5] O, the violence of a Day when the minds of the Prophets themselves are dazed, and when their knowledges are erased by overwhelming dread! '*What response did you receive*', they shall be asked, 'you who were sent out to creation?' Already had they known [the response], but yet their minds are overcome with dismay and consternation, and they know not how to make reply, saying fearfully, '*No knowledge have we; truly You, only You, are the All-Knower of the Unseen*'. In this they only speak the truth, as their hearts leap and as their knowledges are wiped away, until such time as God (Exalted is He!) restores to them their strength.

Then Noah (upon whom be peace) is summoned, and is asked, 'Delivered you your message?' 'Yes,' he replies. Then his people are asked, 'Did a message come to you?' and they reply, 'There came to us no warner.' Then Jesus (upon whom be peace) is brought, and God (Exalted is He!) asks him '*Did you say to people:*

Take me and my mother as two gods besides God?'[6] And he remains writhing under the force of this question for many years. O, the majesty of that Day, when the Prophets themselves are submitted to judgement by questions such as these!

Now the angels advance and give out their summons, one by one: 'So-and-so, the son of So-and-so, make haste to the place of Presentation!' At this, all are seized by fear and trembling, and every mind is thunderstruck. Some groups of men long to be taken directly to Hell so that their foul actions might not be displayed to the Almighty and that the veil might never be lifted before the congregation of mankind.

Before the Inquisition opens, the Light of the Throne becomes manifest, *and the earth shines forth with the light of her Lord,*[7] and the heart of every bondsman knows with full certainty that the Almighty has come to question His bondsmen, and believes that no other man sees Him, and that he alone has been singled out for questioning and none other. Then the Almighty (Sublime and Exalted is He!) says, 'Gabriel! Bring Hell to Us!' Thither he goes, and, finding it raging and furious, says, 'Obey, Hell, the command of your Creator and King!' And the Inferno does not delay in obeying his summons, but flares up and boils, sighing and braying at mankind, who hear its raging and its sighing clearly.

Then there emerge the Guardians of Hell, bounding towards mankind in rage at those who had disobeyed God (Exalted is He!) and who had rebelled against His ordinances. Fix in your mind and heart the state of the hearts of God's bondsmen as they fill with terror and panic, turning in flight or falling down upon their knees: *On that Day thou shalt behold each nation crouching.*[8] Some collapse upon their faces in their distress, while the sinners and the evildoers cry curses and imprecations, and even the Saints and the Righteous[9] shout aloud, 'Myself! Myself!'

While they are in this condition the Inferno moans a second time, and their fear redoubles and their strength falters as they think that they are to be seized. Then it moans a third time and all men fall down prostrate, fearfully raising their eyes *to watch in timidity*[10] and submission. Then the hearts of the wrongdoers are broken, and *hearts choke gullets*,[11] and the minds of the blessed and the damned alike are dazed.

After this, God (Exalted is He!) approaches the Emissaries and demands, '*What response did you receive?*' And when the sinners behold the judgement which is being made of the Prophets their alarm increases. Father flees from son, brother flees from brother, and husband from wife, as each waits for his turn. Then, one by one, they are taken, and God (Exalted is He!) asks each of them with His own voice of his great and minor deeds, of his secret and his public life, and of [the actions of] his every limb and extremity.

Said Abū Hurayra, '[The Companions] once asked, "O Emissary of God! Shall we behold our Lord on the Day of Arising?" And he replied by asking, "Are you obstructed when looking at the sun when it stands at its zenith, unconcealed by any cloud?" "No," they said. "Are you obstructed when looking at the moon when it is full and unconcealed by any cloud?" "No," they said. And he declared, "By Him in Whose hand lies my soul, you shall not be obstructed from the vision of your Lord. He shall confront His bondsman and ask him, 'Did I not honour you and grant you authority and spouses? Did I not submit horses and camels to your command, and give you mastery and dominion?' And the bondsman shall say, 'Yes, indeed.' And He says, 'Did you not reckon that you would meet Me?' and he replies, 'I did not.' 'I shall forget you', says He, 'even as you did forget Me' ".'[12]

So picture yourself, O unfortunate one, with the angels grasping your upper arms as you stand before God (Exalted is He!), as He, speaking with His voice, demands of you, 'Did I not bless you with youth? How did you employ it? Did I not grant you long life? How did you spend it? Did I not bestow wealth upon you? Whence did you come by it, and how did you expend it? Did I not ennoble you with knowledge? How did you act by what you knew?'

How, then, do you imagine that your shame and humiliation shall be, as He enumerates His blessings upon you and your acts of disobedience against Him; His support and your sins? Should you deny them, your very limbs shall bear witness against you.

Said Anas, 'We were once with the Emissary of God (may God bless him and grant him peace) when he laughed, and said, "Know you what has made me laugh?" "God and His Emissary know best," we replied. "The speech of a bondsman to his Lord," he said. "For he shall say, 'O my Lord! Did You not save me from wrongdoing?' and He shall say, 'Yes, I did.' Then he says, 'I shall allow no testimony against myself save that of a witness of mine.' And He declares, '*Sufficient is thy soul this day as witness against thyself*,[13] and the noble Scribes.' Then a seal is set over his mouth and his various parts are commanded to speak, and they tell of his deeds. Then he is allowed to speak once more, and he says to his limbs, 'Away with you! Curse you! I was speaking in your defence!' " '[14]

We seek refuge in God, therefore, from being shamed before the congregation of mankind by the testimony of our own parts. However, God (Exalted is He!) has pledged that He will screen the secrets of the believer so that no other man shall come to know of them. A man once asked Ibn ᶜUmar what he had heard the Emissary of God (may God bless him and grant him peace) say in private. 'The Emissary of God,' he answered, 'may God bless him and grant him peace, used to say, "One of you shall come close to his Lord until He takes him under His protection.[A] He shall say, 'You did such-and-such a thing,' to which he replies, 'Yes.' 'And you did such-and-such a thing,' He says, and he replies, 'Yes.' Then He declares, 'I concealed these things for you in the world, and today I forgive you them'." '[15]

The Emissary of God (may God bless him and grant him peace) has said, 'Whosoever conceals the faults of a believer shall have his own faults concealed by God on the Day of Arising.'[16] From this we know that it is hoped that the bondsman who has faith will conceal the faults of others and tolerate their shortcomings within himself without wagging his tongue and mentioning their faults or speaking of them in their absence in a way

[A] *ḥattā yaḍaᶜ kanafahu ᶜalayh*: the *kanaf* is a man's flank, or side, but may be used metaphorically (Lane, 3004); Nawawī (Sharḥ, xvii. 87) interprets it as meaning in this context 'protection and forgiveness'.

that they would find disagreeable were they to hear it. Such [a commendable practice] is deserving of a corresponding reward at the Arising. Suppose that one had concealed the faults of another; is not the fearful sound of the Summons to the Presentation battering your ears sufficient payment for your sins? You are seized and led by your forelock while your heart pounds and your mind flies about and your limbs and extremities tremble and the colour of your skin changes. Because of the greatness of the terror, the earth around you lies in darkness. Imagine yourself in this situation, stepping over the shoulders of others and passing through the ranks of men, being led like a wild horse, while people raise up their eyes to watch you. Imagine yourself thus in the hands of those to whom you have been entrusted.

At last you reach the Throne of the All-Merciful, and they throw you from their hands. Then God (Sublime and Exalted is He!) calls you with His august speech, saying, 'O son of Adam, draw thou near!' So you approach him with palpitating, fearful and dismayed heart, humble and abject eye and sundered breast, and are given your book, which *leaves nothing small or large without enumerating it.*[17] Then how many evil acts which you had forgotten shall you recall, and how many defective acts of obedience of which you were neglectful shall now stand revealed! How often did you show timidity and faint-heartedness! How many times did you show inability and weakness! O would that I could know with what feet you shall stand up before Him, with what tongue you shall make reply, and with what heart you shall comprehend that which you say!

Then meditate upon how great will be your shame when He reminds you of your sins with His voice, saying, 'O My bondsman! Are you not ashamed before Me? You challenged Me with foulness, but fearing My creatures showed them only beauty. Was I of less account to you than My bondsmen? You attached no importance and paid no attention to My watching over you, yet showed great respect for the scrutiny of others. Did I not grant you My blessings? What distracted you from Me? Did you imagine that I was not watching you, and that you would never meet Me?'

Said the Emissary of God (may God bless him and grant him peace), 'There is not one amongst you but that God, the Lord of the Worlds, shall question him without any veil or intermediary.'[18] And he said (may God bless him and grant him peace), 'Each one of you shall stand before God (Great and Glorious is He!) with no intervening veil. He will ask him, "Did I not grant you of My blessings? Did I not give you wealth?" and he will reply, "Yes, surely." Then He shall say, "Did I not send an Emissary unto you?" and he will reply, "Yes, surely." Then he will look to his right and see only Hell, and then to his left, and see only Hell. So let each of you ward off Hell, even if only with half a date,[A] and if you have none, then with a kindly word.'[19]

Said Ibn Masᶜūd, 'There is not one among you that shall not be alone with God (Great and Glorious is He!) just as one of you is alone with the moon on the night when it is full. "O son of Adam!" He shall say. "What beguiled you with respect to Me? O son of Adam! To what use did you put your knowledge? O son of Adam! What was your response to the Messengers? O son of Adam! Did I not stand watch over your eyes while you looked at what was forbidden you? Did I not stand watch over your ears?" Thus shall He continue until He has enumerated the remainder of his organs and limbs.'

Said Mujāhid, 'The feet of God's bondsman shall not move from His presence (Great and Glorious is He!) on the Day of Arising until he has been questioned regarding four things: his lifespan, and how he spent it; his works, and how he acted; his body, and how he employed it; and his wealth, whence he came by it and how he expended it.'

Therefore, O unfortunate one, stand in awe of the shameful and perilous condition in which you shall find yourself at that time. For if you are to be told, 'I concealed these things for you in the world, and today I forgive you them', then great will be your rapture and your joy, and you shall be the envy of the first and the last. But should the angels be told, 'Take this bondsman of evil, *and fetter him; then into hellfire cast him*,'[20] then were the very

[A] As charity.

heavens and the earth to weep it would not be out of proportion to the enormity of your misfortune and the intensity of your regret at having neglected the obedience of God, and at having sold your Afterlife for the sake of this base and inferior world which never endured with you.

The Scales

NEXT, be not heedless of the Scales. Think upon the flying of the Books to their left and right sides. For after the Inquisition mankind shall be in three parties.

One party will be composed of those who have not a single good deed to their credit. In their case there shall emerge from Hell a black creature,[A] which shall snatch them as a bird pecks at grain, and grasp them and pitch them into Hell, which engulfs them. A voice calls out to them, 'Sorrow, never to be followed by any joy!'

Another party is composed of those with not a single transgression to their discredit. A voice calls out, saying, 'Let those who did praise God abundantly in every state arise!' and they stand up and hasten to Heaven. Then this is done with regard to the people who used to stand in the night vigil, and then with those whom no worldly *commerce or sale*[1] distracted from the remembrance of God (Exalted is He!). A voice calls out to them, saying, 'Joy, never to be followed by any sorrow!'

But a third party, which constitutes the greater part of mankind, still remains. They have mingled good works with ill,

[A] *ʿunuq aswad.* Referring to the Tradition from which this phrase is directly derived (Tirmidhī, Jahannam, 1) Lane translates *ʿunuq* as 'a portion' (Lane, 2175), but this does not seem to make good sense in the present context; it seems better to opt for the meaning given by the *qāḍī* Abū Bakr ibn al-ʿArabī, who, in his commentary on the *Ṣaḥīḥ* of Tirmidhī, understands it to signify something 'possessed of two eyes, two ears and a tongue' (*dhāt ʿaynayn wa-udhunayn wa-lisān*) (*ʿĀriḍat al-aḥwadhī*, x. 44).

and although it may not be plain to them, it is plain to God (Exalted is He!) which of them are those whose good or evil deeds predominate. God, however, demurs from not giving them to know of this, that He may manifest His generosity in pardon, and His equity in chastisement.

So the books and scrolls which contain the good and evil deeds fly up, and the Scales are erected, and all eyes are upturned towards the books: shall they fall into the left scale or the right? Then they look to the Scales themselves: shall they tip in favour of the evil actions or in favour of the good? This state is fearsome indeed, and dazes the minds of all creatures.

Al-Ḥasan relates that the Emissary of God (may God bless him and grant him peace) once had his head in ᶜĀ'isha's lap (may God be pleased with her), and fell asleep. She remembered the Afterlife, so that she wept, shedding tears that dropped onto the cheek of God's Emissary (may God bless him and grant him peace), who awoke. 'What has made you weep, ᶜĀ'isha?' he asked, and she said, 'I recalled the Afterlife: shall you remember your family on the Day of Arising?' And he replied, 'By Him in Whose hand lies my soul, there shall be three places in which a man shall remember no-one but himself: when the Scales are erected and actions are weighed, so that the son of Adam shall watch to see if his balance shall be heavy or light; and at [the Assessment of] the Scrolls, so that he watches to see if he is to receive his book in his right hand or in his left; and at the Traverse.'[2]

Said Anas, 'Each descendant of Adam will be brought on the Day of Arising and made to stand before the two sides of the Scales, to which an angel has been assigned. Should his balance be heavy, the Angel will call out in a voice heard by all creatures, "So-and-so is joyful, so that he shall never be sorrowful again!" However, if his balance should be light, then he will call out in a voice heard by all creatures, "So-and-so is sorrowful, so that he shall never be joyful again!" And when the scale containing the good deeds is light the Guardians of Hell [*al-zabāniya*] approach bearing *hooked rods of iron*,[3] and attired in garments of fire, and take Hell's lot to Hell.'

Said God's Emissary (may God bless him and grant him peace), regarding the Day of Arising, 'It is the Day on which God (Exalted is He!) shall summon Adam (upon whom be peace) and say to him, "O Adam, arise, and call forth the company of Hell!" And he shall ask, "And how many are the company of Hell?" "From each thousand, nine hundred and ninety-nine," He replies.' When the Companions heard this they were downcast, not one of them smiling. But when the Emissary of God (may God bless him and grant him peace) saw what had befallen them he said, 'Work, and rejoice; for by Him in Whose hand lies the soul of Muḥammad, there shall be with you two creatures who are never present with anyone without multiplying the proportion of those of the sons of Adam and the sons of the devil who shall be destroyed.' 'And who are those two?' they asked. 'Gog and Magog,'[A] he replied. Then he left them, saying, 'Work, and rejoice; for by Him in Whose hand lies the soul of Muḥammad, you shall be among mankind on the Day of Arising no more than such as is the cauterisation mark on the camel's flank, or the mark which is upon the withers of the riding beast.'[B] [1]

[A] Mentioned briefly in the Qur'ān (XVIII:94; XXI:96), Jūj and Ma'jūj are generally understood to be a numerous race of men said to dwell somewhere in Central Asia, the appearance of which, accompanied by great slaughter, is to be one of the signs of the Apocalypse. (Cf. A.J. Wensinck, art. "Yā<u>dj</u>ū<u>dj</u> wa-Mā<u>dj</u>ū<u>dj</u>" in *SEI*, 637; Ibn Ka<u>th</u>īr, *Bidāya*, II. 109-112.)

[B] i.e., a tiny proportion.

The Adversaries, and the Restoration of Wrongs

YOU HAVE come to know the fearsome and perilous nature of the Scales, and of how eyes will be turned upwards to their tongue. Then, *as for him whose scales are heavy; he will live a pleasant life. But as for him whose scales are light; his mother is the Abyss. And what will convey to you what she is? Raging fire.*[1] Know that none shall escape the peril which is the Scales save the man that called himself to account in this world, and weighed up his deeds, statements, ideas and hours in the scales of the Law, as ᶜUmar (may God be pleased with him) said, 'Call yourselves to account before you yourselves are called to account; weigh yourselves up before you yourselves are weighed up'. A man's weighing of himself can only consist in his sincerely repenting of every sin before he dies, and in remedying his inadequacy in discharging his obligations towards God, and in righting the wrongs [that he has committed] grain by grain, and in reconciling himself with all those who were injured by his tongue, his hands, and the bad opinions which he harboured within his breast. He should set their hearts at rest so that when he dies not a single injustice or obligation will remain to his discredit. Such a man will enter Heaven without reckoning. If, however, he should perish before making reparations for his iniquities his adversaries shall surround him, seizing him by the hand, the forelock or the throat, while one of them says, 'You wronged me!' and another, 'You insulted me!' and yet another, 'You mocked me!' and another, 'You mentioned me to my discredit in my absence!' and another, 'You were my neighbour, but treated me badly!' and another, 'You had dealings with me, but cheated me!' and another, 'You sold something to me, but defrauded me, and concealed from me the defects of your merchandise!' and another says, 'You lied regarding the value of your goods!' and another, 'You saw that I was in need, and you were rich, yet did not feed me!' and still another, 'You saw me wronged, and were able to put an end to that wrong, but instead you humoured my persecutor and failed to protect me!'

While you are in this state, and while your adversaries cling to you with their claws and hold on to you by the scruff of your neck, while you are dumbfounded and bewildered by their multitude (for there shall be no-one with whom you had a dirham's worth of dealings during your lifetime, or with whom you sat but once, against whom you did not commit some injury, whether by backbiting or treachery, or a contemptuous glance, while they were too weak to oppose you); at this time you strain your head upwards towards your Lord and Master, that perhaps He may deliver you from their hands. Then your ears are assailed by the call of the Almighty (majestic is His glory!): *Today each soul is requited for that which it acquired. No injustice is there this Day.*[2] Then your heart is divested of all dignity as you tell yourself that your doom is inevitable, and recall that of which God (Exalted is He!) warned you on the tongue of His Emissary, when He said, *Consider not that God is heedless of that which the wrongdoers commit. He only gives them respite until a Day on which eyes shall stare, as they come hurrying on in fear, their heads upraised, their gaze returning not to them, and their hearts as air. So give warning to mankind!*[3]

How great is your pleasure today, as you suck dry people's reputations, and as you appropriate their wealth, but how intense will be your lamentation on that Day when your Lord shall stand upon the carpet of justice, and when you shall be made to speak on your own behalf, even though you shall be bankrupt, indigent, helpless and abased, unable to restore any right or to come forward with any justification. Then your good deeds, for the sake of which you had exhausted yourself in this life, shall be taken from you and made over to your adversaries as a compensation for their rights [which you had abused].

Said Abū Hurayra, 'The Emissary of God (may God bless him and grant him peace) once said, "Do you know who is the bankrupt?" And we replied, "The bankrupt among us, O Emissary of God, is he that has neither dirham nor dinar[4] to his name, nor any property." But he said, "The bankrupt of my nation is he that shall come forward on the Day of Arising with the Prayer, the Fast and the Tithe, but having insulted this man, and abused that man, and having consumed another's wealth, and shed another's blood, and struck yet another. Each one of these shall be given a portion of his good works, and should these be exhausted before his obligation is discharged, then he shall be assigned some of their sins, which will be heaped upon him. Then he shall be cast into Hell." '[5]

See, therefore, how your misfortune shall be on that Day, since you have not one good work that is free from the vice of eyeservice and the subterfuges of the devil. Should, over every lengthy period, you gain one sound good deed, then your adversaries will make haste to seize it. Perhaps if you were to call yourself to account while you persevered in fasting during the day and praying at night you might come to know that not a single day passes without there falling from your tongue some slander against a Muslim which cancels out the entirety of your good deeds; what, then, of your remaining sins, such as consuming what is unlawful or doubtful; and what of the insufficiency of your virtues? How may you hope to escape from your iniquities on a Day when the very hornless sheep shall exact retribution from the sheep that had horns?

Abū Dharr has related that God's Emissary (may God bless him and grant him peace) once beheld two sheep butting one another. 'O Abū Dharr!' he said. 'Do you know over what thing they butt each other?' 'No,' I replied. 'Yet God knows', he said, 'and shall judge between them on the Day of Arising.'[6]

Said Abū Hurayra [commenting upon] His word (Great and Glorious is He!), *And no beast is there upon the earth, neither any bird which flies on its two wings, but that they are nations like unto yourselves:*[A] [7] 'On the Day of Arising, all of creation will be gathered together: the cattle, the riding-beasts, the birds, and every other thing, and it shall be by God's justice[8] (Exalted is He!) that He takes the hornless sheep's case against the horned one.

[A] The verse continues: *We have neglected nothing in the Book. Then unto their Lord shall they be gathered.*

Then He shall say, "Be dust!" which is the time at which the unbeliever says, "*Would that I were dust!*"[A]

So how shall you fare, O unfortunate one, on the Day when you shall behold your scroll empty of those good deeds over which you tired yourself at such length, and ask, 'Where are my good deeds?' to be told, 'They have been transferred to the scrolls of your adversaries'. And you shall behold your scroll all filled with sins which you had long persevered in avoiding, and which you had expended much effort in abstaining from, and you shall say, 'O Lord! These are sins I never once committed!' to be told, 'They are the sins of the people you slandered and insulted, and to whom you intended harm, and wronged when selling, or in neighbourliness, or when holding conversation or an argument, or when you mentioned them, or while you studied, or through any other kind of relation with them.'

Said Ibn Masᶜūd, 'The Emissary of God (may God bless him and grant him peace) said, "The devil has despaired of images ever being worshipped in the land of the Arabs, but he shall be satisfied with you if you commit that which is less heinous: the degrading faults [*al-muḥaqqirāt*], which are the mortal sins [*al-mūbiqāt*]. Therefore avoid injustice as much as you are able, for truly, on the Day of Arising a bondsman shall come with righteous deeds like unto the mountains, believing that they shall save him, but bondsman after bondsman shall come forward, saying, 'O Lord! So-and-so dealt with me unjustly,' and He shall say, 'Erase some of his good deeds!'; and thus shall the matter proceed until none of his good deeds remain. This is akin to a group of travellers who rest in a desert place. Having no firewood, they scatter to look for some, and before long they have made a great fire, and prepare whatever they wish. Thus it shall be with sins".'[9]

[A] Q. LXXVIII:40. This vision of the judgement and subsequent extinction of the animals is part of orthodox doctrine. According to certain Muᶜtazilites, however, gentle and pleasing creatures shall join the faithful in Heaven, while the harmful ones shall be consigned to Hell. The Muᶜtazilite theologian al-Naẓẓām is said to have taught that all animals would enter Heaven, to which eccentricity al-Baghdādī characteristically retorts that 'He is very welcome to a heaven which contains pigs, dogs and snakes'. (*Uṣūl*, 236.)

When His word *Truly you will die, and they will die, then on the Day of Arising before your Lord shall you dispute*[10] was revealed, al-Zubayr asked, 'O Emissary of God! Shall the worst sins which passed between us in the world return to us?' 'Yes,' he replied. 'They shall certainly return to you, until you return to everyone who has a right that which he deserves'. And al-Zubayr said, 'By God, the matter is hard!'[11]

Therefore be in awe of the violence of a Day on which not one footstep will be ignored, nor yet a single blow or word disregarded, in order that the victims of injustice might wreak vengeance upon those that did them wrong. Said Anas, 'I once heard God's Emissary (may God bless him and grant him peace) say, "God shall gather together His bondsmen, who shall be naked, dusty and *buhm*[A]". We asked, "What does *buhm* mean?" and he answered, "That they have nothing with them. Then their Lord (Exalted is He!) shall address them with a voice heard from afar just as it is heard from nearby, saying, 'I am the King! I am the Reckoner! It is not proper for any of Heaven's people, when any one of the people of Hell has been wronged by him, that he should take his place in Heaven until the latter has exacted retribution from him; neither is it right that any of Hell's people should enter Hell when he has a grievance against any of Heaven's people until he has exacted retribution from him, even for no more than a slap.' " And we said, "How shall that be, when we have come to God (Great and Glorious is He!) naked, dusty and *buhm*?" and he replied, "With good and evil works".'[12]

Thus fear God, O bondsmen of God, and beware of committing any injustices against His bondsmen by seizing their property, impugning their reputations, injuring their feelings or dealing with them in an ill-mannered fashion. Forgiveness is most swiftly granted through that which is purely between a bondsman and his Lord. As for the man who has accumulated many wrongs but then turns from them in repentance, and for whom it would be difficult to make amends to all those he had wronged, let him store up an abundance of good works for the Day of

[A] The most obvious sense of this word (here a plural of *bahīm*) in this context is 'without physical defect'; thus is it interpreted in Lane, s.v.

Retaliation, and let him, with perfect sincerity, keep certain of his good works a secret between him and God, so that none shall come to know of them but Him. It may be that this will bring him closer to God (Exalted is He!) so that he thereby wins that grace which He has stored up for His loved ones, who are the believers, that the wrongs which His bondsmen have incurred might thereby be turned aside.

It is as Anas related of God's Emissary (may God bless him and grant him peace): 'While the Emissary of God (may God bless him and grant him peace) was seated once, we saw him laugh so heartily that his eye-teeth were visible. "What has made you laugh, O Emissary of God," asked ʿUmar, "may my father and my mother be your ransom?" And he replied, "I laugh because of two men from my nation, who shall kneel in the presence of the Lord of Power. One of them says, 'O my Lord, grant me retaliation for the wrong [for which I am owed recompense] from my brother,' and God (Exalted is He!) says, 'Give your brother that in which he was wronged.' 'O Lord,' he replies, 'None of my righteous works remain.' Then God (Exalted is He!) says to the man that made the demand, 'What shall you do with your brother,[13] seeing that none of his righteous works remain?' And he replies, 'O my Lord! Let him bear some of my burden in my stead.' " And the Emissary of God (may God bless him and grant him peace) wept, as he said, "Truly, that shall be a mighty Day, a Day when men have need of others to bear their burdens!" Then he [continued, and] said, "And God says to the one who made the request, 'Lift up your head, and look to the Gardens!' This he does, and he says, 'O my Lord! I behold lofty cities of silver, and golden palaces wreathed about with pearls. For which Prophet shall they be, or for which Saint or Martyr?' And He says, 'They belong to whomsoever pays me their price.' 'O my Lord!' he says, 'And who possesses their price?' 'You possess it,' He replies. 'And what might it be?' he asks, and He says, 'Your forgiveness of your brother.' 'O my Lord!' he says, 'I have forgiven him!' Then God (Exalted is He!) says, 'Take your brother's hand and bring him into Heaven.' " Then God's Emissary (may God bless him and grant him peace) said, "*Fear*

God, and make reconciliation amongst yourselves,[14] for God reconciles the believers with one another".'[15]

This [preceding Tradition] is an indication that such a state may only be obtained through 'emulating the ethics of God,'[A] which means reconciliation between men, and the other [divine] proprieties.

Now contemplate your own case: should your scroll be void of injustices, or should God show you His grace by pardoning you so that you become certain of eternal joy, then how abundant will be your happiness upon taking leave of the place of Judgement when the noble robe of God's good-pleasure is conferred upon you and you are promised such felicity as will never be followed by any woe, and pleasure such as will never be assailed on any side by extinction. At this, your heart will fly from happiness and joy, and your face will become radiant until it gleams and shines like the full moon. Imagine how you shall stride proudly in front of creation, head held high, your back free of any burden, with the joyful expression of pleasure and the coolness of satisfaction sparkling from your brow, as the creatures of the former and later generations behold you and your condition, envying you your beauty and your fairness. The Angels are marching before and behind you, crying out over the heads of all present, 'Behold So-and-so, the son of So-and-so! God is well pleased with him, and has made him pleased. His is felicity such as will never be followed by any woe!'

Do you believe that this rank shall be less glorious than the degree you have attained in this world in the hearts of men through hypocrisy, flattery, dissimulation and eyeservice? If you realise indeed that it is better, or rather that between the two there exists no comparison at all, then work to attain this degree though pure sincerity and an honest intention in your dealings with God, for you shall never attain it save in this way. But if (and we seek refuge in God from such a thing!) the matter should be otherwise, and should there proceed from your scroll a crime *which you deemed trivial but which in God's sight is grave,*[16] then you

[A] *al-takhalluq bi-akhlāq Allāh*; i.e. emulating 'those ethics which it is proper for man to emulate' (Sharnūbī, p.3).

shall be made hateful for that reason, and He shall say, 'My curse rests upon you, O bondsman of evil! I do not accept your worship.' No sooner have you heard this call when your face is blackened, and the Angels become wrathful because of the wrath of God (Exalted is He!), and say, 'And upon you rests our curse also, and the curse of all creation!' At this, the Angels of Hell swarm around you, wrathful because of the wrath of their Creator, and draw near to you, with all their uncouthness, viciousness, and loathsome aspect, and seize you by the forelock and drag you along on your face before the concourse of mankind, who behold the blackness of your face and the prospect of your degradation, while you call out, wailing and screaming. '*Do not call today one lament,*' they say to you, '*rather call many laments!*'[17] The angels cry out, saying, 'Here is So-and-so, son of So-and-so. God has disclosed his disgraceful and degrading acts, and has cursed him for his foul transgressions, so that his shall be suffering such as will never be followed by any joy.'

This might be the result of some sin you had committed from fear of God's bondsmen, or out of desire for some status in their eyes, or from fear of being disgraced before them. How great, therefore, is your ignorance, that you should flee from humiliation before a small company of God's bondsmen in this passing world, but do not fear the great disgrace before the mighty throng, and exposure to the wrath and painful chastisement of God, and to being driven by the Angels of Hell to the very centre of the Blaze. Such are your circumstances, although you are yet unaware of the still greater peril, which is that of the Traverse.

The Traverse

THEN, O unfortunate one,[1] after these terrors, think upon the statement of God (Exalted is He!): *On the Day when We shall gather up the Godfearing to the All-Merciful in throngs, and drive the evildoers to the Inferno in a mass,*[2] and His statement (Exalted is

He!): *Guide them to the Traverse of the Blaze. And stay them, for they shall be questioned.*[3] Mankind, after the terrors [mentioned previously], shall be driven to the Traverse, which is a bridge stretched over the gulf of Hell, sharper than a sword and thinner than a hair. Whosoever has in the world kept upright upon the Straight Path [*al-ṣirāṭ al-mustaqīm*] shall bear lightly upon the Traverse [*ṣirāṭ*] of the Afterlife, and will be saved. But whosoever deviates from uprightness in this world, and weighs down his back with burdens, and disobeys his Lord, shall slip upon taking his first step on the Traverse, and shall go to perdition.

Now meditate upon the terror which shall alight upon your heart at the time when you behold the Traverse and its slenderness, and when your eye then falls upon the core of the Inferno beneath you as your ears are assailed by the moaning and raging of Hell.

You are obliged to walk over this Traverse, despite your weak condition, your palpitating heart, your quaking feet and the burdens which lie so heavily upon your back that you would be incapable of walking upon the flat earth, let alone the sharpness of the Traverse. How shall you fare, then, when you have set one of your feet upon it and felt its sharpness, and are compelled to lift your other foot up, while all the time people before you are staggering and slipping off, to be caught by the Angels of Hell with hooks and grapples. You shall watch them toppling over and falling head first towards Hell, with their feet uppermost.

O, how foul is that scene, how difficult that slope, and how narrow that crossing-place! Look to how your condition shall be when you crawl and ascend upon it, weighed down by the burdens which lie upon your back, glancing to your right and left at other men as they tumble into Hell. And the Emissary (upon him be peace) shall be saying, 'O Lord! Deliver! Deliver!' while shrieks of woe and suffering rise up from the bottom of the Inferno (for many there are who have already slipped from the Traverse). How, then, shall you fare, when your own foot slips, and your contrition avails you not, and you cry in woe and sorrow, saying, 'This is what I used to fear! *Would that I had sent before me something for my own life!*[4] *Would that I had taken a path with the Emissary! Woe is me! Would that I had never taken So-and-so as a friend!*[5] *Would that I were dust!*[6] *Would that I were forgotten, forgetting!*[7] Would that my mother had never begotten me!'

Then the fires catch you (and may God protect us!) and the Herald cries out, '*Fall back therein, and speak not!*'[8] and there is nothing to do but to scream, groan, draw breath, and shout for help.

How do you view your thinking now, when these perils are in front of you? Should you not believe in this, then how prolonged will be your abiding with the unbelievers in the Inferno's depths! Should you believe in it, however, but be heedless thereof and of making preparations for it, out of indifference, then how much have you lost, and how great is your sin! Of what use to you is your faith if it does not spur you on to the diligent quest for the satisfaction of God (Exalted is He!) through obedience to Him, and to abandoning acts of rebellion against Him. Were there to lie before you no terror save that of the Traverse alone, and the dismay felt by your heart at the peril of crossing it, then even should you receive deliverance it would provide such horror, fear and panic as would always suffice you.

Said the Emissary of God (may God bless him and grant him peace), 'The Traverse shall be set up between the two edges of the Inferno. Of all the Emissaries that cross with their nations, I shall be the first. That Day none shall speak save the Prophets, whose prayer shall be, "O Lord God, deliver! O Lord God, deliver!" And in the Inferno lie hooks which resemble the thorns of the *saᶜdān* bush[A]. Have you ever seen the thorns of the *saᶜdān* bush?' 'Yes, O Emissary of God,' they replied. 'They are like the thorns of the *saᶜdān* bush,' he said, 'except that their great size is known only to God (Exalted is He!). They snatch at men through their works, whereby some perish, while others are lacerated but escape.'[9]

Said Abū Saᶜīd al-Khudrī, 'The Emissary of God (may God bless him and grant him peace) once said, "Mankind shall pass over the Inferno's Traverse, upon which are thorns, hooks and

[A] A desert shrub with a head of prickles which, when shed, may wound the foot of one who treads upon them. (Lane, 1362.)

grapples, which snatch at them from left and right. On either side are the Angels, who say, 'O Lord God, deliver! O Lord God, deliver!' There are some among mankind who shall cross like a shaft of lightning; others shall pass over like the wind, others like horses at a gallop, others shall run, still others walk, while others crawl on their hands and knees or creep along on their bellies. As regards the people of Hell, those who are deserving of it; they neither live nor die. Some men will be taken on account of their sins and transgressions, and shall burn until they turn to charcoal, at which time Intercession for them shall become permitted".' [And he continued] to the end of the Tradition.[10]

According to Ibn Masᶜūd (may God be pleased with him), [the Prophet] (may God bless him and grant him peace) said, '*God shall gather together the first and the last to the tryst of a known Day:*[11] They shall stand for forty years with eyes raised up to heaven, awaiting the definitive Judgement.' He continued with the Tradition until he mentioned the time when the Faithful shall prostrate, and then said, 'Then He shall say to the Faithful: "Raise up your heads!" This they do, and He vouchsafes them a light in proportion to their works. Some will be given light like a great mountain which coruscates before them. Others are given a lesser light: some receive it in the quantity of a date-palm, while others are given still less, until the last one of them will be a man given light only upon his big toe, which is sometimes illumined and sometimes extinguished. When it is lit, he puts his foot forwards and walks, but when it is in darkness he halts.' Then he mentioned the passage over the Traverse, which shall be in proportion to the light which men have received. Some shall cross in the twinkling of an eye, others like lightning, others like clouds, others like shooting stars, others like a swift stallion, others shall walk rapidly, until he who has been given light upon his big toe shall cross, crawling on his face, his hands and his feet, pushing one hand forward and holding on with the other, clinging with one foot and dragging the other, while Hell assails his flanks. Thus will he progress until he is finished, and when he has done he shall stand up over it and say, 'Praised be God! He has granted me something never given to anyone else, for He has delivered me from Hell after I had beheld it!' Then he shall be taken to a pool at the Gate of Heaven, where he bathes.'[12]

Said Anas ibn Mālik, 'I once heard the Emissary of God (may God bless him and grant him peace) say, "The Traverse is like a sword blade," (or "as sharp as an hair"). "The Angels shall save the believers, both men and women, and Gabriel (upon him be peace) will hold onto me while I say, 'O my Lord! Deliver! Deliver!' Many are the men and women who shall stumble on that Day." '[13]

Such are the terrifying and awesome matters which relate to the Traverse. Let your thoughts dwell at length upon them, for truly, the man who is safest from the terrors of the Day of Arising is he who contemplated them most abundantly in this world. For God never conjoins two fears in His bondsman: whoso fears these terrors in this world shall be safe from them in the next. By 'fear' I do not mean a sensitivity [*riqqa*] like that of women, whereby one's eyes gush tears and one's heart becomes softened upon hearing something, but which is followed only by swift forgetfulness and a resumption of one's indulgence and frivolity, which is not fear at all. Rather, when one has conceived a fear of something one will flee from it, and when one hopes for something one will seek it out. Thus you shall be saved only by a fear which prevents you from disobeying God (Exalted is He!) and which spurs you on towards His obedience.

Of yet less value than the sensitivity of women is the fear harboured by fools, who, upon hearing of these terrors quickly seek refuge in God with their tongues, saying, 'I beseech God for aid! We seek refuge in Him! O Lord God! Deliver! Deliver!' while persisting nonetheless in sins which will be the instruments of their destruction. Satan laughs at their seeking refuge thus with God, just as he might laugh at a man pursued by a dangerous carnivore in the desert, when before him lies a castle and who says, when he beholds from afar the animal's fangs and its savagery, 'I seek refuge in this impregnable castle, and implore the aid of its mighty structure and firm walls!' But he says this with his tongue while sitting quite still; how, then, might this avail him against the beast? The terrors of the Afterlife are similar;

and there is no castle save the sincere declaration that 'there is no deity save God.' Such sincerity means that one should have no goal or object of worship save God (Exalted is He!). The *one who takes his passions to be his god*[14] is far indeed from being sincere in his profession of God's unity, and his condition has exposed his soul to grave peril.

If, however, you are unable to achieve this at all, then harbour love for God's Emissary (may God bless him and grant him peace) and be zealous to honour his Precedent, and long to respect the hearts of the righteous men of his nation, seeking blessings from their supplications. For it may be that you shall thereby be benefited by his, or their, intercession, and gain salvation thereby if your trading-goods are few.

The Intercession

KNOW THAT when certain of the Faithful enter Hell deservedly, God (Exalted is He!) shall through His grace accept the Intercession made on their behalf by the Prophets, the Saints, the Divines and the Righteous. In addition, all those with some standing before God (Exalted is He!) and a goodly relation with Him shall enjoy a right of Intercession on behalf of their families, kinsmen, friends and acquaintances. Be zealous, therefore, of acquiring for yourself the rank which will permit you thus to intercede for them. It is achieved by never despising any human creature, for God (Exalted is He!) has hidden sainthood among His bondsmen, and it may well be that the man your eye scorns is one of His Saints. Likewise, never underestimate any transgression, for God (Exalted is He!) has concealed His wrath among the sins which may be committed against Him, and it may well be that the sin which you now commit entails His anger. And never belittle any act of obedience, for God (Exalted is He!) has hidden His satisfaction among acts of obedience to Him; thus it may be that even if it should constitute no more than a kind word, or a morsel of food, or a good intention, or anything of this nature, that such an act will entail His satisfaction.

Textual proofs of the Intercession in the Qur'ān and the Traditions are legion. God (Exalted is He!) has said, *Your Lord shall surely give to you, and you shall be satisfied.*[A] [1]

ᶜAmr ibn al-ᶜĀṣ related that God's Emissary (may God bless him and grant him peace) once recited the saying of Abraham (upon whom be peace): *'O my Lord, truly they have misled many of the people; but whoso follows me, he is of me, and whoso disobeys me, still You are All-Forgiving, All-Merciful'*,[2] and the saying of Jesus (upon whom be peace): *'If You chastise them, truly they are Your bondsmen.'*[3] Then he lifted up his head and said, 'My nation! O my nation!' and wept. And God (Great and Glorious is He!) said, 'O Gabriel! Go hence to Muḥammad, and ask him what has made him weep'. Thus he came to him, and asked him, and [the Prophet] informed him (although He had known better than he). Then He said, 'O Gabriel! Go [again] to Muḥammad, and tell him that I shall grant him satisfaction regarding his nation, and not wrong him.'[4]

And he said (may God bless him and grant him peace), 'I have been vouchsafed five things which were never granted to anyone before me: I am given victory through fear a month's journey around; war spoils are made lawful to me, although they were not lawful to anyone before me; the whole earth has been made a mosque for me, and its earth made pure, so that any man of my nation who is due to perform the Prayer may do so; and I am given the Intercession; and, while each Prophet [before me] was sent to his own people alone, I am sent to the entirety of mankind.'[5]

And he said (may God bless him and grant him peace), 'On the Day of Arising I shall lead the Prophets in prayer, and shall preach

[A] This verse is sometimes interpreted as a reference to the Intercession: cf. e.g. Bayhaqī, *Iᶜtiqād*, 125.

to them, and shall be the Exerciser of the Intercession; and I do not boast'.[6]

And he said (may God bless him and grant him peace), 'I am the lord of Adam's descendants, and I do not boast. I am the first around whom the earth shall split asunder. I am the first Intercessor. I am the first to be given Intercession. The banner of praise shall lie in my hand[A]; behind it shall be Adam, and then those who came after him.'[7]

And he said (may God bless him and grant him peace), 'Every Prophet has a prayer which must be granted, and it is my wish that I should conceal this prayer and make of it an Intercession for my nation on the Day of Arising.'[8]

Said Ibn ʿAbbās, 'The Emissary of God (may God bless him and grant him peace) once said, "Pulpits of gold shall be erected for the Prophets, who shall sit upon them. But my pulpit shall remain empty, for I shall be standing before my Lord, fearful that He might send me to Heaven while my nation remains behind. I shall say, 'O my Lord! My nation! My nation!' and God (Great and Glorious is He!) shall say, 'O Muḥammad! What would you have me do with your nation?' 'O my Lord!' I reply, 'Make brief their reckoning!' And thus shall I continue to intercede until I am given to release men who have already been sent to Hell, so that Mālik, the guardian of Hell, shall say, 'O Muḥammad! I have not left any remnant of your nation to the wrath of your Lord!' " '[9]

And he said (may God bless him and grant him peace), 'On the Day of Arising I shall intercede for the greater part of what is on the face of the earth, including both desert and town.'[10]

Said Abū Hurayra, 'Some meat was once brought to the Emissary of God (may God bless him and grant him peace). The leg being pleasing to him, he stretched out his hand towards it and took a bite. Then he said, "On the Day of Arising I shall be the Lord of the Messengers. Do you know how that shall be? God shall gather together the first and the last on a single plain, while

[A] Certain early descriptions of the Day of Judgement represent each Prophet as holding a banner (*liwāʾ*): that of Joseph, patron of chaste youths, is green; Noah, patron of those who feared God, bears a multicoloured banner, and so forth. (Cf. *Escatología*, 133n; Schimmel, 86.)

they are made to hear the Herald and are keenly scrutinised, as the sun draws near so that people suffer more misery and pain than they can support or bear, and they say one to another, 'Do you not behold our plight? Will you not look to see who might intercede for you with your Lord?' And someone will say, 'Go to Adam, upon him be peace.' Thus they make their way to him and say, 'You are the father of mankind; God created you with His hand, and blew into you *something of His spirit,*[11] and did command the Angels to fall down before you in prostration.[12] Intercede for us with your Lord! Do you not behold our predicament and plight?' But Adam (upon him be peace) replies to them, saying, 'Truly, my Lord is wrathful today as He has never been before, and as He will never be again.[13] He forbade me the Tree,[14] but I disobeyed Him. Myself! Myself! Go to another! Go to Noah!'

'"And thus they make their way to Noah (upon whom be peace). 'O Noah!' they say. 'You were the first Emissary to the people of the earth. God has called you *a thankful bondsman.*[15] Intercede for us with your Lord! Do you not behold our plight?' But he says, 'Truly, my Lord is wrathful today as He has never been before, and as He will never be again.[16] I used to have a prayer [for which an answer was guaranteed] but I used it against my people.[A] Myself! Myself! Go to Abraham, God's Friend!'

'"And thus they make their way to Abraham, the Friend of God (upon whom be peace) and say, 'You are God's Prophet, and His Friend from amongst all the people of the earth. Intercede for us with your Lord! Do you not behold our plight?' But he says to them, 'Truly, my Lord is wrathful today as He has never been before, and as He will never be again. I told three lies,' (and he named them). 'Myself! Myself! Go to another! Go to Moses!'

'"And thus they make their way to Moses (upon whom be peace) and say, 'O Moses! You are God's Emissary; He honoured you with the bearing of His message and speech to mankind! Intercede for us with your Lord! Do you not behold our plight?' But he says, 'Truly, my Lord is wrathful today as He has never been

[A] Noah having prayed, '*My Lord! Leave not one of the unbelievers in the land!*' (Q. LXXI:26).

been before, and as He will never be again. I once killed a man I had not been commanded to kill.[A] Myself! Myself! Go to another! Go to Jesus (upon him be peace!)'

' "And so they make their way to Jesus and say, 'O Jesus! You are *God's Emissary and His word, which He did convey unto Mary, and a spirit from Him.*[17] You spoke to people from your cradle.[B] Intercede for us with your Lord! Do you not behold our plight?' But Jesus says, 'Truly my Lord is wrathful today as He has never been before, and shall never be again.' (but he mentioned no sin).[18] 'Myself! Myself! Go to another![19] Go to Muḥammad (may God bless him and grant him peace)!'

' "So they come to me, and say, 'O Muḥammad! You are the Emissary of God and the *Seal of the Prophets.*[20] God has forgiven you *your former and forthcoming sins.*[21] Intercede for us with your Lord! Do you not behold our plight?' And so I set off, and go before the Throne, and fall down in prostration before my Lord. Then God inspires in me such praises and great glorification of Him as were never inspired in anyone before me, and it is said, 'O Muḥammad! Lift up your head! Ask, and you will be answered; plead for intercession, and it will be granted you.' So I raise my head, and say, 'My nation! My nation, O Lord!' And I am told, 'O Muḥammad! Bring in those of your nation for whom there need be no reckoning by the right-hand Gate of Heaven! The remaining Gates shall be for the others.' "

'Then he said, "By Him in Whose hand lies my soul, there lies between two door-jambs of the Gates of Heaven a distance greater than that which is between Mecca and Hajar[C],[22] and that which separates Mecca and Bostra." '[23]

The same text is contained in another Tradition, but with the additional mention of the transgressions of Abraham, which were his saying, '*This is my Lord*'[24] of the travelling star, his saying, '*Rather, it was this, the bigger of them, that did it,*'[25] of the gods, and his saying, '*Truly, I am unwell*'.[26]

[A] Before his flight from Egypt. Cf. Q. xxviii:15.

[B] One of the miracles attributed to Jesus in the Qur'ān (Q. xix:29–30).

[C] A complex of oases in eastern Arabia (modern al-Ḥaṣā).

In this wise, then, shall be the Intercession of God's Emissary (may God bless him and grant him peace). But individuals from amongst His nation, including the Divines and the Righteous, shall be possessed of an Intercession also. For God's Emissary (may God bless him and grant him peace) has said, 'By virtue of the Intercession of a man of my community a host greater than that of Rabīʿa and Muḍar shall enter into Heaven.'[A] [27]

And he said (may God bless him and grant him peace) 'A man shall be told, "Arise, So-and-so, and intercede!" and shall get up and exercise Intercession for his tribe or his family, or for one man or two, all in proportion to his works.'[28]

Said Anas, 'The Emissary of God (may God bless him and grant him peace) once said, "On the Day of Arising, one of the people of Heaven shall look out upon the people of Hell, one of whom calls out to him, saying, 'O So-and-so! Do you know me?' 'No,' he shall reply. 'By God, I do not know you. Who might you be?' 'I am the man you once passed in the world,' he says, 'and whom you asked for a drink of water, and who gave you to drink.' 'I know you now,' he says. 'Then intercede through this for me with your Lord,' he entreats him. So he petitions God (exalted is His remembrance!), saying, 'I looked out at the people of Hell, and was called by one of them, who said, "Do you know me?" "No," I replied. "Who might you be?" "I am the man whom, when in the world, you once asked for a drink of water, and who gave you to drink. Thus intercede for me with your Lord!" Permit me, therefore, to intercede on his account.' And God gives him to intercede for him, and the order is issued for him to be removed from Hell".'[29]

Said Anas, 'The Emissary of God (may God bless him and grant him peace) said, "I shall be the first of men to come forth when they are resurrected. I shall be their preacher when they come in throngs. I shall bring them good tidings when they are in despair. On that Day the banner of praise shall be in my hand. I

[A] The texts differ over the identity of this man. According to Ājurrī (p.351) he is the caliph ʿUthmān ibn ʿAffān; Ibn Ḥanbal (*Zuhd*, 158) also mentions the possibility of this, but adds the name of Uways al-Qaranī as an alternative. Rabīʿa and Muḍar were two numerous tribes.

am the noblest of Adam's children in my Lord's sight, and I do not boast".'[30]

Said God's Emissary (may God bless him and grant him peace), 'I shall stand in the presence of my Lord (Great and Glorious is He!) and[31] be given a robe of Heaven to wear. Then shall I stand at the right-hand side of the Throne in a place which shall be occupied by no other man.'[32]

Said Ibn ᶜAbbās (may God be pleased with them both), 'A group of the Companions of God's Emissary (may God bless him and grant him peace) once sat down to wait for him. When he came out and drew near to them, he heard them talking, and could hear one of them saying, "How astonishing it is that God (Great and Glorious is He!) should have taken a Friend from among His creation, for *He did choose Abraham to be His Friend.*"[33] Another said, "But that is no more remarkable than the speech of Moses, for *He spoke unto him directly.*"[34] And another said, "And Jesus was God's Word and Spirit."[35] Said another, "And *Adam was chosen by God.*"[36] Then the Emissary of God (may God bless him and grant him peace) came out to them, and said, "I heard your discoursing and your wonderment that Abraham should have been God's Friend: it was so. And that Moses should have been God's Intimate [*najī*]: it was so. And that Jesus should have been God's Spirit and Word: it was so. And that Adam should have been *chosen by God*: it was so. I am the Beloved of God, and I do not boast. I shall carry the banner of praise on the Day of Arising, and I do not boast. I shall be the first to intercede, and the first to be granted Intercession on the Day of Arising, and I do not boast. I shall be the first to shake the door-rings of Heaven, and God shall open [its gates] for me, and I shall enter with those of the believers that were poverty-stricken, and I do not boast. I am the most noble of the First and the Last, and I do not boast." '[37]

The Pool

KNOW THAT the Pool is a great dignity which God has conferred solely upon our Prophet (may God bless him and grant him peace). A description of it is included in the Traditions. It is our hope that God (Exalted is He!) will grant us to know of it in this world and to taste it in the next, for one of its qualities is that 'whosoever drinks of it shall never thirst again'.

Said Anas, 'The Emissary of God (may God bless him and grant him peace) once dozed off, and then lifted up his head with a smile. "O Emissary of God," [the Companions] asked, "What has made you smile?" "A verse which was revealed to me lately," he replied, and recited, "*In the name of God, the Compassionate, the Merciful. Truly, We have given you al-Kawthar.*"[1] until he had finished the chapter. Then he said, "Do you know what *al-Kawthar* is?" and we replied, "God and His Emissary know best." "It is a river in Heaven", he said, "which God (Great and Glorious is He!) has promised me. Upon it is abundant good: for upon it lies a Pool to which my nation shall repair on the Day of Arising. Its drinking vessels are as the number of stars in the sky." '[2]

Said Anas, 'The Emissary of God (may God bless him and grant him peace) said, "When I was travelling in Heaven I beheld a river whose banks were like domes of hollow pearls. 'What is this, O Gabriel?' I enquired, and he replied, 'This is *al-Kawthar*, which your Lord has granted you.' And the Angel waved his hand, and lo and behold! its mud was of strong musk." '[3]

And he said, 'The Emissary of God (may God bless him and grant him peace) used to say, "The distance between the two sides of my Pool is like that which is between Medina and Ṣanʿā' or Amman".'[A] [4]

[A] Or, 'Oman'.

Ibn ʿUmar related that when His Word (Exalted is He!): *Truly, We have granted you al-Kawthar* was revealed, the Emissary of God (may God bless him and grant him peace) said, 'It is a river in Heaven, the banks of which are of gold, and whose water is whiter than milk, sweeter than honey, and finer-smelling than musk. It flows over stones which are pearls, both large and small.'[5]

Said Thawbān, the *mawlā* of God's Emissary (may God bless him and grant him peace), 'The Emissary of God (may God bless him and grant him peace) said, "My Pool stretches for the distance which is between Aden and Amman of al-Balqā'[A]. Its water is whiter than milk and sweeter than honey. Its drinking vessels are as the number of stars in the sky. Whoever drinks one draught from it shall never thirst again. The first people to reach it will be the poor from among the Emigrants." And ʿUmar ibn al-Khaṭṭāb asked, "Who might they be, O Emissary of God?" and he replied, "They are the wild-haired, dusty-clothed ones, who do not marry women of pleasure, and for whom no portals are opened".' And ʿUmar ibn ʿAbd al-ʿAzīz declared [upon hearing this Tradition], 'By God! I have married women of pleasure! Fāṭima bint ʿAbd al-Malik! And portals have been opened for me! May God have mercy upon me! I have no choice but to cease anointing my head with oil so that I become wild-haired, and not to wash the garment I am wearing until it becomes soiled!'[6]

Said Abū Dharr, 'I once asked, "O Emissary of God! What are the drinking vessels of the Pool?" and he replied, "By Him in Whose hand lies the soul of Muḥammad, its vessels are more numerous than the stars and planets in the sky on a dark and cloudless night. Whoever drinks of it shall never thirst again. There pours into it from Heaven through a spout the width and breadth of which is like the distance between Amman and al-ʿAqaba a liquid that is whiter than milk and sweeter than honey." '[7]

[A] Al-Balqā': a region roughly corresponding to the modern Transjordan. (Cf. Ibn Shaddād, 275.)

Said Samura, 'The Emissary of God (may God bless him and grant him peace) said,[8] "For every Prophet there is a Pool, and they shall boast with one another about which is reached by a greater number of people. It is my hope that I shall be the one with the greatest number of all." '[9]

Such was the hope of God's Emissary (may God bless him and grant him peace). Therefore let every bondsman aspire to be among those who come to it, and beware of all wishful thinking and beguilement in believing that it truly constitutes one's hope. The man who hopes for a harvest is he that sows the seed, clears and irrigates the land, and then sits back with the hope that God will cause the crop to grow through His grace, and that He will ward off rainstorms until the time for harvesting has arrived. As for the man who renounces ploughing, sowing and clearing and irrigating the land, and then takes to hoping that God in His grace will bring forth grain and fruit, he is a man of wishful thinking and beguilement, and is not truly hoping at all. Such are the hopes of the majority of mankind, and they constitute no more than the beguilement of fools. We seek refuge in God from beguilement and heedlessness, for being beguiled [by our virtue] from God is worse even than being beguiled by the things of this world. God (Exalted is He!) has said, *Do not be beguiled by the life of this world, and let not the beguiler beguile you of God.*[10]

The Inferno, and its Terrors and Torments

O YOU who are in heedlessness of your own self, beguiled by the preoccupations of this world, which even now draw nigh to their end and extinction! Renounce all thought upon what you must leave, and turn your mind to thoughts of your final destination. For it has been given you to know that Hell is the destiny of all men, for it is said, *There is not one of you but shall come to it. This is a fixed ordinance of thy Lord. Then shall We deliver those that were Godfearing, and leave the wrongdoers therein crouching.*[1] Thus your coming unto it is certain, while your salvation therefrom is no more than conjecture. Fill up your heart, therefore, with the dread of that destination, that perhaps you may make preparations for deliverance therefrom. Contemplate the plight in which all creatures shall be when they have endured their share of the Arising's calamities. Amidst torment and horror shall they stand, waiting to hear the truth about their condition, and awaiting the Intercession of those that might intercede on their behalf.

The evildoers are whelmed in shadows pierced by sheets of flame, as a flaring blaze overspreads, and they hear it sighing and gurgling from the violence of its wrath and fury. Now the evildoers become certain of their perdition, as the nations crouch down upon their very knees, so that even the innocent are fearful of an evil end. The Herald comes forth from amongst the Guardians of Hell, and demands, 'Where is So-and-so, son of So-and-so, who did procrastinate with his soul in the world through lengthy hopes, who did waste his life in works of iniquity?' And the Angels make haste towards him with rods of iron, and confront him with terrible threats, and drive him away to the fierce torment, casting him head over heels into the Blaze's depths. 'Taste it!' they say to him. 'Truly you are the mighty one, the noble! Dwell now in an abode with straitened sides, gloomy passageways and shadowy dangers. Therein the prisoner shall dwell for evermore. Therein the fires are stoked up. Therein their drink is boiling water, and their place of refuge is the Blaze.' The Guardians of Hell beat them, and the Abyss unites them. They hope only for obliteration, but there is for them no salvation. Their feet are pressed to their forelocks, and their faces are black from their sins. On every side they cry out, from every direction and place they scream aloud, 'O Mālik! The threat has come true for us! O Mālik! We are weighed down with iron! O Mālik! Our skins have become roasted! O Mālik! Release us from here, for we shall not return [to our former sins]!'

But the Guardians of Hell shall say, 'What folly! There is no place of safety, and for you there shall be no escape from the abode of degradation! *Fall back therein, and speak not!*[2] Were you to be released from it you would return to that which was forbidden you!' At this they despair, and for *their unmindfulness of God*[3] they lament. But repentance cannot help them, neither can they be succoured by regret. Instead, they are thrust down upon their faces, chained and fettered, with Hellfire above them, Hellfire beneath them, Hellfire on their right and Hellfire on their left, so that they drown in a sea of[4] fire: their food is fire, their drink is fire, their apparel is fire, their resting-place is fire. They dwell among fragments of flame and *garments of tar*,[5] flayed with rods and weighed down by shackles, as they writhe in its narrow passages and are broken in its depths, cast about from one side to another, boiled in water as water boils in cauldrons. Each time they shriek out in grief and lamentation scalding water is poured over their heads, *melting away their skin and what is in their bellies. There are iron rods for them*[6] which splinter their brows. Pus bursts forth from their mouths, and their livers are lacerated by thirst, as the pupils of their eyes flow out over their cheeks, the flesh of which has peeled away. Their skin and hair are plucked out, but *as often as their skins are consumed We shall exchange them for fresh skins.*[7] Their bones are denuded of flesh, but their spirits remain in their veins and arteries, which hiss as they are scorched by the flames. In the midst of this they long constantly to die; never, however, shall they do so.

How would you be were you to behold them, when their faces have turned blacker than charcoal, and when their eyes have been put out, their tongues struck dumb, their backs broken and their bones snapped, their ears and noses[8] severed, their skin torn, and their hands shackled to their necks, and their forelocks pressed against their feet as they walk upon the fire on their faces, stepping with their eyeballs upon spikes of iron? The raging fire shall have entered into the depths of their every part, as the snakes and scorpions of the Abyss cling to their extremities.

This being a partial[9] summary of their circumstances, you should now look into a detailed exposition of the terrors [to which they are exposed]. Think also upon the valleys of the Inferno and its narrow ravines, for the Prophet (may God bless him and grant him peace) has said, 'In the Inferno there lie seventy thousand valleys, each of which has seventy thousand ravines, in each of which are seventy thousand serpents and seventy thousand scorpions. The unbeliever and the hypocrite shall have not have respite until they have been cast down upon each one of them.'[10]

Said ᶜAlī (may God ennoble his face), 'The Emissary of God (may God bless him and grant him peace) once said, "We[11] seek refuge in God from the Chasm of Grief." or "the Vale of Grief." And he was asked, "O Emissary of God, what is the Chasm of Grief?" or "the Vale of Grief?" and he replied, "A vale in the Inferno from which the Inferno itself seeks God's protection seventy times each day, which God (Exalted is He!) has prepared for the ostentatious reciters of the Qur'ān." '[12]

Thus is the compass of the Inferno, and of its ramifying valleys, which are in proportion to the number of worldly passions; just as the number of its gates is seven, being the number of the parts with which a man sins. They are layered one above the other: the uppermost is the Inferno [*Jahannam*], then comes the Blaze [*Saqar*], the Flame [*Laẓā*], the Furnace [*al-Ḥuṭama*], the Fire [*al-Saᶜīr*], Hellfire [*al-Jaḥīm*] and the Abyss [*al-Hāwiya*].[A] Contemplate the depth of the Abyss, which is without limit, just as there is no limit to the desires of this world; for just as one worldly desire ends only in another which is yet stronger, so the Abyss of the Inferno ends only in another Abyss which is yet more profound.

Said Abū Hurayra, 'Once, when we were with the Emissary of God (may God bless him and grant him peace) we heard the sound of something falling. "Do you know what that was?" he asked, and we replied, "God and His Emissary know best." "That was a rock," he said, "which was cast into the Inferno seventy years ago and which has only now reached its floor".'[13]

[A] These are all terms used in the Qur'ān (respectively, e.g. VIII:16; LXXIV:26; LXX:15; CIV:4; XXII:4; LXXIX:39; CI:9) where, however, no such hierarchical arrangement is specified. Cf. T. O'Shaughnessy, 'The Seven Names for Hell in the Qur'ān', *BSOAS* 24 (1961), 444–469; for the geography of Hell more generally see *Escatología*, 135–63. The first tier is almost always known as Jahannam, and constitutes a temporary purgatory for monotheists guilty of mortal sins.

Then consider the discrepancy which exists between its tiers, for *truly, the Afterlife is greater in degrees and greater in preferment.*[14] Just as the indulgence of men in this world varies, some being engrossed in it and gathering it in as though they were drowning in it, while others plunge into it to a limited depth; in like wise Hell's grasp upon them shall vary, for *in truth, God does not commit injustice, even so much as an atom's weight.*[15] Thus the varieties of punishment do not bear in upon all who are in Hell in every circumstance; rather everyone has a known limit which is proportionate to his rebelliousness and sin. The least tormented of them, however, would gladly renounce the entire world in order to ransom himself therefrom because of the extremity of his plight. Said God's Emissary (may God bless him and grant him peace), 'The least tormented of Hell's denizens shall, on the Day of Arising, wear sandals of fire, the heat of which will cause his brains to boil.'[16] Contemplate the state of this man, who has been dealt with lightly, and consider how must be the state of one who is treated with rigour. And should you ever doubt the intensity of Hell's torment, then merely bring your finger near to a flame and draw a comparison from that. Then know that your comparison is mistaken, for there is no correspondence between the fire of this world and that of the Inferno; but since the pain produced by fire is the greatest in the world, the pain of the Inferno is described in terms thereof. Nay, were Hell's inhabitants to come across fire such as ours they would plunge into it submissively in order to flee from their condition.

This has been expressed in a number of Traditions. It is said that the fire of this world is washed with seventy waters of mercy so that men might abide it.[17] And the Emissary of God (may God bless him and grant him peace) described the nature of the infernal fire quite clearly, saying, 'God (Exalted is He!) ordered Hell to be stoked up for a thousand years until it became red; then it was stoked up for a further thousand years until it turned white; then it was stoked up for another thousand years until it became black. Black it is, and shadowy.'[18]

And he said (may God bless him and grant him peace), 'Hell complained to its Lord, saying, "O my Lord, one part of me has been consumed by another!" and it was allowed two breaths, one in winter and the other in summer. Thus the greatest hardship you endure in summer is from its heat, while the most severe time of winter is from its bitter cold [*al-zamharīr*][A].'[19]

Said Anas ibn Mālik, 'The unbeliever who was the most comfortable of men in the world shall be brought forth, and it shall be said, "Dip him into Hell for one instant!" He is then asked, "Have you ever experienced any comfort?" "No," he replies. Then the man who had suffered most in the world is brought, and it is said, "Dip him into Heaven for one instant!" Then he is asked, "Have you ever experienced any suffering?" and he replies, "No".'[20]

Said Abū Hurayra, 'Were there to be a hundred thousand or more people in the Mosque[B], and only one of the inhabitants of Hell were to exhale, every one of them would perish.'[21]

One of the Divines[C] said [commenting on the text] *Their faces are scorched by Hell, and they scowl therein*:[22] 'It scorches them all at once, and leaves no flesh on their bones without casting it down around their ankles.'[23]

Next look to the foulness of the pus which shall flow from their bodies until they are submerged in it entirely; this is *ghassāq*.[D] Said Abū Saʿīd al-Khudrī, 'The Emissary of God (may God bless him and grant him peace) said, "If one pail of the Inferno's *ghassāq* were to be voided into this world it would pollute the lives of the entirety of its inhabitants".'[24] And this shall be their drink: for as they cry out from thirst each one of them is *given a water of pus to drink, which he gulps down, barely able to swallow it, and death comes to him from every side, but he dies not. And when they cry for help they are succoured with water like molten lead, which burns faces. An evil drink, and a foul place of rest!*[25]

[A] *Zamharīr* is variously understood to mean 'cold', 'cold air', or alternatively an 'icy pit into which the unbeliever is thrown.' (Cf. *Escatología*, 166–8.)

[B] Of Medina.

[C] Ibn Masʿūd, according to Zabīdī (x. 514).

[D] Cf. Q. XXXVIII:57; LXXVIII:25. Interpreted in Lane (p.2258) as 'ichor', 'thick purulent matter', or the 'tears' of the inhabitants of Hell, or an 'intense cold'. Cf. also *Escatología*, 168n.

Then behold their nourishment, which is [the fruit of the tree named] Zaqqūm, as God (Exalted is He!) has said, *Then, O you misguided deniers, shall you eat from a tree of Zaqqūm, filling your bellies therewith, drinking boiling water there, drinking even as does the thirsty camel.*[26] And He has said (Exalted is He!), *It is a tree which grows from the base of Hell, the fruit of which resembles the heads of devils. They shall eat therefrom and fill their stomachs; then theirs is a mixture of boiling water. Then their return shall be to Hellfire.*[27] And He said (Exalted is He!), *They shall enter a roaring fire, and be given boiling water to drink.*[28] And He said (Exalted is He!), *Truly, We have fetters, and Hellfire, and choking food, and a painful torment.*[29]

Said Ibn ᶜAbbās, 'The Emissary of God (may God bless him and grant him peace) said, "If but one drop of Zaqqūm were to fall into the oceans of this world it would pollute them for all its inhabitants. How shall it be, then, for the man whose nourishment it has become?" '[30]

Said Anas, 'The Emissary of God (may God bless him and grant him peace) said, "Desire what God has encouraged you to desire, and beware and fear what God has encouraged you to fear, which is His torment and chastisement, and the Inferno. For truly, were there to be with you in the world in which you live one droplet from[31] Heaven it would sweeten it for you, and if but one droplet from Hell were to be with you in the world it would befoul it for you." '[32]

Said Abu'l-Dardā', 'The Emissary of God (may God bless him and grant him peace) said, "Hunger will be cast upon the people of Hell until it itself becomes equal to the torment they are in. They shall clamour for food, and are given succour with food *from bitter thorn-fruit, which neither nourishes, nor satisfies hunger.*[33] And again they clamour for food, and are given succour with food which chokes them.[34] They remember that in the world they used to drink to relieve choking, so they clamour for a drink,[35] and boiling water is passed up to them with iron hooks, but when it comes near to them it scorches their faces, and when it enters into their bellies their insides become lacerated. 'Call the Guardians of the Inferno!' they say, and they petition them, saying, 'Pray to your Lord to lighten our chastisement for one day!' but they reply, *'Did Emissaries not come unto you with clear proofs?' 'Yes,' they say. 'Pray,' they continue, 'although the prayer of the unbelievers can only go astray'.*[36] Then they say, 'Summon Mālik!' and they call him. *'O Mālik! Let your Lord make an end of us!'* they cry to him, but he says to them, *'You are to remain.'* "[37] And al-Aᶜmash[A] said, "I have been told that between their petition and Mālik's response shall be a thousand years." The Prophet [continued, and] said, "Then they say, 'Call upon your Lord, for none is better than your Lord!' and they say, *'O our Lord! Our evil fortune triumphed over us, and we were a people in misguidance. O our Lord! Bring us hence, and if we return [to sin], then are we wrongdoers.'* And He says in reply, *'Fall back therein, and speak not unto Me.'* At this they despair of any good, and begin to sob, to lament, and to curse.' "[38]

Said Abū Umāma, 'The Emissary of God (may God bless him and grant him peace) said [commenting on] His word (Exalted is He!): *And he shall be given a water of pus to drink, which he gulps down, barely able to swallow it:*[39] "It is brought near to him and he is revolted by it, and when it is brought very close it scalds his face so that its skin peels away; and when he drinks of it it tears his intestines so that they emerge from his rear. God (Exalted is He!) says, *And they are given boiling water to drink, so that their intestines are torn;*[40] and He says (Exalted is He!): *And when they cry for help, they are succoured with water like molten lead, which burns faces.*" '[41]

Thus shall be their food and drink when they hunger and thirst.

Look now at the serpents and scorpions of the Inferno, their strong venom, their great size, and the hideousness of their appearance. They are let loose against its inhabitants and goaded against them, and do not tire of stinging and biting for a single moment.

Said Abū Hurayra, 'The Emissary of God (may God bless him and grant him peace) once said, "Whosoever is given wealth by God but fails to pay the Tithe due thereupon shall find that it appears before him on the Day of Arising as a hairless snake, which puts a collar around his neck on the Day of Arising, and

[A] One of the narrators of this Tradition.

takes him by the corners of his mouth, that is, his jawbones, saying, 'I am your wealth! I am your treasure!' " Then he recited His word (Exalted is He!): *And let not those who hoard up that which God has bestowed upon them of His bounty*[42] [to the end of] the verse.'[A][43]

Said the Emissary of God (may God bless him and grant him peace): 'In Hell there are serpents which resemble the necks of long-necked camels, the bite of which endures for forty autumns. And in it there are scorpions like laden mules, the sting of which endures for forty autumns also.'[44]

These serpents and scorpions are only let loose against one in the way that avarice, bad manners and harmfulness were loosed against one in the world; and whosoever has been protected from [these attributes] will be protected from these snakes also, so that they shall never appear to him.

Then, after all this, think upon how the bodies of Hell's people will be swollen. For God (Exalted is He!) shall cause their frames to grow in length and breadth so that their torment may thereby be intensified. They feel the fire's scorching and the bites of the snakes and the scorpions in all their parts at once and without any interruption.

Said Abū Hurayra, 'The Emissary of God (may God bless him and grant him peace) once said, "In Hell, the unbeliever's molar will be as large as Mount Uḥud, and his skin will be stretched a three day journey's length".'[45]

Said God's Emissary (may God bless him and grant him peace), 'His lower lip shall have fallen down onto his breast, while his upper lip curls back and covers his face.'[46]

And he said (may God bless him and grant him peace), 'On the Day of Arising the unbeliever will drag his tongue on Sijjīn, where people will tread upon it'.[47]

With their bodies thus enlarged Hell shall burn them many times; however their skins and flesh shall constantly be renewed. Said al-Ḥasan [commenting on the text] *As often as their skins are*

[A] The verse continues: *think that it is better for them. Rather, it is worse for them. That which they hoard will be their collar on the Day of Arising. God shall inherit all that is in the heavens and the earth, and He is appraised of what you do.*

consumed We shall exchange them for fresh skins: 'Hell shall consume them seventy thousand times each day, and each time it does so they shall be told "Return", and they return to their previous condition.'

Now contemplate the weeping and sobbing of Hell's inhabitants, and the way in which they shall cry out in grief and lamentation, for this is to be imposed on them as soon as they are cast into Hell. Said the Emissary of God (may God bless him and grant him peace), 'On that Day the Inferno will be brought. It has seventy thousand reins, each of which shall be held by seventy thousand angels.'[48]

Said Anas, 'The Emissary of God (may God bless him and grant him peace) said, "Weeping shall be let loose upon the people of Hell, so that they weep until their tears are exhausted, after which they weep blood until their faces assume the aspect of great trenches, in which ships would float were they to be launched therein".'[49]

For as long as they are granted leave continuously to weep, to sigh, to moan and to cry out in grief and lamentation, they find some relief therein; however they are to be denied this also. Said Muḥammad ibn Kaʿb: 'The inhabitants of Hell will have five prayers, four of which shall be answered by God (Great and Glorious is He!) while after the fifth they shall never speak again. "*O our Lord*" they say, "*Twice You made us die, and twice You gave us life; we have confessed our sins, is there, then, any way to depart?*"[50] And God (Exalted is He!) says to them in response, "*When God Alone was invoked you had no faith, but when partners were ascribed to Him you believed. The command belongs to God only, the Exalted, the Great.*"[51] Then they say, "*O our Lord, we have seen and heard, thus send us back to work righteousness, now we are certain!*"[52] But God (Exalted is He!) replies to them, saying, "*Did you not swear aforetime that you would never pass away?*"[53] Then they say, "*O our Lord, release us, and we shall work righteousness, not that which we used to do!*"[54] and God (Exalted is He!) replies to them, "*Did We not prolong your years long enough for him who reflected to reflect therein? And the Warner came unto you. Now taste, for there is no helper for the wrongdoers!*"[55] Then they say, "*O our Lord, our evil fortune triumphed over us, and we were a people in misguidance. O our Lord, bring us hence, and if we return [to sin] then truly we are wrongdoers!*"[56] But God (Exalted is He!) says in reply, "*Fall back therein, and speak not unto Me*," and thenceforwards they never speak again. This is the utter extremity of punishment.'

Said Mālik ibn Anas (may God be pleased with him), 'Zayd ibn Aslam once said [commenting on] His word (Exalted is He!), *It is the same to us whether we rage or endure, we have no place of refuge*:[57] "They shall endure for a hundred years, then rage for a hundred years, then endure for a hundred years,[58] then say, *It is the same to us whether we rage or endure, we have no place of refuge*".'[59]

Said [the Prophet] (may God bless him and grant him peace), 'On the Day of Arising, death shall be brought in the form of a white ram, which is then slaughtered between Heaven and Hell. And it shall be announced, "O people of Heaven, eternity, and no death!" and "O people of Hell, eternity, and no death!" '[60]

Said al-Ḥasan, 'There is a man who shall emerge from Hell after a thousand years. Would that I were he!'

Al-Ḥusayn (may God be pleased with him) was once seen sitting in a corner and weeping. 'Why do you weep?' he was asked, and he replied, 'I fear that He may cast me into Hell, and not care.'

Such, then, are the varieties of the Inferno's torments described in general terms. The details of the sorrows, laments, trials and sufferings which it shall encompass are without end. Yet despite all the pain that they suffer, their grief over having missed the delight which is in Heaven and the meeting with God (Exalted is He!), and losing His satisfaction, is greater still, for they know that they have sold all of these things *for a paltry price, a few dirhams*,[61] having traded them for nothing more than the base pleasures of the world, for a few short days which themselves were not unsullied, but were instead turbid and spoilt. They say within themselves, 'Alas! O woe! How could we have ruined ourselves by disobeying our Lord? How could we not have charged ourselves with endurance for a few days; had we done so those days would now be past and we would be in the presence of the Lord of the Worlds, delighting in His satisfaction and good-pleasure!'

O the sorrow of those people when they have lost so much, and have been tried by so much, when nothing of this world's delights remains with them! Yet, were they never to behold the rapture which is in Heaven their lamentation would not be complete; thus it is displayed before them. For the Emissary of God (may God bless him and grant him peace) has said, 'On the Day of Arising people will be taken from Hell to Heaven, until, when they draw near thereto, and breathe in its fragrance, and behold its palaces and all that God has prepared for its inhabitants, a voice calls out, "Take them away from it, for they are to have no share therein!" and they return with a grief the likes of which was never known by the first or the last [of mankind]. "O our Lord!" they say. "Had You put us in Hell without revealing to us the reward which You did show us, and that which You have prepared for those who aided Your cause, the matter would have been easier for us." And God (Exalted is He!) says, "Thus was My will in your case. For when you were alone, you challenged Me with mortal sins, but when you met the people you were modest, showing them the opposite of what you displayed to Me in your hearts. You stood in awe of the people, but not of Me; you magnified them, and did not magnify Me. You made bequests to them, but none to Me; today, therefore, shall I cause you to taste the painful chastisement, and deprive you of the reward everlasting." '[62]

Said Aḥmad ibn Ḥarb, 'No-one who prefers shade to sunlight cannot prefer Heaven to Hell.'

Said Jesus (upon whom be peace), 'How many a healthful body, a graceful face, and a skilful tongue, shall tomorrow be woeful among the tiers of Hell!'

Said David, 'My God, no endurance have I before the heat of Thy sun; wherefore then may I endure the heat of Thy Fire? And no endurance have I before the sound of Thy mercy;[A] wherefore then may I endure the sound of Thy chastisement?'

[A] i.e. thunder (thus explained in Ibn Ḥanbal, *Zuhd*, 90).

Contemplate, O unfortunate one, these fearful affairs. Know that God (Exalted is He!) has already created Hell and its terrors,[A] and created people for it whose number can neither rise nor decline, and that the matter has been decided and brought to its conclusion. God (Exalted is He!) has said, *And warn them of the Day of Anguish, when the matter has been decided. They are in heedlessness, and they believe not.*[63] By my life! This is a reference to the Day of Arising, and to eternity, for the Day of Arising shall do no more than make manifest that which has already been decreed.

An astonishing thing it is, that you should laugh and play, and busy yourself with the base things of this world, although you know not how your fate has been determined. And should you say, 'Would that I could know my destiny, and to which goal and place of return I am travelling, and in what fashion my fate has been decreed!' then [know] that there is a token for you from which you may draw comfort and set confidence in your hopes. It is arrived at by looking to your circumstances and works, for in truth, 'everyone is helped towards that for which he has been created.'[64] If you have been helped towards the path of virtue, then rejoice, for you have been distanced from Hell; if, however, when each time you set out to do good you are beset by obstacles which impede you, while whenever you set out to do evil its means become readily available, then you should know that you are doomed. For this is the intimation of an outcome just as much as rain is the intimation of the growth of plants, and as smoke is the intimation of fire. God (Exalted is He!) has said, *Truly, the good are in felicity; and truly, the evil are in hellfire.*[65] Measure yourself by these two verses and you shall know which of these abodes shall be your final destination.

And God knows best.[66]

[A] The Ashʿarite doctrine holds that Heaven and Hell are already created. (Cf. Ashʿari, *Maqālāt*, 475.)

Heaven, and the Varieties of its Bliss

KNOW THAT that Abode, the woes and sorrows of which you now have come to know, is complemented by another Abode. Contemplate, therefore, the felicity and joyfulness which shall therein consist. Whosoever draws away from one of them must needs find residence in the other; occupy your heart therefore with trepidation through long meditation upon the terrors of Hellfire, and with hope through long contemplation of the abiding bliss which is promised the indwellers of the Gardens. Goad your soul onwards with the whip of fear, and lead it by the reins of hope along the Straight Path; thus shall you win a mighty kingdom and be secure from the painful chastisement.

Let your thoughts dwell upon Heaven's people: *upon their faces shall you perceive the expression of delight; they are given to drink of a sealed wine,*[1] seated upon pulpits of rubies in tents of glistening white pearls, among carpets of wondrous green, reclining upon couches placed beside rivers flowing with wine and honey, surrounded by youths and pages, adorned by the large-eyed houris from among the *fine and beautiful,*[2] *who are as sapphires and pearls,*[3] *untouched by either man or jinn,*[4] who walk proudly through the tiers of Heaven,[5] their trains carried by seventy thousand pages. [The couches'] surrounds are of wonderful white silks such as astonish the eyes. [The houris' heads] are wreathed with crowns inlaid with pearls both great and small; flirtatious they are, and coquettish, perfumed and safe from old age or any hardship, *secluded in tents*[6] and palaces of sapphire raised up in the centre of Heaven's gardens; modest of gaze and large-eyed. They and their spouses are served around with goblets, vessels and *a chalice filled with a white wine, which delights those who drink of it.*[7]

They are served around by servants and pages *like hidden pearls, a reward for their former works.*[8] *They are in a secure abode, among gardens and springs,*[9] and *in gardens and rivers, at a seat of truth before a mighty Sovereign*[10] in which they gaze upon the countenance of the Generous King. The *expression of delight*[11] shines upon their faces as they are afflicted by *neither dust nor ignominy,*[12] *rather are they bondsmen honoured*[13] with diverse gifts from their Lord which come without cease. *They abide in that which their souls desired, eternally.*[14] They fear not, neither do they grieve, and are safe from *accident of time.*[15] Therein they rejoice, eating of its various foods, and quaffing its milk, wine and honey from rivers whose beds are of silver, whose pebbles are pearls, and the sand of which is strong musk. Its plants are saffron, and [its people] are showered upon by clouds of rosewater raining down on hills of camphor, and given goblets—and what goblets!—of silver inlaid with pearls, both great and small, and sapphires, one of which contains the *sealed wine*[16] mingled with the sweet water of Salsabīl, and a goblet whose light shines through its gems because of their purity, and through which appears a drink of an exquisiteness and redness never before tasted by man. In the perfection of its design and the superbness of its execution[17] it is borne in the hand of a servant the effulgence of whose face stands challenge to the shining sun. Nay, how could the sun bear any comparison with the sweetness of his aspect, the beauty of his temples and the charm of his eyes?

How astonishing it is that man, who has faith in an abode which may thus be described, and who is certain that its inhabitants shall never pass away, and that misfortunes shall never befall those that occupy its expanses and that they shall never be afflicted by chance happenings, may find solace in an abode permission for whose ruin has been granted by God, and take pleasure in any life which stands outside its boundaries! By God, were there to be [in Heaven] haleness of body alone, together with safekeeping from death, hunger, thirst, and the other varieties of misfortune, it would be worth a man's while to renounce the world solely on its account, and to prefer it to what must necessarily be spoilt and lost.

And how might this be otherwise, when its inhabitants are secure monarchs enjoying diverse pleasures, who shall have therein all that they desire, each day attending before the Throne and gazing upon the noble Countenance of God, winning thereby that which puts an end to their gazing at and attending to all the other delights of the Gardens? Unceasingly they move from one variety of blessing to the next, safe from ever suffering their loss.

Said Abū Hurayra, 'God's Emissary (may God bless him and grant him peace) has said, "On the Day of Arising a herald shall call out, saying, 'You shall be in health, and never fall ill! You shall live, and never die! You shall be young, and never age! You shall be in comfort, and never in any hardship!' This is what He has declared (Great and Glorious is He!): *And they were called: 'This is Heaven; you have inherited it because of what you used to do'.*" '[18]

Whenever you wish to know the attributes of Heaven, read the Qur'ān, for there is no discourse higher than that of God. Read from His statement, *And for him that feared the standing before his Lord shall be two gardens*[19] to the end of the Chapter of the All-Merciful[20]; likewise the Chapter of the Event[21] and certain other Chapters. And should you wish to know the details of its attributes from the Traditions, then consider them now after having discovered them in sum.

Contemplate firstly:

The Number of the Gardens.

Said the Emissary of God (may God bless him and grant him peace) [commenting upon] His statement (Exalted is He!), *And for him that feared the standing before his Lord shall be two gardens*:[22] 'Two gardens whose vessels and their contents shall be of silver, and also two gardens whose vessels and their contents are of gold.[A] In the Garden of Eden,[B] all that shall prevent them from viewing their Lord shall be His Cloak of Glory.'[23]

Then look to the Gates of Heaven, for there are as many of them as there are virtues, just as the gates of Hell are as the number of vices. Said Abū Hurayra, 'The Emissary of God (may God bless him and grant him peace) once said, "Whoever meets the expense of a couple's marriage from his own wealth for the sake of God shall be summoned from every gate of Heaven. Heaven has eight gates: whoever was of the people of Prayer shall be called from the Gate of Prayer; whoever was of the people of Fasting shall be called from the Gate of Fasting; whoever was of the people of Charity [*al-ṣadaqa*] shall be called from the Gate of Charity; and whoever was of the people of the Holy War shall be called from the Gate of the Holy War." And Abū Bakr (may God be pleased with him) said, "By God, not one of us minds from which gate he shall be summoned. But shall anyone be summoned from them all?" "Yes," he replied, "and I hope that you shall be amongst them".'[24]

ʿĀṣim ibn Ḍamra related that "ʿAlī (may God ennoble his face) once made mention of Hell, stressing its enormity in a way I do not now recall, and then said, "*And those that had feared their Lord shall be driven to Heaven in troops*[25] until they reach one of its Gates, where they shall find a tree from the foot of which two springs gush forth. They repair to one of them, as they have been instructed, and drink. Thereby all the grief and hurt which lay in their bellies is removed. Then they make their way to the other where they purify themselves, whereupon the *expression of delight*[26] steals over their faces. From this time on their hair never

[A] Presumably his listeners would have been aware of a subsequent verse: *And beside them shall be two other gardens* (LV:62).

[B] Whether this Eden is identical with that lost by Adam is a matter of dispute among the theologians. Islamic belief has usually set the primordial Garden atop a mountain, perhaps in Syria, Persia, Chaldea or India; 'Adam's Peak' in Ceylon remains to this day a centre of Muslim pilgrimage. (Cf. *Escatología*, 193–6.) According to Ibn al-ʿArabī (apud *Escatología*, 130n; 231–3) Eden is the highest of the heavens, or their citadel (*qaṣba*), and this would seem to be supported by the *ḥadīth* quoted here by our author. Nevertheless, other Traditions (cf. Bayhaqī, *Baʿth*, 158–62) indicate that the *Firdaws* will be the highest of all.

changes, and their heads never become dishevelled; it is as though they had been anointed with oil. Then they come to[27] Heaven, to be told, '*Peace be upon you; good you were, so enter it for evermore.*'[28] Then the Pages meet them, and move around them as the children of the world move around a relation[29] who has returned after a period of absence. 'Rejoice!' they tell him, 'for God has made ready for you such honour!' And a youth goes forth from them to one of his Large-eyed Houri wives, and says, 'So-and-so has arrived!' using the name by which he was called in the world. 'You saw him!' she cries, and he answers, 'I saw him indeed, and he is following me.' And, overcome by rapture, she goes to the threshold. When he arrives at his house he gazes at its foundations, which are of one pearl-stone, over which stands a palace of red, green, yellow, and every other hue; then he raises his head and looks to its roof, which is as lightning, and did not God (Exalted is He!) decree otherwise, it would almost snatch away his sight.

' "Then he lowers his head, and there are his wives, and *goblets set down, and cushions ranged, and silken carpets spread.*[30] He lies back and declares, '*Praised be God, Who did guide us to this; we would not have been guided had He not guided us.*'[31] And a herald calls out, saying, 'You shall live and never die; you shall abide and never depart; you shall be in health and never in any sickness!' " '

Said the Emissary of God (may God bless him and grant him peace), 'On the Day of Arising I shall come to the Gate of Heaven and ask for it to be opened. "Who are you?" the Guardian shall ask. "Muḥammad," I shall reply. "I have been commanded," he says, "never to open this gate for anyone before you".'[32]

Now think upon the number of Heaven's Chambers, and the diverse levels of exaltation therein, for *truly the Afterlife is greater in degrees and greater in preferment.*[33] Just as there exists an external discrepancy between men in their outward good works and in their praiseworthy inward virtues, so shall there exist an external discrepancy in their reward. Thus, if the highest degree should be your quest, then strive to ensure that no-one surpass you in obedience to God (Exalted is He!), for He has enjoined rivalry and competition upon you in this regard, saying (Exalted is He!),

Race one another for forgiveness from your Lord,[34] and *For this, let those who would compete, compete.*[35] It is remarkable that were your companions or neighbours to outstrip you by having a single dirham more than you, or more numerous children, or by building higher edifices, you would be oppressed by this and your breast would be constricted, and your life would be befouled by envy. Yet the best state for you is residence in Heaven, and [even] there you shall not be safe from being outdone by others who have won gifts unparalleled in this world in its entirety.

Said Abū Saʿīd al-Khudrī, 'The Emissary of God, (may God bless him and grant him peace) once said, "The people of Heaven shall behold the people of the Chambers[A] above them just as you behold the morning and evening star when it lies above the horizon; so great is the discrepancy between them in merit." "O Emissary of God," [the Companions] said. "Those shall be the mansions of the Prophets, who alone may attain to them." "But no," he replied. "By Him in Whose hand lies my soul, therein shall be men who had faith in God, and believed the Messengers." '[36]

And he said also, 'The people of the *Highest Degrees*[37] shall be seen by those who are beneath them just as you behold a rising star in the horizons of the sky. Abū Bakr and ʿUmar shall be among them; nay, higher still.'[B] [38]

Said Jābir, 'The Emissary of God (may God bless him and grant him peace) said to us, "Shall I not speak to you of the Chambers of Heaven?" "Please do, O Emissary of God," we replied, "may God bless you and grant you peace, and may our

[A] As so often when discussing the details of the next life, the Islamic authorities have not achieved much in the way of consensus regarding the nature of these 'chambers' [*ghuraf*]. Al-Ḥakīm al-Tirmidhī, who cites this Tradition (*Nawādir*, 273) explains that 'the People of the Chambers are the People of ʿIlliyīn, whose rank is so exalted as to be near the Throne' and asserts that the root *gh-r-f* can bear the meaning of 'exaltation'. Qurṭubī (pp.461–465) also describes the Chambers as the highest reaches of Heaven. According to Zabīdī, however, the *ghuraf* are simply 'high palaces' (Zabīdī, x. 528).

[B] The word *wa-anʿamā*, rendered here as 'higher still,' can equally well be read to mean 'and shall be given felicity'. (Cf. Ibn al-Athīr, *Nihāya*, v. 83.)

mothers and fathers be your ransom!" And he declared, "In Heaven there shall be Chambers of every kind of precious stone. Their exteriors shall all be visible from within and their interiors from without. Inside them shall be joy, pleasures and happiness such as no eye has seen, no ear heard, and which has never occurred to mortal mind."[39] "O Emissary of God!" we said, "For whom shall those Chambers be?" And he replied, "For those who spread abroad the greeting of peace, who give out food, who fast at length and pray at night when the people are asleep." "O Emissary of God!" we said. "And who might sustain such a thing?" "My nation can sustain it," he said, "and I shall tell you how. Whoever meets one of his brethren and greets him or replies to his greeting has spread abroad the greeting of peace. Whoever feeds his family and dependants so that they are satisfied has given out food. Whoever fasts the month of Ramaḍān and three days in every other month has fasted at length. And whoever prays the Night and the Dawn Prayers with a congregation has prayed at night when the people are asleep; meaning the Jews, the Christians and the Zoroastrians." '[40]

The Emissary of God (may God bless him and grant him peace) was once asked about His statement (Exalted is He!), *And goodly dwellings in gardens of Eden*,[41] and he replied, 'They are palaces of pearls, in each of which are seventy ruby mansions, in each of which are seventy emerald rooms, in each of which are seventy beds, on each of which are seventy mattresses of every hue, on each of which is a wife who is one of the Large-eyed Houris. And in every room there are seventy tables, on each of which are seventy varieties of food. In every house are seventy servant-girls. Every morning the believer shall be given strength enough to enjoy all of this.'[42]

The Wall of Heaven, its Land,[1] *Trees and Rivers*

CONTEMPLATE the appearance of Heaven, and meditate upon the rapture of its inhabitants and the sorrow of he who is denied it because of his satisfaction with the world as a substitute.

Said Abū Hurayra, 'The Emissary of God (may God bless him and grant him peace) said, "The Wall of Heaven is of silver and gold bricks, while its soil is of saffron and its earth of musk".'[2]

And he was once asked (may God bless him and grant him peace) about the soil of Heaven, and he replied, 'It is of white flour and pure musk'.[3]

Said Abū Hurayra, 'The Emissary of God (may God bless him and grant him peace) has said, "Whoever would like God (Great and Glorious is He!) to give him wine to drink in the Afterlife should renounce it in this world. Whoever would like God to give him silk to wear in the Afterlife should renounce it in this world. The rivers of Heaven rise beneath hills" (or "mountains") "of musk. And were the finery of the lowliest of Heaven's people to be compared with that of the inhabitants of this world, the finery with which God (Great and Glorious is He!) bedecks one in the Afterlife would prove better than all the finery of this world." '[4]

Said Abū Hurayra, 'The Emissary of God (may God bless him and grant him peace) said, "In Heaven there lies a tree in the shade of which a rider could journey for a hundred years without traversing it. Recite, if you wish, *And shade outspread.*" '[5]

Said Abū Umāma, 'The Companions of the Emissary of God (may God bless him and grant him peace) used to say, "In truth, God (Great and Glorious is He!) will benefit us by the nomads and their questions." For a nomad once came and said, "O Emissary of God! In the Qur'ān God has mentioned a harmful tree, and I had never believed[6] that in Heaven there could be a tree which causes harm." "Which tree is that?" he enquired. "The lote-tree [*sidr*]," he replied, "which has thorns." But he answered, "God (Exalted is He!) has said, *And thornless lote-trees:*[7] He shall remove each thorn and replace it with a fruit, each of which shall open up to provide seventy-two varieties of food no two of which shall be the same." '[8]

Said Jarīr ibn ᶜAbd Allāh, 'Once, when we were resting at al-Saffāḥ, we beheld a man whom the sun had almost reached sleeping beneath a tree. "Take this leather mat and provide him with some shade," I told my servant-boy, and this he did. And when the man awoke it transpired that it was Salmān, so I went over to him to greet him. "O Jarīr," he said. "Be humble before God, for truly, whosoever is humble before God in this world shall be exalted by Him on the Day of Arising. Know you what are the shadows [*ẓulumāt*] on the Day of Arising?" "I do not," I replied, and he declared, "Injustice [*ẓulm*] between men."[A] Then he picked up a twig so small that I could hardly see it, and said, "O Jarīr! Were you to request even this in Heaven you would be unable to find it." "O Abū ᶜAbd Allāh!" I said, "But what of the palms, and the other trees?" "Their roots," he answered, "shall be of pearl and gold, above which shall be the fruit".'

The Raiment of Heaven's People, their Furnishings, Beds, Divans and Tents

GOD (Exalted is He!) has said, *Therein shall they be decked in bracelets of gold and pearl; therein shall their raiment be of silk.*[1] There are a great number of verses pertinent here, although the details are forthcoming only in the Traditions. Abū Hurayra has

[A] Cf. the statement of the Prophet as recorded by Muslim (Birr, 56): 'Injustice [*ẓulm*] will bring shadows [*ẓulumāt*] on the Day of Arising.'

narrated that the Prophet (may God bless him and grant him peace) once said, 'Whoever enters Heaven shall find comfort and no distress; his garments shall not grow threadbare, neither shall his youth ever come to an end. In Heaven there shall be that which no eye has seen, no ear heard, and which has never occurred to mortal mind.'[2]

A man once said, 'O Emissary of God! Tell us of the raiment of Heaven's people: is it to be something created [directly], or shall it be woven?' The Emissary of God (may God bless him and grant him peace) fell silent, as some of the people laughed, but then said, 'Why do you laugh at a man without knowledge of a matter who asks one possessed of it? Nay, rather the fruits of Heaven shall open up to [reveal] it twice [in every day].'[3]

Said Abū Hurayra, 'The Emissary of God (may God bless him and grant him peace) once said, "The aspect of the first throng to enter Heaven shall be as the moon on the night when it is full. Therein shall they never spit, sneeze, or void their bowels. Their vessels and their combs shall be of gold and silver, and their sweat shall be musk. Each one of them shall have two wives the marrow in whose legs is visible through their flesh, so beautiful are they. There arise no differences among them, neither any enmity: their hearts are as one. By morning and eve they proclaim the glory of God." '[4] And in another version [we read], 'And upon each wife shall be seventy gowns.'[5]

And he said (may God bless him and grant him peace) [commenting] upon His word (Exalted is He!), *Therein shall they be decked in bracelets of gold*:[6] 'They shall be wearing crowns the humblest pearl of which would illuminate the earth from East to West.'[7]

And he said (may God bless him and grant him peace), 'Each tent is a hollow pearl whose height shall be sixty miles, and in each corner of which the believer shall have a family unseen by the others.' This has been related by al-Bukhārī in the *Ṣaḥīḥ*.[8]

Said Ibn ʿAbbās, 'A "tent" will be a hollow pearl one league across, and will have four thousand door-flaps of gold.'

Said Abū Saʿīd al-Khudrī, 'The Emissary of God (may God bless him and grant him peace) once said [commenting] on His word (Exalted is He!), *And raised couches:*[9] "The distance between two such couches shall be as the distance between heaven and earth." '[10]

The Food of Heaven's People

IN THE Qur'ān there is a description of the food of Heaven's people, which includes fruit, plump fowl, mannah and quails, honey, milk, and innumerable other varieties. God (Exalted is He!) has said, *As often as they are regaled with food of the fruit thereof they say, This is what was given us aforetime. And it is given to them in resemblance.*[1]

God (Exalted is He!) has also and in many contexts made mention of the drink which Heaven's people shall enjoy. Said Thawbān, the *mawlā* of the Emissary of God (may God bless him and grant him peace), 'I was once with God's Emissary (may God bless him and grant him peace), when one of the rabbis of the Jews came and posed some questions. At length, he asked, "Who shall be the first to cross?"—meaning the Traverse—and he replied, "The poor among the Emigrants". And the Jew inquired, "And what shall be their prize when they enter into Heaven?" "The tip of the fish's liver,"[A] he answered. And he asked, "After that, what shall their nourishment be?" "The bull of Heaven", he replied, "which used to graze at its peripheries, shall be slaughtered for them". "And what shall be their drink?" he enquired. "It shall be from a *spring therein named Salsabīl*,"[2] came his answer. And the rabbi said, "You have spoken truly".'[3]

[A] *ziyāda kabid al-ḥūt*. '*Ziyāda*' (missing in Ṭabarānī's version given in Haythamī, *Majmaʿ*, x. 413) here has the sense of a 'tip', according to Nawawī's commentary (*Sharḥ*, III. 227). In the *Durra* (p. 102) it is asserted that the people of Heaven will eat the liver of the fish which supports the seven earths; however the significance of the event remains somewhat opaque.

Said Zayd ibn Arqam, 'A man from the Jews once came into the presence of God's Emissary (may God bless him and grant him peace) and said, "O Abu'l-Qāsim! Do you not claim that the people of Heaven shall eat and drink therein?" saying to his companions, "If he concedes this to me then I have confuted him!" And God's Emissary (may God bless him and grant him peace) said, "Even so. By Him in Whose hand lies my soul, one of them will be granted the strength of a hundred in eating, drinking and sexual relations." And the Jew said, "The man who eats and drinks must needs relieve nature", but the Emissary of God (may God bless him and grant him peace) replied, "They shall relieve nature by means of a sweat which flows upon their skins like musk, after which their bellies become slender once more".'[4]

Said Ibn Masᶜūd, 'The Emissary of God (may God bless him and grant him peace) said, "You shall only have to behold a bird in Heaven and desire it for it to fall down before you roasted".'[5]

Said Ḥudhayfa, 'The Emissary of God (may God bless him and grant him peace) once said, "In Heaven there shall be birds like great camels." "Will they be tender, O Emissary of God?" asked Abū Bakr, and he replied, "Those that eat of them shall be more so, and you are among those that shall eat of them, O Abū Bakr." '[6]

Said ᶜAbd Allāh ibn ᶜAmr, [commenting] upon His word (Exalted is He!), *They are served around with trays*:[7] 'They will be served around with seventy trays of gold, each of which contains a variety of food the likes of which are not[8] present in the others.'

Said ᶜAbd Allāh ibn Masᶜūd (may God be pleased with him) [commenting upon the text] *Its composition is of Tasnīm*:[9] 'It is to be mixed for the People of the Right Hand, and will be drunk solely by the Ones Brought Nigh.'[A]

Said Abu'l-Dardā' (may God be pleased with him) [commenting] on His word, (Exalted is He!), *Its seal is musk*:[10] 'This is a

[A] See Introduction, p.xxiii. The verse following the one quoted above runs *A spring from which shall drink the Ones Brought Nigh.*

drink which is as white as silver, with which they set a final seal upon their drinking. Were one of the people of the world to dip his hand therein and then bring it forth, no living thing would fail to perceive its fragrance.'

The Large-Eyed Houris and the Pages

THESE ARE described repeatedly in the Qur'ān, and are given a further exposition in the Traditions. Anas has related that the Emissary of God (may God bless him and grant him peace) once said, 'A single morning or evening in the path of God[A] is better than the world and all it contains. An area in Heaven half a bow's length around, or the space which one's foot occupies is better than the world and all it contains. Were but one of the wives of the people of Heaven to look out upon the earth she would illuminate it entirely, and fill [the space] between [heaven and earth] with perfume. The covering [*naṣīf*] which is upon her head'—meaning her scarf [*khimār*]—'is better than the world and all it contains.'[1]

Said Abū Saʿīd al-Khudrī, 'The Emissary of God (may God bless him and grant him peace) said, [commenting] upon His statement (Exalted is He!), *As though they were sapphires and pearls:*[2] "When one comes to behold her face in her tent it is purer than a mirror. The smallest pearl upon her would light up all that is between East and West. She shall be dressed in seventy garments through which his gaze passes until he espies the marrow of her leg underneath." '[3]

Said Anas, 'The Emissary of God (may God bless him and grant him peace) said, "When I was taken on the Night Journey[B]

[A] i.e. participating in the Holy War.

[B] *al-Isrā'*: the Prophet's miraculous journey from Mecca to Jerusalem (Cf. Q. XVII:1) which culminated in the *miʿrāj*, his ascension through the seven heavens. Many Muslim descriptions of Heaven and Hell are drawn from this event: cf. *Escatología*, 9–119; Schimmel, 159–175.

I entered Heaven at a place called al-Bīdukh[A], where there were tents of pearls, sapphires and green chrysolite. And it was said, 'Peace be upon you, O Emissary of God!' 'O Gabriel,' I asked, 'what was that call?' 'It came from the women *secluded in tents*,'[4] he replied, 'who asked leave of their Lord to greet you, which He granted'. And suddenly they began to say, 'We are the contented ones, and shall never be vexed. We are the eternal ones, and shall never pass away.' " And God's Emissary (may God bless him and grant him peace) recited His statement (Exalted is He!), *Houris secluded in tents*.'[5]

Said Mujāhid, [commenting] on His statement (Exalted is He!), *And wives purified*:[6] 'Of menstruation, excrement, mucus, semen and childbearing'.

Said al-Awzāʿī [commenting] on His statement (Exalted is He!), *Happily employed*:[7] 'In the defloration of virgins'.

A man once asked, 'O Emissary of God! Shall the people of Heaven enjoy carnal relations?' and he replied, 'Every man therein shall be given in a single day the capacity of seventy of you'.[8]

Said ʿAbd Allāh ibn ʿUmar, 'The lowest in rank of Heaven's people shall be a man with a thousand servants hastening busily on his account, each of whom is about a different task.'

Said the Emissary of God (may God bless him and grant him peace), 'A single man in Heaven shall wed five hundred houris, four thousand virgins, and eight thousand deflowered women, and shall embrace each one of them for a period equal to his lifetime in the world'.[9]

Said the Prophet (may God bless him and grant him peace), 'In Heaven there is a market in which there is neither purchase nor sale, but only images of men and women. Anyone that desires an image may enter into it. And in Heaven there is a host of the Large-eyed Houris, who lift up their voices in a sound the likes of

[A] (Vocalisation uncertain.) 'Bīdukht' is the Arameo-Persian name of the planet and goddess Venus; cf. D.B. Macdonald, art. 'Budūḥ' in EI^2 (Supplement, fasc. 3), 153–4. The intrusion of lexis of this nature into the less authentic *ḥadīth* material is not at all unusual.

which has never been heard by any creature, saying, "We are the eternal ones, and shall never pass away. We are the joyful ones, and shall never grieve. We are the contented ones, and shall never be vexed. Blessed, therefore, is he who shall be ours, and for whom we shall be." '[10]

Said Anas (may God be pleased with him), 'The Emissary of God (may God bless him and grant him peace) once said, "The Houris of Heaven shall sing, 'We are the houris beautiful, kept hidden for spouses honourable'." '[11]

Said Yaḥyā ibn [Abī] Kathīr [commenting] on His statement (Exalted is He!), *In a garden gladdened*:[12] 'Audition [*samāᶜ*][A] in Heaven.'

Said Abū Umāma al-Bāhilī, 'The Emissary of God (may God bless him and grant him peace) said, "At the head and feet of every man that enters Heaven there shall sit a pair of the Large-eyed Houris, who sing to him in the most beautiful voice ever heard by man or jinn; not the devil's piping, but only the praise and hallowing of God".'[13]

An Exposition of a Diverse Group of the Attributes of Heaven's People for which Accounts are Forthcoming

USĀMA IBN ZAYD has related that God's Emissary (may God bless him and grant him peace) once said to his Companions, 'Ho! Is there anyone that will roll up his sleeves for Heaven? Truly, Heaven is without rival. By the Lord of the Kaᶜba, it is a light which sparkles, and sweet basil which waves, and a *lofty palace*,[1] and a flowing river, and abundant ripe fruit,

[A] *Samāᶜ*: Any Sufi ceremony in which God is invoked collectively. (Cf. Hujwīrī, *Kashf*, 397–413; Qushayrī, *Risāla*, II. 637–659.)

and a beautiful and comely wife, in happiness and ease in an abode everlasting. It is joy in a lofty residence, splendid and secure.' And they said, 'We are the ones who will roll up their sleeves for it, O Emissary of God!' And he said, 'Say, "if God (Exalted is He!) so wills".' Then he made mention of the Holy War, and recommended it.[2]

A man once came to the Emissary of God (may God bless him and grant him peace) and asked, 'Will there be horses in Heaven, for they please me greatly?' 'If you should so desire', he replied, 'you will be brought a horse of ruby which will fly with you in Heaven wherever you please.' Another man said to him, 'I am fond of camels; shall there be any camels in Heaven?' and he answered, 'O bondsman of God; if you are received into Heaven then you shall have therein whatever your soul desires and your eye finds delectable.'[3]

Said Abū Saᶜīd al-Khudrī, 'The Emissary of God (may God bless him and grant him peace) said, "A man in Heaven shall have a child just as he desires, whose gestation, weaning and youth shall be in a single hour".'[4]

Said the Emissary of God (may God bless him and grant him peace), 'When Heaven's people are settled therein, friends will yearn for one another, and the couch of one will travel to that of another so that they meet and discuss what had passed between them in the worldly abode. One of them will say, "O my brother, do you recall such-and-such a day, and such-and-such an assembly, when we prayed to God and He forgave us?" '[5]

And he said (may God bless him and grant him peace), 'The people of Heaven are hairless, beardless, white, compact in limbs, use kohl, and are thirty-three years of age, with the form of Adam. Their height is sixty cubits and their breadth seven'.[6]

Said the Emissary of God (may God bless him and grant him peace), 'The lowliest of Heaven's people shall have eighty thousand servants and seventy-two wives. A dome of pearl, chrysolite and sapphire shall be raised up for him, which is as broad as the distance between al-Jābiya[A] and Ṣanᶜā'. They shall be

[A] A place approximately fifty miles south of Damascus. (Cf. H. Lammens, art. 'al-Djābiya', in *EI*², II. 360.)

wearing crowns the least pearl of which would cast light from East to West.'[7]

And he said (may God bless him and grant him peace), 'I have beheld Heaven: one of its pomegranates is as large as a water skin made from the hide of a large-humped camel. Its birds are as great riding camels. There was a slave-girl there, and I asked her, "O slave-girl! To whom do you belong?" "To Zayd ibn Ḥāritha," she replied. And in Heaven there is that which no eye has seen, no ear heard, and which has never occurred to mortal mind.'[8]

Said Kaᶜb, 'God (Exalted is He!) created Adam with His hand, wrote the Torah with His hand, and then planted Heaven with His hand, saying to it, "Speak!" And it declared, "*The faithful have triumphed*".'[9]

Such are the attributes of Heaven, which we have mentioned both in detail and in sum. Al-Ḥasan al-Baṣrī (may God have mercy upon him) once mentioned them all when he declared, 'Its pomegranates are the size of pails, its rivers are of *water which never stagnates, and of milk the taste of which is never sour,*[10] *and of purified honey,*[11] not cultivated by men, and *of wine a delight to those that drink of it.*[12] Therein minds never grow feeble, and heads never ache. And therein is what no eye has seen, no ear heard, and what has never occurred to mortal mind. They are kings in pleasure, thirty-three years of age. The height of each one will be sixty cubits. They use kohl, and are hairless and beardless. They are safe from the punishment, and the Abode is well-pleased with them. Meads flow for them over pebbles of sapphire and chrysolite. Its roots, palms and vines are of pearl, and its fruit is such as is known only unto God (Exalted is He!). Its fragrance diffuses five hundred years' voyage around. Therein they have swift horses and camels with bridles, reins and saddles of sapphire. Therein they visit one another. Their spouses are *Large-eyed Houris, like hidden pearls.*[13] A woman shall take up between her fingers seventy robes and don them, while the marrow of her leg remains visible beneath. Manners are purified there of coarseness, and bodies of death. They do not blow their noses, neither do they urinate or excrete, but instead they belch and perspire musk. *Therein is their provision morning and night.*[14] There will be no repeated coming and going there.

'The last man to enter Heaven, who is the least of them in degree, will be given to see all that he owns for the distance of a hundred years' journey, all of which is gold and silver palaces, and tents of pearl. His vision will be enhanced, so that he descries its most distant parts as well as he beholds its nearer places.

'Morning and night they shall be served with seventy thousand platters of gold, in each of which is a dish different from the others; the taste of the last shall be as delicious as that of the first. In Heaven there is a sapphire in which are seventy thousand mansions, in each of which lie seventy thousand chambers, in which there is not a single crack or fissure.'

Said Mujāhid, 'The lowliest of Heaven's people shall travel a thousand years in his kingdom, beholding its farthest parts just as he beholds its nearest, while the highest is him that shall gaze upon his Lord morning and night.'

Said Saᶜīd ibn al-Musayyib, 'Every one of Heaven's people shall wear three bracelets: one of gold, another of pearl, and a third of silver.'

Said Abū Hurayra, 'In Heaven there is an houri called al-ᶜAynā'. Whenever she walks seventy thousand maids of honour walk on her right and left, while she asks, "Where are they that enjoined goodness and forbade iniquity?"'

Said Yaḥyā ibn Muᶜādh, 'To renounce this world is a hardship, but to lose Heaven is a hardship greater still. The renunciation of this world is the dowry of the next.' And he said also, 'In the pursuit of this world lies the humiliation of the soul, while in the pursuit of the Afterlife lies its honour. What a marvel it is, then, that one might prefer humiliation for the sake of pursuing something which must pass away, and renounce the honour which is in the pursuit of what must needs abide!'

The Beatific Vision, and the Beholding of the Countenance of God (Blessed and Exalted is He!)

GOD (Exalted is He!) has said, *For those that wrought good shall be the greatest good, and even more.*[1] This 'even more' is the Vision of the Divine Countenance, which is the greatest of all delights, and which shall cause one to be quite oblivious of the pleasures of the people of Heaven. We have mentioned its true nature in the *Book of [Sacramental] Love*[A], and it has been attested to by the Book and the Sunna in a way which refutes what the heretics [*ahl al-bidᶜa*][B] believe.

Said Jarīr ibn ᶜAbd Allāh al-Bajalī, 'We were sitting once with the Emissary of God (may God bless him and grant him peace), when he looked at the full moon, and said, "You shall behold your Lord just as you behold this moon. You shall not be

[A] *K. al-Maḥabba wa'l-shawq wa'l-uns wa'l-riḍā* (*Iḥyā'*, IV. book 6; the Vision is discussed on pp.264–271 [German translation by Gramlich, pp.656–670]).

[B] The Ashᶜarite orthodoxy, which holds the vision [*ru'ya*] of God to be true 'without how' [*bilā kayf*] (Ashᶜarī, *Ibāna*, 9–10; *Maqālāt*, 292–293; Bāqillānī, *Tamhīd*, 266–275) traditionally expressed itself in the form of a polemic specifically or implicitly directed against a variety of early heresies. In particular, the Muᶜtazilites and the Jahmīya, seemingly alluded to here, denied the possibility of the *ru'ya*, (Gardet and Anawati, 58), citing the Qur'ānic verse *Perception cannot reach Him* (VI:103) and God's statement to Moses, '*Thou shalt not behold Me*' (VII:143). The Ashᶜarites replied by asserting that these texts deny only the believer's vision of God in this world (*Ibāna*, 10; *Maqālāt*, 293; *Iqtiṣād*, 67–68), and went on to provide an involved and often brilliant theological explanation of how the *ru'ya* is to be understood. In his earlier works, Ghazālī reiterates this analysis (*Iqtiṣād*, 59–69) but later on, as throughout the *Iljām*, and as in the *Iḥyā'* text from the *K. al-Maḥabba* referred to in this section (esp. IV. 271), regards it as being sufficiently proved by scriptural authority (this representing a more Māturīdite position; cf. Māturīdī, 77) and by *kashf*: the Beatific Vision is none other than the gnosis (*maᶜrifa*) already given in an inferior and more fleeting fashion to the saints in this world (*Iḥyā'*, IV. 270). For his later adumbration of this doctrine see *Escatología*, 251.

obstructed from the vision of Him. Therefore, if you are able to pray before the sun rises and before it sets, then do so." Then he recited, *And proclaim the praise of thy Lord before the sun's rising and at its decline.*'[2] This has been recorded in the two *Ṣaḥīḥs*.[3]

Muslim relates in his *Ṣaḥīḥ* that Ṣuhayb once said, 'The Emissary of God (may God bless him and grant him peace) recited His word (Exalted is He!): *For those that wrought good shall be the greatest good, and even more* [and commented as follows]: "When the people of Heaven enter Heaven and those of Hell enter Hell, a herald shall call out, saying, 'O people of Heaven! There is a tryst for you with your Lord,[4] which He wishes to bring about for you.' 'What might that tryst be?' they enquire. 'Did He not load heavily our scales, and whiten our faces, and bring us into Heaven and deliver us from Hell?' And, the veil is lifted, and they gaze upon the Countenance of God (Great and Glorious is He!), and never had they been given anything more beloved to them than this." '[5]

This Tradition of the Vision, which is narrated by a number of the Companions, reveals the supreme height of the *greatest good*, and the very limit of bliss. All that we have detailed regarding the delights [of Heaven] shall at that moment be forgotten; for the rapture felt by Heaven's people at the Meeting shall be without end; neither shall any of the pleasures of Heaven stand any comparison with it at all.

We have made our discourse here succinct, since we have already provided details in the *Book of* [*Sacramental*] *Love, Affection and Satisfaction*. It is not proper that the bondsman's quest for Heaven should be for anything other than the meeting with his Lord. As for the rest of Heaven's delights, man's participation in them is no more than that of a beast let loose in a pasture.[A]

[A] A favourite Sufi motif. Ghazālī devotes two Expositions to the subject, the first of which (*Iḥyā'*, IV. 264–7; tr. Gramlich, 656–64) shows that gnosis and the vision of the supernal One, Who has neither form nor dimension, constitute the highest form of felicity, while the second (IV. 267–71; Gramlich, 664–70) explains why the Vision is 'clearer' and 'more perfect' in the Afterlife. The argument runs thus: Every organ of perception brings pleasure when its instinctive function is fulfilled. The heart is such an organ, for God has spoken of *him whose breast God has opened to Islam, so that he has a light from his Lord* (Q. XXXIX:22): this divine Light is the Intellect,

And we conclude the Book with A Chapter on the Wide Compass of God's Mercy, for optimism's sake

THE Emissary of God (may God bless him and grant him peace) used to like optimism, and, since we have to our credit no works through which we might hope for forgiveness, we emulate him (may God bless him and grant him peace) and are optimistic, hoping that God may end our courses well in this world and in the next; thus we shall end this book with a commemoration of His mercy (Exalted is He!). For He has said, *Assuredly, God forgives not that partners should be associated unto Him, but He forgives all save that to whomsoever He will.*[1] And He has said (Exalted is He!), *O my bondsmen, who were prodigal with their own selves! Despair not of God's mercy! Truly, God forgives all sins. Truly, He is the All-Forgiving, the All-Merciful.*[2] And He has said (Exalted is He!), *Yet whosoever has wrought evil or has wronged his own self, but then asks for God's forgiveness, shall find Him to be All-Forgiving, All-Merciful.*[3]

We ask forgiveness of God (Exalted is He!) for every stumbling on our part, and for every slip of the pen in this and all our other books. We ask His forgiveness for those of our words which have not been matched by our deeds. We ask His forgiveness for the claims and professions of knowledge and insight into His religion which we have made despite our insufficiencies therein. We ask

which with its intuitive powers is to be distinguished from pure reason (p.264), and may perceive intangibles and know God, which is a fulfillment entailing a pleasure greater than any other, since knowledge of the Creator is superior to any knowledge which may be had of His creation. But this cannot be proved rationally, for 'only he who tastes, knows' (p.266), just as the pleasure of sexual union cannot be explained to children. When the Vision is attained, 'all concerns and desires are extinguished' (p.267). Thus Rābiʿa al-ʿAdawīya could make her famous pronouncement, 'I have not worshipped Him from fear of Hell, nor from longing for Heaven, for thus would I be as a bad hireling; rather have I worshipped Him out of love and yearning for Him alone' (p.266).

His forgiveness for every science we have acquired and every action which we have undertaken for His noble sake, but which was then commingled with something else. We ask His forgiveness for every covenant we made within ourselves but which we then fell short of fulfilling. We ask His forgiveness for every blessing which He bestowed upon us but which we employed in disobedience to Him. We seek His forgiveness for having declared or implied the shortcomings or the inadequacy of anyone. And we ask His forgiveness for every passing notion which induced us to dissemble or be mannered for the sake of playing up to others, in any book which we have written, or any discourse which we have delivered, or any science which we have profited or profited from. And after having asked His pardon for all these things, for ourselves and for whomsoever reads this book of ours, or copies it, or listens to it, we ask that He should honour us with His forgiveness and mercy, and overlook the entirety of our sins, both evident and concealed. For all-encompassing is His generosity, all-abundant is His mercy, and His grace overflows upon all that He has made. And we, who are of His making, find no path to Him but that which lies through His grace and munificence. For the Emissary of God (may God bless him and grant him peace) has said, 'Truly, God (Exalted is He!) is of a hundred mercies, one of which He has sent below to jinn and to mankind, and to the birds and the animals and the vermin, through which is all their mutual dealing with kindness and with mercy. And ninety-nine mercies has He withheld, and by them shall He show mercy to His bondsmen on the Day of Arising.'[4]

And it is related that when the Day of Arising comes, God (Exalted is He!) shall bring forth a book from beneath the Throne, in which it is written: 'My Mercy has outstripped My wrath. I am the Most Merciful of all that show mercy'. And from out of Hell shall proceed the number of Heaven's folk twice multiplied.[5]

And God's Emissary has said (may God bless him and grant him peace), 'On the Day of Arising, God (Great and Glorious is He!) shall joyfully appear before us, and declare, "Rejoice, O assembly of Muslims! For there is not one of you that has not had his place in Hell taken by a Jew or a Christian!" '[A] [6]

Said the Prophet (may God bless him and grant him peace), 'On the Day of Arising, God shall give Adam to intercede on behalf of a hundred and ten million of his seed.'[B] [7]

And the Prophet (may God bless him and grant him peace) has said, 'On the Day of Arising, God (Great and Glorious is He!) shall ask the faithful, "Did you yearn for the meeting with Me?" "Yes, O our Lord!" they reply. And when He asks why, they answer, "Because in Your indulgence and pardon did we set our hopes." And at this He declares, "For you have I decreed that pardon".'[8]

And he said (may God bless him and grant him peace), 'On the Day of Arising, God (Great and Glorious is He!) shall say, "Bring forth from Hell all those who remembered Me on one day, or ever feared the standing before Me".'[9]

And the Emissary of God said (may God bless him and grant him peace), 'When the people of Hell are thronged together in the Inferno with whomsoever God wills of the people of Islam [*ahl al-qibla*], the unbelievers shall say to the latter, "Were you not Muslims?" "Yes," they make reply, to be told, "Your Islam did not avail you, for see, you are with us in Hell!" And they say, "We had committed sins, and were taken to task for them." And God (Great and Glorious is He!) hears what they say, and orders all those of the people of Islam who are in Hell to be brought forth; and this is done. And when the unbelievers behold this they cry out, saying, "Would that we had been Muslims, that we might be fetched hence like them!" And then the Emissary of

[A] Given the title of this chapter, it may be relevant to point out that As̲h̲ʿarite orthodoxy teaches that non-Muslims who have not been exposed to Islam, even after its historical advent, cannot be taken to task for not embracing it. Provided that they believe in the unity and justice of God, they too are candidates for salvation. (Cf. Bag̲h̲dādī, *Uṣūl*, 262–4.)

[B] As Ḥasan K̲h̲ālid points out (pp.185–6, 346–52), the Traditions envisage two quite different classes of intercession: one for relief and mercy on the Day of Judgement, as described previously, and another, to be exercised exclusively by the Prophet Muḥammad, by which sinners shall be delivered from the infernal regions—a belief corresponding to the Catholic doctrine of the 'Harrowing of Hell'.

God (may God bless him and grant him peace) recited, *Presently those that disbelieved shall wish they had been Muslims.*'[A] [10]

And he said (may God bless him and grant him peace), 'God is more compassionate to His believing bondsman than is the loving mother to her child.'[11]

Said Jarīr ibn ᶜAbd Allāh, 'The man whose good deeds outweigh his sins on the Day of Arising shall enter Heaven without reckoning. The man whose good deeds match his sins *shall receive a lenient judgement*,[12] and shall then enter Heaven. The Intercession of God's Emissary (may God bless him and grant him peace) is only for the man that ruined himself and burdened his back.'[B]

It is related that God (Great and Glorious is He!) once said to Moses (upon whom be peace), 'O Moses! Qārūn begged for your aid, but you afforded him none.[C] But by My Glory and Majesty, had he begged for My aid I would have aided him, and would have granted him My forgiveness.'

Said Saᶜd ibn Bilāl, 'On the Day of Arising, an order shall be promulgated for the removal of two men from Hell, and God (Exalted is He!) shall say, "That was for what your hands had wrought, *and never was I unjust to My bondsmen.*"[13] Then He shall decree their restoration into Hell, upon which one of them is covered in shackles up to his neck, while the other holds back. Then the command is given to bring them out anew, and He questions them about what they had just done. The one who had returned to Hell says, "I had feared the evil consequence of sin, and wished never again to expose myself to Your displeasure." And the man who had hesitated declares, "My good opinion of You convinced me that You would never send me back after

[A] The Muᶜtazilite and the Khārijite sects taught that Muslim recidivists would remain in Hell eternally (Ashᶜarī, *Maqālāt*, 474; Rāzī, *Maᶜālim*, 131). This doctrine was rejected by the Ashᶜarites; according to Ghazālī, even the most sinful of the believers will remain in Hell for no more than seven thousand years (*Iḥyā'*, IV. 268).

[B] Cf. the *ḥadīth* 'My Intercession is for those of my nation who are guilty of great sins'. (Abū Dāūd, Sunna, 21; Ibn Māja, Zuhd, 37; cf. Ashᶜarī, *Maqālāt*, 293; Bāqillānī, *Tamhīd*, 365.)

[C] Cf. Q. XXVIII:76–82. Qārūn, the biblical Korah, was swallowed up by the earth for his defiance of God.

having delivered me." Thus it is that God orders that they both be taken to Heaven.'[14]

Said God's Emissary (may God bless him and grant him peace), 'On the Day of Arising, a herald shall cry out from beneath the Throne, saying, "O nation of Muḥammad! All that was due to me from you I grant you now, and only that which follows [of rights unrestored] remains. Thus grant them to one another, and enter Heaven through My mercy." '[A] [15]

It is related that a nomad once heard Ibn ʿAbbās recite *And you did stand on the brink of a fiery chasm, and He did save you therefrom.*[16] 'By God!' he said. 'He would not have saved you therefrom if He wanted to cast you into it!' And Ibn ʿAbbās remarked [to all and sundry], 'Learn this from one who is uneducated!'

Said al-Ṣunābiḥī, 'I came in upon ʿUbāda ibn al-Ṣāmit when he was in his mortal illness. I began to weep, but he said, "Easy now! Why do you weep? For, by God, not one of the Traditions which I heard from God's Emissary (may God bless him and grant him peace) in which there would be benefit for you did I not relate to you, save one alone, which I shall narrate to you today now that my soul is beset on all sides. I heard the Emissary of God (may God bless him and grant him peace) say, 'God has made Hell forbidden for all who declare, "There is no deity save God, and Muḥammad is the Emissary of God".' " '[17]

Said ʿAbd Allāh ibn ʿAmr ibn al-ʿĀṣ, 'The Emissary of God (may God bless him and grant him peace) once said, "On the Day of Arising, God shall choose a man from my nation out of the assembly of all creatures. Ninety-nine books shall be spread out before him, each one of which stretches as far as the eye can see. Then He shall ask him, 'Do you deny any of this? Have my Recording Angels dealt you any injustice?' 'No, my Lord,' he shall reply. Then He shall ask, 'Have you any excuse?' 'No, my Lord,' he shall reply. 'But yes,' says He, 'you have one good action in My sight, and today there shall be no injustice against you.' And He brings out a card upon which is written, 'I bear witness that there is no deity save God, and I bear witness that Muḥammad is the Emissary of God.' 'O my Lord!' he says,

[A] A reference to the principle of 'restoration of wrongs' dealt with on pp.198–205.

'What is that card beside all these books?' 'You shall not be wronged,' says He. And the books are placed in one scale, and the card in the other, and the books rise up while the card descends, for there is nothing which can outweigh God's name." '[A] [18]

Said God's Emissary (may God bless him and grant him peace) at the close of a lengthy[19] Tradition in which he described the Arising and the Traverse, 'God shall say to the Angels: "Wherever you find a dinar's weight of good in anyone's heart, bring that person forth from Hell;" thus they bring forth a great throng. Then they say, "O our Lord! We have left therein none of those whom You ordered us to take." But He says, "Go back, and whenever you find an half-dinar's weight of good in anyone's heart, bring him forth from Hell;" and thus they bring out another great throng. Then they say, "O our Lord! We have left therein none of those whom You ordered us to take." "Return", He says, "and whenever you find half an[20] ant's weight of good in anyone's heart, then bring him forth". Thus they bring out a further great throng, upon which they declare, "O our Lord! We have left therein no good." '[21] And Abū Saʿīd al-Khudrī was wont to declare, 'If you do not believe me in respect of this Tradition, then recite, if you wish, His statement (Exalted is He!): *Truly, God does not work so much as an ant's weight of injustice. If there is a good act, he multiplies it, and bestows from His presence a mighty reward.*'[22] Then he [continued the Tradition, and] said, ' "Then God shall say, 'The Angels have interceded, the Prophets have interceded, the believers have interceded; none remains now except the Most Merciful of the Merciful.' And He takes up a handful, and there emerges a people that never once did good, who have been turned to cinders. He casts them into a river at the mouths of Heaven which is called the River of Life, from which they grow as do seeds cast upon the banks of a flash-flood. Have you not seen that what grows between the stones and the trees is yellow and green,[23] while that which is in the shade is white?" And they said, "O Emissary of God! It is just as though

[A] This, the *ḥadīth al-Biṭāqa*, the '*ḥadīth* of the Card' is among the best-known of all Traditions.

you had been a shepherd in the desert!"[A] And he said, "Then they emerge like pearls. Around their necks are rings, so that they are recognised by the people of Heaven, who say, 'Behold the slaves freed by the All-Merciful, those whom He brought into Heaven although they had never done any praiseworthy thing, nor sent before them the slightest good!' Then He says, 'Enter into Heaven, where whatsoever you see shall be yours.' And they say, 'O our Lord! You have given us that which You never bestowed upon anyone before us!' And God (Exalted is He!) says, 'And I have for you something which is better still.' 'O our Lord!' they say, 'And what could be better still?' 'My Satisfaction with you;' he replies, 'for henceforth I shall never be wrathful against you again'." ' This has been narrated by al-Bukhārī and Muslim in their *Ṣaḥīḥs*.[24]

Al-Bukhārī also narrates on the authority of Ibn ᶜAbbās (may God be pleased with them both) that 'The Emissary of God (may God bless him and grant him peace) came out to us one day, and said, "The nations have been displayed before me, so that one Prophet passed by me accompanied by one man, another Prophet by two, a Prophet by no-one at all, and another by a group. Then I espied a great host, and hoped that it would be my nation, but was told, 'That is Moses and his people.' Then I was commanded to look, and I beheld another great host which filled the horizons. And I was told to look this way and that, until I beheld still another mighty host. 'Behold your nation,' I was told. 'Of them, seventy thousand shall enter Heaven without reckoning.' " At this, the people went apart, none [of the seventy thousand] having been named by the Emissary of God (may God bless him and grant him peace). The Companions discussed this matter amongst themselves, and said, "As for our case, we were born into polytheism, and only later believed in God and His Emissary; those [whom he mentioned] are our descendants." News of this reached the Emissary of God (may God bless him and grant him peace), who declared, "Rather, they are those who do not resort

[A] And so he had, according to the traditional accounts, in his youth.

to cauterisation,[A] or charms, or to drawing omens from birds,[B] and who set their trust in God." Then ʿUkāsha stood up and said, "Pray God to set me among them, O Emissary of God!" and he replied, "You are among them." Another man arose and repeated what ʿUkāsha had said, but the Prophet (may God bless him and grant him peace) declared, "In this, ʿUkāsha has preceded you".'[C] [25]

Said ʿAmr ibn Ḥazm al-Anṣārī, 'The Emissary of God (may God bless him and grant him peace) once retired from us for three days, coming forth only for the prescribed Prayers, following which he would return. When it was the fourth day he came out before us, and we said, "O Emissary of God! You kept from us until we thought that something might have transpired." "Nothing but good has transpired," he said. "My Lord (Great and Glorious is He!) gave me a covenant, saying that He would bring into Heaven seventy thousand of my nation without reckoning. During these three days I petitioned Him for more, and found my Lord Praiseworthy, Self-Sufficient and Generous. For every one of those seventy thousand He gave me seventy thousand more. 'O my Lord!' I said. 'And shall my nation reach such a multitude?' and He replied, 'I shall make up the number for you with the nomads'." '[26]

Said Abū Dharr, 'The Emissary of God (may God bless him and grant him peace) said, "Gabriel appeared to me at the edge of the Ḥarra,[D] and said, 'Give your nation the glad news that whoever dies without having associated any partners unto God shall enter into Heaven.' 'O Gabriel!' I said, 'Even if he had committed theft and adultery?' 'Yes,' he replied, 'even if he had committed theft and adultery.'[27] 'Even if he had committed theft

[A] An explanation for this dislike of cauterisation is given by the Indian sage Shāh Walī Allāh al-Dahlawī, who tells us that the practice drives away the angels (*Ḥujjat Allāh al-Bāligha*, II. 194).

[B] A pagan Arab custom.

[C] 'ʿUkāsha has preceded you' became a proverb with roughly the same meaning as our English idiom 'pipped at the post'. It is still occasionally heard. (Cf. Sakhāwī, 384.)

[D] The basalt plain which surrounds Medina on three sides.

and adultery?' I asked [again], and he replied, 'Even if he used to drink wine'." '[28]

Said Abu'l-Dardā', 'The Emissary of God (may God bless him and grant him peace) once recited, *And for whomsoever fears the standing before his Lord shall be two gardens,*[29] and I asked, "Even if he had committed theft and adultery, O Emissary of God?" And he said, "*And for whomsoever fears the standing before his Lord shall be two gardens,*" and I asked [again], "Even if he had committed theft and adultery, O Emissary of God?" But he said, "*And for whomsoever fears the standing before his Lord shall be two gardens.*" And [again] I asked, "Even if he had committed theft and adultery, O Emissary of God?" And he declared, "Yes, despite Abu'l-Dardā'!" '[30]

And God's Emissary (may God bless him and grant him peace) said, 'When the Day of Arising comes, every believer shall be presented with a man from the people of the other faiths [*ahl al-milal*] and be told, "Behold your ransom from Hell!" '[31]

And Muslim relates in the *Ṣaḥīḥ* that Abū Burda related to ᶜUmar ibn ᶜAbd al-ᶜAzīz on the authority of his father Abū Mūsā [al-Ashᶜarī] that the Prophet (may God bless him and grant him peace) said, 'Never shall a Muslim man die without God (Exalted is He!) setting in his place in Hell a Jew or a Christian'. ᶜUmar ibn ᶜAbd al-ᶜAzīz made him swear three times 'by God, besides Whom there is no other deity' that his father had indeed related this to him on the authority of God's Emissary (may God bless him and grant him peace), and he did so.[A] [32]

It is related that during one of the campaigns a boy was standing and being sold off, this being on an intensely hot summer's day. He was seen by a woman concealed among the

[A] These two well-known Traditions, the second of which was, according to al-Nawawī, described by ᶜUmar ibn ᶜAbd al-ᶜAzīz and al-Shāfiᶜī as being 'of all the Traditions of Islam the most inspiring of hope', (*Sharḥ*, XVII. 86) have been given a necessary gloss by the same commentator, who remarks that their 'purport is that God (Exalted is He!) shall forgive the Muslims their sins and absolve them thereof, and lay upon the Jews and the Christians their like because of their unbelief and their transgressions. Yet it is by their own works that He shall consign them to Hell, not those of the Muslims. This interpretation is indispensable because of His statement (Exalted is He!), *No soul shall bear the burden of another.*' (*Sharḥ*, XVII. 85.)

people, who made her way forwards vigorously with her companions behind her, until she took up the child and clutched him to her breast. Then she turned her back to the valley to keep the heat away from him, saying, 'My son! My son!' At this the people wept, and left what they were doing. Then the Emissary of God (may God bless him and grant him peace) came up and stood before them. They told him of what had transpired, and he was delighted to see their compassion. Then he gave them glad news, saying, 'Marvel you at this woman's compassion for her son?' and they said that they did. And he declared (may God bless him and grant him peace), 'Truly, God (Blessed and Exalted is He!) is even more compassionate towards you all than is this woman towards her son.' At this, the Muslims went apart in the greatest rapture and joy.[33]

These Traditions, together with those which we have related in the *Book of Hope*, give us the glad news of the wide compass of God's Mercy (Exalted is He!). It is our hope that He will not deal with us as we deserve, but will rather grant us that which is appropriate to Him, in His generosity, abundant indulgence, and mercy.

NOTES

PART ONE

Notes to Chapter One

1 This rubric missing in Z.

2 MA, A: 'from palaces into the graves'.

3 'and drink' missing in Z.

4 'and protection' missing in Z.

5 Q. XIX:98.

6 Tirmidhī, Qiyāma, 25; Ibn Mājah, Zuhd, 21.

7 Q. XXI:1.

8 Q. LXII:8.

9 Bukhārī, Riqāq, 41; Muslim, Dhikr, 14.

10 Tirmidhī, Qiyāma, 26; Nasā'ī, Janā'iz, 3.

11 Quḍāʿī, II. 314; Abū Nuʿaym, VI. 392; Wakīʿ. I,285; Ibn al-Mubārak, (*riwāya* Nuʿaym ibn Ḥammād), 38.

12 Ṭabarānī, *al-Muʿjam al-Awsaṭ* (Suyūṭī, *Sharḥ*, 20).

13 Ḥākim, IV. 319; Ṭabarānī, *al-Muʿjam al-Kabīr* (Haythamī, *Majmaʿ*, II. 320; X. 309).

14 A well-known *ḥadīth* of the Prophet (Muslim, Zuhd, 1).

15 Quḍāʿī, I. 133; Abū Nuʿaym, III. 121.

16 Ṭabarānī, *al-Muʿjam al-Awsaṭ* (Haythamī, *Majmaʿ*, X. 308).

17 Ibn Abi'l-Dunyā, *K. al-Mawt* (Zabīdī, X. 228; Suyūṭī, *Jāmiʿ*, II. 208).

18 Ibn al-Sunnī, 164; Ibn Abi'l-Dunyā, *K. al-Birr wa'l-ṣila* (Zabīdī, X. 229).

19 Quḍāʿī, II. 302; Ṭabarānī, *al-Muʿjam al-Awsaṭ* (Haythamī, *Majmaʿ*, X. 308); Ibn al-Sunnī, 164.

20 Ibn Ḥanbal, *Zuhd*, 14, 182; al-Bazzār, *al-Musnad*, (Haythamī, *Majmaʿ*, III. 55).

21 Ibn Ḥanbal, *Zuhd*, 24; Ibn al-Mubārak, 90; Abū Nuʿaym, VII. 299; al-Bazzār, *al-Musnad* (Haythamī, *Majmaʿ*, X. 309).

22 Ṭabarānī, *Ṣaghīr*, II. 87; al-Ḥakīm al-Tirmidhī, 125-126.

23 'misfortunes and' missing in Z.

24 Z: 'power'.

Notes to Chapter Two

1 Assigned to the Prophet in Ibn Abi'l-Dunyā, *Qiṣar al-amal* (Zabīdī, X. 237; Ibn al-Jawzī, *ʿIlal*, II. 329); the first half is given as such in Qushayrī, *Risāla*, II. 440; but more commonly held to be a saying of the caliph ʿAlī; cf. Ibn Ḥanbal, *Zuhd*, 162–163; Ibn al-Mubārak, 86; Abū Nuʿaym, I. 76; Ḥalīmī, III. 395.

2 Quḍāʿī, I. 345; Bayhaqī, *Shuʿab al-īmān* (Zabīdī, X. 237). The final three phrases became fairly popular: cf. e.g. Ibn Qutayba, *ʿUyūn*, II. 331, where they form part of a homily delivered by Abu'l-Dardā' to the people of Damascus.

3 Abū Nuʿaym, VI. 91. The Qur'ānic passage is from Q. VI:134.

4 Ibn al-Mubārak, 99.
5 Ibn al-Mubārak, 86; Wakīʿ, II. 436–437.
6 Tirmidhī, Qiyāma, 22.
7 Bukhārī, Riqāq, 4.
8 Ibn Ḥanbal, *Musnad*, III. 115; Ibn al-Mubārak, 87; Wakīʿ, II. 433.
9 Muslim, Zakāt, 115.
10 Ibn Ḥanbal, *Zuhd*, 16; Ṭabarānī, *al-Muʿjam al-Awsaṭ* (Haythamī, *Majmaʿ*, x. 286); al-Ḥakīm al-Tirmidhī, 345.
11 Ibn Ḥanbal, *Musnad*, I. 387; Tirmidhī, Qiyāma, 24.
12 Ibn Ḥanbal, *Zuhd*, 472.
13 Given as a saying of the Prophet in Ḥalīmī, III. 386.
14 Q.XXXIX:69
15 Q.XXXIX:75
16 'ibn ʿAlī' missing in Z.
17 Q. II:197.
18 Ṭabarānī, *Ṣaghīr*, I. 251; Ḥākim, IV. 325.
19 Q. XXXIII:71.
20 Q. IV:119.
21 Q. II:96.
22 Q. XXXVIII:25. The *ḥadīth* is related in al-Ḥakīm al-Tirmidhī, 79; Ibn al-Mubārak, 87.
23 Ibn ʿUmar.
24 See above, p.15.
25 See above, p. 16.
26 Q. XCIX:7.
27 Z: 'He therefore makes'.
28 Q. LIV:46. The *ḥadīth* is given in Tirmidhī, Zuhd, 3.
29 Ibn al-Mubārak, 2; Wakīʿ, I. 223–4; Ḥākim, IV. 306; Ḥalīmī, III. 379.
30 Bukhārī, Riqāq, 1.
31 Tirmidhī, Qiyāma, 18.
32 Tirmidhī, Qiyāma, 23.
33 Z: 'in the people'.
34 Abū Nuʿaym, VII. 304.
35 Quḍāʿī, I. 218; Ṭabarānī, *al-Muʿjam al-Awsaṭ* (Haythamī, *Majmaʿ*, x. 228).
36 al-Bazzār, *al-Musnad*, (Haythamī, *Majmaʿ*, x. 311); Ibn Abī ʿĀṣim, *Zuhd*, 75.
37 Ibn Abi'l-Dunyā, *Qiṣar al-amal* (Zabīdī, x. 254).
38 Muslim, Jumuʿa, 52.
39 Q. VI: 125.
40 Ibn al-Mubārak, 106–107; al-Ḥakīm al-Tirmidhī, 126; Ḥalīmī, III. 384; Ḥākim, IV. 311
41 Q. LXVII:2.
42 Q. LXXIV:35–7
43 'the profusion of' missing in Z.
44 Q. XIX:84.
45 '*and vain . . . you*' missing in MA and A.
46 Q. LVII:14. 'By the devil' missing in Z.
47 MA, A: 'al-Bājī', which seems unlikely.

Notes to Chapter Three

1 *balagha*. (Z: *ghalaba ʿalā*: 'overwhelms'.)
2 Ḥākim, IV. 257.
3 Q. IV:18.
4 Ibn Māja, Janā'iz, 64; Tirmidhī, Janā'iz, 7.
5 Ibn Abi'l-Dunyā, *K. al-Mawt* (Zabīdī, x. 260; Suyūṭī, *Sharḥ*, 33).
6 Ibn Abi'l-Dunyā, *K. al-Mawt* (Zabīdī, x. 260; Suyūṭī, *Sharḥ*, 31). A similar *ḥadīth* is related in the *Ḥilya* of Abū Nuʿaym (VIII. 201), where the number of blows is given as one thousand.
7 Ibn Abi'l-Dunyā, *K. al-Mawt* (Zabīdī, x. 260; Suyūṭī, *Sharḥ*, 31).
8 al-Bazzār *al-Musnad* (Haythamī, *Majmaʿ*, II. 322); Abū Nuʿaym, VIII. 201.
9 Abū Dāūd, Janā'iz, 10.

10 Ibn Abi'l-Dunyā, *K. al-Mawt* (Zabīdī, x. 262).
11 Bukhārī, Riqāq, 42.
12 Ibn Māja, Janā'iz, 65.
13 Daylamī, *Musnad al-Firdaws* (Zabīdī, x. 263; Suyūṭī, Sharḥ, 34); Qushayrī, *Risāla*, II. 589.
14 Ibn Abi'l-Dunyā, *K. al-Mawt* (Zabīdī, x. 266).
15 Muslim, Dhikr, 15.
16 Ibn Abi'l-Dunyā, *K. al-Mawt* (Zabīdī, x. 267).
17 'rapture, security, glory and honour' missing in Z.
18 al-Ḥakīm al-Tirmidhī, 125.
19 Muslim, Janā'iz, 1.
20 Muslim, Īmān, 43.
21 Ṭabarānī, *al-Muʿjam al-Kabīr* (Zabīdī, x. 275).
22 Ibn Ḥanbal, *Musnad*, II. 251; Dārimī, Raqā'iq, 22.
23 Tirmidhī, Janā'iz, II; Ibn Māja, Zuhd, 31.
24 Q. LXX:15,16.

Notes to Chapter Four

1 This rubric missing in Z.
2 Q. LV:70.
3 Q. LIV:55.
4 *al-khalq*. (A: *al-Ḥaqq*: "the Truth".)
5 Q. XXXIV:28.
6 *fīmā nalqāhu*. (MA: *fīmā laqiyahu*: 'what he encountered'.)
7 Q. LIII:15.
8 Q. LI:50.
9 Q. LIII:14.
10 Q. LIII:15.
11 al-Bazzār, *al-Musnad* (Haythamī, *Majmaʿ*, IX. 25).
12 Ṭabarānī, *al-Muʿjam al-Kabīr* (Zabīdī, x. 286).
13 Dārimī, Muqaddima, 14.
14 Bukhārī, Riqāq, 42; ibid., Maghāzī, 83. 'And I said' to the end missing in Z.
15 Z has in place of this sentence, ' "What are they saying?" he asked, and they replied, "They are saying that they fear that you shall die".'
16 Q. CIII:1–3.
17 Q. LIX:9.
18 Q. VI:129. This *ḥadīth*, with some variations, is to be found in Bukhārī, Manāqib al-Anṣār, 11. Cf. Zabīdī, x. 290.
19 Q. XXXIII:43.
20 'May God bless them all' missing in Z.
21 al-Bazzār, *al-Musnad* (Haythamī, *Majmaʿ*, IX. 25).
22 Bukhārī, Anbiyā', 19; Muslim, Jihād, 76.
23 This *ḥadīth* is to be found with some variations in Ṭabarānī, *al-Muʿjam al-Kabīr*, (Haythamī, *Majmaʿ*, IX. 23); al-Bazzār, *al-Musnad* (Haythamī, *Kashf*, I. 398).
24 Z: 'her daughter', identified by Zabīdī (x. 293) as Umm Kulthūm bint ʿAlī.
25 Z: 'her fragrance'.
26 Ṭabarānī, *al-Muʿjam al-Kabīr* (Zabīdī, x. 293–294).
27 MA: 'and on it my husband was killed'. A: 'and on it ʿAlī was killed'.
28 Q. XXXIX:30–31.
29 Q. III:144.
30 *yabkī*. (Z: *yukabbir*: 'declaring, "God is Most Great!"'.)
31 *wa'khlufhu fīnā*. (MA, A: *wa'ḥfaẓhu fīnā*: 'safeguard him [his memory?] amongst us'.)
32 Q. III:185.
33 Q. IV:135.
34 Q. XXXIX:30.
35 Q. II:156
36 Q. L:19.
37 This last phrase is an echo of Q. LXXXV:15: *He is the One Who acts as He will.*

38 *rāghiban rāhiban*: so in MA, A. This is confirmed in Abū Nu^c^aym, I. 36 and Ibn al-Mubārak, 319. Z has *zāhidan*: 'be ascetic' in place of 'fear'.

39 Cf. Q. II:195: *Be not cast by your own hands into ruin.*

40 'of God' missing in Z.

41 *khalaqta*. (Z: *ja^c^alta*: 'set'.)

42 Q. LIX:9.

43 Ājurrī (Zabīdī, x. 315).

44 Q. XXI:87.

45 Z: 'Ibn al-Bannāj'.

46 MA, A: 'ibn al-Ḥasan'.

Notes to Chapter Five

1 Z, A: 'ibn ^c^Utba'.

2 Q. VI:94.

3 'Whereupon he passed away' missing in Z.

4 Q. XXVIII:83.

5 Q. LXIX:28–29.

6 *jary*: so in all three texts. Zabīdī (x. 328) also mentions a variant reading *kary*, which would mean 'excavation and direction'.

7 Ḥākim, IV. 317; Abū Nu^c^aym, I. 196; Ibn Ḥibbān (Haythamī, *Mawārid*, 614); Ibn Abī ^c^Āṣim, *Zuhd*, 65.

8 Q. XXXVII:61.

9 Q. XXIV:15.

10 Q. V:27.

11 'When ... al-Rūdhbārī' missing in Z. The version given is that of Qushayrī, *Risāla*, II. 593.

12 'Godfearing' missing in Z.

Notes to Chapter Six

1 'before long' missing in Z.

2 'O Lord!' missing in MA, A.

3 Ibn Ḥanbal, *Zuhd*, 14.

4 Tirmidhī, Zuhd, 5; Ibn Māja, Zuhd, 32.

5 Ḥākim, II. 336; a similar *ḥadīth* is given in Muslim, Janā'iz, 108.

6 Tirmidhī, Zuhd, 5; Ibn Māja, Zuhd, 32.

7 Unrepeated in Z.

8 Q. XXIII:99–100.

9 Q. XIII:6.

10 Zabīdī suggests that this should read, '. . . Fāṭima bint al-Ḥusayn, while watching the funeral of her husband al-Ḥasan ibn al-Ḥasan'.

11 Al-Farazdaq, *Dīwān*, II. 39, with the sequence of the verses reversed.

12 MA, A: 'my son!' The version in Z is confirmed in Ibn Qutayba, *^c^Uyūn al-akhbār*, II. 302.

13 *a^c^mār*. (Z, A: *a^c^māl*: 'works'.)

14 Q. I:1.

15 'sorrow and' missing in A.

16 Ibn Māja, Janā'iz, 58.

17 Bukhārī, Janā'iz, 6; Muslim, Birr, 150.

18 Muslim, Janā'iz, 100.

19 Ḥākim, I. 376; Ibn Ḥibbān (Haythamī, *Mawārid*, 201).

20 Ḥākim, I. 376.

21 Ḥākim, I. 377; IV. 330.

22 Ibn Ḥanbal, *Musnad*, III. 38; V. 356; Ṭabarānī, *al-Mu^c^jam al-Kabīr* (Haythamī, *Majma^c^*, III. 58).

23 Ṭabarānī, *Ṣaghīr*, II. 69; *al-Mu^c^jam al-Awsaṭ* (Haythamī, *Majma^c^*, III. 59).

24 Ibn Abi'l-Dunyā, *K. al-Qubūr* (Zabīdī, x. 363).

25 Dāraquṭnī, Mawāqīt, 194; al-Ḥakīm al-Tirmidhī, 148; al-Bazzār, *al-Musnad* (Haythamī, *Majma^c^*, IV. 2).

26 Bayhaqī, *Shu^c^ab al-īmān* (Zabīdī, x. 364).

27 Ibn Abi'l-Dunyā, *K. al-Qubūr* (Suyūṭī, *Sharḥ*, 202; Zabīdī, x. 367).

28 Daylamī, *Musnad al-Firdaws*; Bayhaqī, *Shuʿab al-īmān* (Zabīdī, x. 367).

29 Al-Awdī: so in Z, MA and A. Zabīdī (x. 368) also finds the variant reading 'al-Azdī'.

30 Ṭabarānī, *al-Muʿjam al-Kabīr* (Haythamī, *Majmaʿ*, II. 324; III. 45).

31 'Aḥmad' missing in A.

32 *Sūras* CXIII and CXIV.

33 *Sūra* CXII.

34 'to pray' missing in MA, A.

35 'where . . . spent' missing in MA, A.

36 Abū Dāūd, Adab, 46.

37 Bukhārī, Janā'iz, 97.

38 Ibn Abi'l-Dunyā, *K. al-Mawt* (Zabīdī, x. 374; Suyūṭī, *Sharḥ*, 297). 'Do ... advantage' is to be found in Nasā'ī, Janā'iz, 51.

39 Bukhārī, Janā'iz, 85; Muslim, Janā'iz, 78.

40 Ibn Ḥanbal, *Musnad*, II. 384, 408; al-Bazzār, *al-Musnad* (Haythamī, *Majmaʿ*, III. 4–5).

Notes to Chapter Seven

1 This rubric missing in Z.

2 'power and' missing in Z.

3 Q. XVII:14.

4 Q. XVII:85.

5 Q. III:170–171.

6 Muslim, Janna, 91.

7 Tirmidhī, Qiyāma, 26.

8 Daylamī, *Ma'thūr*, I. 285; Ibn Abi'l-Dunyā, *K. al-Mawt* (Zabīdī, x. 380).

9 Bukhārī, Janā'iz, 90; Muslim, Janna, 80. 'And he will be told ... Arising' missing in Z.

10 Ibn Māja, Janā'iz, 62.

11 Q. XVI:57.

12 Q. XXXIV:54.

13 Tirmidhī, Tafsīr Sūrat Āl ʿImrān, 18; Ibn Māja, Jihād, 16.

14 'mightiness and' missing in MA, A.

15 Ibn Abi'l-Dunyā, *K. al-Mawt* (Zabīdī, x. 384).

16 Ibn Abi'l-Dunyā, *K. al-Mawt* (Zabīdī, x. 384).

17 Bukhārī, Riqāq, 42; Muslim, Janā'iz, 61.

18 al-Ḥakīm al-Tirmidhī, 213.

19 Ibn Abi'l-Dunyā, *K. al-Mawt* (Zabīdī, x. 385; Suyūṭī, *Sharḥ*, 264); Daylamī, *Ma'thūr*, V. 29.

20 *Tārīkh Baghdād*, XII. 212; Ibn Ḥanbal, *Musnad*, III. 68.

21 Q. II:156.

22 Ḥākim, I. 353; Ṭabarānī, *al-Muʿjam al-Kabīr; al-Muʿjam al-Awsaṭ* (Haythamī, *Majmaʿ*, II. 327).

23 al-Ḥakīm al-Tirmidhī, 161; Abū Nuʿaym, VI. 90; Abū Yaʿlā, *al-Musnad* (Haythamī, *Majmaʿ*, III. 45–46).

24 'al-Laythī' missing in Z.

25 *falā anīsa laka'l-yawma ghayranā* (MA,A: *falā anīsa laka'l-yawma ʿindanā*: 'so that today you have no companion amongst us.').

26 Ibn al-Mubārak, (*riwāya* Nuʿaym ibn Ḥammād), 41; Ibn Abi'l-Dunyā, *K. al-Qubūr* (Zabīdī, x. 397; Suyūṭī, *Sharḥ*, 114).

27 Q. XX:55.

28 Q. XIV:27.

29 Q. IX:21.

30 Q. LXVI:6.

31 Q. XXII:19.

32 Q. XIV:50.

33 'and blind' missing in Z.

34 Ḥākim, I. 37–38; Ājurrī, 367–370; Ṭayālisī, 102–103; Bayhaqī, *Ithbāt*, 38–39.

35 Q. LXXXIX:27.

36 Q. LXXXIX:28.

37 Q. XXIII:100.
38 'Nay' missing in A.
39 Q. XXIII:100.
40 Q. XX:124.
41 al-Ḥakīm al-Tirmidhī, 159; Ājurrī, 358; Ibn Ḥibbān (Haythamī, *Mawārid*, 198–199).
42 *maqāmāt* (MA: *muqaddimāt*: 'preliminaries').
43 Q. LXXXIII:15–16.
44 Q. XXXVII:61.
45 *yatasallā* (Z: *yubtalā*: 'be tried with').
46 Ibn Ḥanbal, *Zuhd*, 184; Abū Nuᶜaym, I. 164.
47 Q. X:7.
48 MA, A: 'Abū Saᶜīd al-Khudrī'.
49 Ājurrī, 365; Ibn Ḥibbān (Haythamī, *Mawārid*, 197); Bayhaqī, *Ithbāt*, 56.
50 'And a span' missing in Z.
51 Ājurrī, 366–367; Bayhaqī, *Iᶜtiqād*, 148–149.
52 Z adds: 'from my direction.'
53 Ibn Ḥanbal, *Musnad*, V. 407; al-Ḥakīm al-Tirmidhī, 159.
54 Ibn Ḥanbal, *Musnad*, VI. 55; Bayhaqī, *Ithbāt*, 106–107.
55 Ṭabarānī, *al-Muᶜjam al-Kabīr* (Haythamī, *Majmaᶜ*, III. 47).

Notes to Chapter Eight

1 Q. V:27.
2 *falā tarā bi'l-ᶜayn al-ẓāhira wa-innamā yarā bi-ᶜayn ukhrā*. (Z: *falā tara'l-ᶜayn al-ẓāhira wa-innamā yudriku bi-ᶜayn ukhrā*.)
3 Bukhārī, Taᶜbīr, 2; Muslim, Ru'yā, 6.
4 Cf. Bukhārī, Wuḍū', 75; Muslim, Dhikr, 76.
5 Q. XLVIII:27.
6 Q. LXXXV:22.
7 Q. VI:59; X:61 etc.
8 Q. XXXVI:12.
9 'whereby . . . seen' missing in Z.
10 A *ḥadīth* of the Prophet (Abū Nuᶜaym, VII. 90; Ṭabarānī, *al-Muᶜjam al-Awsaṭ* [Haythamī, *Majmaᶜ*, X. 415]). Cited also in the *Risāla* of al-Qushayrī (II. 717), without reference to an authority.
11 Q. L:22.
12 Q. LII:15–16.
13 Q. XXXIX:47.
14 Ḥākim, IV. 325; Ṭabarānī, *al-Muᶜjam al-Awsaṭ* (Haythamī, *Majmaᶜ*, X. 219).
15 Tirmidhī, Manāqib, 14; Ibn Māja, Muqaddima, 11.
16 Q. III:31.
17 Q. LXXIX:37–39.
18 Q. LXVIII:35–36.
19 'In his sleep' missing in Z.
20 Bukhārī, ᶜIlm, 38; Muslim, Ru'yā, 10.
21 Q. II:156.
22 MA, A: 'al-Bazzār'. The version given is that of Qushayrī (*Risāla*, II. 724).
23 Bukhārī, Adab, 96; Muslim, Birr, 165.
24 Z: 'Bishr'.
25 Q. IV:69. Z adds '*and the Martyrs and the Righteous*'.
26 Ar: *min ishārāt al-qawm ilayy*. The *Risāla* (II. 728) omits *ilayy*.
27 Q. XXXVII:61.
28 Q. XVII:100.
29 A: 'al-Shakhkhām.'
30 Q. IV:69.
31 Q. III.33.
32 Q. IV:69.
33 Q. XXV:3.

PART TWO

Notes

THE TRUMPET-BLAST

1 Bukhārī, Tafsīr Sūrat al-Baqara, 8.
2 'worldly' missing in Z.
3 Q. XXXVI:77.
4 Q. LXXV:36–39. '*Making . . . female*' missing in Z.
5 Q. XXXVI:29.
6 Q. XXXIX:68.
7 Q. LXXIV:7–9.
8 Q. XXXVI:48–52.
9 Tirmidhī, Qiyāma, 8.
10 Q. XXXIX:68.
11 Q. XXXIX:68.
12 Q. XXXIX:69.
13 ʿAbd ibn Ḥumayd, *Tafsīr* (Zabīdī, X. 453).
14 Q. LXXXI:5.
15 Q. XIX:68.

THE LAND AND PEOPLE OF THE CONCOURSE

1 Q. XX:107.
2 Q. LXXIX:5,6.
3 Q. LXXIX:7.
4 Cf. Q. LXXIX:8.
5 Bukhārī, Riqāq, 44; Muslim, Qiyāma, II.
6 Q. XIV:48.
7 Z: 'you'.
8 Q. LV:37.
9 Q. LXX:8.
10 Q. LXX:9.
11 Q. CI:4.
12 Q. LXXX:37. The *ḥadīth* is given by Bukhārī, Anbiyā', 48; Muslim, Janna, 67.
13 Tirmidhī, Tafsīr Sūrat al-Isrā', 17; Ibn Ḥanbal, *Musnad*, II. 354.

THE PERSPIRATION

1 Q. LIII:9.
2 Q. LXXXIII:6.
3 Bukhārī, Riqāq, 47; Muslim, Janna, 6.
4 Bukhārī, Riqāq, 70; Muslim, Janna, 75.
5 Bayhaqī, *Baʿth* (Zabīdī, X. 458).
6 'the waist' missing in Z.
7 Ḥākim, IV. 571; Ibn Ḥibbān (Haythamī, *Mawārid*, 640); Abū Yaʿlā, *al-Musnad* (Haythamī, *Majmaʿ*, X. 335).
8 As related in a *ḥadīth* of the Prophet; cf. Ṭabarānī, *al-Muʿjam al-Kabīr*; Abū Yaʿlā, *al-Musnad* (Haythamī, *Majmaʿ*, X. 336).
9 'in might' missing in Z.

THE LENGTH OF THE DAY OF ARISING

1 Q. LXXXIII:6.
2 Ḥākim, IV. 572; Ṭabarānī, *al-Muʿjam al-Kabīr* (Haythamī, *Majmaʿ*, VII. 135).
3 Q. LXXXVIII:5.
4 Q. XX:109.
5 Ibn Ḥanbal, *Musnad*, III. 75; Ibn Ḥibbān (Haythamī, *Mawārid*, 638); Abū Yaʿlā, *al-Musnad* (Haythamī, *Majmaʿ*, X. 337).

THE DAY OF ARISING, AND ITS CALAMITIES AND NAMES

1 Cf. Q. LXXXII:1.
2 Cf. Q. LXXXII:2.
3 Cf. Q. LXXXI:2.
4 Cf. Q. LXXXI:1.

5 Cf. Q. LXXXI:3.
6 Cf. Q. LXXXI:4.
7 Cf. Q. LXXXI:5.
8 Cf. Q. LXXXI:6.
9 Cf. Q. LXXXI:7.
10 Cf. Q. LXXXI:11.
11 Cf. Q. LXXXI:12.
12 Cf. Q. LXXVII:9.
13 Cf. Q. LXXXIV:3.
14 Q. XCIX:1,2.
15 Q. XCIX:6.
16 '*to your Lord*' missing in MA, A.
17 Q. LXIX:14–18.
18 Q. XVIII:47.
19 Q. LVI:4–6.
20 Q. CI:4–5.
21 Q. XXII:2.
22 Q. XIV:48.
23 Q. XX:105–107.
24 Q. XXVII:88.
25 Q. LV:37.
26 Q. LV:39.
27 Q. LV:41.
28 Q. III:30.
29 Q. LXXXI:14.
30 Q. LXXXII:5.
31 'and its sisters, which are' missing in MA, A.
32 *sūras* XI, LVI, LXXVII, LXXVIII, and LXXXI respectively. The *ḥadīth* is found in Tirmidhī, Tafsīr Sūrat al-Wāqiʿa, 6.
33 *tumajmij*. (Z: *tajmaʿ*: 'gathering up'.)
34 'the Barren Day' missing in Z.
35 A: 'of the Dawn'; Z: 'of Closing'.
36 Q. III:9; III:25.
37 Q. LXXXVI:9.
38 Q. II:48; II:123.
39 Q. XIV:42.
40 Q. XLIV:41.
41 Q. LXXXII:19.
42 Q. LII:13.
43 Q. LIV:48.
44 Q. XXXIII:66.
45 Q. XXXI:33.
46 Q. LXXX:34–35.
47 Q. LXXVII:35–36.
48 Q. XXX:43; XLII:47.
49 Q. XL:16.
50 Q. LI:13.
51 Q. XXVI:88.
52 Q. XL:52.
53 'men's' missing in Z.
54 Q. LXXXII:6.
55 Q. XXI:1–3.
56 Q. LIV:1.
57 Q. LXX:5–6.
58 Q. XXXIII:63.

THE INQUISITION

1 Abū Dāūd, Sunna, 18; Ibn Ḥanbal, *Musnad*, II. 26.
2 Q. VII:6–7.
3 Q. XV:92–93.
4 'with the Angels' missing in MA, A.
5 Q. V:109. '*Truly You . . . Unseen*' missing in Z.
6 Q. V:116.
7 Q. XXXIX:69.
8 Q. XLV:28.
9 'and the Righteous' missing in MA, A.
10 Q. XLII:45.
11 Q. XL:18.
12 Muslim, Īmān, 306.
13 Q. XVII:14.
14 Muslim, Zuhd, 17.
15 Muslim, Tawba, 52.
16 Ibn Māja, Ḥudūd, 5.
17 Q. XVIII:49.
18 Bukhārī, Manāqib, 25; Muslim, Zakāt, 67.
19 Tirmidhī, Zuhd, 37.
20 Q. LXIX:30–31.

THE SCALES

1 Q. XXIV:37.
2 Ājurrī, 385; Bayhaqī, *Iʿtiqād*, 139.
3 Q. XXII:21.
4 Bukhārī, Riqāq, 46; Muslim, Īmān, 423.

THE ADVERSARIES, AND THE RESTORATION OF WRONGS

1 Q. CI:6–11.

2 Q. XL:17

3 Q. XIV:42–44. '*So give warning to mankind!*' missing in Z.

4 'nor dinar' missing in Z.

5 Muslim, Birr, 60.

6 al-Bazzār, *al-Musnad*; Ṭabarānī, *al-Muᶜjam al-Awsaṭ* (Haythamī, *Majmaᶜ*, X. 352).

7 Q. VI:38.

8 *ᶜadl*. Z has *ᶜadhāb*, 'punishment', which Zabīdī says is a copyist's error.

9 Ibn Ḥanbal, *Musnad*, I. 402.

10 Q. XXXIX:30–31.

11 Ibn Ḥanbal, *Musnad*, I. 168; Ḥākim, II. 435, IV. 572; Abū Nuᶜaym, I. 91.

12 Ibn Ḥanbal, *Musnad*, III. 495; Bayhaqī, *Asmā'*, I. 139–140; Ḥākim, IV. 575; Ṭabarānī, *al-Muᶜjam al-Awsaṭ* (Haythamī, *Majmaᶜ*, X. 345–346).

13 'with your brother' missing in Z.

14 Q. VIII:1.

15 Ḥākim, IV. 576.

16 Q. XXIV:15.

17 Q. XXV:14

THE TRAVERSE

1 'O unfortunate one' missing in MA, A.

2 Q. XIX:85–86.

3 Q. XXXVII:23–24.

4 Q. LXXXIX:24.

5 Q. XXV:27–28.

6 Q. LXXVIII:40.

7 Q. XIX:23.

8 Q. XXIII:108.

9 Bukhārī, Adhān, 129; Muslim, Īmān, 229.

10 Ibn Ḥanbal, *Musnad*, III. 25.

11 Q. LVI:49–50.

12 Ḥākim, II. 376–377.

13 Ibn Ḥanbal, *Musnad*, VI. 110.

14 Q. XXV:43; XLV:23.

THE INTERCESSION

1 Q. XCIII:5.

2 Q. XIV:36.

3 Q. V:118.

4 Muslim, Īmān, 346.

5 Bukhārī, Tayammum, 1; Muslim, Masājid, 3, 5.

6 Tirmidhī, Manāqib, 1; Ibn Māja, Zuhd, 37.

7 Muslim, Faḍā'il, 3.

8 Bukhārī, Tawḥīd, 31; Muslim, Īmān, 334.

9 Ṭabarānī, *al-Muᶜjam al-Kabīr*; *al-Muᶜjam al-Awsaṭ* (Haythamī, *Majmaᶜ*, X. 380).

10 Ibn Ḥanbal, *Musnad*, V. 347.

11 Q. XXXII:9.

12 Cf. Q. II:34; XV:30.

13 'and as He will never be again' missing in Z.

14 Cf. Q. II:35; VII:22.

15 Q. XVII:3.

16 'and as He will never be again' missing in Z.

17 Q. IV:171.

18 'but he mentioned no sin' missing in Z.

19 'Go to another!' missing in Z.

20 Q. XXXIII:40.

21 Q. XLVIII:2.

22 MA, A: 'Ḥimyar'.

23 Bukhārī, Anbiyā', 3.

24 Q. VI:77.

25 Q. XXI:63.

26 Q. XXXVII:89. The Tradition with this addition is to be found in Muslim, Īmān, 328.

27 Ḥākim, I. 71; Ājurrī, 351; Ibn Ḥanbal, *Zuhd*, 157–158, 412–413; Ibn Ḥibbān (Haythamī, *Mawārid*, 645–646).

28 Tirmidhī, Qiyāma, 12; Ibn Ḥanbal, *Musnad*, III. 20.

29 Abū Yaᶜlā, *al-Musnad* (Haythamī, *Majmaᶜ*, X. 382).

30 Tirmidhī, Manāqib, 1; Dārimī, Muqaddima, 8.

31 'stand . . . and' missing in Z.

32 Tirmidhī, Manāqib, 1.
33 Q. IV:125.
34 Q. IV:164.
35 Q. IV:171.
36 Q. III:33.
37 Tirmidhī, Manāqib, 1.

THE POOL

1 Q. CVIII:1.
2 Muslim, Ṣalāt, 56, 57.
3 Bukhārī, Riqāq, 53.
4 Muslim, Faḍā'il, 34, 41.
5 Tirmidhī, Tafsīr Sūrat al-Kawthar, 3.
6 The Tradition and the accompanying anecdote are related in Tirmidhī, Qiyāma, 15.
7 Muslim, Faḍā'il, 37.
8 'The . . . said' missing in Z.
9 Tirmidhī, Qiyāma, 14.
10 Q. XXXI:33.

THE INFERNO, AND ITS TERRORS AND TORMENTS

1 Q. XIX:71–72.
2 Q. XXIII:108.
3 Q. XXXIX:56.
4 'a sea of' missing in MA, A.
5 Q. XIV:50.
6 Q. XXII:20–21.
7 Q. IV:56.
8 'and noses' missing in MA, A.
9 'partial' missing in Z.
10 Ibn Qāniᶜ, *al-Muᶜjam* (Zabīdī, x. 511); BAYHAQĪ, *Baᶜth*, 275. According to Qurṭubī (p.386) this is not a *ḥadīth* at all, but a saying of one of the early Muslims.
11 'We' missing in Z, where the imperative seems to be intended.
12 Ibn Māja, Muqaddima, 23.
13 Muslim, Janna, 36.
14 Q. XVII:21.
15 Q. IV:40.
16 Bukharī, Riqāq, 51; Muslim, Īmān, 364.
17 A Tradition of the Prophet with almost the same wording is related by Ibn Ḥibbān (Haythamī, *Mawārid*, 648).
18 Ibn al-Mubārak (*riwāya* Nuᶜaym ibn Ḥammād), 88; Abū Nuᶜaym, VI. 139; Ibn Abī Shayba, XIII. 167.
19 Bukhārī, Bad' al-khalq, 10; Muslim, Masājid, 185, 186.
20 A *ḥadīth* of the Prophet (Muslim, Ṣifat al-Qiyāma, 42).
21 A *ḥadīth* of the Prophet (al-Bazzār, *al-Musnad*; Abū Yaᶜlā, *al-Musnad* [Haythamī, *Majmaᶜ*, x. 391]); Abū Nuᶜaym, IV. 307; Bayhaqī, *Baᶜth*, 330).
22 Q. XXIII:104. '*and they scowl therein*' missing in A.
23 A similar saying is ascribed to the Prophet in Abū Nuᶜaym, IV. 363.
24 Tirmidhī, Jahannam, 4; Ibn Ḥanbal, *Musnad*, III. 28.
25 Q. XIV:16–17.
26 Q. LVI:51–55.
27 Q. XXXVII:64–67. '*Then* ... *Hellfire*' missing in Z.
28 Q. LXXXVIII:4–5.
29 Q. LXXIII:12–13.
30 Tirmidhī, Jahannam, 4; Ibn Māja, Zuhd, 38.
31 *qaṭra*. (A: *naẓra*: 'one glimpse of'.)
32 Ibn Abī Shayba, XIII. 175; Bayhaqī, *Baᶜth*, 303.
33 Q. LXXXVIII:6.
34 Cf. Q. LXXIII:13.
35 'so ... drink' missing in A.
36 Q. XL:50.
37 Q. XLIII:77.
38 Tirmidhī, Jahannam, 5.
39 Q. XIV:16–17.
40 Q. XLVII:15.
41 Q. XVIII:29. The *ḥadīth* is narrated in Tirmidhī, Jahannam, 4,5; Ibn Ḥanbal, *Musnad*, v. 265.
42 Q. III:180.
43 Bukhārī, Zakāt, 3.
44 Ibn Ḥanbal, *Musnad*, IV. 191.

45 Muslim, Janna, 54.

46 Tirmidhī, Jahannam, 5; Ibn Ḥanbal, *Musnad*, III. 88.

47 Tirmidhī, Jahannam, 3; Ibn Ḥanbal, *Musnad*, II. 92.

48 Muslim, Janna, 33.

49 Ibn Māja, Zuhd, 38.

50 Q. XL:11.

51 Q. XL:12.

52 Q. XXXII:12. '*Now we are certain*' missing in MA, A.

53 Q. XIV:44.

54 Q. XXXV:37.

55 Q. XXXV:37.

56 Q. XXIII:106–108.

57 Q. XIV:21.

58 'then . . . years' missing in Z, and in version of Bayhaqī (*Baʿth*, 329).

59 '*we . . . refuge*' missing in MA, A.

60 Bukhārī, Tafsīr Sūrat 19, 1; Muslim, Janna, 40.

61 Q. XII:20.

62 Bayhaqī, *Baʿth*, 328; Abū Nuʿaym, IV. 124–5.

63 Q. XIX:39.

64 A *ḥadīth* of the Prophet (Bukhārī, Adab, 120; Muslim, Qadar, 6,7).

65 Q. LXXXII:13–14.

66 This phrase missing in Z.

HEAVEN, AND THE VARIETIES OF ITS BLISS

1 Q. LXXXIII:24. This section is particularly rich in Qur'ānic resonances; the reader's attention has been drawn only to the more obvious of these.

2 Q. LV:70.

3 Q. LV:58.

4 Q. LV:74.

5 'walking . . . Heaven' missing in Z.

6 Q. LV:72. '*tents* and' missing in Z.

7 Q. XXXVII:45–46.

8 Q. LVI:23–24.

9 Q. XLIV:51–52.

10 Q. LIV:54–55.

11 Q. LXXXIII:24.

12 Q. X:26.

13 Q. XXI:26.

14 Q. XXI:102.

15 Q. LII:30.

16 Q. LXXXIII:25.

17 'and . . . execution' missing in Z.

18 Q. VII:43; Muslim, Janna, 27.

19 Q. LV:46.

20 Q. LV.

21 Q. LVI.

22 Q. LV:46.

23 Bukhārī, Tawḥīd, 24; Muslim, Īmān, 296.

24 Bukhārī, Bad' al-khalq, 9; Muslim, Zakāt, 85.

25 Q. XXXIX:73.

26 Q. LXXXIII:24.

27 MA and A add here: 'the Guardians of', a phrase absent from Bayhaqī, *Baʿth*, 172, which is almost certainly Ghazālī's source here.

28 Q. XXXIX:73.

29 *qarīb*. (MA, A: *ḥabīb*: 'a loved one'.)

30 Q. LXXXVIII:14–16.

31 Q. VII:43.

32 Muslim, Īmān, 333.

33 Q. XVII:21.

34 Q. LVII:21.

35 Q. LXXXIII:26.

36 Bukhārī, Bad' al-khalq, 8; Muslim, Janna, 14.

37 Q. XX:75.

38 Tirmidhī, Manāqib, 14; Ibn Māja, Muqaddima, 11.

39 'and which . . . mind' missing in Z.

40 Abū Nuʿaym, II. 356. Bayhaqī, *Baʿth*, 176–7.

41 Q. IX:72.

42 Ṭabarānī, *al-Muʿjam al-Awsaṭ* (Haythamī, *Majmaʿ*, X. 420); Ibn al-Mubārak, 550–551; Bayhaqī, *Baʿth*, 178.

THE WALL OF HEAVEN, ITS LAND, TREES AND RIVERS

1 *arḍihā*. (MA: *arāḍīhā*: 'Lands'.)
2 al-Bazzār, *al-Musnad* (Haythamī, *Majma*, x. 397); Abū Nuʿaym, II. 249; Bayhaqī, *Baʿth*, 179.
3 Muslim, Fitan, 92.
4 Ṭabarānī, *al-Muʿjam al-Awsaṭ* (Haythamī, *Majmaʿ*, x. 401); Bayhaqī, *Baʿth*, 184.
5 Q. LVI:30. The Tradition is from Bukhārī, Bad' al-khalq, 8; Muslim, Janna, 8.
6 *ma kuntu arā*, so in Z and Bayhaqī, *Baʿth*, 187. (MA,A: *mā kuntu adrī*: 'I never knew'.)
7 Q. LVI:28.
8 Ḥākim, II. 476; Bayhaqī, *Baʿth*, 187.

THE RAIMENT OF HEAVEN'S PEOPLE, THEIR FURNISHINGS, BEDS, DIVANS AND TENTS

1 Q. XXII:23; XXXV:33.
2 Ibn al-Mubārak, 512; Bayhaqī, *Baʿth*, 194–5.
3 Ibn Ḥanbal, *Musnad*, II. 225; Ṭabarānī, *Ṣaghīr*, I. 47; Ṭayālisī, 300; Bayhaqī, *Baʿth*, 195.
4 Bukhārī, Bad' al-khalq, 8; Muslim, Janna, 14.
5 Tirmidhī, Qiyāma, 60; Ibn Ḥanbal, *Musnad*, VI. 345.
6 Q. XVIII:31; XXII:23; XXXV:33.
7 Tirmidhī, Janna, 23; Ibn Ḥanbal, *Musnad*, III. 75.
8 Bukhārī, Tafsīr Sūrat al-Raḥmān, 2; Bad' al-khalq, 8.
9 Q. LXXXVIII:13.
10 Ibn Ḥibbān (Haythamī, *Mawārid*, 653); Bayhaqī, *Baʿth*, 201. A nearly identical Tradition is given in Tirmidhī, Janna, 8.

THE FOOD OF HEAVEN'S PEOPLE

1 Q. II:25.
2 Q. LXXVI:18.
3 Muslim, Ḥayḍ, 36.
4 Ibn al-Mubārak, 512–513; Ṭabarānī, *al-Muʿjam al-Awsaṭ* (Haythamī, *Majmaʿ*, x. 416); Ibn Ḥibbān (Haythamī, *Mawārid*, 655); Ibn Abī Shayba, XIII. 108–9.
5 Ibn al-Mubārak, 510; al-Bazzār, *al-Musnad* (Haythamī, *Majmaʿ*, x. 414); Ibn Abī Shayba, XIII. 99; Bayhaqī, *Baʿth*, 206.
6 Ibn al-Mubārak, 525; Ḥākim, II. 537.
7 Q. XLIII:71.
8 'the likes of which åre not' missing in Z, A; given in Bayhaqī, *Baʿth*, 207.
9 Q. LXXXIII:27.
10 Q. LXXXIII:26.

THE LARGE-EYED HOURIS AND THE PAGES

1 Bukhārī, Jihād, 5.
2 Q. LV:58.
3 Tirmidhī, Qiyāma, 60; Ibn Ḥanbal, II. 230.
4 Q. LV:72.
5 Bayhaqī, *Baʿth*, 215.
6 Q. III:15.
7 Q. XXXVI:55.
8 Tirmidhī, Janna, 6.
9 Bayhaqī, *Baʿth*, 224.
10 Tirmidhī, Janna, 15; Ibn Ḥanbal, *Musnad*, I. 156.
11 Ṭabarānī, *al-Muʿjam al-Awsaṭ* (Haythamī, *Majmaʿ*, x.419); Ibn Abī Shayba, XIII. 106.
12 Q. XXX:15.
13 Ṭabarānī, *al-Muʿjam al-Awsaṭ* (Haythamī, *Majmaʿ*, x. 418); Bayhaqī, *Baʿth*, 228.

AN EXPOSITION OF A DIVERSE GROUP OF THE ATTRIBUTES OF HEAVEN'S PEOPLE FOR WHICH ACCOUNTS ARE FORTHCOMING

1 Q. XXII:45.
2 Ibn Māja, Zuhd, 39
3 Tirmidhī, Ṣifat al-Janna, 11; Ibn Ḥanbal, V. 352.
4 Ibn Māja, Zuhd, 39; Tirmidhī, Janna, 23.
5 al-Bazzār, *al-Musnad* (Haythamī, *Majmaʿ*, X. 421); Abū Nuʿaym, VIII. 49; Bayhaqī, *Baʿth*, 237.
6 Ibn Ḥanbal, *Musnad*, II. 295; Ibn Abī Shayba, XIII. 114; Ṭabarānī, *Ṣaghīr*, II. 17; Bayhaqī, *Baʿth*, 245.
7 Tirmidhī, Janna, 23; Ibn Ḥanbal, *Musnad*, III. 76.
8 Bayhaqī, *Baʿth*, 143–4.
9 Q. XXIII:1.
10 Q. XLVII:15.
11 Q. XLVII:15.
12 Q. XLVII:15.
13 Q. LVI:22–23.
14 Q. XIX:62.

THE BEATIFIC VISION

1 Q. X:26.
2 Q. XX:130.
3 Bukhārī, Tawḥīd, 24; Muslim, Masājid, 211.
4 'with your Lord' missing in Z.
5 Muslim, Īmān, 297.

THE WIDE COMPASS OF GOD'S MERCY

1 Q. IV:48.
2 Q. XXXIX:53.
3 Q. IV:110.
4 Muslim, Tawba, 22.
5 A *ḥadīth* of the Prophet(Bukhārī, Tawba, 15; Muslim, Tawba, 14).
6 Ibn Ḥanbal, *Musnad*, IV. 407; Ājurrī, 280.
7 Ṭabarānī, *al-Muʿjam al-Awsaṭ* (Haythamī, *Majmaʿ*, X. 381).
8 Ibn Ḥanbal, *Musnad*, V. 238.
9 Tirmidhī, Jahannam, 9.
10 Q. XV:2. The *ḥadīth* is given in Ḥākim, II. 242; Bayhaqī, *Baʿth*, 91; Ṭabarānī, *al-Muʿjam al-Awsaṭ* (Haythamī, *Majmaʿ*, VII. 45); Ibn Abī ʿĀṣim, *Sunna*, II. 405.
11 Bukhārī, Adab, 18; Muslim, Tawba, 21.
12 Q. LXXXIV:8.
13 Q. L:29.
14 Tirmidhī, Jahannam, 10.
15 Abu'l-Asʿad al-Qushayrī, *Samāʿīyāt* (Zabīdī, X. 561).
16 Q. III:103.
17 Muslim, Īmān, 49.
18 Tirmidhī, Īmān, 17; Ibn Māja, Zuhd, 25.
19 'lengthy' missing in Z.
20 'half an' missing in Z.
21 MA, A: (instead of 'no good'), 'none of those whom You ordered us to take'.
22 Q. IV:40.
23 *akhḍar*. (MA, A: *abyaḍ*: 'white'.)
24 Bukhārī, Īmān, 15; Muslim, Īmān, 299.
25 Bukhārī, Anbiyā', 31.
26 Ṭabarānī, *al-Muʿjam al-Awsaṭ* (Haythamī, *Majmaʿ*, X. 310); al-Ḥakīm al-Tirmidhī, 84.
27 MA, A add here: 'Even if he had committed theft and adultery?' I asked. 'Yes,' he replied, 'even if he had committed theft and adultery.'
28 MA, A have here: 'Yes, even if he had committed theft and adultery, and even if he used to drink wine'. The *ḥadīth* in Z is given in Bukhārī, Tawḥīd, 33; Muslim, Īmān, 164. Curiously enough, MA and A are

here reproducing a slightly different version of the *ḥadīth* (Muslim, Īmān, 163).

29 Q. LV:46.

30 Ibn Ḥanbal, *Musnad*, II. 357; Bayhaqī, *Baʿth*, 69.

31 Ibn Ḥanbal, *Musnad*, IV. 410; Bayhaqī, *Baʿth*, 94; a similar *ḥadīth* is given by Muslim (Tawba, 56).

32 Muslim, Tawba, 57.

33 Bukhārī, Adab, 18; Muslim, Tawba, 26.

APPENDIX

PERSONS CITED IN TEXT — EXCLUDING PROPHETS

AL-ᶜABBĀS ibn ᶜAbd al-Muṭṭalib (d. 32 [652/3])—61, 63, 69. The uncle of the Prophet, before whom he was born, it is sometimes said, by two years. An important personality at Mecca, he held the ancient office of providing water (*siqāya*) to the pilgrims. While always tolerant of his nephew's cause, he joined it only upon the conquest of Mecca in 8 AH. (*EI*², I. 8–9 [W. Montgomery Watt]; *Iṣāba*, II. 263.)

ᶜABD ALLĀH IBN ᶜABBĀS—77. See 'Ibn ᶜAbbās'.

ᶜABD ALLĀH IBN ᶜAMR IBN AL-ᶜĀṢ (d. *c* 65 [684/5])—128, 131, 243, 256. A Companion of the Prophet, and an authority on the Tradition. He was celebrated for his austere lifestyle, which he was enjoined by the Prophet to temper. (Nawawī, *Tahdhīb*, 361–2.)

ᶜABD ALLĀH IBN MASᶜŪD—243. See 'Ibn Masᶜūd'.

ᶜABD ALLĀH IBN AL-MUBĀRAK ibn Wāḍiḥ al-Ḥanẓalī (d. 181 [797/8])—89, 164. An influential saint and scholar of the Law. Originally of Merv in Central Asia, he travelled to study with Mālik ibn Anas in Medina and al-Awzāᶜī in Syria before he died in combat against the Byzantines. His works on renunciation and the Holy War have been published and are still popular. (*GALS*, I. 256; Ṣafadī, XVII. 419–20; Abū Nuᶜaym, VIII. 162–91; ᶜAṭṭār, 124–8.)

ᶜABD ALLĀH IBN RAWĀḤA al-Khazrajī (d. 8 [629])—131. An early Medinese convert chiefly remembered for his heroism at the battle of Mu'ta, where, after assuming the command after the deaths of Zayd ibn Ḥāritha and Jaᶜfar ibn Abī Ṭālib, he too joined the ranks of the martyrs. (*EI*², I. 50–1 [A. Schaade]; *Iṣāba*, II. 298–9.)

ᶜABD ALLĀH IBN SALĀM ibn al-Ḥārith al-Qaynuqāᶜī (d. 43 [663/4])—81. Said to have been a rabbi of aristocratic stock before converting to Islam, he is credited with a large corpus of Judaic tales, many of which are to be found in al-Ṭabarī's commentary on the Qur'ān. He participated in the conquest of Syria and Palestine, but died in Medina. (*EI^2*, I. 52 [J. Horovitz]; *Iṣāba*, II. 312–3.)

ʿABD ALLĀH IBN SUMAYṬ (d. 181 [797/8])—21. A respected traditionist of Basra. (Zabīdī, X. 242.)

ʿABD ALLĀH IBN THAʿLABA al-ʿUdhrī (d. *c* 87 [705/6])—23. A Follower (*tābiʿī*), and a 'weeper' (*bakkā'*), whose tears are said to have left permanent marks on his cheeks. A pupil of Ibn ʿUmar and Abū Hurayra in *ḥadīth*, he left a number of sayings on the subject of death. (*Kāshif*, II. 68; Abū Nuʿaym, VI. 245-6; Ṣafadī, XVII. 99.)

ʿABD ALLĀH IBN ʿUBAYD IBN ʿUMAYR al-Laythī (d. 113 [731/2])—135. An early ascetic and renowned preacher of Mecca, as well as a highly-regarded traditionist who studied under Ibn ʿAbbās. (*Mashāhīr*, 83; Abū Nuʿaym, III. 354–9; Ṣafadī, XVII. 304-5.)

ʿABD ALLĀH IBN ʿUMAR—15, 29, 79, 182, 245. See 'Ibn ʿUmar'.

ʿABD ALLĀH IBN ZAMʿA ibn al-Aswad ibn al-Muṭṭalib al-Qurashī (d. *c* 35 [655/6])—64, 65. A Companion, and a prolific narrator of Traditions. His father is said to have died with the idolators at the battle of Badr. (*Iṣāba*, II. 303–4; *Istīʿāb*, II. 298–300.)

ʿABD ALLĀH AL-ZARRĀD—159. Possibly ʿAbd Allāh ibn Abān al-Zarrād, a traditionist who died in 287 (900/1) at Baghdad. (*Tārīkh Baghdād*, IX. 421.)

ʿABD AL-MALIK IBN MARWĀN (*regn.* 65–86 [685–705])—86–7. The fifth Umayyad caliph, remembered for administrative reforms and a number of successful campaigns against the Khārijite rebels and Byzantine encroachment.

ʿABD AL-RAḤMĀN IBN AL-ʿALĀ' IBN AL-LAJLĀJ—117.

A traditionist of Aleppo, whose father was also a respected scholar. (*Kāshif*, II. 160.)

ᶜABD AL-RAḤMĀN ibn Abī Bakr al-Qurashī (d. *c* 54 [673/4]) —61, 112. The elder son of Abū Bakr, he participated in his father's campaign in the Yamāma, where he acquired some fame as an archer. (*Iṣāba*, II. 399–401; *Istīᶜāb*, II. 391–4.)

ᶜABD AL-RAḤMĀN IBN ᶜAWF al-Qurashī (d. 31 [652])—77, 80. One of the first to respond to the Prophet's call in Mecca, he took part in the migration to Abyssinia. A wealthy merchant, he donated huge sums in charity, and was one of the council of six nominated by ᶜUmar to choose his successor, as well as being one of the ten men assured of Heaven by the Prophet while they still lived. (*EI²*, I. 84 [M.Th. Houtsma—W. Montgomery Watt]; *Iṣāba*, II. 408–10.)

ᶜABD AL-RAḤMĀN IBN YŪSUF—22. Unidentified: many figures with this name are recorded.

ᶜABD AL-WĀḤID IBN ZAYD (d. *c* 177 [793/4])—157. A companion of al-Ḥasan al-Baṣrī and al-Dārānī chiefly remembered for the importance which he attached to solitude. According to Abū Nuᶜaym, he was partially paralysed, from which affliction he was released only at the time of prayer. (Abū Nuᶜaym, VI. 155–65; *Bidāya*, X. 171; Massignon, *Essai*, 194.)

ABU'L-ᶜABBĀS IBN ᶜAṬĀ' (d. *c* 309 [921/2])—93. A Sufi of Baghdad and a companion of al-Junayd. He is said to have written a number of works, but these are now lost. (Sulamī, 260–8.)

ABU'L-ᶜABBĀS AL-DĪNAWARĪ (d. *c* 340 [951/2])—91. A Sufi who preached at Nīsābūr and Samarqand. He was a companion of al-Jurayrī and Abū Saᶜīd al-Kharrāz. (Sulamī, 500–4; Abū Nuᶜaym, X. 383.)

ABŪ ᶜALĪ AL-RŪDHBĀRĪ (d. 322 [933/4])—91. The well-known Sufi of Baghdad, who also spent time in Egypt. He was associated with the circle of al-Junayd and al-Nūrī. He was also a *ḥadīth* scholar and a jurist who studied under Ibrāhīm al-Ḥarbī. (Qushayrī, I. 185–6; Sulamī, 362–9; *Tārīkh Baghdād*, I. 329–33.)

ABŪ ʿAMR IBN AL-ʿALĀ' ibn ʿAmmār al-Māzinī (d. 154 [770/1])—98. A traditionist of Basra, who was also an authority on Arabic grammar. (*Mashāhīr*, 153–4.)

ABŪ ASHʿATH—11. Identified by Zabīdī (x. 231) as a traditionist by the name of Ibn ʿAbd al-Malik al-Ḥamrānī.

ABŪ AYYŪB AL-ANṢĀRĪ, Khālid ibn Zayd al-Najjārī (d. *c* 52 [672])—132. One of the first Medinese Muslims, present at the first 'Pledge of al-ʿAqaba' and host to the Prophet before the construction of the latter's house. In later years he was the caliph ʿAlī's governor over Medina, and died during a seige of Constantinople. His tomb remains to this day the spiritual hub of Istanbul. (*EI*^{2}, I. 108–9 [E. Lévi-Provençal *et al.*]; *Iṣāba*, I. 404–5.)

ABŪ BAKR AL-KATTĀNĪ—162. See 'al-Kattānī.'

ABŪ BAKR IBN ʿABD ALLĀH AL-MAZANĪ—114. A mistake for Bakr ibn ʿAbd Allāh al-Mazanī, for whom see s.v.

ABŪ BAKR IBN ABĪ MARYAM al-Ghassānī (d. 256 [868/9]) —167. A prolific narrator of Tradition sometimes cited by al-Tirmidhī, although generally considered to be unreliable (*ḍaʿīf*). A well-known ascetic, who lived and taught at Ḥimṣ (Syria). (Abū Nuʿaym, VI. 88–91; *Ḍuʿafā'*, 262; Ṣafadī, x. 230.)

ABŪ BAKR AL-RASHĪDĪ—166. A jurist of Nīsābūr. (Zabīdī, x. 438.)

ABŪ BAKR AL-ṢIDDĪQ ibn Abī Quḥāfa al-Taymī (d. 13 [634])—24, 60, 61, 63, 64, 69, 70, 71–3, 74–7, 81, 82, 114, 158, 159, 163, 185, 237, 243. A small businessman of Mecca who personally accompanied the Prophet on his emigration to Medina, Abū Bakr became the Prophet's closest advisor, and after his death became the first caliph. His short reign (11/632–13/634) saw the quelling of an uprising in Central Arabia and the beginnings of the conquest of Iraq and Palestine. (*EI*^{2}, I. 109–111 [W. Montgomery Watt].)

ABŪ BURDA ibn Abī Mūsā al-Ashʿarī (d. 104 [722/3])—260. A traditionist and chief judge of Kūfa in the reign of ʿAbd al-Malik, from which post he was dismissed by al-Ḥajjāj. (*Mashāhīr*, 104; *Bidāya*, IX. 231; *EI*^{2}, I. 693–4 [J. Schacht].)

ABU'L-DARDĀ', ʿUwaymir al-Khazrajī (d. 32 [652/3])—14, 102, 128, 131, 225, 243, 260. A celebrated Companion of the Prophet who joined Islam sometime after the battle of Badr, whereupon he is said to have given up commerce in order to occupy himself with worship with the *ahl al-Ṣuffa*. He was one of those who gathered together the text of the Qur'ān during the Prophet's lifetime. He died in Damascus, where he was buried, and is venerated in particular by the Sufis (*EI*², I. 113–4 [A. Jeffery]; Abū Nuʿaym, I. 208–27.)

ABŪ DHARR, Jundub ibn Junāda al-Ghifārī (d. *c* 32 [652/3])—102, 112, 200, 218, 259. One of the earliest Muslims, his shyness and devout temperament made him the protagonist of a rich variety of legendary material. He also transmitted a large number of Traditions: al-Bukhārī and Muslim between them include thirty-one of these. (*EI*², I. 114–5 [J. Robson]; Massignon, *Essai*, 158–9; *Istīʿāb*, IV. 62–5.)

ABŪ HĀSHIM AL-RUMMĀNĪ—19. Possibly to be identified with Abū Hāshim Yaḥyā al-Zummānī, a highly-regarded traditionist of Wāsiṭ, who died in 122 (739/40). (Zabīdī, X. 241; *Kāshif*, III. 341.)

ABŪ ḤĀTIM AL-RĀZĪ, Muḥammad ibn Idrīs al-Ḥanẓalī (d. 277 [890/1])—164. A respected scholar with a fine memory who taught Ibrāhīm al-Ḥarbī and Ibn Abi'l-Dunyā in Baghdad. (*Bidāya*, XI. 59; *Tārīkh Baghdād*, II. 73–8.)

ABŪ ḤĀZIM, Salama ibn Dīnār al-Madanī (d. 140 [757/8])—86. An ascetic who became an important figure for the early Sufis. 'Everything which does not bring you to God', he said, 'can only bring you to destruction'. (*GAS*, I. 634–5; *Mashāhīr*, 79; Abū Nuʿaym, III. 229–59.)

ABŪ HURAYRA al-Dawsī al-Yamānī (d. *c* 58 [677/8])—32, 43, 46, 48, 97, 114, 120, 127, 131, 137, 138, 144, 146, 179, 180, 191, 199, 200, 212, 222, 224, 226, 234, 240, 249. One of the most copious narrators of Tradition, and also a model of poverty and the fear of God's chastisement. He is said to have joined Islam during the Khaybar expedition (7/629); after which he became one of the *ahl al-Ṣuffa*. After the Prophet's death he was appointed governor of Baḥrayn by ᶜUmar. (Azami, 35–7; *EI*², I. 129 [J. Robson]; *Iṣāba*, IV. 200–8.)

ABŪ JAᶜFAR—73. See 'Muḥammad ibn ᶜAlī.'

ABŪ JAᶜFAR AL-ṢAYDALĀNĪ—160. A Sufi of Baghdad, a companion of al-Sarrāj and a spiritual instructor of Ibn al Aᶜrābī. He spent many years in Mecca. (*Tārīkh Baghdād*, XIV. 416.)

ABŪ LAHAB, ᶜAbd al-ᶜUzzā ibn ᶜAbd al-Muṭṭalib (d. 2 [623/4])—157. A patrician of Mecca who became one of the leading persecutors of the Prophet when he made his mission public. His sons, ᶜUtba and Muᶜattib eventually joined Islam. (*EI*², I. 136–7 [W. Montgomery Watt].)

ABŪ LU'LU'A (d. 23 [644])—77. A slave who killed the Caliph ᶜUmar, whom, he believed, had failed to rectify a tax grievance. (Cf. e.g., Ibn Aᶜtham, II. 83–6.)

ABŪ MUḤAMMAD IBN ᶜALĪ—23. Unidentified.

ABŪ MŪSĀ AL-ASHᶜARĪ, ᶜAbd Allāh ibn Qays (d. *c* 42 [662/3])—34, 260. Abū Mūsā joined Islam during the Khaybar campaign. During the caliphate of ᶜUmar he was responsible for the conquest of Khūzistān, and was made governor of Basra. Later he became ᶜAlī's representative at the arbitration following the battle of Ṣiffīn (37/657), after which he took no further part in public life. (*EI*², I. 695–6 [L. Veccia Vaglieri].)

ABŪ MŪSĀ AL-TAMĪMĪ—105. A traditionist of Basra. (Zabīdī, x. 355.)

ABŪ QAYS, ᶜAbd al-Raḥmān ibn Thābit (d. 54 [673/4])—127. A *mawlā* of ᶜAmr ibn al-ᶜĀṣ, he transmitted Traditions from ᶜAmr and Umm Salama; he is also reported to have been well versed in *fiqh*. (*Kāshif*, III. 326.)

ABŪ QILĀBA—118. Probably ᶜAbd Allāh ibn Zayd al-Jarmī, (d. 104 [722/3]), a traditionist of Basra, who is said to have fled to Syria to escape being made a judge. He is said to have known the caliph ᶜUmar II and ᶜAnbasa ibn Saᶜīd. (Ṣafadī, XVII. 185; Azami, 63; *Mashāhīr*, 89.)

ABŪ SAᶜĪD AL-KHARRĀZ, Aḥmad ibn ᶜĪsā (d. 277 [890/1])—90, 91, 143, 163. An important Sufi who, according to Hujwīrī, was 'the first to explain the doctrine of annihilation (*fanā'*) and subsistence (*baqā'*).' He was a close companion of Dhu'l-Nūn, Bishr al-Ḥāfī, and al-Sarī al-Saqaṭī, and was renowned for the emphasis he placed on *ᶜishq*, the passionate love of God, and upon the scrupulous observance of the Law. (Sulamī, 223–8; Hujwīrī, 143; Qushayrī, I. 161–2; *GAS*, I. 646.)

ABŪ SAᶜĪD AL-KHUDRĪ, Saᶜd ibn Mālik al-Khazrajī (d. *c* 64 [683/4] or 74 [693/4])—15, 48, 132, 207, 224, 237, 242, 244, 247, 257. A Companion who was considered too young to participate in the battle of Uḥud, in which his father was killed. He related a large corpus of *ḥadīths* to Ibn ᶜAbbās and Saᶜīd ibn al-Musayyib, and was buried in Medina. (*Iṣāba*, II. 32–3; Nawawī, *Tahdhīb*, 723–4.)

ABŪ SAᶜĪD AL-ṢAFFĀR—166. Unidentified.

ABŪ SAᶜĪD AL-SHAḤḤĀM—166. A Sufi of the circle of al-Qushayrī (who died 465 [1072]). (Zabīdī, x. 438.)

ABŪ SINĀN, Ḍirār ibn Murra al-Shaybānī (d. 132 [749–50])—110. One of the 'weepers' (*bakkā'ūn*), who is recorded as having achieved sanctity through serving his family. A respected traditionist of Kūfa. (Abū Nuᶜaym, v. 91–4; *Mashāhīr*, 164; *Kāshif*, II. 34.)

ABŪ SULAYMĀN AL-DĀRĀNĪ, ᶜAbd al-Raḥmān (d. 205 [820/1] or 215 [830/1])—12, 92, 162. Well-known to the Sufis for his piety and renunciation, he was responsible for characteristic maxims such as 'The heart is ruined when fear departs from it even for one moment', and 'The sign of perdition is the drying-up of tears'. (Qushayrī, I. 108–10; Sulamī, 68–73; Hujwīrī, 112–3; Abū Nuᶜaym, IX. 254–80.)

ABŪ ᶜUBAYDA AL-NĀJĪ, Bakr ibn al-Aswad (d. *c* 170 [786/7])—35. An ascetic, and a traditionist usually considered to be unreliable. (Ṣafadī, x. 202; *Ḍuᶜafā'*, 261.)

ABŪ UMĀMA, Asᶜad ibn Sahl ibn Ḥanīf al-Najjārī (d. 100

[718/9])—114. An early Muslim who is sometimes held to have been a Companion of the Prophet. (*Iṣāba*, IV. 10; *Mashāhīr*, 28.)

ABŪ UMĀMA AL-BĀHILĪ, Ṣudayy ibn ʿAjlān (d. 81 [700/1] or 86 [705/6])—116, 226, 239, 246. A companion of the Prophet who related a large number of Traditions. He was sent to certain of the desert tribes, and won many converts with the aid of miracles. He later removed to Ḥimṣ; according to Ibn ʿUyayna he was the last Companion of the Prophet to die in Syria. (*Iṣāba*, II. 175–6; *Istīʿāb*, IV. 4; *Mashāhīr*, 50.)

ABŪ ʿUMAR ṢĀḤIB AL-SUQYĀ—130. Unidentified.

ABŪ YAḤYĀ AL-MAZANĪ—95. Unidentified.

ABŪ YAʿQŪB AL-QĀRI' AL-DAQĪQĪ—167. Unidentified.

ABŪ ZAKARĪYĀ AL-TAYMĪ, Yaḥyā (d. 200 [815/6])—21. Born in Kūfa, this traditionist and Qur'ānic exegete travelled to Basra, Egypt and North Africa, dying in Mecca on pilgrimage. (*GAS*, I. 39.)

AḤMAD IBN ABI'L-ḤAWĀRĪ, Abu'l-Ḥasan (d. *c* 230 [844/5])—162. An early Syrian exponent of Sufism, a disciple of al-Dārānī and a companion of Ibn ʿUyayna. He is said to have thrown away his books and lived the life of a wandering ascetic. (Hujwīrī, 118–9; Qushayrī, I. 117; Sulamī, 88–92.)

AḤMAD IBN ḤANBAL (d. 241 [855])—117. The great *ḥadīth* scholar after whom the Ḥanbalī school of law is named. He travelled extensively in search of Traditions, of which he is said to have committed over three hundred thousand to memory. A companion of Bishr al-Ḥāfī and Maʿrūf al-Karkhī, he was held in high regard by the Sufis, who attribute a number of miracles to him. His tomb became one of the most frequented centres of pilgrimage in Baghdad. (*EI*², I. 272–7 [H. Laoust]; Abū Nuʿaym, IX. 161–234; Hujwīrī, 117–8.)

AḤMAD IBN ḤARB al-Marwazī (d. 234 [848/9])—104, 230. A traditionist who studied under Ibn ʿUyayna and Abū Dāūd al-Ṭayālisī, and who was sometimes accused of sympathy with the Murji'ite heresy. (*Tārīkh Baghdād*, IV. 118–9; ʿAṭṭār, 146–9.)

AḤMAD IBN KHIḌRAWAYHI (d. 240 [854/5])—95. A prominent Khurāsānī Sufi, born in Balkh, who lived and taught at Merv, where he died at the age of 95. He was a disciple of Ḥātim al-Aṣamm and a companion of Abū Turāb al-Nakhshabī. (Sulamī, 93–7; Qushayrī, I. 115–6; Ṣafadī, VI. 373.)

ᶜĀ'ISHA bint Abī Bakr (d. 58 [678])—9, 11, 40, 59, 60, 61, 64, 65, 66, 67, 73, 74, 79, 112, 119, 129, 146, 196. The third and most beloved wife of the Prophet. During his final illness he asked his other wives for leave to stay in her house, where he died. After his death she was involved in the revolt of Ṭalḥa and al-Zubayr against the caliph ᶜAlī, after which she lived quietly at Medina until she died. She was well-versed in Arab history and in poetry, and some of her verses have been preserved. (*EI*², I. 307–8 [W. Montgomery Watt].)

AL-ᶜALĀ' IBN ZIYĀD ibn Maṭar al-ᶜAdawī (d. 94 [712/3])—160. An early ascetic of Basra, who remained solitary all his life, only going out to the mosque, or to funerals or to visit the sick. He had a vision in which the world appeared to him in the shape of a misshapen hag wearing fine jewellery. (*Mashāhīr*, 90; Abū Nuᶜaym, II. 242–9; *Kāshif*, II. 309.)

ᶜALĪ IBN ABĪ ṬĀLIB (d. 40 [660])—15, 41, 61, 68, 73, 80, 81, 83–4, 101, 112, 127, 157, 158, 222. The cousin and son-in-law of the Prophet, having married his daughter Fāṭima. He was usually the Prophet's standard-bearer on expeditions, and became the model of the Muslim knight for later generations. He lived a life of austerity and piety. Upon the death of ᶜUthmān (35/656) he accepted, with some reluctance, the office of Caliph, which he held for five years disturbed by several rebellions, including that of Muᶜāwiya, the governor of Syria. He was assassinated at Kūfa by a member of the extreme Khārijite sect, which repudiated him for having agreed to negotiate with Muᶜāwiya. (*EI*², I. 381–6 [L. Veccia Vaglieri]; *Istīᶜāb*, III. 26–67.)

ᶜALĪ IBN ᶜĀṢIM ibn Ṣuhayb al-Wāsiṭī (d. 201 [816/7])—168. A traditionist who taught at Baghdad. Although considered unreliable by some authorities, a number of his *ḥadīths* are to be found in the *Musnad* of Ibn Ḥanbal. (*Tārīkh Baghdād*, XI. 446–58; Azami, 119–20; *Bidāya*, X. 248.)

ᶜALĪ IBN MŪSĀ AL-ḤADDĀD—117. Unidentified.

ᶜALĪ AL-ṬALḤĪ—161. Unidentified.

ᶜALQAMA ibn Qays al-Nakhaᶜī (d. *c* 62 [681/2])—000. A pupil of Ibn Masᶜūd, who called him the most erudite of his disciples. He also related traditions from ᶜAlī, Saᶜd ibn Abī Waqqāṣ and ᶜUthmān. (*Tārīkh Baghdād*, XII. 296; Abū Nuᶜaym, II. 98-102; *GAS*, I. 398.)

AL-AᶜMASH, Sulaymān ibn Mihrān al-Asadī (d. 147 [764/5])—55, 98, 226. A Qur'ān specialist of Persian origin who studied under Mujāhid at Kūfa. One of the fourteen canonical readings of the Qur'ān bears his name. In addition, Sufyān al-Thawrī and Ibn ᶜUyayna both studied *ḥadīth* under him. (Azami, 101–2; *Tārīkh Baghdād*, IX. 3–13; *Mashāhīr*, 111. *EI*², I. 431 [C. Brockelmann—[Ch. Pellat]].)

ĀMINA BINT WAHB al-Zuhrīya (d. *c* 575 AD)—101, 157. The mother of the Prophet, she died when he was about six. She was probably buried at a place known as al-Abwā' between Mecca and Medina. The historians record a number of miracles surrounding her pregnancy and the Prophet's birth. (*EI*², I. 438 [W. Montgomery Watt].)

ᶜĀMIR IBN ᶜABD ALLĀH ibn al-Zubayr ibn al-ᶜAwwām (d. 121 [738/9])—33. An ascetic of Medina, who is recorded as having kept his hands raised in supplication between the night and morning prayers. He is said to have died in prayer. He also transmitted a number of Traditions which are recorded by both al-Bukhārī and Muslim. (Ṣafadī, XVI. 589; *Kāshif*, II. 51; Abū Nuᶜaym, III. 166–8.)

ᶜĀMIR IBN ᶜABD AL-QAYS (d. *c* 41–60 [661–80])—89. A *tābiᶜī* of Basra who died at Damascus, where he had become famous for his austere and eloquent sermons. A number of miracles are recorded of him—he is said to have lived in the desert where wild beasts came tamely to him. He was also known for his charity towards orphans. These and other aspects of his life are often cited by the Sufis. (Abū Nuᶜaym, II. 87–95; Ṣafadī, XVI. 585–6; Ibn Marthad, 37–8.)

ᶜAMR IBN AL-ᶜĀṢ al-Sahmī (d. 42 [663/4])—88, 102, 211. A Companion of the Prophet and a politician and general of great skill. To him goes the credit for the conquest of Palestine (12 [633]) and Egypt (19–21 [640–2]), where he founded the city of Fusṭāṭ, which was to grow into Cairo. He sided with Muᶜāwiya at the battle of Ṣiffīn, and represented him at the arbitration which followed. (*EI*², I. 451 [A. J. Wensinck].)

ᶜAMR IBN DĪNĀR al-Jumaḥī (d. 126 [743/4])—130. A scholar of the Law in Mecca, where he learnt the recitation of the Qur'ān and a number of Traditions from Ibn ᶜAbbās. (*Mashāhīr*, 84; Abū Nuᶜaym, III. 347–54; *Ghāya*, I. 600–1.)

ᶜAMR IBN ḤAZM AL-ANṢĀRĪ al-Khazrajī (d. 51 [671/2])—259. A Companion who distinguished himself in the 'Battle of the Trench', and who became the Prophet's governor of Najrān. A number of *ḥadīths* are related on his authority by al-Nasā'ī. (*Iṣāba*, II. 525; *Kāshif*, II. 282.)

ᶜAMR IBN MAYMŪN al-Awdī (d. *c* 74 [693/4])—77. A 'Follower' who was present at the murder of ᶜUmar, and who later moved to Kufa. He transmitted a number of *ḥadīths* which have been recorded by al-Bukhārī, and was much given to devotional practices. (*Mashāhīr*, 99; Abū Nuᶜaym, IV. 148–54; *Kāshif*, II. 296.)

ANAS ibn Mālik ibn al-Naḍr (d. 91–3 [709/10–711/2])—10, 17, 114, 119, 127, 146, 192, 196, 202, 209, 215, 224, 228, 244, 246. A celebrated Companion of the Prophet, he had been presented to the Prophet by his mother at an early age in fulfilment of a vow. After the Prophet's death he participated in the wars of conquest. One hundred and twenty eight Traditions on his authority are to be found in the collections of al-Bukhārī and Muslim. (*Iṣāba*, I. 84–5; *EI*², I. 482 [A. J. Wensinck—J. Robson].)

ᶜANBASA ibn Saᶜīd (d. 100 [718/9])—12. A respected traditionist, originally of Kūfa, who taught Ibn al-Mubārak and was a judge at Rayy. (*Kāshif*, II. 304; Zabīdī, X. 232.)

AL-AṢBAGH AL-ḤANẒALĪ, ibn Nubāta—83. An unreliable

traditionist of Kūfa accused of S͟hīʿite tendancies. (Zabīdī, X. 318; ʿUqaylī, I. 129–30; *Tahd͟hīb al-Tahd͟hīb*, I. 362–3.)

AS͟HʿATH IBN ASLAM—50–1. Unidentified.

ʿĀṢIM IBN ḌAMRA (d. 174 [790/1])—235. A traditionist of Kūfa, generally regarded as reliable. (*Kās͟hif*, II. 45; *G͟hāya*, I. 349.)

ʿĀṢIM AL-AḤWAL, ibn Sulaymān (d. *c* 141 [758/9])—36. A traditionist from Basra who became chief judge of al-Madāʾin. (*Mas͟hāhīr*, 98; *Bidāya*, X. 78; Ṣafadī, XVI. 568.)

ʿĀṢIM AL-JAHDARĪ, ibn al-ʿAjjāj (d. 129 [746/7])—114. An ascetic of Basra and an authority on the reading of the Qurʾān; he had his own reading which is considered one of the *qirāʾāt s͟hādhdha*. (*G͟hāya*, I. 349; Ṣafadī, XVI. 568; *Mas͟hāhīr*, 94.)

AL-ASWAD—30. Possibly a reference to al-Aswad ibn Yazīd al-Nak͟haʿī (d. *c* 80 [699/700]), an ascetic who is said to have performed the Pilgrimage eighty times, and to have slept only between the sunset and night prayers. (Abū Nuʿaym, II. 102–5; *Kās͟hif*, I. 80; Ibn Mart͟had, 53–5.)

ʿAṬĀʾ AL-K͟HURĀSĀNĪ, ibn Abī Muslim (d. 135 [752/3])—10. A traditionist who was a *mawlā* of al-Muhallab ibn Abī Ṣufra; a number of his narratives are to be found in the *Ṣaḥīḥ* of Muslim. (*Kās͟hif*, II. 233; *Bidāya*, X. 57; *GAS*, I. 33–4.)

ʿAṬĀʾ AL-SALĪMĪ (d. 121 [738/9])—103, 160. An ascetic and traditionist of Basra. (Abū Nuʿaym, VI. 215–27; *Mas͟hāhīr*, 152.)

ʿAṬĀʾ IBN YASĀR al-Hilālī (d. *c* 103 [721/2])—54, 90, 145. A Follower who spent his life in Medina and Syria. He transmitted *ḥadīt͟hs* from Abū D͟harr and Zayd ibn T͟hābit, some of which are to be found in the collections of al-Buk͟hārī and Muslim. (*Mas͟hāhīr*, 69; *Kās͟hif*, II. 233.)

AL-AWZĀʿĪ, ʿAbd al-Raḥmān ibn ʿAmr, Abū ʿAmr (d. 157 [774])—41, 161, 245. The principal authority on the s͟harīʿa in Syria of his generation, who placed especial emphasis on the 'living tradition' of the Muslim community as an authoritative source of law. His *mad͟hhab* also spread in North Africa and Spain, where it was then replaced by that of Mālik. His tomb near Beirut is still visited. (*EI*², I. 772–3 [J. Schacht]; *GALS*, I. 308–9; *Fihrist*, 227.)

AYYŪB AL-SAKHTIYĀNĪ ibn Abī Tamīma (d. 131 [748/9])—165. A pupil of Anas ibn Mālik, he was a reputable narrator of Traditions, and is recorded as having been particularly scrupulous about the *sunna*. A number of miracles are reported of him. (*Mashāhīr*, 150; Azami, 81; Abū Nuᶜaym, III. 3–14; *GAS*, I. 87–8.)

BAKR IBN ᶜABD ALLĀH AL-MAZANĪ (d. 106 [724/5] or 108 [726/7])—52. A 'Follower' of Basra, who, despite his considerable wealth, spent much time teaching and sitting with the poor. A prolific narrator of Tradition, he was known for the importance he attached to the fear of Hell. (*Mashāhīr*, 90; Ṣafadī, X. 207; Abū Nuᶜaym, II. 224–32; *Kāshif*, I. 108.)

BAKR AL-ᶜĀBID, ibn ᶜAmr al-Nājī (d. 108 [726/7])—103. A Follower who related *ḥadīths* from ᶜĀ'isha, in particular to Qatāda and ᶜĀṣim al-Aḥwal; considered a sound authority. (*Kāshif*, I. 108; Abū Nuᶜaym, III. 101–2.)

BAKRĀN AL-DĪNAWARĪ—92. A Sufi of the circle of al-Shiblī (d. 334 [945/6]). (Qushayrī, I. 183.)

AL-BARĀ' IBN ᶜĀZIB al-Awsī (d. *c* 72 [691/2])—135. A Companion of the Prophet, who is said to have taken part in all his expeditions save that of Badr, for which he was considered to be too young. Later he was set in charge of the armies which conquered Rayy and Qazwīn. (*EI*², I. 1025 [K. V. Zettersteen]; *Iṣāba*, I. 146–7.)

BASHSHĀR IBN GHĀLIB AL-NAJRĀNĪ—116. Unidentified.

BILĀL ibn Rabāḥ (d. 17–21 [638/9–642/3])—64, 89. Usually held to have been the second adult convert to Islam, Bilāl was born in Mecca into slavery, and was tortured by his master Umayya ibn Khalaf when he refused to renounce his new faith. He was purchased by Abū Bakr, who set him free. He became the Prophet's muezzin at Medina, and later moved to Syria, where he died. (*EI*², I. 1215 [W. ᶜArafat].)

BISHR IBN AL-ḤĀRITH 'al-Ḥāfī' (d. *c* 227 [841/2])—92, 162. One of the most celebrated figures of early Sufism, he was a companion of Fuḍayl ibn ʿIyāḍ. Formerly given to riotous living, his repentance is said to have come when, in a state of inebriation, he picked up a scrap of paper on which was written the name of God, which he perfumed and put in a clean place. That night he received a dream in which God told him that He would perfume his name as a reward for his act. Many other tales of his charismatic and devout life have found their way into the classical works on Sufism. (Qushayrī, I. 84–8; Hujwīrī, 105–6; *Siyar*, x. 469; Abū Nuʿaym, VIII. 336–60; Sulamī, 33–40; *EI*², I. 1244–6 [F. Meier]; Dermenghem, 67–78.)

BISHR IBN MANṢŪR al-Azdī (d. 180 [796/7])—115. A Follower much given to devotional practices in private, who was a recognised authority on *ḥadīth*. He lived in Basra, but is said to have spent some time in Syria. (Ṣafadī, x. 156; *Kāshif*, I. 104; Abū Nuʿaym, VI. 239–43.)

AL-ḌAḤḤĀK ibn Muzāḥim al-Hilālī (d. 105 [723/4])—100, 115. A traditionist of Balkh (and later Merv) whose material was used by al-Bukhārī, and who was particularly erudite in Qur'ānic exegesis. According to some authorities he met one or more of the Prophet's Companions. (*Mashāhīr*, 194; Azami, 64; *Ghāya*, I. 337.)

DĀŪD AL-ṬĀ'Ī, ibn Nuṣayr (d. *c* 165 [781/2])—19, 23, 34, 105, 166. A companion of Ibrāhīm ibn Adham, and an ascetic of whom many anecdotes are told in the early works on Sufism. He placed emphasis on poverty as an aid to the struggle against the lower self, gave all he had to the poor, and is said to have subsisted on a diet of barley bread and water. He was also an outstanding authority on the Law, which he studied under Abū Ḥanīfa. (*Siyar*, VII. 423; *Tārīkh Baghdād*, VIII. 347–55; Qushayrī, I. 92–5; Abū Nuʿaym, VII. 335–367; *Tahdhīb al-Tahdhīb*, III. 203.)

DHU'L-NŪN al-Miṣrī, Thawbān (d. 245 [859/60])—91. Born in Upper Egypt, he travelled to Mecca and Damascus, and became a leading exponent of Sufism. It is said that he was the first to give a systematic explanation of the *aḥwāl* ('states') and *maqāmāt* ('stations') encountered on the spiritual path. A number of miracles are attributed to him, as well as some fine poetry. (*EI*², II. 242 [M. Smith]; Sulamī, 23–32; Qushayrī, I. 67–70; Hujwīrī, 100–3; Massignon, *Essai*, 206–13.)

AL-FAḌL ibn al-ᶜAbbās ibn ᶜAbd al-Muṭṭalib (d. 13 [634])—61. A Companion of the Prophet who died fighting the Byzantines at the battle of the Yarmūk at the age of 22. (*Mashāhīr*, 9.)

AL-FARAZDAQ, Abū Firās Tammām ibn Ghālib, (d. *c* 110 [728/9])—105. A poet of Bedouin origin who wrote verse chiefly of a satirical and panegyric nature. Many of his poems are directed against his great rival Jarīr. (*EI*², II. 788–9 [R. Blachère].)

FĀṬIMA (d. 11 [632])—, 42, 66, 84, 113 The youngest and best-loved of the daughters of the Prophet. He once told her that 'God is angry when you are angry, and glad when you are glad'. In the year 2 she married ᶜAlī ibn Abī Ṭālib in the union which was to produce al-Ḥasan and al-Ḥusayn. Her piety made her a figure greatly revered by later generations. (*Iṣāba*, IV. 365–8; *EI*², II. 841–50 [L. Veccia Vaglieri].)

FĀṬIMA, Umm Salama bint Aḥmad—91. The sister of the famous Sufi Abū ᶜAlī al-Rūdhbārī, of an aristocratic and wealthy family; she is remembered for her sanctity and devoutness. (*Tārīkh Baghdād*, I. 330.)

FĀṬIMA BINT ᶜABD AL-MALIK—87, 218. The wife of the caliph ᶜUmar II and the sister of his successor Yazīd II. When ᶜUmar assumed power he is said to have given away all his wealth, and asked her whether she still wished to remain with him: she chose to remain. She reported many of his secret prayers and devotions after his death. (*Bidāya*, IX. 198–201.)

FĀṬIMA BINT AL-ḤASAN—104. As Zabīdī points out, this is a mistake for Fāṭima bint al-Ḥusayn, the granddaughter of the caliph ᶜAlī and of Ṭalḥa ibn ᶜUbayd Allāh. She married her cousin al-Ḥasan ibn al-Ḥasan, and related a number of *ḥadīths*. (*Tahdhīb al-Tahdhīb*, XII. 442–3.)

FUḌAYL ibn ᶜIyāḍ (d. 187 [803/4].)—89. A brigand who repented and became a pioneer of early Sufism. He studied *ḥadīth* under Sufyān al-Thawrī and Abū Ḥanīfa, and became well-known for his sermons on the worthlessness of the world, which he likened to 'a madhouse, the people in which are lunatics wearing the shackles of desire and sin'. (Hujwīrī, 97–100; Sulamī, 7–12; *Mashāhīr*, 149; *EI*², II. 936 [M. Smith]; *GAS*, I. 636; Dermenghem, 51–66.)

FUḌAYL AL-RUQĀSHĪ (d. 95 [713/4])—36. A *ḥadīth* scholar and ascetic of Basra, remembered for a number of fine sayings on the devotional life. (*Mashāhīr*, 98; Abū Nuʿaym, III. 102–3.)

ḤAFṢA bint ʿUmar ibn al-Khaṭṭāb (d. *c* 45 [665/6])—79. An early Muslim who married the Prophet in the year 3. After the death of her father she inherited the copy of the Qur'ān prepared by the Prophet's secretary Zayd ibn Thābit, which became the 'authorised version' approved by ʿUthmān. (*Iṣāba*, IV. 264; *EI*², III. 63–5 [L. Veccia Vaglieri].)

AL-ḤAJJĀJ ibn Yūsuf al-Thaqafī (d. 95 [714])—88. An Umayyad general notorious for his ruthlessness. Of humble origins, he was born near al-Ṭā'if, and became a policeman at Damascus. He attracted the attention of the caliph ʿAbd al-Malik, who put him in charge of a campaign against Ibn al-Zubayr, whom he defeated and killed at Mecca. He also fought extensively against the Khārijites. (*EI*², III. 39–43 [A. Dietrich].)

AL-ḤAKAM IBN AL-MUṬṬALIB al-Makhzūmī—94. An early traditionist of Manbij in northern Syria. (Zabīdī, X. 343.)

ḤAMZA ibn ʿAbd al-Muṭṭalib (d. 3 [625])—84, 113. The paternal uncle of the Prophet, he helped to arrange his first marriage. A brave warrior, his conversion greatly heartened the early Muslim community in Mecca. He was killed at the battle of Uḥud by an Abyssinian slave who had been promised his freedom should he accomplish this deed. (*EI*², III. 152–4 [G. M. Meredith-Owens].)

HĀRŪN AL-RASHĪD (*regn.* 170–193 [786–809])—88. Perhaps the best-known ʿAbbāsid caliph, whose cultured and sumptuous court presided nevertheless over an empire troubled by rebellion and Byzantine encroachment.

AL-ḤASAN IBN ʿALĪ (d. *c* 50 [670/1])—84, 157. Grandson of

the Prophet, and second Imām of the Shīʿa. Until the reign of ʿAlī he lived a secluded life at Medina, which was interrupted by a short period in which he claimed the Caliphate. (*EI*², III. 240–3 [L. Veccia Vaglieri].)

AL-ḤASAN al-Baṣrī (d. 110 [728/9])—11, 12, 18, 19, 21, 34, 35, 41, 46, 54, 90, 105, 164, 167, 182, 196, 227, 229, 248. Perhaps the best known personality among the second generation of Muslims, he was born in Medina and took part in the conquest of eastern Iran. He then moved to Basra, where his sanctity and great eloquence attracted great numbers to his circle. He was also a judge and an authority on *ḥadīth*. His tomb at Basra remains an important centre for devout visits. (Hujwīrī, 86–7; Abū Nuʿaym, II. 131–61; ʿAṭṭār, 19–26; *EI*², III. 247–8 [H. Ritter].)

AL-ḤASAN IBN AL-ḤUSAYN—104. Probably a mistake for al-Ḥasan ibn al-Ḥasan (ibn ʿAlī ibn Abī Ṭālib), a *ḥadīth* scholar who died *c* 97 (715/6). (*Tahdhīb al-Tahdhīb*, II. 263.)

AL-ḤASAN IBN ṢĀLIḤ ibn Ḥuyayy al-Thawrī (d. 167 [783/4])—103. An ascetic of Kūfa of Shīʿite leanings, who spent all of his nights in prayer. (*Mashāhīr*, 170; *Bidāya*, X. 150; Abū Nuʿaym, VII. 327–35.)

ḤĀTIM AL-AṢAMM al-Balkhī (d. 237 [851/2])—103. A disciple of the Khurāsānī Sufi Shaqīq al-Balkhī, he was known as the 'Luqmān of this nation' for his wise sayings. (Hujwīrī, 115; Ṣafadī, XI. 233–4; Sulamī, 80–7; Abū Nuʿaym, VIII. 73–84.)

ḤUDHAYFA ibn al-Yamān al-ʿAbasī (d. 36 [656/7])—8, 33, 46, 48, 146, 243. One of the earliest converts to Islam, whose father was martyred at the battle of Uḥud. He is particularly revered by the Sufis. He related a considerable number of *ḥadīths*, particularly those relating to eschatology: according to the sources he said that 'the Prophet told me all that would occur from the present until the Day of Judgement'. (*Iṣāba*, I. 316-7; Massignon, *Essai*, 159–61; Nawawī, *Tahdhīb*, 199–201; Abū Nuʿaym, I. 270–83.)

ḤUDHAYFA—94. Unidentified.

AL-ḤUSAYN IBN ʿALĪ ibn Abī Ṭālib (d. 61 [680])—84, 159, 229. A grandson of the Prophet, who, although he acquiesced in the caliphate of Muʿāwiya, refused to recognise his son al-Yazīd upon his accession in 60 AH (680 AD). Against the advice of Ibn ʿAbbās and ʿAbd Allāh ibn ʿUmar, al-Ḥusayn marched with a handful of supporters to Kūfa, where he believed that he could muster support; the Kūfans, however, intimidated by Yazīd's governor, met him in battle at nearby Karbalā', where he was slain. (*EI*², III. 607–15 [L. Veccia Vaglieri].)

IBN ʿABBĀS, ʿAbd Allāh (d. 68 [687/8])—16, 31, 44, 72, 81, 156, 158, 178, 212, 216, 225, 241, 256, 258. A cousin and close companion of the Prophet respected for his piety and commonly acknowledged as the greatest scholar of the first generation of Muslims, a narrator of *ḥadīth* and the founder of the science of Qur'ānic exegesis. He fought alongside ʿAlī at Ṣiffīn, and died at al-Ṭā'if, where the site of his grave is still visited. (Nawawī, *Tahdhīb*, 351–4; Abū Nuʿaym, I. 314–29; *Mashāhīr*, 9; *Iṣāba*, II. 322–6; *EI*², I. 40–1 [L. Veccia Vaglieri].)

IBN ABĪ MULAYKA, ʿAbd Allāh ibn ʿUbayd Allāh (d. 117 [735/6])—112, 113. A prominent Follower (*tābiʿī*) of Mecca who joined the revolt of Ibn al-Zubayr, who made him a judge. He is said to have met eighty Companions of the Prophet. (*Tahdhīb al-Tahdhīb*, V. 306; *Mashāhīr*, 82–3.)

IBN MASʿŪD, ʿAbd Allāh al-Hudhalī (d. 32–3 [652/3–653/4])—14, 17, 33, 35, 46, 59, 63, 194, 201, 208, 243. Of Bedouin origin, Ibn Masʿūd is said to have been either the third or the sixth convert to Islam; he became one of the most erudite Companions. He was particularly well versed in the recitation and interpretation of the Qur'ān, and was an expert in matters of law. In addition, he related a number of the most important eschatological *ḥadīths*. (*EI*², III. 873–5 [J.-C. Vadet]; *Iṣāba*, II. 360–62; *Istīʿāb*, II. 308–16.)

IBN AL-MUBĀRAK—90, 166. See 'ʿAbd Allāh ibn al-Mubārak'.

IBN MULJAM, ʿAbd al-Raḥmān al-Murādī (d. 40 [661])—83, 157. The Khārijite assassin of the caliph ʿAlī, he was caught and put to death after carrying out his mission. (*EI*², III. 887–90 [L. Veccia Vaglieri].)

IBN AL-MUNKADIR, Muḥammad al-Taymī (d. 130 [747/8])—89. A prominent Follower and reciter of the Qur'ān, who transmitted a number of *ḥadīths*. (*Mashāhīr*, 65; Abū Nuᶜaym, III. 146–58.)

IBN MUṬĪᶜ—14. Possibly ᶜAbd Allāh ibn Muṭīᶜ al-ᶜAdawī (d. 73 [692]), one of the leaders of the Medinese insurrection against Yazid I. Defeated at the battle of the Ḥarra in 63 (683) he became governor of Kūfa for Ibn al-Zubayr, with whom he was killed at Mecca. (*EI*², I. 50 [K. V. Zettersteen—Ch. Pellat].)

IBN RĀSHID, Muḥammad, al-Makḥūlī (d. *c* 170 [786/7])—166. A respected traditionist of Damascus, who later moved to Basra. A number of his *ḥadīths* are cited by Abū Dāūd, al-Nasā'ī and al-Tirmidhī. (*Kāshif*, III. 37; *Tahdhīb al-Tahdhīb*, IX. 158–60.)

IBN AL-SAMMĀK, Muḥammad ibn Ṣabīḥ (d. 183 [799/800])—107. A traditionist and preacher of Baghdad who delivered a famous sermon before Hārūn al-Rashīd, and who wrote to the wealthy urging them to renounce their riches in favour of poverty and the religious life. He was a disciple of Sufyān al-Thawrī in *ḥadīth*, and taught Ibn Ḥanbal. (*Siyar*, VIII. 291–3; *Tārīkh Baghdād*, V. 368–73; *Taᶜjīl*, 364–5.)

IBN SĪRĪN, Muḥammad, al-Anṣārī (d. 110 [728/9])—11, 113, 153. Born during the caliphate of ᶜUthmān, his father was clerk to Anas ibn Mālik. He moved to Basra, where he preached in the marketplaces and where he became known as an authority on law. He is also remembered as a master interpreter of dreams, and a book on the subject is attributed to him. (*Mashāhīr*, 88; Azami, 94–5; Abū Nuᶜaym, II. 263–82; *EI*², III. 947–8 [T. Fahd]; *GAS*, I. 633–4.)

IBN AL-TAYYĀḤ—83. Unidentified.

IBN ᶜUMAR, ᶜAbd Allāh (d. 73 [693/4])—10, 32, 70, 113, 114, 117, 130, 180, 192, 218. A Companion of the Prophet who, at the age of fourteen asked to be permitted to fight at Uḥud, which permission was denied. Possessed of high moral qualities he commanded universal deference and respect. Although it is said that he was offered the caliphate on three separate occasions he kept himself aloof from politics and occupied himself instead with study and instruction. (*EI*², I. 53–4 [L. Veccia Vaglieri]; *Iṣāba*, II. 338–41; Abū Nuʿaym, I. 292–314.)

IBN ʿUYAYNA, Sufyān al-Hilālī (d. *c* 198 [813/4])—161, 163. An influential *ḥadīth* specialist born in Kūfa and reared in Mecca, who studied under Ibn Shihāb al-Zuhrī. 'But for Mālik and Ibn ʿUyayna', al-Shāfiʿī is represented as saying, 'the knowledge of the Ḥijāz would have been lost'. He is a principal source of *ḥadīth* in the *Musnad* of al-Ḥumaydī. (*Mashāhīr*, 149; *GAS*, I. 139; Azami, 169–70.)

IBRĀHĪM IBN ISḤĀQ AL-ḤARBĪ (d. 285 [898/9])—161. A grammarian, historian and traditionist of Baghdad, an important disciple of Ibn Ḥanbal, and an admirer of Bishr al-Ḥāfī. His book on the Pilgrimage has recently been published. (Ṣafadī, v. 320–4; *Bidāya*, x. 297; Zabīdī, x. 434.)

IBRĀHĪM AL-NAKHAʿĪ, ibn Yazīd (d. *c* 96 [714/5])—89. A devout and learned scholar of Kūfa who opposed the writing of *ḥadīth* as an unjustified innovation. He studied under al-Ḥasan al-Baṣrī and Anas ibn Mālik, and taught Abū Ḥanīfa, who may have been influenced by his extensive use of personal judgement (*ra'y*) in matters of jurisprudence. (*Mashāhīr*, 101; Azami, 65–6; *Ghāya*, I. 29.)

IBRĀHĪM AL-TAYMĪ, ibn Yazīd (d. *c* 93 [711/2])—11. An ascetic of Kūfa who is said to have placed great emphasis on 'short hopes' (*qiṣar al-amal*). He figures in many hortatory tales with his father, Yazīd ibn Sharīk. A respected traditionist, he taught al-Aʿmash, and use is made of his *ḥadīths* by al-Bukhārī and Muslim. (Abū Nuʿaym, IV. 210-19; *Mashāhīr*, 101; *Kāshif*, I. 50.)

IBRĀHĪM AL-ZAYYĀT—98. Unidentified.

ʿIKRIMA, *mawlā* Ibn ʿAbbās (d. *c* 105 [723–4])—44. Said to have been of Berber origin, he was a manumitted slave of Ibn ʿAbbās, whose exegesis of the Qur'ān he passed on to Mujāhid. Although accused of Khārijite sympathies, he is regarded as a reliable authority on *ḥadīth*. (Azami, 66–7; *Ghāya*, I. 515; *EI*², III. 1081–2 [J. Schacht]; Abū Nuʿaym, III. 326–47.)

JĀBIR ibn ʿAbd Allāh al-Khazrajī al-Anṣārī (d. 68–78 [687/8–

697/8])—32, 129, 150, 157, 237. A Companion of the Prophet whose father died at the battle of Uḥud. He participated in nineteen of the expeditions of the Prophet, and related a sizeable number of Traditions. (*Iṣāba*, I. 214–5; Nawawī, *Tahdhīb*, 184–6; *Mashāhīr*, 11.)

JĀBIR IBN WADĀʿA—50. Unidentified.

JĀBIR IBN ZAYD al-Azdī (d. 93 [711/2])—46. Usually known as Abu'l-Shaʿthā'. A Basran authority on the *sharīʿa* and the interpretation of the Qur'ān, and a leader of the Ibāḍī branch of the Khārijite movement. He was a pupil of Ibn ʿAbbās, and related *ḥadīths* to Qatāda. (*Kāshif*, I. 121; Abū Nuʿaym, III. 85–92; *Mashāhīr*, 89.)

JAʿFAR ibn Abī Ṭālib (d. 8 [629])—84. A cousin of the Prophet and the elder brother of ʿAlī. It was he that led the emigration to Abyssinia, whence he returned in time for the Khaybar expedition (7/628). He was known as 'Abu'l-Masākīn' because of his concern for the poor. (*EI*², II. 372 [L. Veccia Vaglieri]; *Istīʿāb*, I. 211–4.)

JAʿFAR IBN MUḤAMMAD ibn ʿAlī ibn al-Ḥusayn, 'al-Ṣādiq' (d. 148 [765])—102, 113. A major authority on law and *ḥadīth*, he taught both Abū Ḥanīfa and Mālik. His austere and saintly life made him an important ideal for the Sufis, who gathered large numbers of sayings attributed to him. He was later made into the seventh Imām of the Shīʿa: the Jaʿfarīya sect is named after him. (*EI*², II. 374–5 [M.G.S. Hodgson]; *Mashāhīr*, 127; Abū Nuʿaym, III. 192–206; *Tahdhīb al-Tahdhīb*, II. 104.)

JAʿFAR IBN NUṢAYR al-Khuldī (d. 348 [959/60])—92. (Correct name: Jaʿfar ibn Muḥammad ibn Nuṣayr al-Khuldī.) A major Sufi of Baghdad, a companion of Ruwaym, al-Junayd and al-Nūrī, who spent much of his life engaged in extensive travels. He left a number of aphorisms which are much quoted in the classical works on Sufism. (*GAS*, I. 661; Qushayrī, II. 443; Hujwīrī, 156–7; *Tārīkh Baghdād*, VII. 226–31; Abū Nuʿaym, X. 381.)

JAʿFAR IBN SAʿĪD—132. As Zabīdī remarks (X. 394), this is probably an error for 'Jaʿfar *ʿan* Saʿīd' (ibn al-Musayyib), a reference to Jaʿfar ibn Sulaymān (d. 178 [794/5]), a Shīʿite traditionist and ascetic of Basra. (*Kāshif*, I. 129; *Bidāya*, X. 173; *Mashāhīr*, 159.)

AL-JĀḤIẒ (d. 255 [868/9])—165. One of the finest Arabic prose stylists, he left a wealth of elegant and witty books, such as the *Animals* and the *Misers* which have furnished much information about early Islamic society. Although originally of Basra he wrote principally in Baghdad. In addition to his literary tastes he was a theologian of the Muᶜtazilite school. (C. Pellat, *Le Milieu basrien et la formation de Ǧāḥiẓ*.)

JARĪR IBN ᶜABD ALLĀH al-Bajalī (d. 51 [671/2])—240, 250, 255. A Companion of the Prophet. Of an aristocratic family, he was renowned for his handsomeness. A number of *ḥadīths* were related by him. (*Mashāhīr*, 44; *Kāshif*, I. 126.)

JARĪR ibn ᶜAṭīya al-Khaṭafī (d. 110 [728–9])—98. With al-Farazdaq and al-Akhṭal, Jarīr represents the last flowering of the Bedouin poetic tradition. His work is composed primarily of panegyrics, and ruthless broadsides directed against his rival al-Farazdaq. (*GALS*, II. 53–5.)

AL-JUNAYD, Abu'l-Qāsim ibn Muḥammad (d. 298 [910/11])—90, 91, 92, 93, 160, 162, 165. The best known of the Sufis of Baghdad. A nephew and disciple of al-Sarī al-Saqaṭī, he vowed that would not teach during the latter's lifetime out of deference to his preceptor; however he received a vision of the Prophet, who told him that 'God shall make your words the salvation of a multitude of mankind'; he then began to teach. His gatherings 'were attended by jurists and philosophers (attracted by his precise reasoning), theologians (drawn by his orthodoxy) and Sufis (for his discoursing upon the Truth)'. In addition, he was an authority on theology and law, in which he followed the school of Abū Thawr. (Sulamī, 141–50; *GAS*, I. 647–50; *EI*², II. 600 [A. J. Arberry]; A. H. Abdel-Kader, *The Life, Personality and Writings of al-Junayd*.)

AL-JURAYRĪ (d. 311 [923/4])—90. A companion of Junayd, sometimes said to have been his successor. He was also a theologian and a jurist. (Hujwīrī, 148; Qushayrī, I. 166–7; Sulamī, 253–9; *Tārīkh Baghdād*, IV. 430–4.)

KAᶜB al-Aḥbār, ibn Mātiᶜ al-Ḥimyarī (d. 32 [652/3] or 34 [654/5])—11, 42, 113, 129, 134, 182, 248. A rabbi from the Yemen who converted to Islam during the caliphate of ᶜUmar. (*EI*², iv. 316–7 [M. Schmitz]; *Mas͟hāhīr*, 118.)

AL-KATTĀNĪ, Muḥammad ibn ᶜAlī (d. 322 [933/4])—94, 162. A Baghdad Sufi of the circle of al-Junayd and al-K͟harrāz; he spent much of his life in Mecca, where he died. (Sulamī, 386-91; *Tārīk͟h Bag͟hdād*, iii. 74–6; Abū Nuᶜaym, x. 357–8; ᶜAṭṭār, 253–6.)

K͟HADĪJA BINT K͟HUWAYLID (d. 3 BH [619])—84. The first wife of the Prophet. She was a businesswoman of Mecca, and married him after having been impressed with his efficiency and honesty in the matter of a caravan to Syria which he had supervised for her. (*EI*², iv. 898–9 [W. Montgomery Watt].)

K͟HAYT͟HAMA ibn ᶜAbd al-Raḥmān al-Kūfī (d. *c* 80 [699/700])—55. A traditionist who studied under ᶜAbd Allāh ibn ᶜAmr and ᶜAlī. A wealthy man, he is said to have given lavish banquets for the poor. (*Mas͟hāhīr*, 103; Abū Nuᶜaym, iv. 113–126.)

LUQMĀN—37. A sage of pre-Islamic Arabia who figures prominently in Arab legend and proverbs. He is shown in the Qur'ān as a monotheist giving advice to his son. (*EI*², v. 811–3 [B. Heller—[N. A. Stillman]].)

AL-MAG͟HĀZILĪ—94. Possibly a reference to Banān ibn Yaḥyā al-Mag͟hāzilī (d. 264 [877/8]), a traditionist. (*Tārīk͟h Bag͟hdād*, vii. 99–100.)

MAJNŪN—164. The protagonist of a Bedouin love story. A shepherd, he falls in love with the girl Laylā. When he loses her he turns mad, wandering in the desert and communing with wild beasts. The tale was later turned into a symbol of the Sufi love of God. (*EI*², v. 1102–7 [C. Pellat *et al.*].)

MAKḤŪL, Abū ᶜAbd Allāh al-Dimas͟hqī (d. 112 [730/1])—42, 97. A prisoner of war taken at Kabul and given to an Egyptian woman, who set him free. He later became one of the more prominent jurists of Damascus, where he influenced al-Awzāᶜī. (*Kās͟hif*, iii. 152; *Fihrist*, 227; *Mas͟hāhīr*, 114.)

MĀLIK IBN ANAS al-Aṣbaḥī (d. 179 [795/6])—131, 164, 229.

The founder of one of the four main schools of Islamic law. Born into a family of *ḥadīth* scholars at Medina, he studied the recitation of the Qur'ān with Nāfiᶜ and heard *ḥadīths* from al-Zuhrī and Ibn al-Munkadir. He taught al-Shāfiᶜī, al-Thawrī and Ibn al-Mubārak. His book, the *Muwaṭṭa'*, is the earliest surviving work of Muslim law, and places great emphasis on the actual practice of Islam in Medina in Mālik's time. (*SEI*, 320–4 [J. Schacht].)

MĀLIK IBN DĪNĀR al-Nājī (d. 131 [748/9])—34, 98, 106. An ascetic of Basra who made a living by copying the Qur'ān. A companion of al-Ḥasan al-Baṣrī, he was credited with a number of miracles, including the ability to walk on water. (*Mashāhīr*, 90; Hujwīrī, 89–90; *Ghāya*, II. 36; Abū Nuᶜaym, II. 357–88.)

AL-MA'MŪN (*regn.* 198–218 [813–833])—88. The caliph who presided over the zenith of Abbasid civilisation. He led a number of successful campaigns against the Byzantines and provincial rebels. His adoption of Muᶜtazilite theology may have been an attempt to reconcile both the Shīᶜa and the emerging Sunni orthodoxy to the ruling dynasty.

MANṢŪR IBN ISMĀᶜĪL al-Maghribī—159. A Sufi who taught al-Qushayrī. (Zabīdī, x. 433.)

MAᶜRŪF AL-KARKHĪ, ibn Fīrūz (d. 200–1 [815/6–816/7])—24. One of the major early Sufis. His parents are said to have been Christians. He was a major influence on al-Sarī al-Saqaṭī, but also instructed Ibn Ḥanbal in *ḥadīth*. His grave, restored in 1312 AH, is an important focus of the religious life of Baghdad, and many miraculous cures are said to be worked there. (Hujwīrī, 113–5; Sulamī, 74–9; Qushayrī, I. 74–8; Ibn al-Jawzī, *Manāqib Maᶜrūf al-Karkhī wa-akhbāruhu*.)

MARWĀN ibn al-Ḥakam (*regn.* 64–5 [684–5])—46. An Umayyad caliph whose reign stands out only for his defeat of the forces of the rebel Ibn al-Zubayr at the battle of Marj Rāhiṭ.

MASRŪQ ibn al-Ajdaᶜ (d. 63 [682/3])—127. Chiefly resident in Kūfa, he was a respected traditionist and 'Follower' who taught Ibrāhīm al-Nakhaᶜī. He is said to have fought on the side of ᶜAlī against the Khārijites. (*Mashāhīr*, 101; *Tārīkh Baghdād*, XIII. 232–5; *Kāshif*, III. 120.)

AL-MASŪḤĪ, al-Ḥasan ibn ʿAlī—163. A Sufi who was a follower of Bishr al-Ḥāfī and who taught al-Jurayrī. It is said that he was the first to give lessons on Sufism in Baghdad. Having no house, he slept in the portico of a mosque. (*Tārīkh Baghdād*, VII. 366–67; Abū Nuʿaym, X. 322.)

MAYMŪN IBN MIHRĀN al-Jazarī (d. *c* 117 [735/6])—104. An ascetic of Raqqa on the upper Euphrates, he was a pupil of al-Ḥasan al-Baṣrī and a traditionist who became secretary to the caliph ʿUmar ibn ʿAbd al-ʿAzīz. (*Mashāhīr*, 117; *Bidāya*, IX. 314; Abū Nuʿaym, IV. 82–97.)

MUʿĀDH IBN JABAL al-Khazrajī (d. *c* 18 [639/40])—29, 88. An early convert to Islam, he became well versed in *fiqh* in a short space of time. He was the Prophet's governor of the Yemen, and died in Syria. (*Iṣāba*, III. 406–7; *Mashāhīr*, 50.)

MUʿĀWIYA IBN ABĪ SUFYĀN ibn Ḥarb ibn Umayya (*regn.* 40–60 [661–80])—85, 86, 158. The first caliph of the Umayyad dynasty, able and astute, he continued the conquests of his predecessors.

MUBASHSHIR IBN ISMĀʿĪL AL-ḤALABĪ (d. 200 [815/6])—117. A traditionist of Aleppo who studied under al-Awzāʿī and taught a number of ʿIraqī scholars. He is usually accounted a reliable authority. (*Kāshif*, III. 104; *Bidāya*, X. 247.)

AL-MUFAḌḌAL IBN FAḌĀLA (d. 181 [797/8])—19. A somewhat unreliable traditionist of Basra, remembered for his love of prayer. (Abū Nuʿaym, VIII. 321–3; *Kāshif*, III. 150; *Ḍuʿafāʾ*, 226.)

AL-MUGHĪRA IBN SHUʿBA al-Thaqafī (d. 50 [670/1])—78. A Companion of the Prophet. He took part in a number of the early conquests, and lost an eye at the battle of Yarmūk. The caliph ʿUmar made him governor of Basra and then of Kūfa; he subsequently retired from politics until it became clear that Muʿāwiya had won, when he again assumed the governorship of the latter city. (*Iṣāba*, III. 432–3.)

MUḤAMMAD IBN ABĪ TAWBA—24. Unidentified.

MUḤAMMAD IBN AḤMAD AL-MARWAZĪ—117. Probably a reference to a certain Shāfiʿite jurist and ascetic of this name who died at Merv in 371 (981/2). (*Tārīkh Baghdād*, I. 314.)

MUḤAMMAD IBN ʿALĪ ibn al-Ḥusayn ibn ʿAlī ibn Abī Ṭālib, 'al-Bāqir'. (d. *c* 114 [732/3])—84, 137. The father of the traditionist Jaʿfar al-Ṣādiq, he taught al-Zuhrī and al-Awzāʿī. He was later made into the fifth Imām of the Shīʿa. (*Mashāhīr*, 62; *Kāshif*, III. 71.)

MUḤAMMAD IBN AL-ḤUSAYN—84. Unidentified.

MUḤAMMAD IBN KAʿB AL-QURAẒĪ (d. 108 [726/7] or 118 [736/7])—138, 228. A Follower (*tābiʿī*) of Kūfa (later of Medina) much given to worship and the recitation of the Qur'ān. He related a number of *ḥadīth*s to Ibn al-Munkadir. (Abū Nuʿaym, III. 212-21; *Mashāhīr*, 65; *Ghāya*, II. 233.)

MUḤAMMAD IBN AL-MUNKADIR—145, 157. See 'Ibn al-Munkadir'.

MUḤAMMAD IBN QUDĀMA AL-JAWHARĪ (d. 237 [851/2])—117. A traditionist of Baghdad who studied under Ibn ʿUyayna. His reliability is sometimes questioned. (Zabīdī, X. 370; *Kāshif*, III. 80.)

MUḤAMMAD IBN ṢABĪḤ—133. See 'Ibn al-Sammāk'.

MUḤAMMAD IBN SULAYMĀN ibn ʿAlī ibn ʿAbd Allāh ibn ʿAbbās (d. 173 [789/90])—110. A traditionist of doubtful reliability who was governor of Basra for a period. (*Bidāya*, X. 103, 162–3; ʿUqaylī, IV. 73.)

MUḤAMMAD AL-ṬŪSĪ, ibn Aslam (d. 242 [856/7])—166. A traditionist said to have been one of the first to write on the subject of weak *ḥadīths*. He was known for the sermons he preached against the Murji'ite heresy. (Ṣafadī, II. 204; Abū Nuʿaym, IX. 237–54; *Bidāya*, X. 344.)

MUḤAMMAD IBN WĀSIʿ al-Azdī (d. 127 [744/5])—47, 115, 160. An early *ḥadīth* scholar noted for his asceticism. His statement, 'I never saw anything without seeing God therein' was much discussed by later Sufis. He fought under Qutayba ibn Muslim during the conquest of Transoxiana, and later became a judge. (Hujwīrī, 91–2; Abū Nuᶜaym, II. 345–57; *Ghāya*, II. 274; *Mashāhīr*, 151.)

MUḤAMMAD IBN ᶜUQBA—86. A *qāḍī* and traditionist. (Zabīdī, x. 322; *Kāshif*, III. 70; *Tahdhīb al-Tahdhīb*, IX. 347.)

MUḤAMMAD IBN YŪSUF—22. Possibly a reference to Muḥammad ibn Yūsuf ibn Yaᶜqūb, a chief judge of Baghdad (d. 320 [932/3]), known for his retiring disposition and friendship with the traditionist Ibn Maniᶜ. (Ṣafadī, v. 245–6; *Bidāya*, XI. 76.)

MUJĀHID ibn Jabr al-Makkī (d. 104 [722/3])—40, 102, 132, 194, 245, 249. Sometimes considered the most learned authority among the 'Followers' (*tābiᶜūn*) on the exegesis of the Qur'ān, which he learnt from Ibn ᶜAbbās, he was particularly concerned to establish the circumstances under which each verse had been revealed. He was also respected for his austere and pious lifestyle. (*Mashāhīr*, 82; *Fihrist*, 33; *Ghāya*, II. 41–2; Abū Nuᶜaym, III. 279–310.)

MUJAMMIᶜ ibn Ṣamghān al-Taymī—160. An ascetic of Kūfa who associated with Sufyān al-Thawrī. He is recorded as having been a person of simplicity and generosity, who would unhesitatingly allow strangers lodging in his house. (Abū Nuᶜaym, v. 89–91.)

MUMSHĀD AL-DĪNAWARĪ (d. 299 [911/2])—91, 94. A Sufi of the circle of Ibn al-Jallā'. (Abū Nuᶜaym, x. 353–4; Sulamī, 318–20.)

AL-MUNDHIR ibn Mālik al-ᶜAbdī (d. 108 [726/6])—34. A respected traditionist of Basra, who was present at the death of al-Ḥasan al-Baṣrī. (Abū Nuᶜaym, III. 97–101; *Kāshif*, III. 154.)

AL-MUNTAṢIR ibn al-Mutawakkil (*regn.* 247–8 [861–2])—88. An Abbasid caliph, who came to power after inducing the Turkish palace guards to assassinate his father.

MUQĀTIL ibn Sulaymān al-Azdī (d. 150 [767/8])—175. A theologian and exegete from Balkh in Cental Asia who taught principally in Baghdad. He knew a large amount of Jewish lore, and compiled a commentary on the Qur'ān. (*GAS*, I. 60; *Tārīkh Baghdād*, XIII. 160–9; *Tahdhīb al-Tahdhīb*, X. 284.)

MŪSĀ IBN ḤAMMĀD—168. Unidentified.

AL-MUʿTAMIR IBN SULAYMĀN al-Taymī (d. 187 [802/3]) —50, 94. An ascetic and a reliable traditionist of Basra who associated with al-Ḥasan al-Baṣrī. His father, Sulaymān ibn Tarkhān (d. 143 [760/1]) was also a *ḥadīth* scholar. (*Mashāhīr*, 161; Ibn Qutayba, *Maʿārif*, 240.)

MUTAMMIM AL-DAWRAQĪ—159. Unidentified.

MUṬARRIF IBN ʿABD ALLĀH IBN AL-SHIKHKHĪR al-ʿĀmirī (d. *c* 87 [806/7])—12, 18. An ascetic and a traditionist of Basra. Many miracles and famous prayers are attributed to him. (*Mashāhīr*, 88; Abū Nuʿaym, II. 198–212; *Kāshif*, III. 132.)

MUṬARRIF ibn Maʿqil al-Tamīmī—11. A traditionist who studied under Ibn Sīrīn. (Zabīdī, X. 231.)

MUṬARRIF IBN ABĪ BAKR AL-HUDHALĪ—118. An early ascetic of Basra. (Zabīdī, X. 373; Massignon, *Essai*, 164.)

AL-MUʿTAṢIM (*regn.* 218–27 [833–42])—88. An Abbasid caliph, remembered for his victory over the Byzantines at Amorium and his regularising of the use of Turkish palace guards.

NĀFIʿ, *mawlā* ibn ʿUmar. (d. 119 [737])—113, 114. An important *ḥadīth* scholar of Medina, who studied under Ibn ʿUmar and Abū Hurayra, and who taught Mālik ibn Anas and al-Layth ibn Saʿd. (*Mashāhīr*, 80; *Kāshif*, III. 174.)

NAṢR ibn Ṭarīf al-Bāhilī—90. An unreliable traditionist accused by Ibn al-Mubārak of 'Qadarite' leanings. (ʿUqaylī, IV. 296–8.)

AL-NAṢRĀBĀDHĪ, Ibrāhīm ibn Muḥammad (d. *c* 367 [977/8]) —165. A Sufi of Khurāsān, who associated with al-Shiblī and Abū ʿAlī al-Rūdhbārī. He was also a prolific traditionist. (Qushayrī, I. 222–3; Sulamī, 511–5; *GAS*, I. 663; Hujwīrī, 159–60.)

AL-NUʿMĀN IBN BASHĪR al-Khazrajī (d. *c* 74 [693/4])—

131. A Companion of the Prophet who became governor of Ḥimṣ for Yazīd I. He was killed by the populace of the latter city when he tried to raise support for the rebellion of Ibn al-Zubayr. (*Iṣāba*, III. 529–30; *EI*, III. 952–3 [K. V. Zettersteen].)

AL-NŪRĪ, Abu'l-Ḥusayn (d. 295 [907/8])—95. An important Sufi of the Baghdad school. A companion of al-Junayd, he left a number of poems on Divine love. (Sulamī, 151–8; *GAS*, I. 650; *Tārīkh Baghdād*, V. 130; ʿAṭṭār, 221–30; Ernst, 97-101.)

QABĪṢA IBN ʿUQBA al-Kūfī (d. 215 [830/1])—164. A traditionist and exegete who studied under Sufyān al-Thawrī and taught Ibn Ḥanbal and Ibn Abī Shayba. A number of *ḥadīths* related on his authority are given by al-Bukhārī. (*GAS*, I. 40–1; *Tārīkh Baghdād*, XII. 473–6; *Bidāya*, X. 269.)

AL-QAʿQĀʿ IBN ʿAMR al-Tamīmī—71. A noted warrior who distinguished himself at the battle of al-Qādisīya. The story of his presence at the Prophet's death is usually regarded as a fiction. (*Istīʿāb*, III. 252; *Iṣāba*, III. 230.)

AL-QAʿQĀʿ IBN ḤAKĪM al-Kinānī—23. A pious and highly-regarded traditionist of the second generation of Muslims, who related *ḥadīths* from Abū Hurayra and Ibn ʿUmar. (*Mashāhīr*, 77; *Kāshif*, II. 346; *Tahdhīb al-Tahdhīb*, VIII. 383.)

QATĀDA ibn Diʿāma al-Baṣrī (d. 117 [735/6])—182. Although blind from birth, he became an authority on the exegesis of the Qur'ān. He was an associate of al-Ḥasan al-Baṣrī, and is sometimes accused of Muʿtazilite sympathies. (*Fihrist*, 34; *Mashāhīr*, 96; *GAS*, I. 31–2; Massignon, *Essai*, 200.)

RĀBIʿA AL-ʿADAWĪYA, bint Ismāʿīl (d. 185 [801/2])—116. The most famous woman Sufi. It is said that she was stolen as a child and sold into slavery, but was released on account of her piety. She lived for a time in the desert, where she was fed miraculously by God. She later moved to Basra, where she taught Sufyān al-Thawrī and Shaqīq al-Balkhī, emphasising the importance of divine love. She left a number of fine prayers. (M. Smith, *Rābiʿa the Mystic and her Fellow-Saints in Islam*.)

AL-RABĪᶜ IBN KHUTHAYM (or 'KHAYTHAM'), al-Thawrī (d. *c* 63 [682/3])—11, 12, 103. A pupil of Ibn ᶜAbbās and a famous ascetic of Kūfa. Constantly ill with a form of palsy, he became for later generations a symbol of endurance in the face of suffering. He emphasised the importance of silence, scrupulousness in religious observance, and the fear of Hell. Many traditions in the collection of al-Bukhārī are given on his authority. (*Mashāhīr*, 99–100; *Ghāya*, I. 283; Abū Nuᶜaym, II. 105–19; *Kāshif*, I. 235; Ibn Marthad 41–3.)

AL-RABĪᶜ IBN SULAYMĀN al-Murādī (d. *c* 270 [883/4])—166. A pupil of al-Shāfiᶜī, and his messenger to Ibn Ḥanbal when this latter had been incarcerated by al-Ma'mūn. He was also the muezzin of the mosque of ᶜAmr in Egypt. (*Kāshif*, I. 236; *Bidāya*, X. 162, 331.)

RUWAYM ibn Aḥmad al-Baghdādī (d. 303 [915/6])—90, 94. A Sufi of the circle of al-Junayd, who stressed the importance of *tajrīd* (divestment from worldly attachments). He is said to have written books on Sufism. Additionally, he was a noted expert on the exegesis of the Qur'ān, and an adherent of the literalist Ẓāhirī school of law. (Hujwīrī, 135–6; Qushayrī, I. 144–6; Abū Nuᶜaym, X. 296–302.)

SAᶜD ibn Abī Waqqāṣ al-Murrī (d. 50 [670/1] or 55 [674–5])—80. One of the ten Companions assured of Heaven by the Prophet, he distinguished himself particularly as a brilliant politician and soldier. To him goes the credit for the defeat of the Persians at al-Qādisīya (16/637), one of history's most decisive battles, and the subsequent founding of Kūfa as a military base. He remained governor of that city until the year 20 [640/1] when he was recalled to Medina following allegations, not credited by the Caliph, of misrule. ᶜUmar later made him one of the six men who were to choose the new caliph. (*SEI*, 482 [K. V. Zettersteen].)

SAᶜD IBN BILĀL—255. According to Zabīdī this is a mistake for Bilāl ibn Saᶜd (d. *c* 120 [737/8]), an ascetic and preacher of Damascus who was also regarded as the greatest Syrian authority on the readings of the Qur'ān at that time. (Ṣafadī, X. 277; *Kāshif*, I. 111; *Tahdhīb al-Tahdhīb*, I. 503.)

SAᶜD IBN MUᶜĀDH al-Awsī (d. 5 [626])—146, 150. The head of an important clan at Medina, he was an early and enthusiastic convert. During the Battle of the Trench he was wounded, and after the fighting had subsided was asked by the Prophet to pass judgement on the Jewish clan of Qurayẓa, which had been accused of dealing secretly with the enemy. He found them guilty, and sentenced their menfolk to death and their women and children to slavery. He himself died shortly afterwards. (*SEI*, 482–3 [K. V. Zettersteen]); *Istīᶜāb*, II. 25–30.)

ṢAFĪYA bint Ḥuyayy ibn Akhṭab (d. 50 [670/1] or 52 [672/3])—11. A Jewish woman who joined Islam and married the Prophet following the Khaybar expedition. She became particularly close to his daughter Fāṭima and showed great devotion to the Prophet, particularly during his final illness. (*SEI*, 487–8 [V. Vacca].)

SAHL AL-ṢUᶜLŪKĪ ibn Muḥammad (d. 404 [1013/4])—166. A prominent Shāfiᶜī jurist of Nīsābūr, whose classes were regularly attended by over five hundred students, among whom was the great traditionist al-Ḥākim. He is said to have written on theology and literature. (Subkī, IV. 393; Ṣafadī, XVI. 12–13; Zabīdī, X. 438.)

SAᶜĪD IBN ᶜABD ALLĀH ibn Jurayj—61. A traditionist who taught al-Aᶜmash. (*Kāshif*, I. 289; *Tahdhīb al-Tahdhīb*, IV. 51.)

SAᶜĪD IBN ᶜABD ALLĀH AL-AWDĪ—116. Unidentified.

SAᶜĪD IBN ᶜABD AL-RAḤMĀN al-Jumaḥī (d. 176 [792/3])—18. A respected traditionist who became Hārūn al-Rashīd's chief judge at Baghdad. A number of traditions in the *Ṣaḥīḥ* of Muslim are given on his authority. (Ṣafadī, XV. 237; *Kāshif*, I. 290; *Ghāya*, I. 306.)

SAᶜĪD IBN AL-MUSAYYIB al-Makhzūmī (d. 93–4 [711/2–712/3])—75, 249. A major genealogist and legal expert of Medina, held by some to have been the most erudite of the second Muslim generation. He refused to marry his devout and learned daughter to the caliph al-Walīd ibn ᶜAbd al-Malik, for which he was flogged. (Abū Nuᶜaym, II. 161–76; Hujwīrī, 83; *Mashāhīr*, 63.)

ṢĀLIḤ IBN BASHĪR al-Murrī (d. *c* 172 [788/9])—160. A 'weak' traditionist of Basra who studied under Ibn Sīrīn and Yazīd al-Ruqāshī. Famed for his sermons, he was invited to Baghdad to preach before the caliph al-Mahdī. (Ṣafadī, XVI. 252; *Bidāya*, X. 170; *Ḍuʿafāʾ*, 136; Abū Nuʿaym, VI. 165–77.)

ṢĀLIḤ AL-MURRĪ—132. See previous notice.

ṢĀLIḤ IBN MISMĀR al-Marwazī (d. 246 [860/1])—92. A traditionist who learnt *ḥadīths* from Ibn ʿUyayna; some of his material is incorporated in the *Ṣaḥīḥ* of Muslim. (*Kāshif*, II. 22.)

SALMĀN AL-FĀRISĪ (d. 36 [656/7])—19, 74, 89, 240. 'Salmān the Good.' A Persian convert to Islam who became one of the most celebrated Companions of the Prophet. It was upon his counsel that the famous 'Fosse' was dug to defend the city from the Meccan army. Later he participated in the conquest of Iraq. His asceticism and devotion to the Prophet made him an ideal for later generations, and in particular the Sufis, to whom he is held to have transmitted much of the Prophet's esoteric knowledge. (*Iṣāba*, II. 60–1; Abū Nuʿaym, I. 185–208; *SEI*, 500–1 [G. Levi della Vida].)

SAMURA ibn Jundub al-Fazārī (d. 51–60 [671/2–679/80])—219. A Companion of the Prophet who transmitted a number of Traditions used by al-Bukhārī and Muslim. He served as governor of Basra and then of Kūfa for a short period. (*GAS*, I. 84–5; *Mashāhīr*, 38.)

AL-SARĪ AL-SAQAṬĪ, ibn al-Mughallis (d. *c* 251 [865/6])—93. The maternal uncle of al-Junayd, and one of the first to present Sufism in a systematised fashion. According to Hujwīrī, his conversion to Sufism was instigated by the Baghdad saint Ḥabīb al-Rāʿī, who, upon being given a crust of bread by al-Sarī, said, 'May God reward you!' 'From that time on', al-Saqaṭī later remarked, 'my worldly affairs never prospered again'. He was perhaps the most influential disciple of Maʿrūf al-Karkhī. (*EI*, IV. 171 [L. Massignon]; *Tārīkh Baghdād*, IX. 187–62; J. al-Murābiṭ, *al-Sarī al-Saqaṭī*; Dermenghem, 115–28.)

SAWDA bint Zamʿa al-Qurashīya (d. 54 [673/4])—178. The second wife of the Prophet, she was one of the earliest converts to

Islam. She is remembered for her charitable and amiable temperament. (*SEI*, 503–4 [V. Vacca].)

SHADDĀD IBN AWS (d. 58 [677/8])—41. A Medinese companion of the Prophet whose father died at the battle of Badr. He narrated a number of *ḥadīths*, and is buried at Jerusalem. (*Iṣāba*, II. 138; Nawawī, *Tahdhīb*, 312; *Mashāhīr*, 50.)

AL-SHĀFIʿĪ, Muḥammad ibn Idrīs al-Qurashī (d. 204 [820])—95, 166, 168. The founder of the Shāfiʿite school of Islamic law. Although born in Gaza he was brought up with a Bedouin tribe, which gave him a good grounding in poetry and the Arabic language. He later studied *fiqh* with Sufyān ibn ʿUyayna and Mālik ibn Anas, developing a legal theory that stood halfway between literalism and personal opinion. He travelled extensively in Iraq and Egypt, where he died; his tomb is today one of the centres of Cairene religious life. (*GAS*, I. 484–90; *Tārīkh Baghdād*, II. 56–73; *SEI*, 512–5 [W. Heffening].)

SHAQĪQ AL-BALKHĪ, al-Azdī (d. 194 [809/10])—19. One of the founders of the Khurāsānī school of Sufism, he was the disciple of the ascetic Ibrāhīm ibn Adham. He was known for his discourses on the nearness of the Resurrection and the importance of reliance (*tawakkul*) upon God. He was also a noted scholar of the *sharīʿa*. (Qushayrī, I. 96–9; Abū Nuʿaym, VIII. 58-73; Sulamī, 54–9; Hujwīrī, 111–2.)

AL-SHIBLĪ, ibn Jaḥdar (d. 334 [945/6])—92, 93, 164. Formerly a chamberlain at the Caliph's palace, he converted to Sufism and became a follower of al-Junayd, whose teachings he later communicated to al-Naṣrābādhī. Well-known for his acts of asceticism and renunciation, it is said that he put salt in his eyes to stay awake for his nocturnal devotions. He was also an authority on the Mālikite school of law. His tomb at Baghdad is still venerated. (Qushayrī, I. 182–3; Sulamī, 340-55; Hujwīrī, 155–6; *Tārīkh Baghdād*, XIV. 389–97; *EI*, IV. 360–1 [L. Massignon]; Dermenghem, 201–30.)

ṢILA IBN ASHYAM al-ʿAdawī (d. 76 [695/6])—100. A Follower (*tābiʿī*) of Basra who fought in the conquest of Sijistān and Ghazna, where he was killed. He was known for his gentle sermons and advice. (Abū Nuʿaym, II. 237–42; *Mashāhīr*, 89; *Bidāya*, IX. 15.)

AL-SUDDĪ—33. Two men with this *nisba* are commonly recorded: (i) Ismāʿīl ibn ʿAbd al-Raḥmān, 'al-Suddī al-Kabīr' (d. 127 [744/5]), an exegete of Kūfa (*Mashāhīr*, 111; *Siyar*, V. 264: *GAS*. I. 32–3); (ii) Muḥammad ibn Marwān, 'al-Suddī al-Ṣaghīr' an early traditionist of Kūfa who lived in Baghdad and taught al-Aṣmaʿī. (*Tārīkh Baghdād*, III. 291–3; *Siyar*, V. 265.)

SUFYĀN—103, 146. See next notice.

SUFYĀN AL-THAWRĪ, ibn Saʿīd (d. 161 [777/8])—162, 163, 164, 166, 168. A scholar and well-known saint of Kūfa, of whom a great number of anecdotes are recorded. He was one of the 'Eight Ascetics,' who included (usual list) ʿĀmir ibn ʿAbd Qays, Abū Muslim al-Khawlānī, Uways al-Qaranī, al-Rabīʿ ibn Khuthaym, al-Aswad ibn Yazīd, Masrūq, and al-Ḥasan al-Baṣrī. It is said that he was offered high office under the Umayyads but consistently declined. (*Fihrist*, 225; Abū Nuʿaym, VI. 356–93, VII. 3–144; *EI*, IV. 500–2 [M. Plessner].)

SUFYĀN IBN ʿUYAYNA—157. See 'Ibn ʿUyayna'.

ṢUHAYB ibn Sinān, 'al-Rūmī' (d. *c* 38 [658/9])—251. An Arab from the Mosul region captured and enslaved as a child by Byzantine raiders. He was brought up in the Byzantine empire, and then taken to Mecca and sold. Here he joined the new Muslim community at the house of al-Arqam, and was persecuted for his faith until he made the Emigration to Medina in the company of ʿAlī. (Ṣafadī, XVI. 335–8; *Iṣāba*, II. 188–9; Abū Nuʿaym, I. 151-6.)

SUḤAYM—33. Possibly a reference to Suḥaym al-Madanī, a reputable traditionist who studied under Abū Hurayra and taught Ibn Shihāb al-Zuhrī. (*Kāshif*, I. 274; *Tahdhīb al-Tahdhīb*, III. 454.)

SULAYMĀN IBN ʿABD AL-MALIK (*regn.* 97–99 [715–7])—21. An Umayyad caliph remembered for his gluttony and licentiousness.

SULAYMĀN IBN SUḤAYM al-Madanī—114. A traditionist who taught Ibn ʿUyayna; some of his *ḥadīths* are to be found in the collection of Muslim. He died during the reign of al-Manṣūr. (*Kāshif*, I. 314; *Tābiʿīn*, I. 95; *Tahdhīb al-Tahdhīb*, IV. 193.)

AL-ṢUNĀBIḤĪ, ʿAbd al-Raḥmān al-Murādī (d. 70–80 [689/90–699/700])—256. A Yemenite who went to Medina to meet the Prophet but who arrived five days after his death. He later moved to Syria, where he gained the confidence and respect of the caliph ʿAbd al-Malik. (*Mashāhīr*, 111; Abū Nuʿaym, V. 129–31; *Kāshif*, II. 157.)

ṬALḤA ibn ʿUbayd Allāh al-Qurashī (d. 36 [656–7])—80. One of the ten Companions assured of Paradise by the Prophet; called 'one of the pillars of Islam' by ʿUmar. He distinguished himself at the Battle of Uḥud, where he personally defended the Prophet. One of the six men chosen to elect ʿUmar's successor, he was killed at the Battle of the Camel at the age of 64. His grave is still visited at Basra. (*Iṣāba*, II. 220–2; *Mashāhīr*, 7.)

THĀBIT AL-BUNĀNĪ, ibn Aslam (d. 127 [744/5])—49, 98, 104. A Follower (*tābiʿī*) of Basra who kept the company of Anas ibn Mālik for forty years. One of the 'Weepers', he was much given to prayer and other devotional acts. A number of *ḥadīths* are related on his authority. (*Tahdhīb al-Tahdhīb*, II. 2–4; *Mashāhīr*, 89; Abū Nuʿaym, II. 318–33.)

THAWBĀN ibn Yuḥdad (d. 54 [673/4])—218, 242. A slave purchased and freed by the Prophet, whom he served until the latter's death. He later removed to Ḥimṣ, where he died. The *ḥadīth* collection of Muslim contains material given on his authority. (*Iṣāba*, I. 205; *Mashāhīr*, 50; *Kāshif*, I. 119.)

AL-THAWRĪ—18, 19, 23, 164. See 'Sufyān al-Thawrī.'

THUMĀMA IBN ḤAZN AL-QUSHAYRĪ—82. A companion of the caliph ʿUmar, from whom he related a number of *ḥadīths*; later he moved to Basra. (*Tahdhīb al-Tahdhīb*, II. 27; Ṣafadī, XI. 18; *Mashāhīr*, 92.)

ʿUBĀDA IBN AL-ṢĀMIT al-Khazrajī (d. *c* 34 [654/5])—256. An early convert who took part in the battle of Badr. In later years he participated in the conquest of Egypt, and was made the first *qāḍī* of Palestine by the caliph ᶜUmar. (*Iṣāba*, II. 260–1; *Mashāhīr*, 51.)

ᶜUBAYD ALLĀH—48. Unidentified.

ᶜUBAYD IBN ᶜUMAYR al-Laythī (d. 74 [693/4])—132, 133. A respected traditionist of Mecca who taught the exegesis of the Qur'ān to Mujāhid. He is said to have been unusually thin as a consequence of much fasting and self-denial. (*Mashāhīr*, 82; Abū Nuᶜaym, III. 266–279; *Ghāya*, I. 496–7.)

ᶜUKĀSHA (or ᶜUKKĀSHA) ibn Miḥṣan al-Asadī (d. 12 [633])—259. An early convert who fought at Badr. He was killed in the *ridda* wars during the caliphate of Abū Bakr. (*Iṣāba*, II. 487-8; Abū Nuᶜaym, II. 12–13; *Mashāhīr*, 16.)

ᶜUMAR IBN ᶜABD AL-ᶜAZĪZ ibn Marwān (*regn*. 99–101 [717–20])—11, 12, 14, 20, 22, 24, 87–8, 102, 104, 118, 158, 218, 260. Sometimes called 'the fifth rightly-guided Caliph' for his piety, he was concerned to implement the *sharīᶜa* in a number of neglected areas, such as the equal treatment of converts; he also ended the public cursing of ᶜAlī from the pulpits. A large body of sermons and anecdotes connected with him soon found its way into religious literature.

ᶜUMAR IBN DHARR al-Hamadhānī (d. *c* 156 [772/3])—99, 110. A respected traditionist of Kūfa, and a companion of Sufyān ibn ᶜUyayna. A number of fine prayers for forgiveness are ascribed to him. He is said to have been a member of the Murji'ite sect. (*Tahdhīb al-Tahdhīb*, VII. 444; Abū Nuᶜaym, V. 108–19; *Kāshif*, II. 269.)

ᶜUMAR IBN AL-KHAṬṬĀB (*regn*. 13–23 [634–44])—34, 42, 48, 64, 68, 72, 77–81, 101, 145, 156, 163, 218, 237. At first an enemy of the Prophet's mission, he became one of its staunchest defenders. His daughter Ḥafṣa married the Prophet after the Emigration. When he succeeded Abū Bakr as caliph, he showed considerable brilliance in the face of the new circumstances arising as a result of the conquests, regulating the status of minorities, arranging a military pensions system and founding a number of garrison towns (*amṣār*). He was universally respected for his integrity and uncompromising devotion to the faith. (*Iṣāba*, II. 511–2; *Istīʿāb*, II. 450–66; *SEI*, 600–1 [G. Levi della Vida].)

UMM KULTHŪM bint ʿAlī—68, 83. The daughter of ʿAlī and Fāṭima, she was born during the lifetime of the Prophet. She was married first to ʿUmar ibn al-Khaṭṭāb, and later on to a son of Jaʿfar ibn Abī Ṭālib. (*Iṣāba*, IV. 468–9; *Istīʿāb*, IV. 467–9.)

UMM HĀRŪN—12. Unidentified; said by Zabīdī (X. 232) to have been a Sufi.

UMM AL-MUNDHIR bint Qays al-Anṣārīya—15. A Muslim woman of Medina and a Companion of the Prophet. A number of *ḥadīths* are given on her authority in the collections of Abū Dāūd and al-Tirmidhī. (*Kāshif*, III. 444; *Iṣāba*, IV. 477.)

ʿUQBA IBN ʿĀMIR al-Juhanī (d. 58 [677/8])—181. A Companion who led a campaign for the Prophet and was present at the battle of Tabūk. He later became governor of Egypt, where he is said to be buried. (*Mashāhīr*, 55; *Kāshif*, II. 237.)

USĀMA IBN ZAYD ibn Ḥāritha (d. 54 [673/4])—16, 246. Described by the Prophet as the most beloved of his Companions, he was set in charge of an expedition to Syria, preparations for which began during the Prophet's final illness. He later moved to Damascus. (*Mashāhīr*, 11; *Kāshif*, I. 57; *Iṣāba*, I. 46.)

USAYD IBN ḤUḌAYR al-Ashhalī (d. *c* 20 [640/1])—97. One of the seven Medinese Muslims present at the first ʿAqaba pledge, he was severely wounded at the battle of Uḥud. A number of *ḥadīths* on his authority are extant. (*Iṣāba*, I. 64; *Kāshif*, I. 82.)

ʿUTBA AL-GHULĀM, ibn Abān (d. *c* 153 [770/1])—165, 167. An ascetic of Basra, where he associated with al-Ḥasan al-Baṣrī. It is said that he received a dream in which he was told that he would gain martyrdom; he later travelled to northern Syria where he was attached to the garrison of a frontier fortress, and shortly afterwards was killed in a cavalry sortie near Adana. (*Bidāya*, X. 150; Abū Nuʿaym, VI. 226–38.)

ʿUTHMĀN ibn ʿAffān ibn Abi'l-ʿĀṣ ibn Umayya (*regn.* 23–35 [644–56])—48, 68, 69, 80, 81–3, 101, 164. A wealthy merchant who became a Muslim before the Emigration. He became known as 'Dhu'l-Nūrayn'—'the man of the two lights' because he married two of the Prophet's daughters: firstly Ruqayya, and then, after her death, Umm Kulthūm. During the latter years of his caliphate he was accused of nepotism, a charge which brought about his murder by a group of dissidents from Egypt, who beseiged his house, it is said, for forty-nine days, and then stormed it and stabbed him to death while he was reading the Qur'ān. (*SEI*, 615–7 [G. Levi della Vida]; *Mashāhīr*, 5–6; *Iṣāba*, II. 455–6.)

UWAYS AL-QARANĪ, ibn ʿĀmir al-Murādī (d. 37? [657?])—167. A Yemeni, who although he never met the Prophet, was mentioned and praised by him, and was promised that he would exercise a special intercession for the believers on the Day of Judgement. Ṣafadī tells us that 'most of his discourses concern the remembrance of death'. (Ṣafadī, IX. 456–7; Abū Nuʿaym, II. 79–87; *Mashāhīr*, 100; Ibn Marthad, 71–4.)

WAHB IBN MUNABBIH, ibn Kāmil (d. *c* 110 [728/9])—21, 51. A Yemeni sage possibly of Persian origin, who is said to have prayed all night for forty consecutive years. A number of sermons are ascribed to him, which make considerable use of Jewish lore. He was made a judge during the reign of ʿUmar II. (*Tahdhīb al-Tahdhīb*, XI. 166; Abū Nuʿaym, IV. 23–82; *Mashāhīr*, 122–3.)

WARAQĀ' IBN BISHR AL-HAḌRAMĪ—167. Unidentified.

AL-WĀSIṬĪ, Muḥammad ibn Mūsā (d. *c* 320 [932])—92. A Sufi who associated with al-Junayd and al-Nūrī at Baghdad, and who later moved to Merv, where he died. He was also an authority on *fiqh*. (Qushayrī, I. 174–5; Sulamī, 302–7.)

WĀTHILA IBN AL-ASQAʿ al-Laythī (d. *c* 85 [704])—49. A Companion of the Prophet, and one of the *ahl al-Ṣuffa*. He took part in the Tabūk expedition and in due course moved to Syria, where he narrated *ḥadīths* to Makḥūl. (*Ghāya*, II. 358; *Kāshif*, III. 204; *Mashāhīr*, 51; Abū Nuʿaym, II. 21–3.)

WUHAYB ibn al-Ward al-Makkī (d. *c* 153 [770/1])—45. A *ḥadīth* scholar who spent his life in mortification and worship, and to whom a number of miracles are attributed. He taught Ibn ᶜUyayna and Ibn al-Mubārak, and a few *ḥadīth*s are given on his authority by Muslim and al-Tirmidhī. (Abū Nuᶜaym, VIII. 140–62; *Mashāhīr*, 148; Massignon, *Essai*, 169; *Kāshif*, III. 216.)

YAḤYĀ IBN ABĪ KATHĪR (d. 129 [746/7])—246. A *mawlā* of Ṭayyi'; an ascetic and a traditionist of the Yemen. (*Kāshif*, III. 233; Abū Nuᶜaym, III. 66–75; *Bidāya*, x. 34.)

YAḤYĀ IBN MUᶜĀDH al-Rāzī (d. 258 [871/2])—103, 249. A Sufi who taught in Central Asia. One of the first to teach Sufism in mosques, he left a number of books and sayings. Despite the emphasis he placed on *rajā'*: the hope for Paradise and for God's forgiveness, he was renowned for his perseverence in worship and his great scrupulousness in matters of religion. (Abū Nuᶜaym, x. 51–70; Sulamī, 98–104; *Fihrist*, 184; *GAS*, I. 644; Hujwīrī, 122–3; Massignon, *Essai*, 268–72.)

YAᶜLĀ IBN AL-WALĪD—128. Unidentified.

YAZĪD ibn Muᶜāwiya (*regn.* 60–3 [680–3])—86. The second caliph of the Umayyad dynasty, he sent the army which killed the Prophet's grandson al-Ḥusayn.

YAZĪD IBN MADHᶜŪR—161. Unidentified.

YAZĪD IBN NAᶜĀMA al-Ḍabbī—167. A Follower (*tābiᶜī*) who studied *ḥadīth* under Anas ibn Mālik. (*Kāshif*, III. 251; Zabīdī, x. 439.)

YAZĪD AL-RUQĀSHĪ, ibn Abān (d. *c* 115 [733/4])—54, 103, 134. A traditionist and judge who taught Ṣāliḥ al-Murrī. One of the 'Weepers', he abandoned his studies to devote himself to worship. (*Kāshif*, III. 240; *Ḍuᶜafā'*, 253; Abū Nuᶜaym, III. 50–5; *Tahdhīb al-Tahdhīb*, XI. 309.)

YŪSUF IBN ASBĀṬ al-Shaybānī (d. 196 [811/2])—94. Dominated by the fear of God and of the Judgement, he influenced Bishr al-Ḥāfī. He also related a number of *ḥadīth*s from al-Thawrī. (Abū Nuᶜaym, VIII. 237–53; Zabīdī, x. 343.)

YŪSUF IBN AL-ḤUSAYN al-Rāzī (d. 304 [916/7])—159. A disciple of Dhu'l-Nūn al-Miṣrī and an associate of al-Kharrāz, he is remembered for the emphasis he laid upon sincerity: 'That I should meet God with every sin', he is represented as saying, 'would be preferable to me than to meet him with an atom's weight of affectation'. (Qushayrī, I. 158; Sulamī, 175–82; *Tārīkh Baghdād*, XIV. 314–9; Hujwīrī, 136.)

ZAYD IBN ARQAM al-Khazrajī (d. *c* 65 [684/5])—243. A Companion of the Prophet and a close associate of ᶜAlī, for whom he fought at Ṣiffīn. Thirteen of his *ḥadīths* are to be found in the collections of al-Bukhārī and Muslim. (*Iṣāba*, I. 542; *Mashāhīr*, 47.)

ZAYD IBN ASLAM al-ᶜAdawī al-Ṭūsī (d. 136 [753/4])—41, 110, 229. A respected traditionist and jurist who is said to have taught Mālik ibn Anas. A number of sayings on *rajā'*, hope for God's forgiveness, are ascribed to him. (*Mashāhīr*, 80; Abū Nuᶜaym, III. 221–9; *Ghāya*, I. 296.)

ZAYD IBN ḤĀRITHA al-Kaᶜbī (d. 8 [629])—248. A very early convert to Islam, given as a slave by Khadīja to the Prophet, who set him free. So close was he to him that he was called 'Zayd ibn Muḥammad.' He died leading the Muslim army at Mu'ta. (*Iṣāba*, I. 545–6.)

ZAYD IBN THĀBIT al-Khazrajī (d. 45 [665/6])—16. A Companion who joined Islam at the age of eleven. He was one of those that wrote down the verses of the Qur'ān as these were revealed. (*Iṣāba*, I. 543–4; *Mashāhīr*, 10.)

ZAYNAB bint Muḥammad (d. 8 [629/30])—146, 150. The eldest of the Prophet's daughters, she was married to her cousin Abu'l-ᶜĀṣ[ī] ibn al-Rabīᶜ, and came to Medina after the battle of Badr. Her daughter Umāma married ᶜAlī after the death of Fāṭima. (*SEI*, 653 [V. Vacca]; *Iṣāba*, IV. 306; *Istīᶜāb*, 304-5.)

ZUBAYDA bint Jaᶜfar ibn Manṣūr (d. 216 [831/2])—161. Married to Hārūn al-Rashīd in 165 AH, she became the best known of the Abbasid princesses. It is said that her palace 'sounded like a beehive' because she employed as maids a hundred women who had memorised the Qur'ān. She is particularly remembered for the donations she made to the ulema and to the poor, and for the improvements she effected to the road from Iraq to Mecca and Medina, which was renamed the 'Zubayda Road' in her honour. (Ṣafadī, XIV. 176–8; *Tārīkh Baghdād*, XIV. 433–4; *Bidāya*, X. 271.)

AL-ZUBAYR ibn al-ʿAwwām (d. 35 [655/6])—80, 202. One of the ten Companions who were guaranteed salvation. Perhaps the fifth convert to Islam, he was a cousin of the Prophet, who called him his 'apostle' (*ḥawārī*). His grave is said to be in the vicinity of Basra. (*Iṣāba*, I. 526–8; *SEI*, 660–1 [A. Wensinck].)

ZURĀRA IBN ABĪ AWFĀ al-ʿĀmirī (d. 93 [711/2])—19, 161. A judge at Basra and a respected traditionist. He was renowned for his fear of Hell and the Resurrection: it is said that he once acted as Imām for the dawn prayer at Basra, and that when he reached the verse *When the Trumpet shall sound* he fell dead from fright. (*Mashāhīr*, 95; Abū Nuʿaym, II. 258–61; *Kāshif*, I. 250.)

INDEX TO QUR'ĀNIC QUOTATIONS

QUR'ĀNIC CHAPTER TITLES CITED

BIBLIOGRAPHY

Abdelkader, A.H. *The Life, Personality and Writings of al-Junayd.* London, 1962.

Ahsan, M.M. *Social Life under the Abbasids.* London, 1979.

Ājurrī, Muḥammad b. al-Ḥusayn, al-. *K. al-Sharīʿa.* Partial ed. by M. Ḥ. al-Fiqī. Cairo, 1369/1950.

Allard, M. *Le problème des attributs divins dans la doctrine de al-Ašʿarī et de ses premiers grands disciples.* Beirut, 1965.

Anawati, G.C. 'Introduction historique à une nouvelle traduction de la Métaphysique d'Avicenne'. *MIDEO* 13 (1977), pp.171–252.

——*Etudes de philosophie musulmane.* Paris, 1974.

Arberry, A.J. *Revelation and Reason in Islam.* London, 1957.

——'Ibn Abi'l-Dunyā on penitence'. *JRAS* (1951) pp.48–58.

——*Muslim Saints and Mystics. Episodes from the Tadhkirat al-Auliya' ("Memorial of the Saints") by Farid al-Din Attar.* London, 1979.

Ashʿarī, Abu'l-Ḥasan, al-. *Maqālāt al-Islāmīyīn wa'khtilāf al-muṣallīn.* Ed. H. Ritter. Istanbul, 1929–1930.

——*al-Ibāna ʿan uṣūl al-diyāna.* Cairo, 1348 AH.

Asín Palacios, M. *La Escatología Musulmana en la Divina Comedia.* 2nd. (extended) ed. Granada, 1943.

——*La Espiritualidad de Algazel y su sentido Cristiano.* Madrid & Granada, 1934–1941.

——*Algazel, Dogmática, Moral y Ascética.* Saragossa, 1901.

Azami, M.M. *Studies in Early Hadith Literature.* Indianapolis, 1978.

Badawī, ʿAbd al-Raḥmān. *Mu'allafāt al-Ghazālī.* Cairo, 1380/1961.

Baghdādī, ʿAbd al-Qāhir b. Ṭāhir, al-. *al-Farq bayn al-firaq.* Ed. M. ʿAbd al-Ḥamīd. Cairo, n.d.

——*Uṣūl al-dīn.* Istanbul, 1346/1928.

Bāqillānī, Muḥammad b. al-Ṭayyib, al-. *K. al-Tamhīd.* Ed. R.J. McCarthy. Beirut, 1957.

Bayḍāwī, ᶜAbd Allāh b. ᶜUmar, al-. *Anwār al-tanzīl wa-asrār al-ta'wīl*. Istanbul, 1329 AH.

Bayhaqī, Aḥmad b. al-Ḥusayn, al-. *al-Asmā' wa'l-ṣifāt*. Beirut, 1405/1985.

——*Ithbāt ᶜadhāb al-qabr*. Ed. S. M. al-Quḍāt. Amman, 1403/1983.

——*al-Iᶜtiqād wa'l-hidāya ilā sabīl al-rashād*. Ed. K. al-Ḥūt. Beirut, 1403/1983.

——*K. al-Baᶜth wa'l-nushūr*. Ed. A. A. Ḥaydar. Beirut 1406/1986.

Bouyges, M. *Essai de chronologie des oeuvres de al-Ghazālī (Algazel)*. Ed. and revised by M. Allard. Beirut, 1959.

Brockelmann, C. *Geschichte der arabischen Litteratur*. 2nd. ed. Leiden, 1943–1949; *Supplement*. Leiden, 1937–1942.

Bukhārī, Muḥammad b. Ismāᶜīl, al-. *al-Jāmiᶜ al-Ṣaḥīḥ*. Cairo, 1309 AH.

Calverley, E.E. 'Doctrines of the Soul (*nafs* and *rūḥ*) in Islam'. *MW* 33 (1943) pp.254–264.

Dahlawī, Shāh Walī Allāh, al-. *Ḥujjat Allāh al-Bāligha*. Cairo, 1952–3.

Dāraquṭnī, ᶜAlī b. ᶜUmar, al-. *K. al-Sunan*. Cairo, n.d.

——*Dhikr asmā' al-Tābiᶜīn*. Ed. B. al-Ḍannāwī and K. al-Ḥūt. Beirut, 1406/1985.

Dārimī, Abū Muḥammad, al-. *K. al-Sunan*. Cawnpore, 1293 AH.

Daylamī, Abū Shujāᶜ Shīrawayhi, al-. *al-Firdaws bi-ma'thūr al-khiṭāb*. Ed. al-Saᶜīd Zaghlūl. Beirut, 1406/1986.

Dermenghem, E. *Vies des saints musulmans*. (Edition définitive). Paris, 1983.

Dhahabī, Muḥammad b. Aḥmad, al-. *Siyar aᶜlām al-nubalā'*. Ed. S. al-Arnā'ūṭ *et al.* Beirut, 1401– AH.

——*al-Kāshif fī maᶜrifa man lahu riwāya fi'l-kutub al-sitta*. Beirut, 1403/1983.

Eklund, R. *Life between Death and Resurrection according to Islam*. Uppsala, 1941.

Encyclopaedia of Islam, The. Ed. by M. Houtsma *et al.* Leiden, 1927. New edition, ed. by J.H. Kramers, H.A.R. Gibb *et al.* Leiden, 1954– . *Supplement*, 1980– .

Ernst, C. *Words of ecstasy in Sufism*. Albany (USA), 1985.

Farazdaq, Abū Firās Hammām, al-. *Dīwān*. Beirut, 1400/1980.

Gardet, L. *La Pensée Religieuse d'Avicenne (Ibn Sīnā)*. Paris, 1951.

Gardet, L, and Anawati, M.-M. *Introduction à la théologie musulmane. Essai de théologie comparée*. Paris, 1970.

Ghazālī, Abū Ḥāmid Muḥammad b. Muḥammad, al-. *Tahāfut al-falāsifa*. Ed. M. Bouyges. Beirut, 1927.

——*al-Iqtiṣād fi'l-iᶜtiqād*. Ed. M. Abu'l-ᶜAlā. Cairo, 1972.

——*Iḥyā' ᶜulūm al-dīn*. Cairo, 1347 AH.

——*Faḍā'iḥ al-Bāṭinīya*. Ed. A. Badawī, Cairo, 1964.

——*Fayṣal al-tafriqa bayn al-Islām wa'l-zandaqa*. Ed. S. Dunyā. Cairo, 1961.

——*al-Munqidh min al-ḍalāl wa'l-mūṣil ilā dhi'l-ᶜizza wa'l-jalāl*. Ar. ed. and French trans. by Farid Jabre. Beirut, 1959.

——*Iljām al-ᶜawāmm ᶜan ᶜilm al-kalām*. Ed. M. Abu'l-ᶜAlā, in *al-Quṣūr al-ᶜawālī min rasā'il al-Imām al-Ghazālī*. Cairo, 1390/1970.

——(pseudo?) *Mīzān al-ᶜamal*. Ed. M. Abu'l-ᶜAlā. Cairo, 1973.

——(pseudo?) *al-Durra al-Fākhira fī kashf ᶜulūm al-Ākhira*. Partial ed. and French translation by L. Gautier, as *al-Dourra al-Fakhira: La Perle Précieuse de Ghazali. Traité d'Eschatologie Musulmane*. Leipzig, 1877.

Gramlich, R. *Muḥammad al-Gazzālīs Lehre von den Stufen zur Gottesliebe*. Wiesbaden, 1984. (German transl. and introd. of Books 31–36 of the *Iḥyā'*.)

Guillaume, A. *The Life of Muḥammad. A Translation of Ibn Isḥāq's Sīrat Rasūl Allāh*. London, 1955.

Ḥākim al-Nīsābūrī, al-. *al-Mustadrak ᶜalā al-Ṣaḥīḥayn*. Hyderabad, 1334–42 AH.

Ḥakīm al-Tirmidhī, al-. *Nawādir al-uṣūl fī maᶜrifat aḥādīth al-Rasūl*. Istanbul, 1293 AH.

Ḥalīmī, al-Ḥusayn b. al-Ḥasan, al-. *al-Minhāj fī shuᶜab al-īmān*. Ed. Ḥ.M. Fawda. Beirut, 1399/1979.

Haythamī, ᶜAlī b. Abī Bakr, al-. *Majmaᶜ al-zawā'id wa-manbaᶜ al-fawā'id*. Cairo, 1352 AH.

——*Mawārid al-ẓam'ān ilā zawā'id Ibn Ḥibbān*. Cairo, n.d.

——*Kashf al-astār ᶜan zawā'id al-Bazzār*. Ed. Ḥ. al-Aᶜẓamī. Beirut, 1404/1984.

Ibn ʿAbd al-Barr, Yūsuf. *al-Inbāh ʿalā qabā'il al-ruwā*. Ed. I. al-Ibyārī. Beirut, 1405/1985.

——*al-Istīʿāb fī maʿrifat al-Aṣḥāb*. With *al-Iṣāba* of Ibn Ḥajar. Cairo, 1358–9 AH.

Ibn Abī ʿĀṣim, Abū Bakr ʿAmr. *K. al-Sunna*. Ed. M.N. al-Albānī. Beirut, 1400/1980.

——*K. al-Zuhd*. Ed. A.A. al-Aʿẓamī. Beirut, 1405/1985.

Ibn Abi'l-Dunyā, ʿAbd Allāh b. Muḥammad b. ʿUbayd. *K. Dhamm al-dunyā*. Ed. and introd. by E. Appelrot-Almagor as *The 'K. Dhamm al-dunyā' by Ibn Abi'l-Dunyā*. Ann Arbor, Michigan: University Microfilms, 1979.

——*K. al-Shukr*. Ed. and introd. by Y. al-Sawwās and A. al-Arnā'ūṭ. Beirut, 1405/1985.

——*K. Makārim al-akhlāq*. Ed. and introd. by J.A. Bellamy. Wiesbaden, 1973.

——*K. al-Ṣamt wa-ḥifẓ al-lisān*. Ed. and introd. M. A. ʿĀshūr. Cairo, 1406/1986.

Ibn Abī Shayba. *al-Muṣannaf*. Bombay, 1386–1390 AH.

Ibn al-ʿArabī, Abū Bakr (al-Qāḍī). *ʿĀriḍat al-aḥwadhī fī sharḥ Ṣaḥīḥ al-Tirmidhī*. Cairo, 1352/1934.

Ibn Aʿtham, Aḥmad, al-Kūfī. *al-Futūḥ*. Ed. A. Khan. Hyderabad, 1388/1968—1395/1975.

Ibn al-Athīr, Mubārak b. Muḥammad. *al-Nihāya fī gharīb al-ḥadīth wa'l-athar*. Cairo, 1344 AH.

Ibn al-Daybaʿ, ʿAbd al-Raḥmān b. ʿAlī. *Tamyīz al-ṭayyib min al-khabīth fīmā yadūru ʿalā alsinat al-nās min al-ḥadīth*. Cairo, 1382/1962.

Ibn Ḥajar al-ʿAsqalānī, *Fatḥ al-Bārī sharḥ Ṣaḥīḥ al-Bukhārī*. Cairo, 1344 AH.

——*al-Maṭālib al-ʿĀliya bi-zawā'id al-Masānīd al-Thamāniya*. Ed. Ḥ. al-Aʿẓamī. Kuwait, 1393/1973.

——*al-Iṣāba fī tamyīz al-Ṣaḥāba*. Cairo, 1358–9 AH.

——*Tahdhīb al-Tahdhīb*. Hyderabad, 1326 AH.

——*Taʿjīl al-manfaʿa bi-zawā'id rijāl al-a'immat al-arbaʿa*. Hyderabad, 1324 AH.

Ibn Ḥanbal, Aḥmad b. Muḥammad. *al-Musnad*. Cairo, 1313 AH.

——*K. al-Zuhd*. Beirut, 1403/1983.

——*K. al-Wara*ᶜ. Cairo, 1340 AH.

Ibn Ḥazm, ᶜAlī b. Aḥmad. *al-Fiṣal fi'l-milal wa'l-ahwā' wa'l-niḥal.* Cairo, 1321 AH.

Ibn Ḥibbān, Muḥammad, al-Bustī. *Mashāhīr* ᶜ*ulamā' al-amṣār.* Ed. M. Fleischhammer. Cairo, 1959.

Ibn al-Jarrāḥ, Wakīᶜ. *K. al-Zuhd.* Ed. A.A. al-Faryawā'ī. Medina, 1404/1984.

Ibn al-Jawzī. *al-*ᶜ*Ilal al-Mutanāhiya fi'l-aḥādīth al-wāhiya.* Beirut, 1399/1979.

——*Talbīs Iblīs.* Cairo, 1352 AH.

——*Manāqib Ma*ᶜ*rūf al-Karkhī wa-akhbāruhu.* Ed. A. al-Jabbūrī. Beirut, 1406/1985.

Ibn al-Jazarī, Shams al-Dīn Muḥammad. *Ghāyat al-nihāya fī ṭabaqāt al-Qurrā'.* Ed. G. Bergsträsser and O. Pretzl. Cairo, 1352/1933.

Ibn Kathīr, Ismāᶜīl b. ᶜUmar. *al-Bidāya wa'l-nihāya.* Cairo, 1351 AH.

Ibn Khallikān, Aḥmad b. Muḥammad. *Wafayāt al-a*ᶜ*yān wa-anbā' abnā' al-zamān.* Ed. F. Wüstenfeld. Göttingen, 1835.

Ibn Māja al-Qazwīnī. *K. al-Sunan.* Delhi, 1333 AH.

Ibn Marthad, ᶜAlqama. *Zuhd al-thamāniya min al-Tābi*ᶜ*īn.* Ed. A.A. al-Faryawā'ī. Medina, 1404 AH.

Ibn al-Mubārak, ᶜAbd Allāh. *al-Zuhd wa'l-raqā'iq*, including the *riwāya* of Nuᶜaym b. Ḥammād (with separate pagination). Ed. Ḥ. al-Aᶜẓamī. Malegaon (India), 1385/1966.

Ibn al-Nadīm, Muḥammad. *al-Fihrist.* Ed. G. Flügel. Leipzig, 1871–2.

Ibn Qutayba, ᶜAbd Allāh b. Muslim. ᶜ*Uyūn al-akhbār.* Ed. A. al-ᶜAdawī. Cairo, 1343–8/1925–30.

——al-Maᶜ*ārif.* Ed. F. Wüstenfeld. Göttingen, 1850.

Ibn Rajab, ᶜAbd al-Raḥmān b. Aḥmad. *Ahwāl al-qubūr wa-aḥwāl ahlihā ila'l-nushūr.* Beirut, 1405/1985.

Ibn Shaddād, Muḥammad b. ᶜAlī. *al-A*ᶜ*lāq al-Khaṭīra fī dhikr umarā' al-Shām wa'l-Jazīra.* Vol. II. Ed. S. al-Dahhān. Damascus, 1382/1963.

Ibn Sīnā. *al-Shifā'*. Partial ed. by F. Rahman as *Avicenna's De Anima (Arabic text). Being the psychological part of Kitāb al-Shifā'*. Oxford, 1960.

——*al-Risāla al-Aḍḥawīya fī (amr) al-maᶜād*. Ed. and Italian trans. by F. Lucchetta, as *Avicenna, Epistola sulla vita futura*. Padua, 1969.

Ibn al-Sunnī, Abū Bakr. *ᶜAmal al-yawm wa'l-layla*. Ed. A. Ḥajjāj. Cairo, 1982.

Ījī, ᶜAbd al-Raḥmān b. Aḥmad, al-. *K. al-Mawāqif fī ᶜilm al-kalām*. Ed. Soerensen. Leipzig, 1848.

Iṣfahānī, Abū Nuᶜaym, al-. *Ḥilyat al-awliyā' wa-ṭabaqāt al-aṣfiyā'*. Cairo, 1351–7/1932–8.

Iṣṭakhrī, Abū Isḥāq, al-. *Masālik al-mamālik*. Ed. M.J. de Goeje. Leiden, 1870.

Jabre, F. 'La biographie et l'oeuvre de Ghazālī réconsidérées à la lumière des Ṭabaqāt de Sobkī'. *MIDEO* 1 (1954), pp.73–102.

Jarīr, Ibn ᶜAṭīya al-Khaṭafī. *Dīwān*. Beirut, 1403/1983.

Jayūshī, M. I. al-. *al-Ḥakīm al-Tirmidhī. Dirāsa li-āthārihi wa-afkārihi*. Cairo, 1401/1980 (?).

Khālid, Ḥasan. *al-Islām wa-ru'yatuhu fīmā baᶜd al-mawt*. Beirut, 1406/1986.

Khaṭīb al-Baghdādī, al-. *Tārīkh Baghdād*. Cairo, 1349.

Le Strange, G. *Lands of the Eastern Caliphate*. Cambridge, 1905.

Lane, E. *An Arabic-English Lexicon*. London, 1863–1893.

Laqqānī, ᶜAbd al-Salām, al-. *Irshād al-murīd ilā maqām al-tawḥīd*. Printed at margin of *al-Ḥāshiya* of Muḥammad al-Amīr. Cairo, 1373/1953.

Lazarus-Yafeh, H. *Studies in Al-Ghazzālī*. Jerusalem, 1975.

Macdonald, D.B. 'The Life of al-Ghazzālī'. *JAOS* 20 (1899) pp.70–133.

Massignon, L. *Essai sur les origines du lexique technique de la mystique musulmane*. 2nd. ed. Paris, 1954.

——*La Passion d'al-Hallâj*. Paris, 1922.

Māturīdī, Muḥammad b. Maḥmūd, al-. *K. al-Tawḥīd*. Ed. F. Kholeif. Beirut, 1970.

McCarthy, R.J. *Freedom and Fulfillment. An Annotated Translation of al-Ghazālī's* al-Munqidh min al-Ḍalāl *and other Relevant Works of Al-Ghazālī.* Boston, 1980.

Makkī, Abū Ṭālib, al-. *Qūt al-qulūb fī muᶜāmalat al-Maḥbūb wa-waṣf ṭarīq al-murīd ilā maqām al-tawḥīd.* Cairo, 1310 AH.

Montgomery Watt, W. *Muslim Intellectual: A Study of al-Ghazālī.* Edinburgh, 1963.

——'The Authenticity of the Works Ascribed to Al-Ghazālī'. *JRAS*, 1952, pp.24–45.

Morelon, R. *Le livre du licite et de l'illicite. Kitāb al-ḥalāl wa'l-ḥarām.* Paris, 1981. (French tr. and introd. of book 14 of the *Iḥyā'*.)

Muḥāsibī, al-Ḥārith, al-. *K. al-Riᶜāya li-ḥuqūq Allāh.* Ed. M. Smith. London, 1940.

——*K. al-Tawahhum.* Ed. and introd. by A.J. Arberry. Cairo, 1937.

Murābiṭ, J. al-. *Al-Sarī al-Saqaṭī.* Beirut, 1398 AH..

Nakamura, K. *Ghazali on prayer.* Tokyo, 1973. (English tr. with introd. of the *Kitāb al-adhkār wa'l-daᶜawāt* from the *Iḥyā'*.)

Nasā'ī, Aḥmad ibn Shuᶜayb, al-. *al-Ḍuᶜafā' wa'l-matrūkīn.* Ed. B. al-Ḍannāwī and K. al-Ḥūt. Beirut, 1405/1985.

Nawawī, Muḥyi'l-Dīn Yaḥyā, al-. *al-Minhāj fī Sharḥ Ṣaḥīḥ Muslim ibn al-Ḥajjāj.* Cairo, 1347 AH.

——*al-Tibyān fī ādāb ḥamalat al-Qur'ān.* Cairo, 1365 AH.

——*Tahdhīb al-asmā' wa'l-lughāt.* Ed. F. Wüstenfeld. Göttingen, 1842–7.

Nicholson, R.A. *The Kashf al-maḥjúb, the oldest Persian treatise on Sufiism.* Leiden and London, 1911. (Tr. with introd. of the *Kashf al-Maḥjūb* of al-Hujwīrī.)

Pellat, C. *Le Milieu basrien et la formation de Čāḥiẓ.* Paris, 1953.

Pickthall, M.M. *The Meaning of the Glorious Koran.* London, 1934.

Plotinus. *Enneads.* Vol. IV. Ed. and trans. by A.H. Armstrong. (Loeb Classical Library no.443.) Harvard and London, 1984.

Pouzet, L. *Une Herméneutique de la tradition islamique. Le Commentaire des Arbaᶜūn al-Nawawīya de Muḥyī al-Dīn Yaḥyā al-Nawawī.* Beirut, 1982.

Quḍāʿī, Muḥammad b. Salāma, al-. *Musnad al-Shihāb*. Beirut, 1405/1985.

Qurṭubī, Muḥammad b. Aḥmad, al-. *al-Tadhkira fī aḥwāl al-mawtā wa-umūr al-ākhira*. Cairo, 1352 AH.

Qushayrī, Abu'l-Qāsim, al-. *al-Risāla fī ʿilm al-taṣawwuf*. Ed. A. Maḥmūd and M. al-Sharīf. Cairo, 1385/1966.

Rahman, F. *Prophecy in Islam*. London, 1958.

Rawdānī, Muḥammad b. Muḥammad, al-. *Jamʿ al-fawā'id min Jāmiʿ al-uṣūl wa-Majmaʿ al-zawā'id*. Mecca, 1404/1983.

Rāzī, Fakhr al-Dīn, al-. *Maʿālim uṣūl al-dīn*. Ed. T. A. Saʿd. Beirut, 1404/1984.

Rosenthal, F. *"Sweeter than hope": Complaint and Hope in Medieval Islam*. Leiden, 1983.

Ṣafadī, Ṣalāḥ al-Dīn Khalīl b. Aybak, al-. *al-Wāfī bi'l-wafayāt*. Ed. H. Ritter *et al.* Wiesbaden, 1962– .

Sakhāwī, Muḥammad b. ʿAbd al-Raḥmān, al-. *al-Maqāṣid al-Ḥasana fī bayān kathīr min al-aḥādīth al-mushtahira ʿala'l-alsina*. Ed. and introd. by M.U. al-Khusht. Beirut, 1405/1985.

Schimmel, A. *And Muhammad is His Messenger. The veneration of the Prophet in Islamic piety*. Chapel Hill (USA), 1985.

Sezgin, F. *Geschichte des arabischen Schrifttums*. Leiden, 1967– .

Sharnūbī, ʿAbd al-Majīd, al-. *Taqrīb al-maʿānī ilā matn Risālat Ibn Abī Zayd al-Qayrawānī*. Cairo, 1323 AH.

Shawkānī, Muḥammad b. ʿAlī, al-. *al-Fawā'id al-Majmūʿa fi'l-aḥādīth al-mawḍūʿa*. Ed. A. al-Muʿallimī. Cairo, 1380/1960.

Sherif, M.A. *Ghazali's Theory of Virtue*. Albany (USA), 1975.

Shorter Encyclopaedia of Islam. Ed. H.A.R. Gibb and J.H. Kramers. Leiden, 1974.

Sijistānī, Abū Dāūd, al-. *K. al-Sunan*. Cairo, 1369–70/1950–51.

Smith, J. *The Precious Pearl*. Missoula (USA), 1979. (Trans. of *al-Durra al-Fākhira* attributed to al-Ghazālī.)

——and Haddad, Y. *The Islamic Understanding of Death and Resurrection*. Albany (USA), 1981.

Smith, M. *Al-Ghazālī the Mystic*. London, 1944.

——*Rābiʿa the Mystic and Her Fellow-Saints in Islam*. Cambridge, 1928.

——'The Forerunner of al-Ghazālī (al-Muḥāsibī)'. *JRAS* (Jan. 1936) pp.65–78.

Subkī, Tāj al-Dīn, al-. *Ṭabaqāt al-Shāfiʿīya al-Kubrā*. Cairo, 1324 AH.

Sulamī, Abū ʿAbd al-Raḥmān, al-. *Jawāmiʿ ādāb al-Ṣūfīya* printed together with his *ʿUyūb al-nafs wa-mudāwātuhā*. Ed. & introduced by E. Kohlberg. Jerusalem, 1976.

——*Ṭabaqāt al-Ṣūfīya*. Ed. J. Pedersen. Leiden, 1960.

Suyūṭī, Jalāl al-Dīn, al-. *al-Durar al-muntathira fi'l-aḥādīth al-mushtahira*. Ed. K. M. al-Mīs. Beirut, 1404/1984.

——*al-Jāmiʿ al-Ṣaghīr fī aḥādīth al-Bashīr al-Nadhīr*. Beirut, 1401/1981.

——*Sharḥ al-ṣudūr bi-sharḥ ḥāl al-mawtā wa'l-qubūr*. Beirut, 1404/1984.

——*Al-Ḥāwī li'l-fatāwī*. Cairo, 1352 AH.

——*al-Mujtabā min Sunan al-Nasā'ī*. Cairo, 1383–4/1964–5.

Ṭabarānī, Sulaymān b. Aḥmad, al-. *al-Muʿjam al-Ṣaghīr*. Cairo, 1388 AH.

Ṭabarī, Ibn Jarīr, al-. *Jāmiʿ al-bayān fī ta'wīl āī al-Qur'ān*. Cairo, 1323–9 AH.

Tāshköprüzāde. *Miftāḥ al-saʿāda wa-miṣbāḥ al-siyāda*. Hyderabad, 1328–1336 AH.

Ṭayālisī, Muḥammad b. Jaʿfar, al-. *al-Musnad*. Hyderabad, 1321 AH.

Tritton, A. 'Man, *nafs*, *rūḥ*, *ʿaql*'. *BSOAS* 34 (1971) pp.491–495.

ʿUqaylī, Muḥammad b. ʿAmr, al-. *K. al-Ḍuʿafā' al-Kabīr*. Ed. A. Qalʿajī. Beirut, 1404/1984.

Wensinck, A.J. *et al. Concordance et indices de la tradition musulmane*. Leiden, 1936–1969.

——*The Muslim Creed*. Cambridge, 1932.

——'On the Relation between Ghazālī's Cosmology and his Mysticism'. *Verhandelingen der Koninklijke Akademie van Wetenschappen te Amsterdam*, 75 (1933), A6, 183–209.

Wiener, A. 'Die Farağ ba'd aš-šidda Literatur'. I/II. *Der Islam* 4 (1913) pp.270–298, 387–420.

Wolfson, H.A. *The Philosophy of the Kalam*. Harvard and London, 1976.

Yāqūt al-Ḥimyarī. *Muʿjam al-buldān*. Ed. F. Wüstenfeld. Leipzig, 1866.

Zabīdī, al-Murtaḍā, al-. *Itḥāf al-sādat al-muttaqīn bi-sharḥ asrār Iḥyāʾ ʿulūm al-dīn*. Cairo, 1311 AH.

GENERAL INDEX

al-ʿAbbās, 61, 63, 69, 78, 157
ʿAbd Allāh ibn ʿAbbās, 16, 31, 44, 72, 77, 81, 156, 158, 178, 212, 216, 225, 241, 256, 258
ʿAbd Allāh ibn ʿAmr, 128, 131, 243, 256
ʿAbd Allāh ibn Masʿūd, 14, 17, 33, 35, 46, 59, 63, 194, 201, 208, 224n, 243
ʿAbd Allāh ibn al-Mubārak, xiv, xxiv, 89, 90, 164, 166
ʿAbd Allāh ibn Rawāḥa, 131
ʿAbd Allāh ibn Salām, 81
ʿAbd Allāh ibn Sumayṭ, 21
ʿAbd Allāh ibn Thaʿlaba, 23
ʿAbd Allāh ibn ʿUbayd ibn ʿUmayr, 135
ʿAbd Allāh ibn ʿUmar, 10, 15, 29, 32, 70, 79, 113, 114, 117, 130, 180, 182, 192, 218, 245
ʿAbd Allāh ibn Zamʿa, 64, 65
ʿAbd Allāh al-Zarrād, 159
ʿAbd Allāh ibn Zayd (Abū Qilāba), 118
ʿAbd al-Malik ibn Marwān, 86–7
ʿAbd al-Qays, 118
ʿAbd al-Raḥmān ibn al-ʿAlā' ibn al-Lajlāj, 117
ʿAbd al-Raḥmān ibn Abī Bakr, 61, 112
ʿAbd al-Raḥmān ibn ʿAwf, 77, 80
ʿAbd al-Raḥmān ibn Thābit (Abū Qays), 127
ʿAbd al-Raḥmān ibn Yūsuf, 22
ʿAbd al-Wāḥid ibn Zayd, 157
Abu'l-ʿAbbās ibn ʿAṭā', 93
Abu'l-ʿAbbās al-Dīnawarī, 91
Abū ʿAlī al-Rūdhbārī, 91
Abū ʿAmr ibn al-ʿAlā', 98
Abū Ashʿath, 11
Abū Ayyūb al-Anṣārī, 132
Abū Bakr ibn ʿAbd Allāh al-Muzanī, 114
Abū Bakr ibn Abī Maryam, 167
Abū Bakr al-Rashīdī, 166
Abū Bakr al-Ṣiddīq, xiv, 24, 60, 61, 63, 64, 73, 81, 82, 114, 158, 159, 163, 185, 237, 243; speech at Prophet's death 69–72; death of, 74–7
Abū Burda, 260
Abu'l-Dardā', 14, 102, 128, 131, 225, 243, 260
Abū Dharr, xiv, 102, 112, 200, 218, 259
Abū Hāshim al-Rummānī, 19
Abū Ḥātim al-Rāzī, 164
Abū Ḥāzim, 86
Abū Hurayra, 32, 43, 46, 48, 97, 114, 120, 127, 131, 137, 138, 144, 146, 179, 180, 191, 199, 200, 212, 222, 224, 226, 234, 240, 249
Abū Jābir, 129, 150
Abu Jaʿfar (Muḥammad ibn ʿAlī), 73, 84, 137
Abū Jaʿfar al-Ṣaydalānī, 160
Abū Lahab, 157
Abū Lu'lu'a, 77,
Abū Muḥammad ibn ʿAlī, 23
Abū Mūsā al-Ashʿarī, 34, 260
Abū Mūsā al-Tamīmī, 105
Abū Nuʿaym al-Iṣfahānī, xix, xxviii
Abū Qays, 127
Abū Qilāba, 118
Abū Saʿīd al-Kharrāz, 90, 91, 143, 163
Abū Saʿīd al-Khudrī, 15, 48, 132, 207, 224, 237, 242, 244, 247, 257
Abū Saʿīd al-Ṣaffār, 166
Abū Saʿīd al-Shaḥḥām,166
Abū Sinān, 110
Abū Sulaymān al-Dārānī, xiv, 12, 92, 162
Abū Ṭālib al-Makkī, xiv, xix
Abū ʿUbayda al-Nājī, 35
Abū Umāma (ibn Sahl), 114
Abū Umāma al-Bāhilī, 116, 226, 239, 246

Donne, ix
dragon (*tinnīn*), 138
dreams, 19, 20, 44, 116, 124, 140, 149–69; interpretation of, xxii, 153; Prophet seen in, 81, 156–8, 163
al-Durra al-Fākhira ... (attributed to Ghazālī), xxvi-xxvii, 131n, 138n, 242n

earthquakes, 184
Eden, 235, 238
Egypt, xvi, 214n
Egyptian Book of the Dead, ix
Eklund, R., xxiv
Elias (al-Yasaᶜ), 61
Elisabeth (mother of St. John the Baptist), 167n
Emigrants (*al-Muhājirūn*), 61, 62, 80, 218, 242
Eve, 117
'evil end' (*sū' al-khātima*), 47, 49

Faḍā'iḥ al-Bāṭinīya (of Ghazālī), xxvi
al-Faḍl ibn al-ᶜAbbās, 61
Fakhr al-Mulk, xxv
al-Fārābī, 122n
al-Farazdaq, 105
farḍ ᶜayn, xxvii
fasting, 134, 146, 153, 156, 181, 200, 235, 238
Fāṭima (daughter of the Prophet), 42, 66, 84, 113
Fāṭima (sister of al-Rūdhbārī), 91
Fāṭima bint ᶜAbd al-Malik, 87, 218
Fāṭima bint al-Ḥasan, 104
fatra, 101
Fayṣal al-tafriqa (of Ghazālī), xxvi
filial piety, 110, 113
fiqh (jurisprudence), xviii, 99
Firdaws, 235n
fish which supports the seven earths, 242n
fiṭra, 151
Followers (*al-Tābiᶜūn*), xiv
forty, xxvii
Friday, 115, 166
[al-]Fuḍayl ibn ᶜIyāḍ, 89
Fuḍayl al-Ruqāshī, 36
funerals, 23, 27, 97–100, 113, 117, 127, 135, 146, 165

Gabriel, 60, 64, 66, 67, 80, 139, 154n, 176, 190, 217, 245, 259
Garden of the Refuge, 59, 63
Gardet, L., xxv, 122n
Gardet and Anawati, xxv
Gehenna, see 'Hell'
ghassāq, 224
al-Ghazālī, xv-xxiii; life of, xv-xvii
ghuraf, 236–8
gnostic(s), xxiii, 7, 8, 250n, 251n
Gog and Magog, 197
Gospel, 59
Greek philosophy, xiv
guardians of Hell, 196, 205, 206, 225

ḥadīths, x, xiii, xiv, xx, xxiv, xxix, 73, 122, 129, 176n, 211, 217, 223, 234, 240, 244, 245n, 254n; *ḥadīth qudsī*, xxvii
Ḥaḍramawt, 131n
Ḥafṣa, 79
Hajar, 214
al-Ḥajjāj, 88
al-Ḥajj ('the Pilgrimage'), xvi, 134, 157, 181
al-Ḥakam ibn al-Muṭṭalib, 94
al-Ḥākim al-Nīsābūrī, xxv
al-Ḥakīm al-Tirmidhī, xix, 33n, 59n, 237n
ḥāl, 50n
Ḥamza, 84, 113
ḥanūṭ, 135n
al-Ḥārith ibn al-Khazraj, 69
al-Ḥarra, 259
'Harrowing of Hell', 254n; see also '*Shafāᶜa*'
Hārūn al-Rashīd, 88
al-Ḥaṣā, 214n
al-Ḥasan ibn ᶜAlī, 84, 157
al-Ḥasan al-Baṣrī, xiv, 11, 12, 18, 19, 21, 34, 35, 41, 46, 54, 90, 105, 164, 167, 182, 196, 227, 229, 248
al-Ḥasan ibn al-Ḥusayn, 104
al-Ḥasan ibn Ṣāliḥ, 103